Chaucer's Legendary Good Women

Chaucer's *Legend of Good Women* is a testament to the disparate views of women prevalent in the Middle Ages. Dr Percival contends that the complex medieval notion of Woman informs the structure of the poem: in the Prologue Chaucer praises conventional ideas of female virtue, while in the Legends he shows a humorous scepticism, apparently influenced by contemporary antifeminist traditions. The debate Chaucer thus promotes could be relied on to entertain many medieval readers, while at the same time it demonstrates the power of the vernacular translator/poet to handle language wittily and to play with the august texts of the past. This is a comprehensive account of the *Legend*'s interpretative puzzles, which does not ignore the element of political writing, and adds to a close and nuanced reading of the text an examination of literary, historical and social contexts.

Dr Florence Percival's special interests, apart from Chaucer, are in the field of Arthurian literature, in particular the Tristan legend and Sir Thomas Malory. She is at present collaborating on an annotated bibliography of Middle English Bible translations.

CAMBRIDGE STUDIES IN MEDIEVAL LITERATURE

General editor
Alastair Minnis, *University of York*

Editorial board
Patrick Boyde, *University of Cambridge*
John Burrow, *University of Bristol*
Rita Copeland, *University of Minnesota*
Alan Deyermond, *University of London*
Peter Dronke, *University of Cambridge*
Professor Simon Gaunt, *King's College, London*
Nigel Palmer, *University of Oxford*
Winthrop Wetherbee, *Cornell University*

This series of critical books seeks to cover the whole area of literature written in the major medieval languages – the main European vernaculars, and medieval Latin and Greek – during the period c. 1100–1500. Its chief aim is to publish and stimulate fresh scholarship and criticism on medieval literature, special emphasis being placed on understanding major works of poetry, prose, and drama in relation to the contemporary culture and learning which fostered them.

A complete list of titles in the series can be found at the end of the volume.

Chaucer's Legendary Good Women

FLORENCE PERCIVAL

CAMBRIDGE
UNIVERSITY PRESS

PUBLISHED BY THE PRESS SYNDICATE OF THE UNIVERSITY OF CAMBRIDGE
The Pitt Building, Trumpington Street, Cambridge CB2 1RP, United Kingdom

CAMBRIDGE UNIVERSITY PRESS
The Edinburgh Building, Cambridge CB2 2RU, United Kingdom
40 West 20th Street, New York, NY 10011–4211, USA
10 Stamford Road, Oakleigh, Melbourne 3166, Australia

First published 1998

Printed in the United Kingdom at the University Press, Cambridge

Typeset in Adobe Garamond 11.5/14pt [CE]

A catalogue record for this book is available from the British Library

ISBN 0 521 41655 8 hardback

*For Norman and Edith Weber
and Maud Morrison*

Contents

Note on the text

I refer to the two Prologues to the *Legend of Good Women* as Prologue F and Prologue G, or simply F and G, especially when prefacing line numbers. *LGW* is sometimes used before line numbers, if it is not otherwise clear that the lines are from the *Legend of Good Women*.

I often use 'the *Legend*' as an abbreviation for the *Legend of Good Women* as a whole, but an unitalicised use of 'Legend' refers to a story in the poem's tale collection, one of the Legends of good women, e.g., 'Legend of Cleopatra'.

Chaucer sometimes uses spellings for the names of the heroines and heroes of his Legends which differ from the generally accepted spellings of these characters from mythology. Where this is the case, I use Chaucer's spellings to refer to his characters, and the usual spellings for other versions of the classical stories; thus Phillis and Demophon are the protagonists of Chaucer's tale, but Phyllis and Demophoon refer to Ovid's characters.

Abbreviations

BD	*The Book of the Duchess*
Bo	*Boece*
CA	*Confessio Amantis*
CFMA	Les classiques français du moyen âge
ChauR	*Chaucer Review*
DNB	*Dictionary of National Biography*
EETS	Early English Text Society
ELH	*English Literary History*
HF	*The House of Fame*
JEGP	*Journal of English and Germanic Philology*
JWCI	*Journal of the Warburg and Courtauld Institutes*
KnT	*The Knight's Tale*
LGW	*The Legend of Good Women*
MÆ	*Medium Ævum*
MED	*A Middle English Dictionary*
MkT	*The Monk's Tale*
MLN	*Modern Language Notes*
MLR	*Modern Language Review*
MLT	*The Man of Law's Tale*
MP	*Modern Philology*
MS	*Mediaeval Studies*
N&Q	*Notes and Queries*
OED	*The Oxford English Dictionary*
PMLA	*Publications of the Modern Language Association*
PL	*Patrologia latina*
PQ	*Philological Quarterly*
RES	*Review of English Studies*
Romaunt	*The Romaunt of the Rose*
RPr	*The Reeve's Prologue*
RR	*Roman de la Rose*
SAC	*Studies in the Age of Chaucer*

Abbreviations

SATF	Société des Anciens Textes Français
SNT	*The Second Nun's Tale*
SP	*Studies in Philology*
SqT	*The Squire's Tale*
TC	*Troilus and Criseyde*
WBPr	*The Wife of Bath's Prologue*

Introduction

No – just a defence of textual representations of women in Chaucer's poems

Chaucer's *Legend of Good Women* purports to be a defence of women. A defence presupposes that a charge has been levelled, or that a slander requires an answer. In the fiction of this poem, it is Chaucer himself who is accused of perpetrating a slander on women's reputation, since he chose to write of the unfaithful Criseyde in an earlier work. He must therefore make amends for this sin against the God of Love by composing an exemplary collection of stories of women who 'were true in loving all their lives'. Thus the *Legend* is a palinode and sits squarely in an ancient literary tradition which commonly concerned itself with the relative merits and demerits of women and men.

palinode

The palinode or poetic recantation is above all a display of rhetorical skill in pleading a case, and from the time the palinode form made its first appearance in ancient Greek literature – when in a new poem Stesichorus recanted the 'sin' of slandering the archetypally feminine Helen of Troy with a new poem in her favour – the cause which was taken up was the defence of women or of love.[1] Two poems likely to have influenced Chaucer's *Legend* are considered palinodes: Book III of the *Ars Amatoria* by Ovid, and *Le Jugement dou Roy de Navarre* by Chaucer's near contemporary Guillaume de Machaut. In both of these the topic is the 'war of the sexes'; both use the exemplum technique, and indeed draw attention to its limitations as a method of valid proof; both make use of the stories of the traditional 'heroines' in versions

---

[1] See Eleanor J. Winsor, 'A Study in the Sources and Rhetoric of Chaucer's *Legend of Good Women* and Ovid's *Heroides*', Dissertation, Yale, 1963, pp. 1–3; Elizabeth D. Harvey, 'Speaking of Tongues: the Poetics of the Feminine Voice in Chaucer's *Legend of Good Women*', in E. E. Dubruck, ed., *New Images of Medieval Women: Essays Toward a Cultural Anthropology* (Lewiston: Mellen, 1989), pp. 50–1.

I

marked by amusing distortions which reflect the biased point of view their teller wishes to affect. Many in Chaucer's audience would have been familiar with these poetic 'recantations' – indeed the late fourteenth and early fifteenth centuries mark a period when several other palinodes were composed.

The *Legend of Good Women* exhibits other traditional motifs of the palinode form: the hostility and threats of the God of Love or Venus, the poet's consciousness that he has been wrongly accused, the need for literary recompense in kind (indeed the poet is compelled to perform such recompense), and above all the comically maintained partisanship for the opposite side. One motif often seen in the medieval period is the statement that the poet has been forced to recant his sin because of the anger of the ladies of the court, as is suggested at the end of *Troilus and Criseyde*. These stories can invariably be shown to be pure invention, a rhetorical ploy, for the poet's earlier work creates for the palinode its own adequate frame of reference.

Palinodal in form or not, all cases of medieval or renaissance defences of women must be seen as operating in a climate of debate. Sometimes there is a recantation of one's own poem as here. Sometimes the new work is a response to another author, as when Christine de Pizan was stimulated to write *The Book of the City of Ladies* after reading 'Matheolus', a famous compendium of antifeminist tenets. Sometimes, as in Boccaccio's *Concerning Famous Women*, the writer persistently counterpoints his retelling of tales about women against the accepted views of what it meant to be virile or womanly. And, in a world where 'men write the books', Chaucer is of course self-consciously espousing in the *Legend* the less common, less authoritative side of the debate.[2]

Moreover, in the Prologue to the *Legend of Good Women* Chaucer makes frequent allusion to several other topics which were traditionally debated. Thus he juxtaposes such polarities as authority and experience, summer and winter, youth and age, mercy and judgement, and, of

---

[2] See A. Blamires with Karen Pratt and C. W. Marx, eds., *Woman Defamed and Woman Defended: an Anthology of Medieval Texts* (Oxford: Clarendon, 1992), a useful anthology of the antifeminist and feminist works with which the men of Chaucer's time were more than familiar.

course, flower and leaf – all subjects of debates which have their own literary expression elsewhere, and, as Thomas L. Reed recently pointed out, debates which are often in Middle English left humorously unresolved and unresolvable.[3] Reed proposes a context for these debates which is essentially recreational, ludic, even carnivalesque. For either side to win or lose unequivocally, or in accordance with the normal hierarchies, is unnecessary in such contexts, because each participant in the debate is presented as having an understandably justifiable point of view. Rather than concentrating on the merits of the relative debating positions, attention focuses on the dialectics of the argument and the competing interests of the disputants. It may well be that, for the original audience of the *Legend of Good Women*, such allusions to the ludic debate tradition, along with the fictionalised demand for a poetic retraction in praise of women, were signal enough that an orthodox courtly treatment of women was not to be expected.

The *Legend of Good Women* is not formally a debate in the sense that opposing arguments are put forward and argued. It is rather that the attitude the poet expresses towards women in the exemplary tales of which the *Legend* is composed contrasts uncomfortably with that expressed in their Prologue. In the Prologue we hear the idealising orthodox voice of traditional *louange des dames* or praise of women. In the Legends, purportedly composed as the penitential response to *Troilus and Criseyde*, Ovidian sympathy for women is mingled with Ovidian cynicism. With its three contrasting spokespersons – the God of Love, the harassed and reluctant male poet, and Alceste as representative woman – the *Legend* partakes of that kind of debate which does not seek to resolve but to exploit the biased interests and personalities of the participants.

In the Prologue the poet dreams of a queen, whom he thinks is his 'lady sovereyne' because of her beauty and evident goodness and who in her mercy takes it upon herself to intercede for him before the God of Love. Her clothing of green and white makes her look like the humble

---

[3] See T. L. Reed, *Middle English Debate Poetry and the Aesthetics of Irresolution* (Columbia: University of Missouri Press, 1990), for discussion and bibliographic references to Middle English debates on these topics.

daisy of the fields, which the poet has been admiring in his waking life. The God of Love finally reveals to him that she is actually the legendary Queen Alceste of Thrace, in remembrance of whose goodness the daisy was created. In the course of the poet's dream he thus comes to understand that in some way the little flower and the queen-like lady dressed like a daisy are one in exemplary female virtue with the ancient heroine Alceste.

good

The attributes which the poet gives the daisy in the *Legend of Good Women* are symbolic of all a woman should be – humble, pure (as the daisy's petals are white), blushingly modest (as the petals have red tips), obedient (as the daisy opens and follows the sun), careful of her reputation (as the daisy closes at night), above all faithful (as the daisy blooms in winter as well as summer). The story of Alceste concerns a heroine who was so devoted to her husband that she chose to die in his place and was turned into a daisy because of her virtuous love. She is the embodiment of 'trouthe of womanhede', she 'knows al the bounds that she oghte to kepe', and she is thus an example to all other women in the practice of love and 'wyfhod'. In the action of the Prologue, this composite female personage shows mercy to the suffering poet and is described as the source of his poetic inspiration. This is straightforward encomium. All the descriptions of daisy, 'lady sovereyne', and good Alceste display no hint of irony, even if the traditional models of feminine worth, found for example in the poet's balade *Hyd Absolon*, are naively decorative rather than seriously examined. They certainly cannot be simply assumed ironic because the female virtues so lauded are not generally valued today.

In the Legends, on the other hand, Chaucer presents us with a collection of stories about women whose exemplary status as instances of legendary virtue was far from assured and whose suffering at the hands of men is often treated by Chaucer with flippancy, sometimes with sexual double entendre, and finally with a show of boredom. Pretending to praise, pretending to sympathise, is a well-known technique of irony, especially when the topic is the praise or 'dispraise' of women. The stance which Chaucer adopts has similarities with other medieval defences of women, which operate by superficially opposing the view that women are naturally bad, while at the same time condemning their characteristic virtues as foolish. Chaucer may well save women from the charge of native untrustworthiness, for example, only to lay them open to the charge of gullibility, of trusting men too much:

> O sely wemen, ful of innocence,
> Ful of pite, of trouthe and conscience,
> What maketh yow to men to truste so?
> 1254–6[4]

The epithets 'sely' (blessed, hapless) and 'innocent', which often collocate in the *Legend,* are entirely appropriate terms for describing women saints, but frequently bear the connotations 'simple, guileless, naive, gullible'.[5] It is clear that in this poem's strategy Chaucer is more than happy for such ambiguity to stand unresolved.

Chaucer has been commanded to compose a Legendary of good women, or a secular version of a collection of saints' lives. The God of Love has suggested that suitable subjects would be the heroines of the poet's own books, whom he featured in his balade, *Hyd Absolon,* and who are the ladies heading the crowd surrounding the Daisy Queen in his vision. While it is just possible to see a connection between the story of Alceste's sacrificial death and those of other women who 'died for love' or otherwise suffered, nevertheless many questions come to mind when some of these exemplary women turn out to be the like of Cleopatra and Medea. Why, if Chaucer genuinely wished to write about good women, choose to adapt the biographies of women generally thought to be bad? Cleopatra and Medea were serial killers, Medea and Philomela were infanticides, and close female associates of Hypsipyle and Hypermnestra were involved in mass murder. Such details are glossed over but not entirely suppressed in Chaucer's portraits – what unsavoury light, for example, would be thrown on the goodness of women (one thinks of the death of the men of Lesbos at the

---

[4] All Chaucer quotations are taken from L. D. Benson, ed., *The Riverside Chaucer,* 3rd edn (Oxford University Press, 1987). Because of its date of publication, I have not been able to consider extensively the text in Janet Cowen and G. Kane's *Geoffrey Chaucer: the Legend of Good Women* (East Lansing: Colleagues Press, 1995). I have, however, consulted the occasional reading which I thought crucial, and removed from my own commentary on the Prologues any observation which depended on a small verbal deviation between the two versions, since Cowen and Kane (pp. 124–39) believe small variations in the G Prologue are more likely to be scribal than authorial.

[5] See *MED* for the meaning of 'sely' in *LGW* 2532 and 'innocent' in *LGW* 1546.

hands of its women), if we took Chaucer's advice in *Hypsipyle* and consulted the original for *all* the facts (1557–8)? Even when the heroines are as genuinely virtuous as Lucrece, may not their deaths be considered foolish and reprehensible suicides rather than the sacrifices of holy martyrs?

How, moreover, should we respond to the persistently fluctuating tone in the Legends? To take one example: Chaucer defuses the mood of pathos and horror which dominates his story of Tereus' rape and mutilation of his sister-in-law, Philomela, with an unexpectedly flippant concluding 'moral' for women, which trivialises the heroine's experience and that of all women at the hands of all men (2384–93). By contrast, his version of the Ariadne story is shaded with a measure of cynicism, but his treatment of Ariadne's eventual abandonment by Theseus on a deserted isle (2187–97) is not unsympathetic towards his heroine's anguish. Indeed, satire or even irony is far too blunt an instrument with which to dissect the peculiar effect of this and other of the Legends, for the occasional pathos seems intended genuinely to move its audience. Critics have too often tried to level out the differences in tone – to accept Cleopatra and her companions as in some sense the equal in virtue of the good Alceste, or else to respond to the evident comedy in some of the Legends by denigrating the goodness of other heroines such as Lucrece to make them fit the ironic model. Feminist critiques are only the latest in a long line of reductionist approaches to the *Legend of Good Women*, which take at face value its stated subject of defending women, while ignoring the effect on the poem's meaning of the frequently flippant stance the narrator adopts. There are, on the other hand, many critics whose assessment of the Legends is overwhelmingly affected by the many comic asides and cynical 'morals' which decorate the tales and who have finally concluded that the *Legend* is an 'unmerciful satire' on women.

How then are we to reconcile the opposing responses which the poem evokes? I believe that the Prologue to the *Legend of Good Women* offers us at least three contexts which should shape our interpretation of the uneasy clash obtaining in the *Legend* between the orthodox literary ideals of the gentleman-poet, *la louange des dames*, and the humorous allusions which are normally associated with other registers entirely, those in which women are comprehensively mocked. The first and

[handwritten margin note: No – Critics are better than this / straw men (or women) here]

overarching context is that of the joke.[6] It is difficult to identify the "joke"
nuances of social intercourse of a former time, but it is not impossible.
Jokes at the expense of the opposite sex are a common pastime in any
age, and are particularly easy to trace in the Middle Ages. The joke
hinted at in the *Legend* is the one which said that while the existence of
good women was conceivable, in practice none was likely to be found
today. The position is adumbrated in the opening lines of the *Legend*,
where Chaucer gives a carefully reasoned statement of the necessity and
rationality of believing more things than can be validated by the
evidence of one's eyes. As, in the nature of things, nobody can have any
personal experience of the joys of heaven and the pains of hell, this is a
case where it is necessary to accept the authority of scripture (F/G
17–28). It is a perfectly orthodox position, but the passage undoubtedly
sets up a climate of scepticism which is intensified later in the Prologue
when Chaucer tells us he is going to translate some old books, and we
can believe them if we like, he doesn't care (G 88)! What then is the
inherent improbability that the old authorities are asking us to believe?
That it is the goodness in women that is the important but unverifiable
tenet of faith in the 'religion' of the God of Love is suggested by the title
and central situation of the poem.

Chaucer would not have been the first to suggest that the existence of
good women was a phenomenon of which the ordinary man had no
experience, nor could put to the test. Indeed, the brotherhood of men
in the Middle Ages made many joking allusions to what everyone
'knew', that there are no good women, that all women talk too much,
are inquisitive, extravagant, too interested in adornment, and cannot be
trusted. They would have agreed with their modern descendants that
there are no good women drivers or mothers-in-law. There had been, of
course, some good women in the past, which we can read about, but
there are few Lucreces or Penelopes, Alcestes or Griseldas today, as Jean
de Meun made his Jealous Husband say.[7] The Good Woman is to be
thought of as a legendary beast, a rare bird, a black swan: one can

---

6 Cf. Janet M. Cowen, 'Chaucer's *Legend of Good Women*: Structure and Tone', *SP* 82
(1985): 416–36.

7 F. Lecoy, ed., *Le Roman de la Rose* (Paris: CFMA, 1965–70), 8621–76; H. W. Robbins,
trans., *The Romance of the Rose by Guillaume de Lorris and Jean de Meun* (New York:
Dutton, 1962), pp. 174–5.

theoretically conceive of such a fabulous creature, as one can *imagine* a black swan by mentally combining the idea of blackness with the idea of a swan, but one would not expect to find one on earth. Chaucer thus may dream of a fabulously virtuous woman and gracefully hint that he knows at least one good woman in reality, the one he praises as the daisy and confuses with the good Alceste. (This is possibly a compliment to Richard II's wife, Anne of Bohemia, to whom the poem is dedicated in the F Prologue.) But the notion of any large number of good and faithful women invites polite incredulity; indeed the narrator of the *Legend* pretends that his audience may be amazed at his claim of a vision of an enormous number of women, 'And trewe of love thise women were echon' (F 282–91/G 185–94). It is not so much the huge number of women in the vision, but the fact that they were all faithful in love that is so difficult to believe.

Two attitudes to women are thus united in the voice of the narrating male poet. As true believer and orthodox adherent of the 'religion of love' he praises and honours the goodness of women – the daisy, his 'lady sovereyne', the good Alceste. But, as ordinary man, he understands the involuntary doubts of those who must accept by faith those tenets of religion which cannot be tested by experience, a scepticism which he expects may be shown towards his own recounting of stories of the virtuous women which inhabit old books.

This stance is common to both versions of the Prologue. The ludic context, however, is not developed the same way in the two Prologues, each of which was possibly designed for a different audience or readership, and consequently employed differing rhetorical strategies.[8] In the F Prologue the narrating voice draws much of its character from the dialogue in which it engages with its implied audience. The F Prologue conveys a lively sense of a courtly audience at play which augments the bantering references in the Legends to 'ye wemen' and 'us men'. Its characteristic ambience is captured most evocatively in a long but obscure passage dealing with the courtship of the birds (F 125–70). Perhaps youthful and light-hearted flirtation would be a better term

---

[8] D. W. Rowe comes to a similar view of the relationship of the Prologues in *Through Nature to Eternity: Chaucer's Legend of Good Women* (Lincoln: University of Nebraska Press, 1988), pp. 141–55. The F Prologue is usually thought to date from about 1386, the G Prologue from the early 1390s.

than courtship because, for all the conventional talk about choosing mates 'withouten repentyng' (F 146–7), the passage is not about serious troth-plighting, and certainly not about marriage. The transitory nature of the devotion promised by these servants of Love is pointed up with a gentle irony at several points, as when the avian suitors seek their mates' love by swearing 'on the blosmes to be trewe' (F 153–8). Hymning the courtly 'saint', St Valentine, Chaucer's birds hint that the alliances associated with his feast day were not only temporary but also extra-licit, love that accords with nature rather than human law (F 148–52). The matter and tone of many of the poems associated with St Valentine's Day suggest that a carnivalesque and 'up-so-doun' spirit was of its essence. Even Chaucer's contemporary Sir Oton de Grandson, considered the most gentlemanly and courtly of poets connected with the French and English courts, could indulge in antifeminist comments in his poetry for St Valentine – 'Who would ever trust a woman? . . . certainly no wise man, if he does not wish to spend his life in great suffering and sorrow!'[9]

The mode of courtly game established in this passage of the *Legend*, maintained by the narrator's comments on the Legends, seriously diminishes the tragic effect of their heroines' plights. The more vigorously Chaucer attacks the villains in his rogues' gallery, in the context of the *Legend of Good Women* the more likely they are to receive admiration (at least from the men in the audience, supposedly under attack along with them) for being competent exponents of the game of seduction. Chaucer suggests that there are Jasons enough among the men in his audience (1554–7). The unfortunate heroines of the Legends are only too full of mercy and pity for the feigned suffering of their would-be suitors (cf. F 160–5), but the ladies whom Chaucer addresses in his audience seem less 'innocent' and better armed against natural male duplicity. He does not believe they will so gravely misread the intentions of their lovers as Phillis did Demophon's (2401–2).

Thus part of the peculiar flavour of the *Legend of Good Women*, part of the larger context, that is, by means of which we interpret its component parts, is this sense of lively dialogue between men and

---

[9] *Complainte Amoureuse de Sainct Valentin* 67–77, see A. Piaget, ed., *Oton de Grandson: sa vie et ses poésies* (Lausanne: Société d'Histoire de la Suisse Romande, 1941), p. 483.

women, who of their nature espouse different points of view. There is evidence that just such literary duels between the sexes constituted a fair proportion of the entertainment of late medieval courts, alongside the activity of composing lyrics in praise of women, that which is often thought of as 'courtly poetry'. The kind of material that makes up the majority of the manuscripts in which the *Legend of Good Women* appears tells us something about such games, showing us courtly participants answering riddles, learning their fortunes at the 'chance of the dice' and debating questions about love. Glending Olson has proposed that medieval people did not perceive this kind of entertainment as totally frivolous. The mirth such pastimes occasioned was regarded as therapeutic and an antidote to the debilitation of melancholy.[10]

The G Prologue suppresses much of this sense of courtly audience and intimate game. Gone also is the dedication to the queen, extended praise of the daisy, and pervasive use of terminology associated with the religion of love. In its place is evoked a third context which enhances the other significant component of the *Legend of Good Women*, the poet's professional standing, his social role, his responsibility for choice of subject matter, his poetic integrity. Prologue G, generally thought to be a revision of Prologue F, is extant in only one manuscript. In leaving out some of the more obscure references to service of the Flower and cheeky allusions to the interests of a coterie audience, it presents a rather tidier structure and probably opens up the meaning of the poem to a wider readership. The G Prologue does no more than change the emphasis in the central scene of the *Legend of Good Women*, and it does not modify the basic intention conveyed by the F Prologue and the Legends (which are unaltered in both versions). Indeed, the intention is probably made clearer, and the G Prologue is almost invariably quoted in preference to F when the conceptual structure of the Prologue is at issue. There is a shift in register from the F Prologue's sense of light courtly entertainment towards one where the formal lines of the 'debate about women', as indulged in by men of learning, dominates the exposition of the G Prologue. The second mode, while still light-

---

[10] G. Olson, *Literature as Recreation in the Later Middle Ages* (Ithaca: Cornell University Press, 1982), esp. pp. 164–204.

hearted and humorous, is more recognisably aligned with the claims of
the serious male poet to debate and write effectively than are the slightly
obscure allusions to courtly gameplaying of the former. It underlines
the fact that the fictional debate about women is only an excuse to
discuss the poetic craft, a topos which has enabled Chaucer to draw
attention to his poetic output and the skill required not only to choose
one's matter but to draw new meaning from it. It is generally agreed
that Chaucer's original audience was particularly well equipped to
appreciate the details of poetic technique and linguistic manipulation
as well as the simple pleasure of story-telling,[11] and the shift between
courtly game and broader intellectual context is an easy one. There is an
interesting parallel in Christine de Pizan's decision to present the
collection of documents which she had assembled on the Debate about
the *Roman de la Rose* not only to the courtly audience surrounding
Isabeau of Bavaria but also to a learned professional audience represented by Guillaume de Tignonville, Provost of Paris.[12]

Inasmuch as it is the poet's clerkly service of love which is at issue, the
God of Love in the G Prologue is given a much longer speech in which
to arraign the poet. His charge is more precisely one of defaming the
goodness of women in general than it is in Prologue F. And this was, it
must be said, the great topos by means of which the wit and ingenuity
of the man of learning could be displayed:

> Hast thow nat mad in Englysh ek the bok
> How that Crisseyde Troylus forsok,
> In shewynge how that wemen han don mis?
> G 264–6

Chaucer's so-called bias against women and love in *Troilus and Criseyde*
is characterised in the G Prologue as the traditional stance of the old
and impotent man of learning (G 258–63). Moreover, the God of Love
in the G Prologue invokes the whole corpus of clerical antifeminism

11 Cf. P. M. Kean, *Chaucer and the Making of English Poetry*, 2 vols. (London: Routledge, 1972), I, p. 4; E. Reiss, 'Chaucer and his Audience', *ChauR* 14 (1980): 390–402, esp. p. 396; P. Strohm, 'Chaucer's Fifteenth Century Audience and the Narrowing of the "Chaucer Tradition"', *SAC* 4 (1982): 3–31, esp. pp. 26, 28.
12 See J. L. Baird and J. R. Kane, eds. and trans., *La Querelle de la Rose: Letters and Documents* (Chapel Hill: North Carolina Studies in the Romance Languages and Literatures, 1978), p. 12.

when he calls as witnesses to the virtue of women the hallowed names of Walter Map and St Jerome (G 270–81). Jerome and Map do mention good women like Lucrece and Penelope, but only to liken them to legendary beasts no longer to be found on earth, as I have mentioned above.

When Chaucer gets a chance to answer the charge brought against him in the *Legend*, he takes issue with the simplistic notion of both Alceste and the God of Love (cf. G 270–2) that the meaning of a poem is to be equated with the poet's choice of subject matter. Not so, says Chaucer. The ultimate meaning depends on the poet's intention which he imposes upon his subject matter (F 471–4/G 461–4). Because a poem like *Troilus and Criseyde* is *about* unfaithfulness in love does not mean such unfaithfulness is being endorsed. Chaucer here appears to be claiming an eminently serious ethical intent for his previous work, a moral *utilitas*, the mark of a certain *auctoritas* which was normally only accorded the authorities of the illustrious past, who most certainly did not write in English, a language heretofore offered little respect.

The relevance can now be seen of the mysterious reference to Chaucer's translation of the *Roman de la Rose* which is yoked with the composition of *Troilus and Criseyde* in the God of Love's initial accusation against Chaucer (G 253–66). We do not know if Chaucer completed his *Romaunt of the Rose*; the significance of its citation, however, is in the poet's aligning of his *Troilus and Criseyde* with the French masterpiece as a work of infinite complexity, demanding subtle and sophisticated interpretation by its readers. Chaucer's association of *Troilus* with the *Rose* is a claim that its readers, too, must observe the rules of poetic decorum which demand that the parts be interpreted in light of the intention of the whole work, as well as a realisation that works that capitalise on irony and other means of indirection leave themselves open to misinterpretation. This is the burden of the arguments adduced in defence of the *Roman* in the famous *querelle de la Rose*,[13] of which we have the early fifteenth-century documents, and which affords an interesting comparison with the defence of the poet offered in the Prologue to the *Legend of Good Women*.

---

[13] See E. Hicks, ed., *Le Débat sur le Roman de la Rose* (Paris: Champion, 1977); for English translation, see note 12.

Alceste's long speech in defence of Chaucer makes many of the same points as did the defenders of Jean de Meun in the *querelle de la Rose* – even to the instancing of the woman question, and in the point that he did not initiate the sin against the God of Love since he was a mere translator (G 340–5). The idea that translation was an act involving little intelligence or personal responsibility on behalf of the translator was transparently disingenuous. In fact, the transference of the cultural riches of the past from one language into another tongue and time was considered an endeavour of the highest worth. Other aspects of Alceste's defence of the poet show how little the issue at stake is a 'sin' against love and how much it is a declaration of the English poet's own sense of worth and social value. In partial mitigation of Chaucer's crime she enumerates the significant items of his poetic corpus (F 417–30/G 405–20), by means of which, she informs the God of Love, he 'hath maked lewed folk to delyte/ To serven yow, in preysynge of youre name' (G 403–4). Some of the works on the list have nothing to do with the service of love, for example, the translation of *Boethius*. In addition, some passages of the *Parliament of Fowls* or of *Palamon and Arcite*, which are tendered as part of the 'defence', slander the God of Love as grievously as anything in *Troilus and Criseyde*. This adds weight to the suspicion that Chaucer is simply setting up a straw man when he has the God of Love enunciate the charge against him, and Alceste defend him.

Moreover, Alceste's defence is embedded in an extremely long speech, of doubtful relevance, in which she admonishes the God of Love to beware of judging an accused man thoughtlessly and mercilessly, in short, of behaving like a tyrannical lord. While she hesitates at first to offer advice to a God, it is clear that she soon thinks of him as any other medieval ruler. The speech is a carefully constructed patchwork of quotations from cardinal works of the *de regimine principum* tradition, betraying an intimate familiarity with the kind of views expressed by Seneca, John of Salisbury, Giles of Rome, and in the pseudo-Aristotelian *Secretum Secretorum*. Literature of this kind was extensive in the Middle Ages, and as popular with ordinary men as with rulers. If it does nothing else, Alceste's speech enhances the poet's implicit claim to learning and high seriousness.

It is hard to see today how the components fuse in this curious amalgam of courtly writing about love and relatively serious moral instruction on the duties of kings, but there is clearly a sense in which the service of the God of Love stands for the pursuit of the noble life. A gentleman aspired to be able to speak of love out of 'sentement' (F 69) but also to view the transient delights of the world from the perspective of Boethius (F 425/G 413). The man of learning, the scholarly poet, the 'servant of the servants of love', facilitated all these aspirations both with his graceful, courtly 'making' and with his other translations of more serious works. Both his stance as adviser to princes and his demonstrable ability to engage wittily in the debate about women functioned as markers of his usefulness to courtly society.

From at least the time of Ovid, Love and Woman were topics constituting the raw matter on which the male poet imposed form, his love poetry the ultimate witness to his creative power. Indeed, I have invented the phrase, the 'matter of Woman', by analogy with other great medieval 'matters' with which writers dealt, like the 'matter of Arthur' or the 'matter of Charlemagne', as a punning reference to the popular medieval discourse on the nature of Woman, a discourse gloriously stereotyped in joke and anecdote and pseudo-scientific understanding of Woman's close affinity with things material. The rhetorical exploitation of women as subject matter is particularly clearly exemplified in Chaucer's versions of the Lucretia and Dido stories.

We are becoming increasingly aware how thoroughly the discourse of writing, reading, interpreting, translating was permeated from ancient to modern times with metaphors derived from the commerce between women and men.[14] Both Ovid's *Ars Amatoria* and Jean de Meun's *Roman de la Rose* claimed to be, and were frequently enough accepted as, arts of poetry as much as arts of love or arts of seduction. In yet another important antecedent to the *Legend of Good Women*, the palinodal *Jugement dou Roy de Navarre*, Machaut humorously defended the honour of men in general and of himself as a poet when he defended his treatment of women in his earlier debate poem, *Le Jugement dou Roy de Behaingne*. In the *Legend of Good Women*, too, the male poet displays his mastery of the matter of Woman and of love poetry; in the tradition

---

[14] See Carolyn Dinshaw, *Chaucer's Sexual Poetics* (Madison: University of Wisconsin Press, 1989).

of the late medieval gentleman and poet the praise of women and the scepticism at women's virtue do not sit uncomfortably together; indeed, Chaucer's facility in handling both modes draws attention to his poetic skill.

The surface of the text of the *Legend of Good Women* is cheerfully biased in favour of the poet's own gender. Both in its stance of gentlemanly praise of women and in its occasional scepticism, it colludes with the expectations of a preponderantly male audience. That is, to be a poet and to be male are not rigorously distinguished in the *Legend*. It is a voice apologetic towards women, but not overwhelmingly so. It pities woman's plight, but sees no remedy for woman's situation beyond her return to quite traditional behavioural standards, to less wandering on the seashore, less trusting of strangers, less readiness to believe the promises of men. In endorsing Alceste's self-sacrifice Chaucer equates feminine goodness (see G 533–4) with confinement within 'the bounds that she ought to keep' and marginalises women in passivity (like Hypermnestra imprisoned) or silence (like Philomela with her tongue wrenched out by the man who raped her).[15] Where a heroine like Phillis is allowed expression, much of her complaint is truncated, except for the well-written parts! Moreover, it has been noted over the years that the strongest thematic link between the Legends is the comic abuse of men, and women as the victims of men. That is, Lucrece and Hypermnestra are not martyrs to their own service of love in the same sense that Dido and Medea are, but both are pawns in larger masculine enterprises. Though the male protagonists of the tales are ostensibly condemned, Chaucer usually devotes a fair portion of each narrative to the situation in which the 'hero' finds himself, in the world of action and affairs; the relevance to the account of the heroines' sufferings is not immediately obvious in, for example, the brilliant sea-battle in *Cleopatra* or the long description of Jason's adventures in *Hypsipyle and Medea*. Even the inner workings of the minds of the rapists, Tarquin in *Lucrece*, and Tereus in *Philomela* are vividly imagined and carefully rendered.[16] By the time Chaucer comes to the

---

15 For a feminist reading of the silencing of the female voice in the *Legend*, see Harvey, 'Speaking of Tongues', pp. 52–7.
16 Cf. R. W. Frank, Jr, *Chaucer and the 'Legend of Good Women'* (Cambridge, Mass.: Harvard University Press, 1972), pp. 43, 81; R. M. Lumiansky, 'Chaucer and the Idea

second last Legend of unhappy Phillis, he dismisses the wickedness of men in terms of the 'natural' opposition between the sexes, mere instinctive, animal-like behaviour, nothing worth worrying about. Women, their bodies and their property, are presented as fair game to naturally predatory males who take to seduction as ducks to water (2450–1).

In almost every aspect, however, the narrator's masculine bias is an essentially literary stance, a fact easily demonstrated by both internal and external evidence. The narrator's voice is biased in the kinds of ways that Alceste and the God of Love have commented on. That is, all the possibilities for partiality which Alceste enumerates in defence of Chaucer's composition of *Criseyde* and the *Rose*, instead ironically apply to the *Legend*. His responsibility for the work is seriously compromised, because his subject matter has been chosen for him and he has been, moreover, commanded to write by 'som persone and durste yt nat withseye' (F 367/G 347). Alceste notes that he is unlikely to be a lover, but commands him nevertheless to 'spek wel of love' (F 490–1/G 480–1), a phrase which perhaps carries the connotation of the *ars bene dicendi* (Quintilian's term describing rhetoric)[17] – the act of conducting the best advocacy possible on a case with which one is not necessarily sympathetic, and the fiction of course implies that the interests of men do not coincide with the interests of women. Since he is 'nyce' (F 462/G 340) and 'kan nat wel endite' (F 414/G 402), it is not surprising if his difficulties with moulding recalcitrant subject matter are well marked. As Robert Frank so cogently noted, it is to these aspects of the narratorial persona that the many expressions of haste and weariness are to be attributed, not to the poet's genuine boredom with the poem and its subject: 'indeed, the fictive situation that makes the narratives a penance which he must perform demands that he shall groan now and then'.[18] The 'Legend of Chaucer's Boredom', as Frank called it, was a concept which helped to conceal from critics the full implications of what the biased narration does to the meaning of the poem.

Among all the topics for literary conflict, the polarity of male and

of Unfaithful Men', *MLN* 62 (1947): 560–2; Elaine Tuttle Hansen, 'Irony and the Antifeminist Narrator in Chaucer's *Legend of Good Women*', *JEGP* 82 (1983): 11–31.

[17] Winsor, 'Study', pp. 41–2.

[18] Frank, *Chaucer and the Legend*, pp. 207–8.

female is the most engaging, the least amenable in some ways to being confined within purely literary bounds. There tends to be more emotion invested in discussing the faith of women and the infidelity of men (or vice versa) than there is in debates about winter and summer or youth and old age. There can be little doubt, for example, that misogynist writing was indulged in with more enthusiasm than the literary project strictly required, as Christine de Pizan said of Jean de Meun's efforts.[19] Jean himself uttered the standard disclaimer that if women find some of his writing malicious or satirical it was only written for instruction's sake. He was simply translating what other wise men had written from their experience of the ways of women. However, he does admit that he has made a few additions, as poets are wont to do, 'for my game' (*RR* 15195–225, Robbins' translation). Chaucer enters the same game in the *Legend of Good Women*. The jokes characteristic of this genre are of course more appealing to men than to women, and Chaucer was well aware that amusing stories about women were actually taunts, as the tale of Jankyn, laughing as he read his Book of Wicked Wives to the Wife of Bath, makes clear. If nothing else, that episode in the *Canterbury Tales* suggests that Chaucer was prepared to take the consequences of teasing female listeners with stories that often were only ostensibly favourable to the concept of women's goodness, and knew that a vigorous response might be expected, in the context of the courtly gameplaying that he had promoted. It is not impossible that Chaucer, however, like the opponents in the *querelle de la Rose* and as his own God of Love intimates, had some concern that the surface meaning of a literary fiction may have undesirable consequences in the real world.[20] Indeed, the narrator of the *Legend of Good Women* is at times somewhat defensive in his identification with the male oppressors of women and anxious about the responsibility borne by the male poet in promoting the ill-fame so frequently bestowed on women by literature. Such anxiety focuses not only on his treatment of Criseyde in his earlier poem, but also applies to his present enterprise. Thus Chaucer caps his tale of poor Phillis with a joke which hinges on his

19 Hicks, *Débat sur le Roman*, p. 140; Baird and Kane, *Querelle de la Rose*, p. 137.
20 Cf. D. Mehl, 'The Audience of Chaucer's *Troilus and Criseyde*', in Beryl Rowland, ed., *Chaucer and Middle English Studies in Honour of Rossell Hope Robbins* (London: Allen, 1974), p. 186.

own male trustworthiness towards women (in the context of the *Legend of Good Women* the phrase is an oxymoron, for 'male' and 'trustworthy' are mutually contradictory terms):

> Be war, ye wemen, of youre subtyl fo,
> Syn yit this day men may ensaumple se;
> And trusteth, as in love, no man but me.
> 2559–61

Feminist analyses suggest that behind the ironic reference in these lines to sexual relationships (in which realm Chaucer has proved beyond doubt that no man is to be trusted), there may also be a wry acknowledgement of Chaucer's own lack of reliability, pretending as he does to praise women, while at the same time promoting scepticism of their goodness. The 'natural' falseness of men towards women is not unlike a certain inevitable poetic faithlessness towards one's source, one's matter, incurred whenever the poet employs his craft and subtlety, his art and feigning, to translate and make his source new and relevant.[21] The narrator of the *Legend of Phyllis* treats his matter with the same callousness and cleverness that Demophon used to betray Phillis.

Again I stress that this is a stance, a mask, a strategy, which the poet adopts at this point in the poem. It tells us little about Chaucer's actual attitude towards women,[22] although much about an attitude towards women with which many men have colluded. My study will not attempt to connect the *Legend of Good Women* with the world of real women and real anger, although Christine de Pizan in the early fifteenth century provides a potent enough example that the kind of matter used in the *Legend* caused real women to be really angry. Yet even here Christine transformed her anger at the traditional masculine treatment of the matter of Woman into an occasion to enhance her own

[21] See D. A. Favier, '*Anelida and Arcite*: Antifeminist Allegory, Pro-feminist Complaint', *ChauR* 26 (1991): 83–94, esp. pp. 89–90.
[22] A. J. Minnis' thoughtful discussion of the 'structural antifeminism' which pervaded the culture of which Chaucer was part is useful and timely, see Minnis, *The Shorter Poems*, Oxford Guides to Chaucer (Oxford: Clarendon, 1995), pp. 423–34. Minnis notes that the term is 'coined on the analogy of the economist's term "structural unemployment". The ideas in question are dictated and required by the structure; the structure itself must change before its characteristic ills can disappear . . . The male-oriented morality assumed in the *Legend* is, therefore, utterly typical. Chaucer did not invent it; neither did he exaggerate it', p. 427.

professional standing as a writer; in engaging in the traditional debate about women she found a place in the masculine preserve of serious literature.

I do not address the *Legend* primarily as a historical document nor as a socio-feminist case study, although the poem urgently throws up questions relevant to such disciplines; with Chaucer I claim that 'I may not al at-ones speke' (*LGW* F 102). Among the many possible readings of the *Legend of Good Women*, I have limited myself to identifying and elucidating major aspects of the literary context in which I think the *Legend of Good Women* locates itself; in particular, the role that humorous antifeminist/feminist debate plays in the self-definition of the learned poet, in the contexts both of courtly recreation and of scholarly *jeu d'esprit*. Given the comic masculine triumphalism of the Legends, I find it difficult to agree that Chaucer is attempting, for example, any serious analysis of the regrettable 'feminisation of men', as is maintained in a recent feminist reading.[23] Rather, in intimating that his audience will not view the lies and stratagems of the Legends' seducers too severely, he is directing attention to the productive and necessary deceitfulness of the male rhetor and poet.

Thus my study deals with the *Legend of Good Women*'s praise of women implicit in the courtly service of the God of Love, and its interesting counterpoint in the cynical attitudes towards women which were a marker traditionally of the learned writer. To this end I examine the two protagonists with which the poet has to deal in the Prologue to the *Legend*, and the task they impose upon him. In my first section I consider the good woman Alceste, transcendent marguerite and legendary heroine, but also the jokes which the concept of the mythical Good Woman attracted. In the second section I turn to the God of Love, patron of women, poetry and the pursuit of the noble life, and his invocation of scholarly antifeminist debate in the G Prologue (since the enterprise in which Chaucer is engaging is presented more straightforwardly in this version). I then discuss the palinode form, the device by means of which the poet can appear to accede to his sovereign's requests, while drawing attention to his own virtuosity, in the skill with

[23] Elaine Tuttle Hansen, *Chaucer and the Fictions of Gender* (Berkeley: University of California Press, 1992), pp. 1–15.

which he avoids true repentance. Next I deal with the Legends of the so-called good women, identifying some of the strategies by means of which Chaucer subverts the praise of women. There are very great practical difficulties inherent in discussing a poem furnished with two prologues, of different but complementary emphases: there is merit, indeed insight to be gained, in drawing on both together, but also in treating each as a work in its own right. In the last section of this book, therefore, following on my discussion of the Legends, I return to the charming but frequently obscure Prologue F, with its intimate allusions to courtly games and poetry-making. My hope is that insights drawn from discussion of the Legends will elucidate the alternative interpretative context, or framework of expectation, which Chaucer has designed for the small coterie audience for which the *Legend of Good Women* was originally designed.

PART I

Chaucer's Good Woman

I

The Good Woman: the daisy

In the Prologue to the *Legend of Good Women* there are two significant narrative motifs. The one involves the poetic service of the Flower, and includes the praise of Ideal Woman under the figure of the daisy, and the poet's vision of an all but perfect woman from the mythological past. He is initially ignorant of this lady's name but finally comes to recognise her true identity. The second motif involves the God of Love's accusation against Chaucer and is made up of the charge that the poet had written poetry which defames women, his defence by the mysterious Daisy Queen, and the imposition of his penance, a new poem in which he will recant his former sins. Both the recognition motif and the accusation motif are common in the works of fourteenth-century French poets. For example, Machaut's *Jugement dou Roy de Navarre* has both an accusation and a recognition scene, and is also a recantation poem.

The Good Woman is thus represented in the Prologue to the *Legend* under two major literary figures, the marguerite of contemporary French poetry, and as a classical story the poet has read about in his old books. In the F Prologue there is an additional element: the sense that, when Chaucer praises the daisy, he is honouring a particular lady, and that, when he has his vision of a lady dressed like a daisy, he at first believes it is this same lady, who is the subject of his balade *Hyd Absolon*, where she is praised for virtues which outshine those of the heroines of the past. In this belief the poet is wrong; he finds out that the Daisy Queen of his dream is actually the legendary Queen Alceste of Thrace and not the one he calls 'my lady', but the mistake is nevertheless a compliment to the shadowy woman who lies behind the daisy and the visionary queen, whose virtues are so readily mistaken for hers.[1] The F Prologue is almost certainly designed as a tribute to Richard II's wife, Anne of Bohemia, to whom Alceste commands the completed poem is to be presented. There is no way of proving this attribution conclusively, but it seems likely in light of the dedication to her in the F Prologue. (Would the poem have been designed to honour some other lady and simultaneously dedicated to the queen?) Much of the poet's fiery devotion to the daisy is missing from Prologue G, as is the mistaken identity and the dedication. One cannot be sure whether the G version was pared down to its essentials for an occasion where the compliment to the queen was no longer appropriate (possibly after her death), or whether the briefer G Prologue was revised and expanded in F to make it fit an occasion suitable for honouring Anne. The first possibility is most likely.[2]

Of the three poetic modes Chaucer adopted from contemporary French *louange des dames* or praise of women – marguerite poetry, free adaptation of Ovidian transformation myth, and the lyric which combines a catalogue of traditional feminine virtues with a catalogue of classical heroines – it is the first which is least well understood and has led to much aberrant criticism of the *Legend* over the years. The praise

---

[1] Cf. S. Moore, 'The Prologue to Chaucer's "Legend of Good Women", in Relation to Queen Anne and Richard', *MLR* 7 (1912): 488–93; E. T. Donaldson, *Speaking of Chaucer* (London: Athlone, 1970), p. 958.

[2] In retrospect it seems that the credit for convincing English speaking readers that Prologue F preceded Prologue G must go to J. L. Lowes in J. L. Lowes 'The Prologue to the *Legend of Good Women* as Related to the French *Marguerite* Poems and to the *Filostrato*', *PMLA* 19 (1904): 593–683, and J. L. Lowes 'The Prologue to the *Legend of Good Women* Considered in its Chronological Relations', *PMLA* 20 (1905): 749–864. Much of Lowes' evidence has been disallowed since 1904–5, and the fact that his opinion prevailed was probably due to the fact that it was finally accepted by W. W. Skeat, and adopted in F. N. Robinson's *Works of Geoffrey Chaucer*, 2nd edn (Houghton Mifflin: Boston, 1957). Lowes later argued the case much more cogently in 'The Two Prologues to the *Legend of Good Women*: a New Test', in *Anniversary Papers by Colleagues and Pupils of George Lyman Kittredge* (Boston: Ginn, 1913), pp. 95–104. See also J. S. P. Tatlock, *The Development and Chronology of Chaucer's Work* (London: Chaucer Society, 1907), pp. 86–120. Cowen and Kane make the tacit assumption that G is the revision, *Legend of Good Women*, p. 124. For recent dissenting voices, see M. C. Seymour, 'Chaucer's *Legend of Good Women*: Two Fallacies', *RES* NS 37 (1986): 528–34; J. Eadie, 'The Author at Work: the Two Versions of the Prologue to the *Legend of Good Women*', *Neuphilologische Mitteilungen* 93 (1992): 135–44; and Sheila Delany, *The Naked Text: Chaucer's 'Legend of Good Women'* (Berkeley: University of California Press, 1972), pp. 34–43.

of the daisy does not imply a 'fresh appreciation of the beauties of nature' as turn-of the-century critics believed, nor is it a matter of a genuine love affair (particularly inappropriate if Anne of Bohemia was concerned), nor does the hyperbolic nature of its praise of women indicate parody. When Chaucer abandons his study for the daisy-studded fields of spring he is not setting up a significant contrast between authority and experience, as some have said, particularly since daisy worship turns out to be a very much more bookish experience than at first appears. This is a case where it is necessary to understand the 'game' (F/G 33) to which Chaucer alludes as the only activity which could draw him away from his delight in old books (F/G 29–39).

In fashionable, courtly society of the late fourteenth century a more conventional literary pose could hardly have been adopted than this one the poet draws of himself in love with the humble daisy of the meadows. But not, at this time, in English. If Chaucer's affection for 'thise floures white and red' has little to do with nature, and not even much to do with women, it has everything to do with the poetic representation of women, and with the difficult feat of translation which lies ahead:

> Now have I thanne eek this condicioun,
> That, of al the floures in the mede,
> Thanne love I most thise floures white and rede,
> Swiche as men callen daysyes in our toun.
> To hem have I so gret affeccioun,
> As I seyde erst, whanne comen is the May,
> That in my bed ther daweth me no day
> That I nam up and walkyng in the mede
> To seen this flour ayein the sonne sprede,
> Whan it upryseth erly by the morwe.
> F/G 40–9

Chaucer is here signalling his intention to emulate his French contemporaries, Machaut, Froissart and Deschamps, in composing a marguerite poem in English. Indeed, part of the charm of the *Legend* must have lain in hearing in English the commonplaces of this favourite courtly genre of contemporary French poetry. In relation to the newly self-conscious usage of English for sophisticated courtly poetry, 'thise floures . . . swiche as men callen daysyes in our toun' is more than a literal translation of Froissart's *flours petites/ Que nous appellons margher-ites* (*Paradis d'Amour* 1621–2), it is a claim that English poetry too is a fit vehicle for the grace and wit of the poetic worship of ladies, that index of the noble life. The pleasure of the listeners was matched by the difficulty which the poet experienced in attempting to translate the phraseology of a genre (F 66 ff.) which depended so much on a linguistic correspondence between the popular feminine name, Mar-guerite (meaning Pearl), and the little daisy of the fields.

The cult of the marguerite is a minor genre of late fourteenth-century French love poetry whose meaning and development were little understood before the thorough study of James I. Wimsatt.[3] It was probably initiated by Machaut in about 1366, clearly to praise someone named Marguerite, and the fashion lasted for at least two more decades. The poetry seems somewhat obscure today; but as it is usually occasional poetry, it becomes more comprehensible when the occasion and the protagonists are identified. This is certainly true for Machaut and Deschamps. With Froissart, who used the symbol of the marguerite extensively, one is not so sure which, if any, Marguerite was to be identified with the object of the poet's love; moreover, there is a sense in which he thinks of the marguerite as a woman who is the source of his poetic inspiration, or even with the poetic product itself. Thus at the end of his early *Paradis d'Amour* Froissart composes his famous balade *Sur toutes flours j'aimme la margerite*, while at the same time his lady weaves a chaplet of daisies as his reward (*Paradis d'Amour* 1602 ff.). The scene sums up the themes of the poem, the poet's learning how to be a good lover and a good poet; the lady with her complexion of pink and white is identified with the flower of the same colours and the poem woven like a daisy-chain. In *La Prison Amoureuse*, Froissart affixes the sign of the marguerite to a poem by means of his signet ring, in token that the poem is well made.[4] Froissart's use of the marguerite motif helps to explain how the daisy that Chaucer worships can be thought of

---

[3] J. I. Wimsatt, *The Marguerite Poetry of Guillaume de Machaut* (Chapel Hill: University of North Carolina, 1970).

[4] P. F. Dembowski, ed., *Jean Froissart: Le Paradis d'Amour, L'Orloge Amoreus* (Geneva: Droz, 1986); A. Fourrier, ed., *La Prison Amoureuse* (Paris: Klincksieck, 1974). For the significance of the marguerite signet ring, see S. Lanier, 'The Flower of the Imagination: French Marguerite Poetry and Chaucer's Prologue to *The Legend of Good Women*', Dissertation, Santa Barbara: University of California, 1976, pp. 184–8.

as a symbol of feminine perfection and poetic inspiration, not, however, necessarily connected with a woman called Margaret. In the case of Chaucer no 'Margaret' has ever been identified as a suitable candidate, although the F Prologue gives every indication that an actual woman was in mind.

Although marguerite poetry presents itself as love poetry, written in the first person, we should note that in the original poems by Machaut the poet himself is not the lover. It is now generally accepted that Machaut wrote the first marguerite poems on behalf of Pierre de Lusignan (Pierre of Cyprus), with whom Machaut was certainly acquainted and in whom both Chaucer and Froissart showed strong interest.[5] The rather odd references to Cyprus and Egypt in marguerite poetry derive from this connection with Pierre, along with other motifs such as the vaguely oriental atmosphere which produces, for example, the crown made of 'o perle fyn, oriental' worn by Chaucer's Alceste (F 221/G 153) – the wearing of garments lavishly decorated with pearls was characteristic of Pierre. Marguerite was an extraordinarily popular name among the nobility of fourteenth-century France, but Wimsatt postulates plausibly that Marguerite of Flanders was the most likely candidate for Pierre's homage. In the early 1360s she was a young widow and immensely wealthy heiress, whose inheritance was coveted by both France and England. Wimsatt does not suggest that Marguerite was Pierre's mistress in any ordinary sense (he had a wife and several mistresses back home), and he did not necessarily ever meet her. Wimsatt believes Pierre went to the trouble of employing Machaut to praise her effusively, in order to gain her support for his Crusade to reconquer the Holy Land. Machaut's marguerite poems are the result more of political expediency than love, although the narrator constantly refers to himself as the marguerite's lover.

In sum, it appears that in 1366 Machaut composed, on Pierre of Cyprus's behalf, a poem in praise of the marguerite, *Dit de la Marguerite*, where it is clear that a woman rather than a flower is the referent.[6] This poem lays down the features of the description of the marguerite which are to become standard: its devotion to the sun, its

---

[5] Wimsatt, *Marguerite Poetry*, pp. 40 ff.; see also Lowes, 'French *Marguerite* Poems', pp. 595–6.
[6] Wimsatt, *Marguerite Poetry*, p. 47.

colours, its humility, its miraculous powers of healing, the poet's delight in its presence:

> J'aim une fleur, qui s'uevre et qui s'encline
> Vers le soleil de jours quant il chemine,
> Et, quant il est couchiez sous sa courtine
>   Par nuit obscure,
> Elle se clot, einsois que li jours fine;
> Ses fueilles ont dessus couleur sanguine,
> Blanche dessous plus que gente n'ermine
>   De blancheur pure . . .
> Sa grant douçour garist les mauls d'amer,
> Sa grainne puet les mors ressusciter,
> Car elle m'a gari d'outre la mer
>   De ma doulour,
> Si la doy bien servir et honnourer
> Et mettre en li cuer et corps et penser
> Et dessus tout li chierir et amer
>   De fine amour.
> Ce qu'elle s'uevre et s'encline au soleil,
> C'est a dire qu'en li n'a point d'orgueil
> Et qu'elle est humble et de courtois acueil.
> 1–35[7]

[I love a flower which opens and inclines towards the sun during the day while the sun traverses the heavens, and when it is set, underneath its curtain of dark night, she closes up before the day comes to an end. Her petals are of a pink colour above, and underneath whiter than ermine in pure whiteness . . . Her great sweetness cures the ills of love, and her golden centre can raise the dead to life, for she cured me from beyond the sea of my sorrow. And I should certainly serve and honour her and put heart, body and thought in her, and love and cherish her above all with a pure love. That she opens and inclines towards the sun means that there is no pride in her, and that she is humble and courteously welcoming] trans. Windeatt, p. 145

The phrases in this poem recur again and again in Machaut's

---

[7] *Dit de la Marguerite* is printed as an appendix in A. Fourrier, ed., *Jean Froissart: Dits et Débats* (Geneva: Droz, 1979), pp. 147–53. The appendix also includes Machaut's *Dit de la Fleur de Lis et de la Marguerite*. Translations of all the marguerite poems are from B. A. Windeatt, ed. and trans., *Chaucer's Dream Poetry: Sources and Analogues* (Cambridge: Brewer, 1982). Henceforth: Windeatt.

marguerite poetry and that of his successors, so much so that their use designates a poem a marguerite poem, even if the name of the flower is not mentioned.

Wimsatt suggests that Machaut's *Dit de la Lis et la Marguerite* (1369) was also written for Marguerite of Flanders, on behalf of the French royal family when she was being courted by the brother of the French king.[8] Machaut had been connected with the families of both bride and groom for many years, and Pierre was now dead. In the new poem, the lady is praised not only in the symbolic phrases connected with the marguerite, but also the lily (*'lis'*), the French royal symbol; and the qualities of both flowers feed into later marguerite poetry. That it is symbolic value which overrides any sense of botanic fidelity is evident when, much later, Deschamps in *Lay de Franchise* 29–39[9] explains the moral virtues of the marguerite by taking the *fermeté* of its green stalk and the *purté* of its white flower from the qualities Machaut had given the lily in *Lis et Marguerite*, but its *honte et paour*, signified by the red tips of the white petals, from the praise of the marguerite in the same poem. This colour symbolism, fairly standard in marguerite poetry, should be seen behind Chaucer's portrait of Queen Alceste, blushing in her green gown beneath her crown of white and gold. Machaut's marguerite had fallen heir to all the symbolic properties of the literary rose, even its sweet odour (*Dit de la Marguerite* 22), which Chaucer also praises (F 120–3), but which is again quite at odds with a real daisy, ordinarily considered odourless. Deschamps alone approaches reality when he says the marguerite's fragrance is not 'haughty or fierce' (*Lay de Franchise* 64).[10] In the developing cult, the marguerite had become more and more an ideal concept, its links to a real flower or a real woman more and more tenuous. In point of fact, Marguerite of Flanders, as a great and powerful lady in her own right, was not a conspicuously humble and obedient 'marguerite', but, with

[8] Wimsatt, *Marguerite Poetry,* pp. 44–5.
[9] A. Q. de Saint-Hilaire and G. Raynaud, eds., *Œuvres Complètes de Eustache Deschamps,* II vols. (Paris: SATF, 1878–1903), I, pp. 204–5.
[10] Lowes, 'French *Marguerite* Poems', p. 629. Beryl Rowland, however, notes that the daisy does have a faint grassy smell, 'Chaucer's Daisy: Prol. *LGW*, F 120–3; G 109–11', *N&Q* 10 (1963): 210.

Deschamps's *Lay de Franchise*, continued to inspire poetic homage, some twenty years after the first marguerite poem.[11]

I have already noted how for Froissart the marguerite seemed to represent more than any ordinary woman, and indeed, from the earliest marguerite poem, the potential for the little flower to become a symbol of perfection is evident. In *Lis et Marguerite* 263–74, Machaut refers to the various significations of the word marguerite as flower but also as pearl, the primary referent of *margarita*: it designates, he says, a powerful and precious stone with which lords and ladies adorn themselves, it is a saint in heaven, and the most beautiful of women's names. (Even today dictionaries cite a colloquial meaning for 'daisy' as 'something fine or first-rate'.) As a fashionable icon the marguerite in the second half of the fourteenth century was everywhere, and triumphant in areas other than poetry. The daisy was used as a device in decorative art and clothing, as Deschamps notes in *Lay de Franchise* 53–9. Machaut talks of making a gown for his lady out of marguerites (*Lis et Marguerite* 385–8), Froissart wears a marguerite on his signet ring (*Prison Amoureuse* 898–9, 986–7), and Gower in the *Confessio Amantis* associates great pearls and multi-coloured garlands of the leaf and the flower with the new fashions associated with the arrival of Anne of Bohemia and her retinue at the English court (*CA* VIII 2467–70).[12] The daisy is figured in the Wilton Diptych, among the roses, violets and lilies. Even as early as Machaut's *Dit de la Marguerite* 177–92, the hyperbole in his praise of the marguerite knew no bounds: 'It is the sun that gleams, it is the moon that makes the night clear, it is the star which guides me across the sea, it is the ship, strong, secure, and full of delight, it is the steersman who guides me . . . it is the food on which I live, it is the sweet and lovely water that refreshes and revives me and is always pure, clear and fresh . . .' (trans. Windeatt, p. 147). The little daisy bids fair to outshine not only the rose but the pearl also and the Virgin herself. Machaut's original marguerite poems may have been a dutiful reflection of Pierre of Cyprus's desire to flatter the powerful Marguerite of Flanders. But with Pierre dead, the symbolism of the marguerite,

---

[11] Wimsatt, *Marguerite Poetry*, p. 57; Lowes, 'French *Marguerite* Poems', pp. 603–7; Saint-Hilaire and Raynaud, *Deschamps: Œuvres*, XI, pp. 45–6.

[12] References to the *Confessio* are from vols. II and III of G. C. Macaulay, ed., *The Complete Works of John Gower* (Oxford: Clarendon, 1901).

always more applicable to an ideal than limited to a particular occasion and person, was readily adaptable by the later poets.[13]

The fashion for marguerite poetry must to some extent have depended on a pleasure in paradox. On the one hand, the name of many important female personages and the exalted symbolism connected with the *margarita*/pearl. On the other hand, the insignificant daisy of the fields. Apart from the fact that daisy chaplets could be made in winter, probably the only virtue attaching to the real daisy was its reputed medicinal powers, and as it was thought literally to have power to heal the heart, its metaphorical extension to the amatory sphere was hardly surprising, as indeed Machaut says explicitly in *Lis et Marguerite* 275–330. A great deal of poetic ingenuity was expended by Machaut, Froissart, Deschamps and Chaucer on elaborating the symbolism of its faithfulness in blooming winter and summer, its obedience to the sun, its purity and modesty, and its healing powers for the heart as well as the body. All this coincides neatly with what was meant by a 'good woman' in medieval eyes. The Knight of La Tour-Landry calls a good woman, like the soul, a 'precious margarite vnto God'. The Knight is thinking of the marguerite as a pearl: 'Oure Lorde . . . spake vpon the mater of women that liueden in clennesse, he likened suche a woman vnto a precious margarite, the whiche is a bright thinge, rounde, white, and clene, a stone so clere and faire that there is no tache therein, nor spotte of vnclennes.'[14] Such ideas clearly fed the concepts in marguerite poetry.

The significance of all this seems clear for Chaucer's daisy worship and presentation of himself as passionate lover – 'ther loved no wyght hotter in his lyve' (F 59). Many modern critics, even from among those who consider the *Legend* totally serious, cannot see the daisy passages as anything other than burlesque of the courtly lover, 'charming nonsense'.[15] I see no sign of parody, unless exaggerated language be considered parodic in itself. Chaucer's praise of the daisy reproduces

---

13 Wimsatt, *Marguerite Poetry*, p. 65.
14 T. Wright, ed., *The Book of the Knight of La Tour-Landry*, rev. edn (London: EETS 33, 1906), p. 163.
15 R. B. Burlin, *Chaucerian Fiction* (Princeton University Press, 1977), p. 38; cf. Frank, *Chaucer and the Legend*, p. 22, and J. Gardner, 'The Two Prologues to the *Legend of Good Women*', *JEGP* 67 (1968): 606–7.

with care the correctly fashionable tone and manner of offering praise to an important lady. It is much more likely to be a graceful tribute to a patroness than a description of a genuine love affair.

After the 1360s, many of the other marguerite poems are associated with the 1380s, along with the Flower and Leaf poems, that is, broadly contemporaneous with the *Legend of Good Women*. Chaucer, however, must have been familiar with marguerite poetry almost since its inception. We know that he used Froissart's *Paradis d'Amour* in the *Book of the Duchess*, so the *Paradis* with its balade *Sur toutes flours j'aimme la margerite* must have been one of the earliest marguerite poems, written while Froissart was still in England in the late 1360s,[16] acting perhaps as court poet to Queen Philippa.[17] The *Paradis* and *Dit de la Margherite* are the only poems of Froissart that we are certain Chaucer knew, and it is possible, as Wimsatt suggests, that it is through them that Chaucer first became acquainted with the work of Machaut, Froissart's source.

There are several aspects of Chaucer's vision of a queen who was 'lyk a daysie for to sene' (F 224/G 156) which mark out its affiliation with Froissart's concept of the marguerite. In his *Dit de la Margherite*, Froissart mentions the marguerite's *florons* (166) and later writes:

Car en cascun floron, je vous creant,
Porte la flour un droit dart à taillant,
Dont navrés sui si, en soi regardant,
Que membre n'ai où le cop ne s'espant.
187–90

[For in each petal, I assure you, the flower carries a piercing dart, through which I am so wounded by looking at her that there is no limb in my body where it has not spread.] trans. Windeatt, p. 151

Now the word *floron* in Old French seems to mean 'flower-shaped ornament', as in architecture or printing (the same meaning as in Modern English dictionaries), specifically used of the ornaments of a crown. But it also means a 'floret', or one of the tiny separate flowers of

---

[16] Such a time and place for the *Paradis* is implied in Froissart's chronological list of his major poems (c. 1373), see A. Fourrier, ed., *Le Joli Buisson de Jonece* (Geneva: Droz, 1975), pp. 443–52.

[17] See J. I. Wimsatt, *Chaucer and His French Contemporaries* (University of Toronto Press, 1991), pp. 176–7.

which a member of the botanical family of *compositae* (such as a daisy) is made up.[18] Thus it may be translated 'petal', although Froissart appears to have realised that the marguerite's many petals were actually little flowers themselves. And, not only this, he assimilated the dart-shaped 'petal' of the marguerite (again an accurate botanical observation) to the familiar courtly notion of the arrows of love by which the lover is wounded. Chaucer must have been thinking of Froissart's *florons* when he says that Alceste has as many virtues as there are 'smale florouns in hire corowne' (F 528–9) – 'florouns' is so rare a word in Middle English that this is the only citation of it in *MED*.

Froissart, before Chaucer, had given a pseudo-Ovidian mythological explanation of the marguerite's creation. He writes how the young girl Hero wept so many tears on the grave of her lover that the Earth had pity on them, and Jupiter and Phoebus fostered them, giving birth to a new flower, the marguerite, which sprang from her tears. Mercury discovered the daisies and made from them a chaplet which he delivered to Ceres. As a result Mercury received the love he desired, where he had never been successful before. Among the 'myths' of Froissart's own invention, this is one of his favourites.[19] In the version of the story he gives in *Dit de la Margherite*, Mercury stands for the poet, and the marguerite represents the message about love which he carries. The marguerite does not stand for the object of love, the loved one herself, but for the poetic expression of love.[20] Froissart elsewhere uses his myth to investigate the sources of poetic creativity, the sorrow and desire of the lover which parallels the poet's labour, and his ability to create something new out of traditional matter.[21] Froissart's myth of Hero's tears complements his association of the marguerite motif with the weaving of a poetic daisy-chain, or a seal affirming the completion of a beautiful and well-made poetic object. When Chaucer invents his myth of Alceste's transformation into a daisy, he is emulating the Froissartian

---

[18] See Lowes, 'French *Marguerite* Poems', pp. 631–4.

[19] *Dit de la Margherite* 68–80; cf. *Pastourelle* 61–6 (Fourrier, *Dits et Débats*, pp. 48–9).

[20] See B. Ribemont, 'Froissart, le mythe et la marguerite', *Revue des Langues Romanes* 94 (1990): 129–37, esp. pp. 133–4.

[21] Ibid., p. 135. The most extensive discussion of which I am aware concerning the association of the marguerite and the role of the artist is in Lanier, 'Flower of the Imagination', passim.

method of 'putting together pieces of classical stories in new configura-
tions, readily attributing the product to Ovid'.[22]

The relationship of the *Legend*'s praise of the daisy to that of French
marguerite poetry is one both of precise reference and free development. This is exactly the relationship which the marguerite poems of
Froissart and Deschamps bear to those of Machaut. Machaut's words
are quoted exactly, the traditional symbolism is given a slight twist, the
final poems are quite different from each other. Froissart, for example,
uses even the title of Machaut's original *Dit de la Marguerite* for his own
story of Hero's tears in *Dit de la Margherite*; in his description of the
flower itself he uses Machaut's vocabulary and even his rhymes, he
makes a particularly Machaldian reference to the daisy's habit of
dwelling in Egypt as well as in the meadows, but he bends these motifs
to his own purpose, the association of the marguerite and the poet's
creative imagination. Wimsatt has demonstrated how Chaucer's
version of a narrator completely engrossed in the daisy's habits of
opening to the sun and protecting itself from darkness is mediated
through Froissart from Machaut's original,[23] and suggests that Chaucer
is quite aware of the original source (Machaut) behind his immediate
source (Froissart), and is paying tribute to both. Indeed, in the tiny
corpus of marguerite poetry, we have a chance to observe a miniaturised
example of the chain of creative influence in fourteenth-century French
lyric poetry, in which younger poets learned their craft by imitating the
established masters. The inventive exploitation of the older poet's
choice of words, metrical experiments, symbolic structure, and so on,
has several effects: it compliments the master at the same time that it
makes a claim for a place in a great tradition, a claim, however, only
validated when the novice poet establishes his own voice by making
something completely new out of old material. Chaucer's imitatation of
Froissart, and behind him, Machaut, has the added piquancy of moving
into a new language.

Lowes' famous articles of 1904 put beyond doubt the indebtedness of
the *Legend* to the marguerite tradition, but, apart from identifying
Chaucer's undoubted use of Froissart's term *floron*, his simplistic
attempt to trace Chaucer's words to specific sources (with consequences

---

[22] Wimsatt, *French Contemporaries*, p. 192.   [23] Ibid., pp. 186–7.

for dating, and so on) was misguided, as all subsequent critics who have studied the material have pointed out. The truth is that in the *Legend* Chaucer was not often translating closely. It is futile, for example, to look for the source of 'floures white and red', since all the French poets use the phrase *blanc et vermeil*. Many other such phrases which Lowes believed pointed to a specific source had soon become conventional attributes of the literary marguerite, and were employed by all the marguerite poets. When, in Prologue F, Chaucer can hardly wait for the arrival of dawn to leave home and gain the presence of the daisy, the situation bears some similarity to that of Deschamps at the beginning of *Lay de Franchise*; when, at the end of the Prologue to the *Legend*, Chaucer at first does not recognise Queen Alceste, there is some similarity to the end of Froissart's *Paradis d'Amour*. Most other specific resemblances which have been noted are not compelling. For this reason, it has seemed more relevant to give a general account of the tradition of marguerite poetry, for although reminiscence is everywhere in the *Legend*, precise translation is rare.

This is particularly clear in the F Prologue's passage in extended praise of the daisy and its narrator's passionate devotion to her 'that is of alle floures flour' (F 50–65). The English poet's obsessive desire to gaze at the flower is no doubt an echo of Froissart (for example, *Dit de la Margherite* 162–6), but honour and reverence, praise and fervent love of its virtues are everywhere in marguerite poetry. Many of Chaucer's phrases have religious connotations: 'presence' and 'reverence', 'blisful sighte' and 'softneth al my sorwe', 'evere ilyke faire' and 'ever ylyke newe'.[24] These lexical choices are consistent with the use of religious language characteristic of the F Prologue, but not out of harmony with the tone of marguerite poetry generally. Chaucer's description of the daisy closing 'for fere of nyght, so hateth she derknesse' (F 63) parallels Froissart and Deschamps when they say that it closes to protect itself against all scandal, another admirable feminine virtue (*Dit de la Margherite* 60; *Lay de Franchise* 48–50). All four poets give the daisy's devotion to the sun a moral significance. Naturally enough, it is only in English that the F Prologue's sporadic reference to the daisy as 'she' instead of 'it' is significant (cf. F 52 and 53, 62 and 63), for in French it

---

[24] Gardner, 'The Two Prologues', p. 598.

would not have been possible to distinguish lady from flower by gender.

Chaucer breaks off his first passage in eulogy of the daisy to lament his lack of adequate English to praise the flower rightly. Far from luxuriating in the delights of springtime, Chaucer's main concern with daisy worship is as a literary phenomenon:

> Allas, that I ne had Englyssh, ryme or prose,
> Suffisant this flour to preyse aryght!
> But helpeth, ye that han konnyng and myght,
> Ye lovers that kan make of sentement . . .
> For wel I wot that ye han her-biforn
> Of makyng ropen, and lad awey the corn,
> And I come after, glenyng here and there
> And am ful glad yf I may fynde an ere
> Of any goodly word that ye han left.
> And thogh it happen me rehercen eft
> That ye han in your fresshe songes sayd,
> Forbereth me, and beth nat evele apayd . . .
> F 66–80

The importance of this passage as an indicator of the programme of the *Legend of Good Women* can hardly be overemphasised. The passage speaks of the 'anxiety of influence' which an aspiring poet must feel as he contemplates inserting himself into an illustrious tradition; of the inevitable sense of temerity he experiences as he enters the old fields to gather the materials out of which a new poem must come. The lines work as well at articulating the problematic nature of the wider project of an English writer attempting to 'make' in the fashionable French lyric mode, as they do at expressing the specific undertaking at hand of beginning an English marguerite poem. In the same way, the address to 'ye lovers that kan make of sentement' applies to the acknowledged French poetic masters like Machaut and Froissart, who frequently spoke of the *sentement* out of which they composed their poetry. The wry appeal for help, however, is probably also directed to those lovers and amateur versifiers of the court who knew more about praising women than Chaucer professes and who no doubt made up the initial audience of the F Prologue of the *Legend*. (In the G Prologue there is only a much more impersonal reference to the 'folk' who have already reaped the harvest of 'makyng', in the place of F's invocation to 'ye lovers'.)

The Biblical image in the passage suggests a nice balance between the gleaner's humility before the rightful owners of the field and a self-confident claim that the gleaner too has a divinely sanctioned prerogative.[25] The allusion is to the Old Testament story of Ruth the Moabitess, a foreigner who is given permission to glean those ears of corn the legitimate reapers have been encouraged to leave for her. A recent study has examined the use of this image in the works of twelfth-, thirteenth- and fourteenth-century exegetes of scriptural texts and commentaries.[26] The sense that the harvest has already been brought in, that there is little left to say, is common to the poet attempting a genuinely new but authentic marguerite poem in English, and to the exegetes wishing to contribute their own interpretation to the Biblical texts, which had already gained a huge accretion of authoritative commentary. Both are aware that they 'come after', that they follow along behind the acknowledged masters, but the story of Ruth encourages them that it is possible and desirable to generate newly relevant meaning out of the fragments left behind by their predecessors, and holds out the promise of acceptance, as Ruth was eventually married to the owner of the field.

That the simple reproduction in English of the 'goodly wordes' of marguerite poetry is not really what is at issue, but the whole complex project of the genre (the poetic compliment to patron and poetic forebears, the valorisation of the poet's own skill), is made manifest in a remarkable passage in the F Prologue to the *Legend* where Chaucer renews his attempt to offer adequate service to the one he 'dredeth and loveth so sore', and which also becomes an invocation to the source of, and power behind, his poetic inspiration:

> She is the clernesse and the verray lyght
> That in this derke world me wynt and ledeth.
> The hert in-with my sorwfull brest yow dredeth
> And loveth so sore that ye ben verrayly

[25] See A. J. Minnis, *Medieval Theory of Authorship: Scholastic Literary Attitudes in the Later Middle Ages*, 2nd edn (London: Scolar, 1988), p. 113 and n. 142, p. 256.
[26] See Ellen E. Martin, 'Chaucer's Ruth: an Exegetical Poetic in the Prologue to the *Legend of Good Women*', *Exemplaria* 3 (1991): 467–90.

> The maistresse of my wit, and nothing I.
> My word, my werk ys knyt so in youre bond
> That, as an harpe obeieth to the hond
> And maketh it soune after his fyngerynge,
> Ryght so mowe ye oute of myn herte bringe
> Swich vois, ryght as yow lyst, to laughe or pleyne.
> Be ye my gide and lady sovereyne!
> As to myn erthly god to yow I calle,
> Bothe in this werk and in my sorwes alle.
> F 84–96

His ultimate compliment to the daisy is to think of her not only as his 'lady sovereyne', but as his poetic muse and even as his 'erthly god', a phrase with which Machaut had addressed a royal patron. The power to heal the sorrow of his heart, the mastery over his every action, is an attribute of the beloved lady, and of God or the Virgin. The brightness and true illumination are clearly divine, as is the power to bring forth music from the passive soul, yet both are associated with the ability of the lady to inspire poetry at her will. The poet's sorrow or laughter is closely linked to his 'word', his 'werk'; it is the poetic music she calls forth from him. The role of guide or leader is a divine one, the 'bonds' within which his works are fettered have feudal overtones, yet it is of his 'wit' that she is 'maistresse'. This extraordinary portrayal of poetic inspiration as akin to divine inspiration[27] is not a common one at this period.

Chaucer has compounded this amalgam, as Lowes showed,[28] from a passage I noted above from Machaut's *Dit de la Marguerite* 177 ff. and from a few stanzas of Boccaccio's *Filostrato* not used in *Troilus and Criseyde*. Machaut had said of the marguerite, 'It is the sun that gleams . . . it is the star which guides me across the sea . . . it is the steersman who guides me.' It is likely that these lines, commonplaces as they are in fourteenth-century love poetry (not only marguerite poetry), recall phrases from Boccaccio's address to Fiammetta at the beginning of *Filostrato*, where he calls his lady his 'clear and beauteous light' by whom he lives wisely in the dark world, his 'Jove, Apollo, muse'. He implores her to guide his hand, to govern his wit, in the work he is now

---

[27] Burlin, *Chaucerian Fiction*, pp. 39, 42.
[28] Lowes, 'French *Marguerite* Poems', pp. 618–26.

to write. 'Thy image is fixed so strongly in my sad breast that thou hast greater sway there than I myself.'[29] It seems clear that when Chaucer wrote these lines in the *Legend*, he was associating at least three other passages: that of Machaut, that of Boccaccio, and parts of this same passage in the *Filostrato* which he had already translated in *Troilus and Criseyde*. *Dit de la Marguerite* and *Filostrato* both compare the lady to the star which guides the lover to port, and all three use other similar sea-faring images (conventional enough in love poetry and also associated with the Virgin and again with the composing of poetry); *Filostrato* and *Troilus* both have an appeal to lovers reminiscent of the one just made in the *Legend* to 'ye lovers that kan make of sentement', and in both these there are prayers to the poet's muse (*Filostrato* I 6; *TC* I 22 ff., II 10 ff.). And the change of personal pronoun from 'she' to 'yow' in F 86 occurs at the place where Chaucer starts using the Italian, which employs a second person pronoun.

In placing himself with the lovers and poetic servants of Marguerite and Fiammetta, Chaucer makes an implicit claim to belong with the exponents of high seriousness in vernacular culture. Such passages (with their manifest indebtedness to poetic predecessors) honour the skill of the poet as much as the virtue, power and beauty of the lady who is said to be honoured. How far this passage also relates to a real lady cannot be readily determined, but the sense of strong personal emotion it evinces and the fact that it is missing from the G Prologue suggests that the daisy of the F Prologue had a referent in the real world. One of Chaucer's most original contributions to the cult of the marguerite, albeit a feature only relevant to the English daisy, also occurs in a passage suggesting personal devotion and missing from the G Prologue. This is the etymology for 'daisy', which may well be an attempt to give the English word a symbolic significance of equivalent value to that surrounding the French name, Marguerite. As he leans all day on 'his elbow and his side', gazing at the daisy, the poet/narrator says:

> That wel by reson men it calle may
> The 'dayesye', or elles the 'ye of day',
> The emperice and floure of floures alle.
> F 183–5

[29] R. K. Gordon, trans., *The Story of Troilus* (New York: Dutton, 1964), p. 31; *Filostrato* I. 2, 4, 5, quoted in Lowes, 'French *Marguerite* Poems', p. 619.

At the literal level 'empress and flower of all flowers' could conceivably describe appropriately the rose or lily, but hardly the humble daisy of the meadow. The referent of such a phrase is normally some honoured lady and, more particularly, the Virgin (cf. *An ABC* 4). As noted earlier, marguerite in French denotes both a flower and the pearl. The rich complex of symbols associated with the *margarita*/pearl, while primarily religious, also includes the one 'earthly delights', a signification deriving from the use of pearls as ornaments of fashionable dress[30] as in Alceste's headdress, and a meaning consonant with the practices of courtly love. What could be done, however, with the rather humbler English word 'daisy'?

To think of the daisy as the 'eye of day' (the etymology is, surprisingly, totally correct) is only to give it a meaning quite obvious to any English speaker from Anglo-Saxon times onwards. It refers to the daisy's habit of opening during the day and closing at night, like the human eye. The primary meaning of the Anglo-Saxon 'daeges eage' is the sun, and the likeness perceived between the sun and the form of the daisy, whose petals resemble rays around the sun's disc, gives the daisy its name.[31] If medieval etymologies are always symbolic, then 'day's eye' probably refers to that complex of scriptural references which conceives of the sun as a symbol of God, and of the eye as the sun in microcosm, the source of light for the human body, in a literal and spiritual sense. An extensive exegetical tradition exists concerning this complex of ideas. For example, Augustine appeared to believe, under the influence of Neoplatonism, that there was no essential difference between the divine light which illuminates the human mind and the sunlight which illuminates the sensible world.[32] The human eye was thought to see by illuminating the object of its vision by emitting rays from itself as the sun did (this opinion was current for many centuries after Chaucer's

---

[30] See S. K. Heninger, 'The Margarita-Pearl Allegory in Thomas Usk's *Testament of Love*', *Speculum* 32 (1957): 92–3.

[31] W. W. Skeat gives a reference from Lydgate's *Troy Book*: 'And next, Appollo, so clere, shene, and bright,/ The *dayes eye* and voyder of the night', *Complete Works of Geoffrey Chaucer*, 7 vols. (London: Oxford University Press, 1894), VII, p. 291.

[32] See D. Knowles, *The Evolution of Medieval Thought* (London: Longman, 1962), passim; E. de Bruyne, *Études d'Esthétique Médiévale* (Bruges: De Tempel Tempelhof, 1946), III, pp. 16–29.

time).[33] Thus Chaucer's daisy, with its brightness and true light which leads and governs him (F 84–5), is a fitting symbol of illumination and inspiration. When Chaucer creates his God of Love, moreover, he gives him a sun for a crown and a face shining so brightly that he can hardly be looked at (F 230–3/G 163–5). Marguerite poetry, as we have seen, emphasised the daisy's dependence on the sun, and its heliotropism was there given a ready transference to the moral sphere. When Chaucer says that 'wel by reson' the daisy may be called the eye of day, he is suggesting that as a symbol the English daisy could be seen to have as extensive and exalted areas of reference as the marguerite enjoyed by virtue of its linguistic association with the *margarita*/pearl. Lisa J. Kiser has examined at length this traditional material.[34] It is risky, however, to see such descriptions of the daisy as the 'ye of day' and the 'clernesse and the verray lyght' as intrinsic to the symbol's significance in the *Legend of Good Women*, since they are totally absent from the G version (and were thus never present if G was the original, or were totally suppressed if G is the revision). Later English writers, moreover, did not build on these suggestions, and although references to the daisy in English poetry are frequent enough after the *Legend*, it is the flower's natural characteristics and its medicinal powers, as in French poetry, that are elaborated, rather than its etymology.

What then are the salient points to be drawn from this study of Chaucer's relation to the French marguerite tradition and his statement, 'And I come after, glenyng . . .'? First, there is the compliment to the French masters of courtly lyric poetry inherent in the exercise of imitating in English their devotion to the marguerite. The 'praise of women' is seen to be conducted as elegantly in English as in French or Italian. Along with this is the graceful tribute paid to a patroness, with its implication that the production of poetry results from the intimate connection between the poet and the courtly milieu from which the French masters also emanated – 'My word, my werk ys *knyt* so in youre bond'. The allusion to Ruth's gleaning suggests the sense of awe with

---

33 For ancient theories of vision, i.e. how light is perceived by the eye, whose action was thought to mimic that of the sun, see D. Lee, trans., *Plato: Timaeus* (Harmondsworth: Penguin, 1965), pp. 61–3.
34 Lisa J. Kiser, *Telling Classical Tales: Chaucer and the Legend of Good Women* (Ithaca: Cornell University Press, 1983).

which Chaucer views the prospect of competing with French poetry but, if we may extrapolate from the similar use of the image in exegetical writers, also implies that he is willing to take up the invitation to engage in the harvest of 'makyng' and to be considered worthy of incorporation into the tradition. It may well be, moreover, that Chaucer as a vernacular translator, like many of the exegetes who used the image of Ruth, rejoiced in the imaginative challenge, even the liberty, that their marginalised status as workers in a secondary literary tradition (that is, translation or commentary) enforced upon them.[35] I am encouraged to endorse this contention recently made by Ellen E. Martin, because, although Chaucer is consistently respectful before the poetic tradition of his French masters, the element of unruly challenge becomes more pronounced as the *Legend* develops. As he takes up his penance of translating stories of good women from classical sources his posture of humility becomes more and more specious until he is all but thumbing his nose at the authority of the Latin writers, who were masters even more prestigious than the French. He represents himself no longer as the humble and faithful servant of the daisy but as the unfaithful seducer of women, whose humility is merely a ploy, enabling him to do with women and texts 'what so as hem liste'.

Finding English words to translate effectively the French 'praise of women' may have been difficult, and far more difficult than it appears today, but Chaucer's most original development of the marguerite motif comes with his attempt to create a poetic 'myth' of the daisy from his own invention (in the mode of Froissart), and his incorporation into daisy worship of accurate references to classical poetry (in the mode of Machaut and Jean de Meun), which we see in his balade comparing his lady to the heroines of past literature. It is to this association of motifs drawn from classical literature with contemporary praise of the daisy that we turn in the next chapter.

[35] This is the burden of Martin's article, 'Chaucer's Ruth', passim.

2

Alceste: the Good Woman of legend

I turn now to the dream vision section of the *Legend of Good Women* in which the narrator dreams of a lady dressed like a daisy. In his dreaming imagination he associates the transcendental marguerite of French lyric poetry with a classical story of an all but perfect woman, the legendary Queen Alceste of Thrace.

When night falls and the daisy of the field closes, nothing remains for the poet but to hasten to his own rest in a bed of grass and flowers which he has made up 'in a litel herber that I have/ That benched was on turves fressh ygrave' (F 203–4), where the activities of the day lead him to dream of the God of Love and the object of his devotion:

> Me mette how I lay in the medewe thoo,
> To seen this flour that I so love and drede;
> And from afer com walkyng in the mede
> The god of Love, and in his hand a quene.
> F 210–13

The God of Love and a consort (frequently surrounded by companies of famous lovers, as in Froissart's *Paradis d'Amour*) had been among the most familiar protagonists of literary dream visions for several centuries. Moreover, the connection between the dream and the concerns of the dreamer's waking life are here particularly clearly drawn because it appears to him that the queen's clothing makes her 'lyk a daysie for to sene':

> And she was clad in real habit grene.
> A fret of gold she had next her heer,
> And upon that a whit corowne she beer
> With flourouns smale, and I shal nat lye;

For al the world, ryght as a dayesye
Ycorouned ys with white leves lyte,
So were the flowrouns of hire coroune white.
For of o perle fyn, oriental,
Hire white coroune was ymaked al;
For which the white coroune above the grene
Made hire lyk a daysie for to sene,
Considered eke hir fret of gold above.
F 214–25/G 146–57

Finding out who the daisy is and what she represents constitutes the
first major plot-motif of the Prologue to the *Legend of Good Women*.
The poet had recognised the God of Love in his vision at first sight (F
213); as for the queen whom Love holds by the hand, he could do no
more than describe her daisy-like clothing in detail. Puzzled by her
identity he turns his attention back to her after being momentarily
distracted by the fierce stare of 'this myghty god of Love'. (Love's
disapproving countenance is the harbinger of the second plot-motif,
Chaucer's literary 'sin', to be considered in later chapters). In F 241–6/G
173–8 he now concentrates on aspects of her character, or better, her
observable demeanour, if the fiction of the dreamer watching is to be
maintained. Her beauty is 'so womanly, so benigne, and so meke' that it
leads him to recite the balade *Hyd Absolon*:

Hyd, Absolon, thy gilte tresses clere;
Ester, ley thou thy meknesse al adown;
Hyd, Jonathas, al thy frendly manere;
Penalopee and Marcia Catoun,
Make of youre wifhod no comparysoun;
Hyde ye youre beautes, Ysoude and Eleyne:
My lady cometh, that al this may disteyne . . .
F 247–55/G 203–9

Two more rime royal stanzas, using exactly the same rhymes and refrain
as the first, compare his lady to other famous women of the past. When
his lady appears, the balade says, the brightness of her beauty and
goodness makes that of the heroines of classical literature seem dim.
The catalogue of virtues given by Chaucer in his balade provides an
interesting medieval register of exemplary femininity – not only the
beauty of Lucrece, Isolde and Helen, the 'meknesse' of Esther, the

'wifhod' of Penelope, but also 'trouthe of love', primarily indexed by the suffering and betrayal of Dido, Ariadne, Hypsipyle and many others.

This graceful balade has several analogues in contemporary French poetry, although it is not a precise translation of any. It exemplifies many of the favourite devices of similar poems in French, classical references combined with the laudatory catalogue of items (precious stones or flowers, for example), which the lady surpasses. Skeat was certain that a source for *Hyd Absolon* could be found in an (anonymous?) poem which cites Esther, Helen, Thisbe, Lucrece, Yseult and Absolon as comparing unfavourably with his lady, but Machaut, Froissart and Deschamps each wrote a number of balades with similar features. The portrait of a lady which Deschamps gives in one of his balades begins 'Chief d'Absalon, clere face d'Elayne' (no. 168). Several more of his *balades amoureuses* are in the same vein, like no. 182, headed *Comparaison d'une dame avec les héroines de l'antiquité*.

Chaucer may have been aware of one of Machaut's double balades which consists of two balades exactly similar in metre, rhyme scheme, refrain and theme, and given a musical setting.[1] The first, which begins *Ne quier vëoir la biauté d'Absolon*, had been sent to Machaut by another writer and states that one need not seek the beauty of Absolon, the understanding and verbal dexterity of Ulysses, and so on through other Biblical and mythological figures, each stanza concluding with the refrain, *Je voy assez, puis que je voy ma dame*, I see enough, since I see my Lady. To this Machaut wrote a companion balade, *Quant Theseüs, Herculès et Jason*, and set both pieces to music. In the musical performance the two balades would have been sung simultaneously with a further two independent instruments as accompaniment, four lines of music in all. Wilkins, in his edition of this series, adds, 'After the confusion of the two texts in the main part of the stanzas, Machaut produces a splendid effect of clarity as the two voices come together for the refrain, giving extra point to his catalogue of legendary personages and events: *Je voy assez, puis que je voy ma dame*.'[2] The resulting marvel of polyphonic and polytextual technique could hardly have been

[1] N. Wilkins, ed., *One Hundred Ballades, Rondeaux and Virelais from the Late Middle Ages* (Cambridge University Press, 1969), no. 17 and no. 18, pp. 28–9; musical setting, pp. 152–5.

[2] Ibid., p. 125.

emulated often, but Froissart wrote still another matching balade using the same rhymes and with more examples from mythology – Medea, Orpheus, Lucrece, Penelope, and still, in every comparison, *Je voi assés, puisque je voi ma dame.*[3]

Hyd Absolon is very similar to these French examples and must have been admired for its fashionable theme and its technical facility, especially its use of only three rhymes for its three stanzas, as in Froissart's balade, which makes the balade a difficult form in English. In emulating his illustrious French literary confrères there is a sense in which the English Chaucer continues their poetic dialogue and joins with them not only in praising the lady, but in asserting the excellence of his mother tongue 'that al this may dysteyne'. The balade may have been composed quite independently of the *Legend of Good Women*. It was common for fourteenth-century French poets to incorporate their lyrics into their longer works, although the poems also occur separately. This possibility is suggested by the appearance in Chaucer's balade of Absolon and Jonathon, Esther and several other ladies, who are not especially relevant to the theme of the *Legend*, although not out of place in the similar balades of Machaut, Froissart and Deschamps.

In Prologue F several lines in the passage following the balade echo the earlier 'daisy' passages (cf. F 275 with F 94, F 277 with F 186), and the poet appears to have identified the Daisy Queen of his dream with the one to whom the praise of the daisy was offered:

> This balade may ful wel ysongen be,
> As I have seyd erst, by *my lady* free;
> For certeynly al thise mowe nat suffise
> To apperen wyth *my lady* in no wyse.
> For as the sonne wole the fyr disteyne,
> So passeth al *my lady sovereyne*,
> That ys so good, so faire, so debonayre,
> I prey to God that ever falle hire faire!
> For nadde comfort ben of hire presence,
> I hadde ben ded, withouten any defence,
> For drede of Loves wordes and his chere,
> As, when tyme ys, herafter ye shal here.
> F 270–81 (emphasis mine)

[3] Ibid., no. 36, p. 50–1.

46

The mistaken identity of the Daisy Queen with 'my lady' is absent from the equivalent passage in the G Prologue, as are all other implications that the daisy of the field and the Daisy Queen of the dream have a referent in the poet's real world. Instead it is the crowd of attending ladies rather than the poet who sings the balade in Prologue G, using the refrain, 'Alceste is here, that all this may disteyne'.

I have been proceeding on the assumption that the F Prologue's ambiguous association of 'my lady sovereyne' (the lady dressed like a daisy who intercedes for the poet in his dream) and the daisy of the meadows who is the poet's literary muse is designed as a compliment to the wife of Richard II, Anne of Bohemia. Is there anything in Chaucer's response to his vision of the Daisy Queen and in his balade that lends support to this assumption? Anne had no reputation for beauty, but all evidence to her character suggests that it conformed quite neatly to the feminine ideal expressed in *Hyd Absolon*, particularly the 'mekenesse' and the 'wifhod'. May McKisack says she was 'pious and well-educated, [but] plain and poor . . . Anne soon won Richard's passionate devotion and he would seldom allow her to leave his side; but there is no evidence that she sought to restrain his excesses and it is likely to have been her docility which charmed him.'[4] Anne showed interest in the speaking of English and, given that she came from a royal house known for its literary patronage, may well have espoused a marguerite poem in English and appreciated receiving a balade, in the French style, comparing her to the heroines of the past. While there was no necessary connection between the compliments of a poet and the dedicatee's actual virtues, nevertheless the known details of Anne's character and career are not out of harmony with the role of mediator given to the Daisy Queen in the next section of the poet's dream and alluded to in the lines I have just quoted (F 278–80). On several known occasions Anne publicly prostrated herself in order to obtain mercy for wrongdoers. She interceded in late 1381 for the rebels of the Peasants' Revolt, which had delayed her arrival in England to marry Richard (*DNB* I, p. 420); in 1388 (unsuccessfully) for the life of Sir Simon Burley – 'she was three hours on her knees interceding' (*DNB* I, p. 422); in 1392,

---

[4] May McKisack, *The Fourteenth Century: 1307–1399* (Oxford University Press, 1959), p. 427. Cf. also entry on Anne in the *Dictionary of National Biography*, I, p. 420.

when the City of London was in conflict with Richard, the city appealed to Anne as mediatrix and Richard's wrath was appeased: there was a ceremonious scene in Westminster Hall with Richard on the bench with his sceptre and the queen kneeling at his feet to make her formal intercession (*DNB* I, p. 422). I do not think that there is any point in trying to link the *Legend* to any of these occasions for dating purposes; it is interesting to observe, however, that Queen Anne saw fit to conform herself to this particular ideal of womanhood. She would appear to have been a useful person to postulate having on one's 'defence' before a wrathful monarch (cf. F 278–80). At this point we must leave to one side the central scene of the Prologue to the *Legend of Good Women*, where Chaucer is condemned by the God of Love and defended by the Daisy Queen, in order to conclude the working out of the motif of the significance of the daisy.

Chaucer, then, has begun the *Legend of Good Women* by eulogising the daisy and by favourably comparing the lady in the dream to the heroines of antiquity. The third stage of Chaucer's praise of ladies comes much later, after the accusation motif is complete, when the Daisy Queen has completed her magisterial defence of the poet and suggested he compose a 'Legend of good women' as penance for his sin of slandering women in the past. After performing this light act of penance, the lady says, the poet may expect the servants of the God of Love, and perhaps Queen Anne herself, to reward him well for his labours (clearly, though Anne may be the poet's 'lady sovereyne', she is not the lady in the dream, the one now speaking to him):

> Goo now thy wey, this penaunce ys but lyte.
> And whan this book ys maad, yive it the quene,
> On my byhalf, at Eltham or at Sheene.
> F 495–7

None of Queen Anne's ancestors, well-known patrons of the poets Chaucer admired, ever received a more graceful tribute. The portrayal of true pity, wisdom and fair judgement which the Daisy Queen's speech displays, and to which we will pay attention later, stands up well beside Machaut's tributes in his two *jugement* poems to the kings of Bohemia (Anne's grandfather) and Navarre.

48

The God of Love with a smile invites Chaucer to join him in the delight he takes in the virtue of the daisy-like lady (F 498 ff./G 486 ff.). Does the poet appreciate who she is? He answers: 'Nay, sire, so have I blys/ No moore but that I see wel she is good'(F 505–6/G 493–4). When the visionary queen assigned penance for the poet's sin, the second narrative motif of the Prologue was all but complete. This question from the God of Love marks the transition to the resolution of the other narrative motif, Chaucer's coming to understand the true significance of the lady dressed like a daisy. In an important way, the resolution of this motif depends on the resolution of the other. For it is not just her name that is to be revealed, so much as that the poet is to associate the evident pity and goodness of her behaviour, experienced here with his own eyes ('That maistow seen, she kytheth what she ys' [F 504/G 492]), with the knowledge of her history which he already possesses, tucked away in his books. To this end Love asks another question:

> Hastow nat in a book, lyth in thy cheste,
> The grete goodnesse of the quene Alceste,
> That turned was into a dayesye;
> She that for her housbonde chees to dye,
> And eke to goon to helle, rather than he,
> And Ercules rescowed hire, parde,
> And broght hir out of helle agayn to blys?
> F 510–16/G 498–504

The one detail that Chaucer will never find in his books is the Ovid-like metamorphosis of Alceste into a daisy. Not content to use classical myth merely to illustrate and emphasise like Jean de Meun or Machaut, Chaucer like Froissart takes upon himself the creative mantle of Ovid himself, making a significant new myth out of an old story, with detail which becomes intrinsic to the meaning of the poem.[5] Ovid, of course, narrated many stories of people who were turned into flowers, such as Clytie in *Metamorphoses* IV 256–70, who wasted away from unrequited love for Apollo, her limbs becoming rooted to the ground as her face turned to follow the progress of the sun-god across the sky. Clytie thus became a flower 'both white and red' (the flower reflecting the colours

---

[5] Cf. Ribemont, 'Froissart', pp. 129 ff.

of her complexion), who loved the sun, although the classical story has rather less of the moral significance attributed to the heliotropism of the medieval daisy.

The remainder of the God of Love's smooth summary of Alceste's story was, however, quite accurate. The tale of the happy marriage of Alcestis and Admetus occurs in Greek myth. Euripides' *Alcestis*, for example, the action of which takes place on the day of Alcestis' death and her rescue from hell by Heracles, is a brief but moving account of the story. According to the legend, Apollo returned a favour due to Admetus by allowing him to escape his impending death if another could be found who would take his place. His aging parents and other relatives refused, and only his young wife Alcestis was willing to die for him.[6] Alcestis was incontrovertibly a 'good woman', the ultimate apotheosis of wifely duty. The name of Alcestis was not well known in secular or non-scholarly literature of Chaucer's time, at least not in the sense that those of Dido, Medea and Lucretia were, and it is not likely that Chaucer knew Euripides. Ovid mentioned her in *Ars* III, and Jerome also coupled her name with that of Penelope in *Adversus Jovinianum*, which is likely to have been an important citation for Chaucer. Fuller versions of the story, told quite straightforwardly but still only summaries, could have been found, for example, in Hyginus' *Fabulae*. There were of course allegorical moralisations of the story, which I discount because there appears to be no notice of them in Chaucer's version. This kind of explanation of the story (ultimately based on the interpretation of Fulgentius writing at the turn of the sixth century) focused on the etymology of the names Admetus and Alcestis, and produced readings in which Admetus represented the (fearful) human spirit joined in marriage to Alcestis representing the flesh, the death of which meant life for the spirit.[7] This view was not particularly

---

[6] See P. Vellacott, trans., *Euripides: Three Plays, Alcestis, Hippolytus, Iphigenia in Tauris* (Harmondsworth: Penguin, 1953; rev. 1974).

[7] Shaner reproduces and discusses the versions of Hyginus, Nicholas Trivet, Fulgentius, the three Vatican Mythographers, Walsingham and Salutati, see M. C. Shaner (Edwards), 'An Interpretive Study of Chaucer's *Legend of Good Women*', Dissertation, Illinois at Urbana-Champaign, 1973, pp. 8–13. See also discussion of the Alcestis story and its moralisations in V. A. Kolve, 'From Cleopatra to Alceste: an Iconographic Study of the *Legend of Good Women*', in J. P. Hermann and J. J. Burke, Jr, eds., *Signs and Symbols in Chaucer's Poetry* (University of Alabama Press, 1981), pp. 130–78, esp. 171–3

complimentary to Alcestis. The story, however, could also be understood in simple moral terms; for example, Pierre Bersuire, the early fourteenth-century Benedictine author of an allegorised version of Ovid, adds a series of more straightforward interpretations which value the strength of the love and married faith of good women like Alcestis whose perfect love for their husbands and willingness to expose themselves to death, if necessary, make them worthy of being delivered from hell by Christ:

> Istud allega de affectu bonarum mulierum que viros perfecte diligunt ita quod amore ipsorum, si esset necesse, morti exponere se volunt. Iste igitur digne sunt quod ab inferno i. a purgatorio, Hercules i. Xristus, eas extrahat & propter fidem coniugalem quam habent, sursum ad gloriam secum ducat.[8]

This is the same kind of simple moral significance that Chaucer gives the story, as did Jerome. The christological connotations of Alcestis' substitutionary death and return to life, inevitably made by the medieval Christian, are in harmony with the religious language employed in French marguerite poetry. Chaucer speaks of the daisy's 'resureccioun' (F 110), and one of the key attributes of the marguerite was that it remained alive when all else died in the grip of winter – 'And evere ylike fayr and fresh of hewe,/ As wel in wynter as in somer newe' (G 57–8). Machaut says in *Voir Dit* that the inscription *et en yver et en este* signifies love that is perfectly faithful.[9]

A 'recognition' motif commonly climaxed many of the fourteenth-century French poems that lie behind the *Legend of Good Women*. At the end of *Jugement dou Roy de Navarre* Machaut finds out that the lady who had accused him of slandering women was Bonneürté. Froissart's feminine guide in *Paradis d'Amour* is finally identified as Plaisance. The revelation of the name is a key to understanding the meaning of the preceding narrative action, usually revealing it to have been a kind of epistemological process. Recognition motifs in the fourteenth-century

---

and accompanying notes, and Delany, *Naked Text*, pp. 108–13. Both Kolve and Delany also cite Boccaccio's version of the story in *De Genealogia* 13. 1.

[8] Quoted in Shaner, 'An Interpretive Study', pp. 10–11. There is a translation of the lines and brief discussion of the Alceste figure in D. W. Robertson, *A Preface to Chaucer* (Princeton University Press, 1963), pp. 378–9.

[9] Cited in Lowes, 'French *Marguerite* Poems', p. 618.

French dream vision seem a pale reflection of those which Boitani investigated in Dante;[10] hardly sublime or tragic, but sharing with them an emotive movement from ignorance to knowledge, particularly, as in Froissart's poems which use the marguerite motif, an investigation of the springs of the poet's creative power.[11] The original version of *Jugement dou Roy de Navarre* may have involved a pun on Bonneürté and the name of Bonne of Luxembourg,[12] so that the recognition theme has a secondary function of complimenting an important patron.

Thus this scene in the *Legend* is marked by the language of knowledge – seeing, knowing, considering; like many another medieval dreaming poet Chaucer is questioned about his thoughts, in order for him to be led into active understanding. If we think in the terminology of medieval descriptive psychology, the figure of the God of Love speaks as or to the poet's imagination, his *ingenium*,[13] that faculty of the brain which processes sensory images, including those stored in the mind as memories (some of which are the collective memories of the past stored in old books), and offers them to the judgement of reason. It is the faculty of *ingenium* which is receptive to the visionary messages of dreams, and above all, particularly in a poet, is capable of creating new and meaningful images. The reference to the book about Alceste which lies in the poet's 'cheste' appears to be literal, but is probably also a metaphorical allusion to the poet's memory, commonly thought of as a storage box or treasure chest, and is a clear signal of the epistemological

---

[10] P. Boitani, *The Tragic and the Sublime in Medieval Literature* (Cambridge University Press, 1989), chapters 5 and 6.

[11] Lanier, 'Flower of the Imagination', pp. 92–204.

[12] See J. I. Wimsatt and W. W. Kibler, eds. and trans., *Guillaume de Machaut: Le Jugement du Roy de Behaigne and Remede de Fortune* (Athens: University of Georgia Press, 1988), pp. 33–4.

[13] I am favouring the use of the term *ingenium* over 'imagination' so as to avoid confusion with the latter's modern sense. An account of medieval descriptive psychology and *ingenium* in particular may be found in the early chapters of Kathryn L. Lynch, *The High Medieval Dream Vision* (Stanford University Press, 1988). See also W. Wetherbee, 'The Theme of Imagination in Medieval Poetry and the Allegorical Figure "Genius"', *Medievalia and Humanistica*, NS 7 (1976): 45–64, esp. p. 45. Chaucer elsewhere uses the term 'engyn' in an allusion to the cognitive triad of 'memorie, engyn, and intellect' (*SNT* 339).

dimensions of the scene.[14] The inspirational *marguerite* of French poetry is very strongly associated with memory as well as faithfulness, its winter blooming habit recalling summer in the midst of winter.

The God of Love had *recalled* to Chaucer's mind a story he had already read – it is no new fact. And it is not simply the details of Alceste's story which are important and need to be remembered, but the moral implication which attaches to the story (in medieval terminology, its 'intention'), that is, 'the grete goodnesse of the quene Alceste'. This memory, having been brought to life in his dream and pondered on,[15] initiates in his mind a new understanding of his devotion to the daisy and enables him to perceive an identity of virtue in the legendary figure of Alceste, the humble daisy, and his 'lady sovereyne'. (As Chaucer's dream opened he appears to have possessed a rudimentary apprehension of this, as I have said, since his first thought on seeing the queen dressed like a daisy, now revealed as Alceste, was that she was his 'lady sovereyne', for whom he had written the balade *Hyd Absolon.*) The daisy is probably to be regarded as a kind of natural mnemonic, which should bring to mind and preserve all that is known of the faithfulness, the goodness, of women, as it is recorded in old books, seen in the visions of poets, and known from personal experience. The daisy is also a symbol of the resulting poetic artefact conceived in the poet's imagination/*ingenium* and produced by means of his linguistic skill. In a similar scene with epistemological dimensions, in the *marguerite* poem *Paradis d'amour* 1422, the God of Love gave to Froissart *sens* and *arroi*, insight and poetic form or the power of arrangement.[16]

In his answer, the poet is struck by his new insight, and the meaning which his earlier attitudes and recent experiences have thereby acquired:

> And I answerd ageyn, and seyde, 'Yis,
> Now knowe I hire. And is this good Alceste

---

[14] See Mary J. Carruthers, *The Book of Memory: a Study of Memory in Medieval Culture* (Cambridge University Press, 1990). This work is indispensable for its account of the view of the physiological basis for memory and its ethical significance which lies behind the epistemological process dramatised in this dream vision. For the 'cheste' as memory, see pp. 42 ff. and passim.

[15] Cf. ibid., the account of the importance of 'meditation', passim.

[16] Lanier, 'Flower of the Imagination', pp. 123, 206.

The dayesie, and myn owene hertes reste?
Now fele I weel the goodnesse of this wyf,
That both aftir hir deth and in hir lyf
Hir gret bounte doubleth hire renoun.
Wel hath she quyt me myn affeccioun
That I have to hire flour, the dayesye.
F 517–24/G 505–12

The reawakened memory of the story of Alceste, the apprehension of the exemplary significance of her fame (F 522/G 510), as well as the poet's recent experimental knowledge of her goodness ('fele', F 520/G 508) – that is, her pity and intercessory power – all shed light on his earlier instinctive 'affeccioun' for the daisy. I have not introduced a comma after 'Alceste' in line 518, because the more ambiguous syntax which results conveys Chaucer's meaning better. It is his sudden perception of the congruence in goodness between Alceste and the daisy that he wishes to convey: 'And is this good Alceste the dayesie, and myn owene hertes reste?' It is not simply that he has found out her name, as the usual modern punctuation implies: 'And is this good Alceste?' – with the other two terms in apposition. This latter more rigorously delimited meaning makes little sense, or at any rate is hardly worth presenting as a profound insight, as the poet has already heard Alceste refer to her own name in the poem (F 432/G 422). In the G version the problem so formulated borders on the ridiculous, because Alceste was already the subject of the balade *Hyd Absolon.* If the whole notion of a recognition motif initially implicated Anne of Bohemia, then it is interesting that the G Prologue can function quite well with only the notion of the abstract Good Woman, in the same way that *Le Jugement dou Roy de Navarre* with its Lady Bonneürté (originally a complimentary pun) could be rededicated to Bonne of Luxembourg's son-in-law Charles of Navarre after her death.[17]

The recognition of Alceste is thus a playful and totally secular imitation of the high medieval dream vision's spiritual journey in knowing. The God of Love is a somewhat compromised divine mentor, himself needing admonition, and is limited in the same way that the imagination/*ingenium*, by virtue of its involvement with the senses, was

---

[17] See Wimsatt and Kibler, *Behaigne and Remede*, p. 33.

considered a limited but necessary guide to ultimate understanding in medieval epistemology. In sum, then, this small dialogue between the poet and the Apollo-like God of Love enacts and celebrates the act of poetic imagination which results in the Prologue to the *Legend of Good Women*, and is indexed by the poet's active elaboration of the new myth of the daisy/Alceste, first enunciated by the God of Love (F 510/G 500). That is, both Love and the poet contribute to these previously unknown facts about the daisy. This little motif should be seen in relation to significant French analogues – Machaut's *Fonteinne Amoureuse* and Froissart's marguerite poem *Prison Amoureuse*, which present themselves as poetic artefacts resulting from the fictionalised collaboration of poet and aristocratic patron under the auspices of Love and the Lady.

Thus, as Chaucer continues his speech in honour of the figure of the daisy/Alceste/sovereign lady, he embellishes his myth and memorable exemplary image with a host of seemingly erudite but invented allusions. He says, for example, that he would not be surprised if Jupiter had wished to change her into a constellation (like Ariadne in Ovid's tale):

> No wonder ys thogh Jove hire stellyfye,
> As telleth Agaton, for hire goodnesse!
> Hire white corowne berith of hyt witnesse;
> For also many vertues hadde shee
> As smale florouns in hire corowne bee.
> In remembraunce of hire and in honour
> Cibella maade the daysye and the flour
> Ycrowned al with whit, as men may see;
> And Mars yaf to hire corowne reed, pardee,
> In stede of rubyes, sette among the white.
> F 525–34/G 513–22

It is not known how Chaucer could have been aware that Alcestis' story was related in Plato's *Symposium*, a dialogue dealing with the multifarious aspects of love, known in the Middle Ages as *Agatho's Feast* (*Agathonis Convivium* in Macrobius' *Saturnalia*, where there is also a mention of Alcestis). Chaucer's reference to Agaton is somewhat garbled, but given the Italian spelling of the name, it has been suggested that he encountered discussions of the subject matter of *Symposium* on one of his journeys to Italy, where there is manuscript evidence that the work was known at the time.[18] Not surprisingly, there is no mention there of a 'stellification', although the gods are said to pay supreme honour to the nobility of Alcestis' heroic sacrifice. But as an *auctoritas* Agaton is undeniably impressive and one on which it would be difficult to check up. Cybele, Chaucer's Cibella who gave the daisy its white crown, appears to have been a Ceres figure. In *Prison Amoureuse* 1744–55 Froissart associates Cybele with Phoebus, god of the sun, who nourishes the marguerite as it emerges from the earth. All this lends credence to the belief of some early Chaucer scholars that Alceste (who had been rescued from hell by Hercules) was a kind of Persephone, an embodiment of the return of spring.

This is Chaucer's contribution to the symbolic lore of the cult of the marguerite. If he indeed had in mind a real patroness, then the portrait of Queen Alceste was a compliment marked by grace and charm. In the next lines the Queen prettily acts out the significance of the rosy flush which suffuses the tips of the tiny white petals making up her crown of pearl: 'Therwith this queene wex reed for shame a lyte,/ Whan she was preysed so in hire presence' (F 535–6/G 523–4). Then, after castigating Chaucer for his sinful negligence in forgetting to put Alceste in his balade, the God of Love specifies the chief of those virtues which the multi-petalled crown represents:

> And wost so wel that kalender ys shee
> To any woman that wol lover bee.
> For she taught al the craft of fyn lovynge,
> And namely of wyfhod the lyvynge,
> And al the boundes that she oghte kepe.
> F 542–6; cf. G 525–36

'Kalender' is glossed by Skeat as 'almanac; hence a means by which people are guided in their computation of time, and thus a guide, example, or model'. A calendar also contained a record or list of all the saints whose lives were worthy of imitation. Thus, in the context of the religion of love, Alceste is presented as having the exemplary value of a

---

[18] See R. A. Peck, 'Chaucerian Poetics and the Prologue to the *Legend of Good Women*', in J. N. Wasserman and R. J. Blanch, eds., *Chaucer in the Eighties* (Syracuse University Press, 1986), pp. 39–55; esp. pp. 40–2.

saint; it is suggested that in her life women may find a complete guide to love (spoken of as a 'craft' which can be taught), for she manifests every feminine virtue.

To link the story of Alceste with the connotations recently developed in the cult of the marguerite was a felicitous conception on Chaucer's part. More so than Froissart's rather sterile conception of the genesis of the daisy resulting from the tears of Hero, a lady who also loved her husband dearly, Chaucer's myth fruitfully repays meditation. That it was capable of inspiring a range of interpretations is historically exemplified by the series of articles in the journal *Anglia* by the German scholar Hugo Lange, beginning in 1915 and continuing into the 1920s. Lange was originally interested in the heraldic implications of the God of Love's sun-crown and robe embroidered with 'grene greves', which he believed suggested Richard II's badges of the sun-burst and genista. Later he began to see the green of Alceste's robe as the colour of the beginning of the year, the season of spring and love, and to note the similarity of the myth of the daisy to that of Clytie's love for Apollo, god of the sun. It was natural then, he said, for the God of Love and of spring to wear a sun-crown. He was the first to see Alceste as a Persephone figure, but also recognised Christian symbolism in the sun-crown.[19] None of these connotations of the sun or sun-god, to which the daisy/Alceste was devoted, is out of harmony with hints in the text.

The more recent account of the daisy/Alceste myth by Lisa Kiser explicates it in terms of the poet's engagement with ultimate truth by means of metaphor. As the daisy represents the sun in natural shape and habits as well as linguistic form (day's eye), but is not itself the sun, so the apprehension of truth through the mediation of metaphor stands for the poetic method itself. The figure of Alceste, Kiser says, is also like a metaphor in that her sacrificial death gives life to something else – as Alceste dies so the reader moves on from the metaphor to the 'higher truth' it was designed to convey. Kiser believes that Chaucer insists on finding the source of his art in nature and nature's orderly processes, as the daisy follows the movement across the sky of the sun on whose light it depends.[20] The Froissartian concept of the marguerite as natural

---

[19] *Anglia* 39: 347–55; 42: 142–4, 352–6; 44: 213–16, 373–85; 49: 173–80.
[20] Kiser, *Telling Classical Tales*, esp. pp. 28–62.

symbol of the poetic imagination's desire to be in harmony with God as the ultimate source of creativity[21] finds confirmation in aspects of Chaucer's daisy discussed by both Lange and Kiser. This is not to say that Chaucer had carefully thought out every one of the aspects of the daisy/Alceste story which Lange or Kiser commented on, but that, like all good myths, it was able to accommodate a wide range of interpretations without violating its integrity. All this in addition to those many other resonances of the *margarita*/pearl symbol which the idea of the daisy had accumulated by Chaucer's time.

For all his evident mastery of the courtly modes of praising women in the Prologue to the *Legend of Good Women*, its narrator's commitment to *la louange des dames* is less than wholehearted. From the poem's opening lines, and by means of several narratorial hints and asides, another voice of humorous dissent and scepticism may be heard. This note is particularly strong in the G Prologue and in the Legends, but it is by no means covert in the F Prologue with its many nods to courtly values and pastimes and its dedication to the queen. We must assume that Chaucer expected a mixed courtly audience to admire the narrator's elegant praise of women, but also to appreciate his amusing hints that the humble adoration of women's virtue could at times be difficult. It is to the presence of this minor voice in the Prologue that we turn in the next chapter.

---

[21] See Lanier, 'Flower of the Imagination', p. 186.

3

The Good Woman: a legendary beast?

I can detect no irony in Chaucer's portrayal of Alceste as the apotheosis of true love, and loyal, self-sacrificing, law-abiding, married love at that, her slight imperiousness being no more than expected from a queen-like lady. The poetry devoted to the praise of the daisy was also a faithful reproduction, in English, of French marguerite poetry. This, for all its hyperbole, was a totally non-ironic genre, whether composed in praise of an important lady or of a Froissartian poetic ideal. While Chaucer could have changed the orientation of marguerite poetry if he had wished, the daisy passages in the *Legend* give no indication that he did so. The other motif which is used in the *Legend* to praise an ideal of womanhood, the balade *Hyd Absolon*, is also a straightforward example of graceful encomium and technical facility. Taken together, the three motifs operate at one pole of the traditional debate about the nature of woman.

Nevertheless, as the Prologue draws to a close with these motifs resolved in the figure of Alceste, and with the project of the palinodal praise of ladies about to be confirmed, the notion of the Good Woman shows sign of strain. The paradoxical aspects of the concept of the God of Love become evident, the poet begins to choose words whose import is ambivalent. Take these lines from the God of Love's concluding praise of Alceste,

> For she taught al the craft of fyn lovynge,
> And namely of wyfhod the lyvynge,
> And all the boundes that she oghte kepe
> F 544–6; cf. G 533–6

in which almost every word gives pause. The term 'fyn lovynge' is fraught with ambiguity.[1] Its primary reference is no doubt to the ideal of love which inspired the practice of courtly poetry, and it could have been properly used to describe Alceste's marital love and sacrificial devotion, although its collocation with the practice of 'wyfhod' and the keeping of obligatory bounds seems unusual. Its common association with other forms of passionate love may, however, have created as distinct a sense of dissonance for early audiences as for modern ones.[2] Given that Alceste's practice of 'wyfhod' included dying in her husband's place Chaucer may be underlining Alceste's impossible virtue. Or perhaps not. The point I am making is that in the earlier encomiastic passages we are not presented with similar problems of interpretation.

The love which Alceste represents is in some sense under the patronage of the God of Love in that she is 'his Alceste' (F 432). But insofar as Love admires the ladies who will figure in Chaucer's Legends, what seems uppermost in this final section of the Prologue is his ancient characteristic as personification of the unstable and capricious passions, often immoral and leading to other crimes, the subject I will be discussing in the next chapter. There would seem to be something of a discrepancy between the model behaviour of Alceste and that exhibited by many of the women of the balade *Hyd Absolon*. These are now revealed to be the ladies whom Chaucer had seen sitting in a circle around the daisy-like queen, hymning her as the one who 'bereth our alder pris in figurynge' (F 298). The God of Love commands the poet to call them to mind also, 'goode wommen alle, and trewe of love'. These women whom Chaucer will find in his books are to make up the complete record of the Legendary of Cupid's Saints (F 548–65).

If Chaucer was intending to cap his series of Legends of women of often questionable goodness with the story of Alceste, as it seems clear he did (F 548–50/G 538–40), then he must have conceived of *their* ideals of fidelity to their lovers (which he often treats ironically in the

---

[1] See G. Kane, 'Chaucer, Love Poetry, and Romantic Love', in Mary J. Carruthers and Elizabeth D. Kirk, eds., *Acts of Interpretation: the Text in its Contexts 700–1600* (Norman: Pilgrim, 1982), pp. 237–55.

[2] See J. D. Burnley, '*Fine Amor*: Its Meaning and Context', *RES* 31 (1980): 129–48, esp. pp. 145, 147; E. Reiss, 'Chaucer's *fyn lovynge* and the Late Medieval Sense of *fin amor*', in J. B. Bessinger, Jr and R. R. Raymo, eds., *Medieval Studies in Honor of Lillian Herlands Hornstein* (New York University Press, 1976), pp. 181–91, esp. p. 184.

Legends section) as in some way a pale reflection of the ideal of feminine goodness which he is sworn to honour – 'And serve alwey the fresshe dayesye' (F 565). When the topos of the exemplary roll-call of good women is employed in the form of a simple and exotic-sounding list of names, then this is exactly how the device works. Chaucer's balade *Hyd Absolon* is a not particularly extravagant example, and it is a device of which Lydgate is fond. But it may be seen that it is one thing to mention in passing the virtue of Cleopatra's 'passyoun' (F 259/G 213 – in Lydgate's *Floure of Curtesye* it is her 'constaunce eke and faythe'), and another to submit the details of her story to the manipulation possible in a full narrative account. For Lydgate to refer simply to the 'innocence' and 'womanhede' of Phyllis and Hipsyphelee, or the 'discrecioun' of Ariadne,[3] is one thing, to read Ovid's or Chaucer's accounts of their full stories quite another. When Chaucer sang his balade for the Daisy Queen of his vision and saw the huge crowd of women attending her, the scene was not noticeably ironic except for the mildly anti-feminist quip of F 290–1/G 193–4, expressing amazement at the possibility that so many good women existed – 'And trewe of love thise women were echon./ *Now wheither was that a wonder thing or non . . .*'

It is only at the end of the Prologue that the latent irony in the list of classical heroines begins to be realised. Indeed, the potential paradox is indicated by the God of Love's specification that he begin with Cleopatra, perhaps the worst of his 'good women' and one whose 'wyfhod' and descent into hell are a clear parody of the story of Alceste. It is also only at the end of the Prologue that one begins to understand what is implied when the poet earlier told us of the necessity of trusting old books for stories otherwise incredible:

> For myn entent is, or I fro yow fare,
> The naked text in English to declare
> Of many a story, or elles of many a geste,
> As autours seyn; *leveth hem if yow leste.*
> G 85–8 (emphasis mine); cf. F 97–102

Finally, Love says, he is aware that if the poet is to write a number of stories he will need to keep them brief (F 570–7). *Abbreviatio* was of

---

[3] H. N. MacCracken, ed., *The Minor Poems of John Lydgate*, 2 vols. (London: EETS ES 107, 1911 and OS 192, 1934), II, p. 416.

course a prescribed method of telling a story in a form different from its source, but it is a convenient requirement in the *Legend of Good Women*, as some measure of censorship concerning what 'swiche lovers diden in hire tyme' (F 571) will be necessary if the poet is to have any chance of making 'saints' out of many of the women found in his books.

It is now time to investigate the significance of the dramatic opening of the Prologue to the *Legend of Good Women*. It is virtually the same in the F and G versions. Critics seem unsure of the implication for the rest of the poem of these first twenty-five lines. Yet the passage in itself is not hard to understand. Chaucer has either wasted twenty-five lines in stating the obvious – that we could not know much about the past if it were not for written records – or he is setting up a climate of scepticism for all knowledge not gained from personal experience.

In accordance, therefore, with one of the themes of the *Legend of Good Women*, Chaucer opens with a discussion of the foundations of faith:

> A thousand tymes have I herd men tell
> That there ys joy in hevene and peyne in helle,
> And I acorde wel that it ys so;
> But, natheles, yet wot I wel also
> That ther nis noon dwellyng in this contree,
> That eyther hath in hevene or helle ybe,
> Ne may of hit noon other weyes witen,
> But as he hath herd seyd, or founde it writen;
> For by assay ther may no man it preve.
> F/G 1–9

I think it is important to stress that this striking passage is not an expression of full-bodied religious scepticism as it is often considered. Rather it gives a quite precise account of the nature and experience of religious faith for a medieval Christian; faith involves belief in truths that are unverifiable by ordinary means but does not imply scepticism as a necessary concomitant. In the third line the narrator presents himself as an orthodox adherent of Christianity, a believer in the existence of an afterlife and the moral consequences of such belief – 'And I acorde wel that it ys so'. Even if the dramatic focus of the passage fixes on the impossibility of proving the existence of heaven and hell by personal experience, nevertheless the narrator's stance as true believer (who nevertheless sympathises with the instinctive doubt experienced by some) has implications for the whole poem. It is one of Chaucer's chief means of achieving the palinodal contrast around which the *Legend of Good Women* is structured.

The intellectual climate of the late fourteenth century could certainly be described as an age of uncertainty rather than of assured faith. But in order to locate accurately the register of Chaucer's opening lines, it is not necessary to turn to the subtleties of the epistemological investigations of contemporary philosophers, the Ockhamists or nominalists who were thinking deeply about how and of what it was possible to have certain knowledge. It is doubtful whether the tenets of Ockhamism were well-known or influential in England in the late fourteenth century,[4] and it is no longer considered accurate to characterise the fourteenth-century nominalist as either 'sceptical' or 'fideist',[5] because it was not so much that philosophers like Ockham were arguing for a profound scepticism as that they were debating the *grounds* of certitude for knowledge of what we see.[6] To be sure, a nominalist philosopher could endorse the opening lines of the *Legend*, and they do embody, in the simplest of language, the orthodox Ockhamist position. Even an extreme nominalist, like Nicholas of Autrecourt, moreover, considered it prudent to adhere to a belief in the immortality of the soul and the Biblical doctrine of rewards and punishments after death.[7]

Chaucer's register is quite different. It belongs with the common man's stated problem in believing in anything beyond his everyday

---

[4] See W. J. Courtenay, *Schools and Scholars in Fourteenth-Century England* (Princeton University Press, 1987), pp. 378–9.

[5] See H. A. Oberman, 'Fourteenth-Century Religious Thought: A Premature Profile', *Speculum* 53 (1978): 92; R. A. Peck, 'Chaucer and the Nominalist Questions', *Speculum* 53 (1978): 749–50. The concept of 'sceptical fideism' was popularised for Chaucer scholars by Sheila Delany, *Chaucer's House of Fame: the Politics of Skeptical Fideism* (University of Chicago Press, 1972). Cf. Delany's comments on the context and significance of the opening lines of the *Legend* in Delany, *Naked Text*, pp. 43–59.

[6] See Katherine H. Tachau, *Vision and Certitude in the Age of Ockham: Optics, Epistemology and the Foundation of Semantics 1250–1345* (Leiden: Brill, 1988), pp. 75–81, passim.

[7] See F. Copleston, *A History of Philosophy*, vol. III, *Late Mediaeval and Renaissance Philosophy: Ockham to the Speculative Mystics* (New York: Image Books, 1963), p. 157.

experience. It is the language of the moralising chronicler and poet, or even of the romance, and represents an attitude which predated Chaucer's time by centuries. Throughout the thirteenth, fourteenth and fifteenth centuries moralists grieved over people's lack of faith in religious truths which could not be verified by their own eyes and deeds. Such unbelief was commonly blamed for most defects in morality. Although the haranguings of satirists and preachers hardly offer unprejudiced testimony, nevertheless their illustrative stories suggest that a level of religious scepticism was by no means unknown in medieval times. In the thirteenth and fourteenth centuries especially, both the peasants and the upper classes, clergy and lay-people, even popes at times, were condemned for unbelief, particularly in regard to an afterlife. There are stories of involuntary doubt afflicting the genuine faithful: a pious man grieving over the death of a child, or an old nun whose melancholy and consequent failure in belief resulted in suicide. There is the young novice who Caesarius of Heisterbach said fell into despair after taking her vows. She confessed to the abbot:

> Who knows if there be a God, if there be angels with Him, souls or a kingdom of heaven? Who has seen these things? Who on returning from that place has shown us what he saw? . . . I speak according to the way it seems to me. Unless I should see these things, I will not believe.[8]

There were also drunken revellers who laughed about the clergy's attempts to 'deceive them into believing' in life after death. The critics of Pope Boniface VIII (1228–1303) objected not only to his simony and immorality but to his outright unbelief. He was accused by his enemies of denying immortality and directly quoted as saying: 'You fools stupidly believe a foolish thing! Who ever came back from the other world to tell us anything about it? Happy they who know how to enjoy life.' Although there is no real evidence for this story, the point of view expressed was clearly common enough.[9] These examples are all drawn from the thirteenth century, before the advent of philosophic

[8] *Dialogus* I 207: dis. IV c. xxxix. Quoted in Mary Edith Thomas, *Medieval Skepticism and Chaucer* (New York: William-Frederick Press, 1950), p. 17. This still provides a useful compilation of documents and translations on the subject. For the other stories mentioned here, see pp. 15–18; Latin originals, pp. 137–9.
[9] Ibid., p. 20.

nominalism. Chroniclers of the fourteenth century produce a similar range of stories. The poets too, particularly when in a moralistic frame of mind, refer to the same attitude. Deschamps, for example, frequently attributed a decline in moral standards to lack of faith in a future life.[10]

In characterising the opening of the Prologue to the *Legend of Good Women*, it is clearly not necessary to invoke the advent of the logic of Ockham and the growing empiricism of scientific inquiry, in spite of Chaucer's use of such terms as 'assay' and 'preve'. In the first few lines of the *Legend* it is the language not so much of logic as of the everyday experience of seeing and doing which is appealed to (see 5–6, 11, 13, 15, 16). In the development of the argument about the grounds of belief in lines 10–16, Chaucer goes on to consider the nature of truth that cannot be validated by such materialistic means: he points out that people have to believe more things than they have seen with their own eyes (F/G 10–13). It is a philosophic truth, moreover, that the validity of a proposition does not depend on the fact that it cannot be demonstrated in *anybody's* experience (F/G 14–16). By contrasting, at this point in his argument, the domain of experience with that of rational inference, Chaucer moves closest to the stance of contemporary philosophers. Robert Holcot argues in a similar way on the same subject. Like most nominalists who were both philosophers and theologians, Holcot believed strongly that such tenets of faith could never be proved, just as it was impossible to provide a proof for propositions stating that the world was created or, conversely, that it was eternal, even though one of such statements must necessarily be true – 'yet it's most important to believe it, just as many other things are true, which we cannot prove'.[11] Chaucer, however, quashes any sense of impending profundity in his argument, by capping it with the suspiciously flippant proverbial remark: 'Bernard the monk ne saugh nat all, pardee!' (F/G 16).

After thus dismissing an argument based on pure reason, Chaucer proceeds to his concluding point and recommends written authorities as the basis for faith, where there can be no other proof. This is the type of approach commonly recommended to minds more ordinary than those of philosophers. The preacher, John Bromyard, Chaucer's exact

[10] Saint-Hilaire and Raynaud, *Deschamps: Œuvres* VI, pp. 109, 219–20.
[11] See Beryl Smalley, *English Friars and Antiquity in the Early Fourteenth Century* (New York: Barnes, 1960), p. 184 and Appendix I, pp. 329–30 (Latin).

contemporary, writes in terms very similar to Chaucer's when he commends 'the writings, in reliance on which it is necessary to believe things that are not seen'. He adds, however, that 'the daily experience of men' shows the same necessity to believe in God and in the afterlife, just as a blind man believes a guide who sees the things he can't see himself, or as we believe our parents, or those who read to us about ancient kings or 'chronicles or romances or exploits of Charles and Roland and such', which after all we have never seen: 'And he who does not believe things that are read in the Scriptures [about the way to heaven and the joys of the good and the punishments of the wicked] because he has not seen them is more stupid than any idle listener to the aforesaid exploits.'[12]

Although it is not a 'proof' which Holcot would have found adequately rigorous, Chaucer is perfectly orthodox when he recommends giving credence to the 'doctrine of these olde wyse' found in old books (F/G 17–20), echoing the generally held reverence for the written word, for 'authorities'. He is thinking of the truth of the Scriptures – he uses words like 'doctrine', 'credence', 'holynesse', 'honouren and beleve', 'trowen' – but he undoubtedly means belief in 'these olde appreved stories' (F/G 21) to be extended to a wider context, to all knowledge of the past. That is, it applies to the truths of religion ('of holynesse'), of history ('of regnes, of victoryes'), and of matters concerning love ('of love, of hate'), as F/G 22–4 states. Old books contain the aggregated wisdom of mankind, memory of which can be added to the individual's own store of knowledge, which is itself dependent on the accumulation and mental systematisation of his memories of sense impressions. Chaucer's formulation of the idea that old books were the 'key of remembrance' unlocking the treasures of the past has been a popular one both with Chaucer's immediate successors and scholars of our own day:[13]

---

[12] Thomas, *Medieval Skepticism*, pp. 103–4, 162–3.

[13] R. O. Payne's *The Key of Remembrance* (New Haven: Yale University Press, 1963) is well known, but the phrase was being quoted soon after Chaucer's death, e.g., by Edward Duke of York (1406–13) in *Mayster of the Game* and by Lydgate in *The Debate of the Horse, Goose, and Sheep* 188–9, see Caroline Spurgeon, *Five Hundred Years of Chaucer Criticism and Allusion, 1357–1900*, 3 vols. (Cambridge University Press: 1925), I, p. 18.

And yf that olde bokes were aweye,
Yloren were of remembraunce the keye.
Wel ought us thanne honouren and beleve
These bokes, there we han noon other preve.
F/G 25–8

Calling old things to mind has also a well-marked didactic and devotional aspect, which derives from the primarily exemplarist medieval view of the past. Men need to be 'reminded' of the 'lessons of history'. Reading lives of saints, remembering their faithfulness and endurance in suffering, was a standard means of increasing faith. Even in the matter of faithfulness in love remembrance is important, as Malory wrote in his famous passage about stability and keeping faith in the days of 'the old love' when Queen Guinevere went a-maying.[14] Similarly, in marguerite poetry the daisy provokes memory, preserving faithfulness in love, summer in the midst of winter. The right use of 'remembrance' is a key theme in Gower's *Confessio Amantis*, insofar as confession is remembering.

Is Chaucer then, like Gower, quite traditionally writing an introduction for an exempla collection, in order that the moral truths embodied in its stories be not forgotten? We do well to be suspicious – and this in spite of the total orthodoxy of the sentiments expressed in the introduction to the Prologue to the *Legend*, the clarity with which the argument is developed, the simplicity of the vocabulary, the syntax of ordinary conversation. Behind the untroubled surface many treacherous questions lurk. It is true, as the philosophers pointed out, that men must act in faith on many more things than they have personally experienced, and not only in the realm of the supernatural. We can know that Rome is a big city without having been there, said William of Ockham.[15] The belief that certain knowledge depends on personal experience is an illusion of the unsophisticated. Nevertheless, Chaucer has chosen to formulate this proposition in the same simplistic terminology as did the genuine doubters and sceptics of the Middle Ages, who mistrusted anything they could not see with their own eyes. Moreover, he fixed on

---

[14] See E. Vinaver, ed., *Malory: Works*, 2nd edn (London: Oxford University Press, 1971), p. 649.

[15] Quoted in Peck, 'Nominalist Questions', p. 749.

the very topic which roused their doubts most strongly. The clerics who recorded the stories of scepticism which I quoted earlier despised the crude materialism of those who appealed to everyday experience to invalidate the reality of an afterlife. Yet, far from distancing himself from the point of view of the ordinary doubter, Chaucer remarks innocently that none of his countrymen has paid hell or heaven a visit to offer the proof of first-hand experience. The orthodoxy of his sentiments is somewhat undercut by the appeal to hearsay evidence, and even by the fact that one needs to be told 'a thousand times' about the reality of rewards and punishments after death.

Written evidence is, of course, only slightly more reliable. The authority of the Scriptures themselves might be sacrosanct, although often all the most sophisticated tools of reason were needed to elucidate their truth (cf. 'in every skylful wyse', F/G 20). But the writings of the Fathers frequently appeared to contradict each other, and the poetic witnesses to the past offered disturbingly different perspectives. We know this question absorbed Chaucer, and that the smooth recommendation of faith in the 'doctrine of these olde wyse' (F/G 19) concealed many difficulties for him. All in all, the introduction to the *Legend of Good Women* is an adequate enough summary of the conclusions drawn from contemporary epistemological inquiries. Yet one cannot be certain that a climate of scepticism towards orthodox teaching has not been fostered rather than put to rest. The true purpose of the argument of the first twenty-eight lines is suppressed at this point, until after a longish digression on the narrator's own delight in and pious 'devocioun' to old books, a devotion from which he occasionally plays truant on holidays or in the 'joly tyme of May' when he spends his time worshipping daisies. Only then does he turn to the true intention behind his opening discussion:

> But wherfore that I spak, to yive credence
> To olde stories and doon hem reverence?
> F 97–8/G 81–2

F and G differ from each other at this point, but both answers are flippant. In F he refuses to answer at all – 'I may nat al at-ones speke in ryme' – but makes it clear that he had been talking about the need to believe more than one can see or prove (F 99–100). In G 81–8 (quoted above) he insists that the 'authorities' he is about to translate contain matter almost impossible for the ordinary man to believe.

These opening lines of the *Legend of Good Women* are a preparation for the palinodal contrast which Chaucer's Legends will offer to the praise of ladies so gracefully enunciated in the body of the Prologue. That is, in light of the title, the *Legend of* Good *Women*, and the course that the poem takes, one suspects that the narrator's 'faith' is to be related to the courtly religion of love with its habit of honouring women's goodness. The poet's orthodoxy is demonstrated in his panegyric of the daisy, whose referent is without doubt some kind of ideal of perfect woman, the very model of faithfulness, rather than a humble meadow herb. The literary tradition exemplified thus was in marked contrast to the misogynist tradition (ultimately of classical origin) which, although mainly a learned tradition, often appealed to the 'facts' of daily experience to warn men that there were no good women. This alternative tradition fed the huge store of jokes about women with which medieval men, not only scholars, regaled each other and is alluded to in the G version of the Prologue (G 258–340). The F Prologue exploits a different ludic tradition when the narrator mentions St Valentine's Day pledges in order to remind the audience of the kind of love where ladies are not cold or stand-offish, and where men employ the standard promises of fidelity for the purposes of simple seduction (F 125–70). Chaucer here deliberately juxtaposed the ideal of faithfulness in love represented by the marguerite with a model based on the world of courtly flirtation, where vows were never meant to be taken seriously. The references to the courtly game of the Flower and Leaf, in both versions of the Prologue, suggest that the poet envisaged his poem as partaking in and provoking the kind of recreational debate about the relative merits of women and men that medieval audiences delighted in.

   In sum, then, Chaucer's discussion of the difficulties experienced by the faithful in submitting their faith to the evidence of daily experience was probably alluding to the resistance that men pretended to feel towards acceding to that cardinal tenet of courtly orthodoxy, *la louange des dames*. To be truly courteous the gentleman never ceased to praise the virtues of ladies, at least in poetry. The French poets of the fourteenth century provided endless graceful model lyrics of which the man of gentle birth might avail himself in his personal service of the God of Love. Clearly this service of love and ladies was accorded the deepest regard as a civilising mark which displayed unerringly the gentle heart. Nevertheless medieval gentlemen at times enjoyed portraying themselves as profoundly antifeminist at heart – Guillaume de Machaut himself drops the thin veneer of courtesy several times and launches into a diatribe against the unfaithfulness of woman as does even Sir Oton de Grandson.[16] Like Chaucer's Clerk, medieval gentlemen admitted that the existence of a good woman is a possibility, since authority tells us so, but husbands must not expect to find too many Griseldas around today. Lydgate, who enjoyed the vogue for antifeminist writing more than most, translated the French poem about the fabulous beasts, Chichevache and Bicorne; Chichevache who feeds on patient wives wastes away to nothing, Bicorne who feeds on patient husbands is grotesquely fat. Machaut in *Le Jugement dou Roy de Navarre* had admitted reluctantly that there might be one good woman to be found among 500,000. The element of the ludic in this should be clear.

We are dealing here with a recognisable attitude which men often take towards women, if a not wholly serious one. Yet when it was argued in 1908–9 by H. C. Goddard that the opening lines of the *Legend of Good Women* were suggesting that a good woman was a fabulous animal, not to be found in real life but only in old books, his articles were greeted by the critics of the period with astonished indignation. No one will wish to agree with Goddard that the *Legend* is an 'unmerciful satire on women', but his main adversary, J. L. Lowes, took umbrage even at his usage of the terms 'jocose' and 'facetious'.[17] Such criticism as Goddard's, said Lowes, was unduly modern and quite unhistorical, and had no supporting evidence whatsoever. And indeed Goddard had not. His response to the *Legend* was clearly instinctive and

---

[16] I discuss Machaut's antifeminist outbursts in *Le Jugement dou Roy de Navarre* in my chapter on the palinode; Oton de Grandson's antifeminist remarks are alluded to in my Introduction.

[17] H. C. Goddard, 'Chaucer's *Legend of Good Women*', *JEGP* 7 (1908): 87–129 and 8 (1909): 47–112; J. L. Lowes, 'Is Chaucer's *Legend of Good Women* a Travesty?', *JEGP* 8 (1909): 513–69. Cf. also R. M. Garrett, '"Cleopatra the Martyr" and her Sisters', *JEGP* 22 (1923): 64–74; P. F. Baum, 'Chaucer's "Glorious Legende"', *MLN* 60 (1945): 377–81.

derived from his own turn-of-the-century experience of what men 'facetiously' said about women.

The joke which it is suggested that Chaucer is hinting at in the opening lines of the *Legend of Good Women* is not in fact unhistorical. In one of the earliest comments on the *Legend* Lydgate seems to have something similar in mind when, in the Prologue to the *Fall of Princes* 330–6, he implies that in spite of great labour Chaucer was not able to fill the quota of 'good women' which the queen had requested:

> This poete wrote, at request of the queen,
> A legende off perfite hoolynesse,
> Off Goode Women to fynde out nynteen
> That dede excelle in bounte and fairnesse;
> But for his labour and [his] bisynesse
> Was inportable his wittis to encoumbre,
> In all this world to fynde so gret a noumbre.[18]

Two fifteenth-century poems presented adjacent to each other in Robbins' *Secular Lyrics of the XIVth and XVth Centuries*[19] employ just the same idea. The first, no. 180, is a dialogue between a clerk and a nightingale, occurring in a manuscript otherwise devoted to a collection of lives of saints. The clerk asks the nightingale how he shall know a true and good woman, and the nightingale replies that such an unlikely marvel is not to be found on earth, the only faithful women are dead ones:

> Clerk, ylk trew woman hath vpon,
> With-owt any lesyng,
> A robbe of grey marbyl ston,
> And of gret cumpasyng.
>
> Ylk a woman þat ys good
> May doe gret merveyle:
> A-reche þe sky with hur fote
> With-owtyn any fayle. . .
>
> They schul be god wan god is dede,
> And afterward maad all new.

18 H. Bergen, ed., *Lydgate's Fall of Princes*, 4 vols. (London: EETS ES 121–4, 1924–7).
19 R. H. Robbins, *Secular Lyrics of the XIVth and XVth Centuries*, 2nd edn (Oxford: Clarendon, 1955).

> Now take, clerk, thi best rede,
> ffor women schul neuer be trewe.
> 39–54

The next poem, no. 181, is a dialogue between a clerk and a husbandman,[20] written on the fly-leaf of a manuscript the body of which is
a long stanzaic poem on the life of Christ. In the stanzas where the clerk
praises women and love, the refrain, 'Quia amore langueo', is borrowed
from fervently mystical lyrics in which the Virgin or Christ begs for the
love of man. In contrast, the refrain used in the alternating stanzas by
the plain-speaking husbandman, 'Turn vpe hyr haltur & let hyr goo', is
found in other poems of an antifeminist nature. This poet chooses
terms very similar to Chaucer's:

> That husbande-man sayd, 'womon ys wariat:
> *By daly experiens hyt may be preuyt*;
> ffor be a womanse false delysyn
> Mony a gode man hase byn myscheuyt.
> 3yf I say trowth, be not dysgreuyt;
> And take thys for a conclisiun þer-to,
> Thy louely leuyng schall neuer be releuyt,
> Bot þou turn vpe hyr haltur & let hyr goe!'
>
> The clerke vnsward & sayd, '*in bokys I fynde*
> That gode made woman for mannys relefe,
> Then schoe ys turnid all agaynys kynde
> 3ef schoe be cause of mannys myschefe;
> Ther-for reherse no sych myspreue,
> ffor wethur þou tell me treuth or noe,
> Thou schalte nott make me *myse-beleue*,
> Quia amore langueo!'
> 41–56 (emphasis mine)

The husbandman supports his opinion that woman are untrustworthy
by an appeal to the proof of 'daly experiens', the clerk's belief in the
goodness of women rests only on the authority of 'bokys', and he
refuses to 'myse-beleue', whether he is presented with facts or not. In
the unquoted part of the poem religious language is also used: the
husbandman advises the clerk not to 'gyf credens' to women, and rather
to trust what the gospel says, 'Hyt ys nat all tru that peryth in glasse.'

---

[20] See also Carleton Brown, 'Dialogue between a Clerk and a Husbandman', *MLN* 33
(1918): 415–17.

The clerk calls the husbandan's argument a 'mys-fenyng fabulle'. This poet is spelling out the joke only hinted at in the introduction to the Prologue of the *Legend of Good Women*. No anachronism need attach to the suggestion that Chaucer is proposing, at this early stage in the *Legend*, sympathy with the ordinary man whose everyday experience leads him to be sceptical about the faithfulness of women, the topic which is at issue later in the Prologue and, one suspects, in the Legends dealing with the amazing fidelity of the women inhabiting old books. For our purpose it is important to give equal weight to both points of view: both to the assured validity of the tenets of orthodox faith, and to the cheeky scepticism of the non-philosophic man in the street.

The quotation I cited in my last chapter to illustrate the exemplary value of the Alcestis story at a literal level makes the same point. No sooner has Bersuire praised Alcestis as an example of those *bonarum mulierum que viros perfecta diligunt* than he immediately proceeds to point out humorously that such good women do not exist today. Not only would contemporary women be unwilling to die that their husbands might live, he says, but they desire their deaths so that they may remarry: *Quod tamen est hodie contra multas que non solum pro viris suis mori non volunt ut viri vivant, ymmo mortem eorum appetunt ut aliis ipse nubant.*[21] It is instructive that even for Bersuire the notion of a perfect woman calls forth humorous qualification, so that we have here perfectly reflected the attitude that Chaucer brings to the *Legend of Good Women*. The honour and reverence he bears to 'the good Alceste, the dayesie, and [his] owene hertes reste' are presented as totally genuine as orthodox faith in heaven and hell. But the ideal of the daisy, the Alceste of authoritative story, and the example of his 'lady sovereyne' are all instances of that excessively rare breed, the Good Woman: Walter Map, among many others, talks of the truly good woman as 'rarer than a phoenix' while bad women 'swarm in such numbers that no place is free of their malice'.[22] Chaucer's audience may thus be excused if they are sceptical of that vision of a great multitude of good women, true in love each one, because conventional wisdom stated that such can no longer be found in great numbers. To verify their existence

21 Translated and commented upon in Delany, *Naked Text*, p. III.
22 M. R. James, ed. and trans. (rev. C. N. L. Brooke and R. A. B. Mynors), *Walter Map: De Nugis Curialium, Courtiers' Trifles*, (Oxford: Clarendon, 1983), pp. 292–3.

one must turn to the 'olde appreved stories', in the same way that for proof of the existence of heaven and hell one must rely on scriptural authority. The Good Woman is in effect a legendary beast and Lucreces and Penelopes are not to be found outside fables. This is the subversive attitude that the Prologue to the *Legend* will have induced in many of Chaucer's audience towards the Legends of good women that he is forced to relate. Moreover, as is now frequently pointed out, the Legends themselves have much in them to fuel scepticism, or at the very least, the kind of debate that enlivened *Le Jugement dou Roy de Navarre*. As I have already noted, critics usually feel the need to endorse either the comic or serious side of the *Legend*, to the exclusion of the other. Rather, the two aspects are united in the narrating voice, which in this case it is futile to separate from that of Chaucer himself, who is both the author of the poems mentioned later in the Prologue, and a male, possessed of all the biases in perspective that his audience might have expected male writers to have.

The wider context of the medieval attitude to women, a literary and rhetorical tradition with a long history, must be examined elsewhere.[23] Suffice it to say that jibes about 'all women' such as I have quoted were current over several millennia and can be assumed to be recognisable to most men as jokes, even if they do not coincide precisely with what men actually thought about 'some women'. Minnis has suggested usefully in his concluding discussion of the *Legend* in his *Shorter Poems* that the 'exaggerated praise of women', such as we find in the *Legend* and other medieval and early Renaissance works like Castiglione's *Il Cortegiano*, may represent a 'sophisticated gender game: primarily for recreational purposes and social display, a fashionable grace or licensed foolishness which contains more than a hint of the ridiculous, but never goes so far as to be displeasing and certainly not to be taken too seriously'.[24] When I come to my section discussing Chaucer's Legends of good women, the stories of Cleopatra and her sisters, I will be assuming this sense of the

---

[23] E.g., see the texts and introduction in Blamires, *Woman Defamed*.

[24] 'The World Upside Down: Gender Game as Alternative Art', in Minnis, *The Shorter Poems*, pp. 443–454 esp. p. 446. See also his section, 'Debate Form and Implied Audience' in his discussion of the *Parliament of Fowls*, pp. 290–300. W. A. Quinn discusses the ludic quality of the *Legend* in 'Chaucer's Rehersynges: the Performability of *The Legend of Good Women*' (Washington, D.C.: Catholic University of America Press, 1994).

playful and pointing to the evidence for it which the Legends provide. I will later also explore various ludic contexts, literary and social, which Chaucer's palinode in praise of women hints at, contexts in which such jokes and humorous debates about women's virtue were enjoyed. In the world of courtly behaviour, where gentlemen paid lipservice to the value of women, it was clearly important for Chaucer to praise women's goodness, while at the same time promoting the fiction that he was only embracing the opposite side (from the male point of view) because forced to do so.

First, however, I return in my next four chapters to the second plot motif of the Prologue, the poet's confrontation with the God of Love, where the question of the poet's handling of the matter of the virtue of women acts as the touchstone in an exploration (perhaps representing a debate within himself, at times anxious, at times touched by bravado) of the significance of the role of vernacular poet and skilled translator in England's late fourteenth-century courtly society. I begin with the God of Love himself, a conflicted figure who in a sense stands for the secular value system against which and within which the poet must find his sense of relevance.

PART II

The God of Love

4

The God of Love

Alongside the Good Woman, Alceste, the other major personage that
Chaucer confronts in his dream is the spectacular deity, the God of
Love. Any description of the subtleties of meaning embraced by the
term 'love' in a given medieval context is fraught with difficulty, even
leaving to one side the contrast between earthly and spiritual love. If on
the one hand the God of Love, such as the one praised by Christine de
Pizan in her *Epistre au Dieu d'Amours*, is presented as the patron of the
highest secular ideals of the noble life, on the other hand in Jean de
Meun's section of the *Roman de la Rose* he is the thinly disguised
personification of sexual passion. Where does Chaucer's God of Love
fit? He is clearly a more complex figure than the Cupid whose attributes
Boccaccio authoritatively glosses in a moralistic and pessimistic fashion
in his scholarly work, *De Genealogia Deorum*. Boccaccio says there that
Cupid is depicted as a child to show the age of those whose passions and
behaviour are under his influence; his wings indicate the instability of
the passionate; he carries bows and arrows to demonstrate how suddenly the unwary are captured; he is shown blindfolded to teach us that
lovers do not know where they are going and lack any kind of
judgement.[1]

As turn-of-the-century Chaucerian scholars noted, medieval references to the God of Love drew on three distinct fields of discourse,

---

[1] See V. Romano, ed., *Genealogie Deorum Gentilium Libri*, 2 vols. (Bari: Scrittoria
d'Italia, 1951), II, pp. 453–4. This unflattering view of Cupid's characteristics is quite
typical of scholarly medieval mythographies, many others of which are quoted by
E. Panofsky in 'Blind Cupid', in *Studies in Iconology* (1939; rpt. New York: Harper,
1962), pp. 104–7.

which they termed classical, ecclesiastical and feudal.[2] That is, the classical inheritance provided the notion of Cupid as an all-powerful deity, with the attributes indicated by his youth and nakedness, his blindness, his wings and his quiver of arrows. In medieval times this notion of godhood produced a whole supporting 'religion', with a Paradise and Purgatory, apostles, teachers, worshippers, liturgy, commandments, gospel, sins, penances. This then shaded into the idea of Love as a king, to whom men swore feudal homage and who presided over a court wherein he dispensed justice to his subjects and where he and his barons arbitrated *demandes d'amour* and the merits of competing poetic productions. Movement between the three linguistic areas normally appears quite unselfconscious, as it is in the *Legend of Good Women*, and it is not now easy to tell the extent to which wild exaggeration of the 'religion of love', for example, would have been a marked feature, or merely a cliché. In the *Legend of Good Women* the F Prologue systematically exploits religious terminology in its account of the service of the God of Love; in the G Prologue these features are noticeably absent from the text.

The God of Love often seems to stand for a concept of love in which a severely moralistic view of human nature is overlaid with a compound of psychological observation and a perception of the social utility of love (both in producing civilised or polite behaviour and in simply aiding the procreation of the species). From the standpoint of psychological observation, the God of Love's omnipotence and imperiousness, his capriciousness and even blindness, indicated such maxims as that the power of love could be withstood by no one, especially the young, that it was unpredictable as well as irresistible, and often seemed to reward the undeserving (or ignore the deserving) or cause the unsuitably matched in social terms to love each other. Gower states these ideas over and over again in *Confessio Amantis*.[3] It is the same kind of psychological observation, transmuted now into a set of moral imperatives, that underlies the 'commandments' which in numerous texts the God of Love promulgates. The sleeplessness, the fear, the loss of speech

---

[2] See W. A. Neilson, *The Origins and Sources of the Court of Love* (1899; rpt. New York: Russell, 1967), p. 38; W. G. Dodd, *Courtly Love in Chaucer and Gower* (1913; rpt. Gloucester, Mass.: Peter Smith, 1959), pp. 16–20.

[3] E.g. *CA* I 51–4; III 389–9; IV 1731–9, 4556–60; VII 1761–5; VIII 157–8.

and colour in the beloved's presence, are part of the service of the God of Love from its earliest medieval expression. In the *Roman de la Rose* the God of Love is said to *order* his servant to hide his emotions from others, to be alternately hot and cold, and grow lean and pale and dumb in his lady's presence (*RR* 2265–580). When such behavioural traits are thus codified and objectified, they are features which 'false lovers', such as the *Legend*'s villains, may easily counterfeit in order to appear a true servant of Love.

Another role which the medieval God of Love adopts is that of patron of all the social graces of polite society. He is the lord of courtesy. Many of his commands to the Lover in the *Roman de la Rose* mingle moral and social sanctons indiscriminately and involve such items as cheerfulness, elegant manners, cleanliness, avoidance of pride and avarice, expertise in arms, the possession of a fine singing voice, and so on. By the late fourteenth century, such ingenuous instruction is not common, except perhaps Love's injunction that to honour women and to keep the tongue from ribaldry is the mark of true courtesy, in the words of Chaucer's translation:

> For nothyng eke thy tunge applye
> To speke wordis of rebaudrye . . .
> And alle wymmen serve and preise,
> And to thy power her honour reise;
> And if that ony myssaiere
> Dispise wymmen, that thou maist here,
> Blame hym . . .
> *Romaunt* 2223–33

These sentiments are often repeated, as at the the *cour amoureuse* of the French king Charles VI, founded at the turn of the fifteenth century for the purpose of honouring and defending ladies.

Insofar as an exaggerated sensibility was a requisite for true loving, the service of the God of Love had come to seem a prerogative of aristocratic society. When Plaisance, in Froissart's *Paradis d'Amour* 936–41, describes the retinue of the God of Love she says: 'There are counts, dukes and kings, knights, and from all peoples, and with their number his company is fine and gracious, for whoever is not of very gentle condition cannot be one of my lord's men, nor be entered in his register.'[4] The many references to 'courts of love' in the late Middle Ages suggest that any informal and recreational gathering of aristocratic people, that is, the 'servants of the God of Love', might think of itself as a court of love, in the sense both of being the intimate *familia* of the God of Love and as a court of law, in which cases about love were adjudicated.[5] There is, however, almost no corroborative external evidence as to the existence of actual courts of love, and even the famous *cour amoureuse* of Charles VI seems to have been 'originally little more than a spontaneous parlour game' on which was later erected 'a pompous courtly edifice in which the elements of fact and fiction have become inextricably mixed'.[6] But the frequent references to the court of the God of Love accompanied by lively and realistic accounts of late medieval courtly diversion, which we find, for example, in Gower's *Confessio Amantis*[7] or Machaut's *Remede de Fortune*,[8] suggest that familiar social situations were being re-created in these poems.

In *Remede de Fortune* Machaut presents his courtly audience with an idealised view of itself as a society in the service of love, but love seen as refined emotion rather than sexual conquest.[9] The poem tells how its young and innocent protagonist fell in love and was instructed in virtuous living by Love and the lady the young man serves. As the title suggests, *Remede* includes a closely imitated Boethian *consolatio*, trans-posed however into an amatory framework, where the lady Esperence consoles the lover in his suffering and teaches him about Fortune. The poem incorporates a vivid description, of great historical interest, of a day spent in the presence of the poet's lady: there is dancing and carolling outdoors, and, as the company moves inside, much talking about questions of love and sharing of love poems; there is a celebration of mass and a meal, with a lively account of the noisiness of the

---

[4] Trans. Windeatt, *Chaucer's Dream Poetry*, p. 50.

[5] See Green, 'The *Familia Regis* and the *Familia Cupidinis*', in V. J. Scattergood and J. W. Sherborne, eds., *English Court Culture in the Later Middle Ages* (London: Duckworth, 1983), pp. 87–108, and R. F. Green, *Poets and Princepleasers: Literature and the English Court* (University of Toronto Press, 1980), pp. 120–5.

[6] Green, *Poets and Princepleasers*, p. 122. Cf. Theodor Straub, 'Die Gründing des Pariser Minnehofs von 1400', *Zeitschrift für Romanische Philologie* 77 (1961): 1–14.

[7] Cf. Green, *Poets and Princepleasers*, pp. 122–3; G. Mathew, *The Court of Richard II* (London: Murray, 1968), p. 77.

[8] E. Hœpffner, ed., *Œuvres de Guillaume de Machaut*, 3 vols. (Paris: SATF, 1908–21), II.

[9] Wimsatt and Kibler, *Behaigne and Remede*, pp. 33–4.

conversation and the valets organising their masters' clothing, and of the varieties of musical instruments which provided the after-dinner entertainment. Finally the company divides into groups of two or three who play games like chess or dance or sing to the accompaniment of the musicians until the wine and spices are brought. Into the narrative account of the young man's progress in love are worked examples of lyrical forms (one example of each and some with musical accompaniment), carefully labelled and arranged. Although each lyric fits neatly into its narrative position, there can be no doubt that *Remede* was to be thought of as a reference collection of lyric forms composed by the master, ready to be imitated by the gentlemanly amateurs who made up the audience of such as Machaut and Froissart, Gower and Chaucer.[10] *Remede* is an embodiment of that amalgam of which the vision of the noble life was compounded: symbolically speaking, the God of Love rules over the young man's education in virtue, the development of a Boethian outlook on the problems of temporality, the details of quotidian courtly existence, and the producing of beautiful language.

Along with the praise of women, it is this association of the fourteenth-century God of Love with poetry-making that I wish to emphasise. Machaut is known to have supervised the production of the manuscripts which contain his 'complete works'.[11] To the latest and most complete of these he appended a Prologue which explained how Nature and the God of Love gave him special gifts which peculiarly fitted him for the service of his lord, the God of Love, in the production of poetic and musical works (lays, rondeaux, virelais, balades, complaints, etc), 'to the honour and praise of all ladies' (*Prologue* V 1–23). The association of love and poetry is an important theme in the French marguerite poems, and Froissart's *Paradis d'Amour*, for example, concludes with the poet reciting a lay to the God of Love while sitting at his feet, and the whole poem is capped with the balade in honour of the marguerite. The experience of love was acknowledged to be the proper

[10] Cf. D. Kelly, *Medieval Imagination: Rhetoric and the Poetry of Courtly Love* (Madison: University of Wisconsin Press, 1978), p. 3.

[11] See Sarah Jane Manley Williams, 'Machaut's Self-Awareness as Author and Producer', in M. P. Cosman and B. Chandler, eds., *Machaut's World: Science and Art in the Fourteenth Century* (New York: Annals of the New York Academy of Sciences, 1978), pp. 189–97.

matter of poetry, and Machaut and Froissart tend to portray themselves as lovers as a means of validating their poetic function, although clearly a primary object in their love poetry is the display of their technical poetic facility. During the course of the fourteenth century, however, poets began to draw with some subtlety a distinction between the role of the lover/protagonist (the province of aristocratic youth) and the role of the lover/poet (the province of the clerk), self-confidently claiming for the latter a measure of worth deriving from the gifted poet's superior insight, his powers of expression, his Ovidian creativity. The influence of Jean de Meun's concept of the Poet/Lover was incalculable,[12] and Machaut's work increasingly deals with his sense that the making of a poem about love was as valuable as experiencing love directly. The artefacts of the poetic craftsman were to be regarded as much the service of the God of Love as was the love-service of the *fin amant*.[13] Froissart's poetry alludes persistently to these motifs of Machaut's, as Machaut's had done to Jean de Meun's; in this constant dialogue with the texts of their predecessors, Meun, Machaut, Froissart, and indeed the English Chaucer (the last with a mixture of tentativeness and bravado) 'authorise' yet again their own writing and lay claim to a patrilineal succession of poets.[14] In *Troilus and Criseyde* and the *Legend of Good Women* Chaucer demonstrates how thoroughly he had assimilated the understanding developed by his French antecedents that it was not necessary to masquerade as a lover, often a socially inappropriate role, in order to write about love. When Chaucer offered his daisy poetry to the judgement of those 'lovers' who, presumably by right of birth, 'kan make of sentement' (F 69), he was tacitly marking himself off from them. Yet even within the Prologue to the *Legend* he asserts the force of his creative imagination and his linguistic skill in praising ladies, as well as his moral authority (F 462 ff./G 452 ff.), and in the Legends

---

[12] Cf. K. D. Uitti, 'From *Clerc* to *Poète:* the Relevance of the *Romance of the Rose* to Machaut's World', in Cosman and Chandler, *Machaut's World*, pp. 209–16.

[13] See K. Brownlee, *Poetic Identity in Guillaume de Machaut* (Madison: University of Wisconsin Press, 1984), passim, and 'The Poetic Œuvre of Guillaume de Machaut: the Identity of Discourse and the Discourse of Identity', in Cosman and Chandler, *Machaut's World*, pp. 219–33.

[14] See Sylvia Huot, *From Song to Book: the Poetics of Writing in Old French Lyric and Lyrical Narrative Poetry* (Ithaca: Cornell University Press, 1987), particularly the chapters on Meun, Machaut and Froissart.

demonstrates his power over the matter of women with self-conscious virtuosity.

That many gentlemen associated with the French and English courts possessed a high level of poetic competence has been amply demonstrated.[15] The charter of Charles VI's *cour amoureuse* informs us that it was formed for the specific purpose of adjudicating on poetic matters, including questions of lapses in poetic decorum or of metrical faults.[16] The difficulty, which Green identifies,[17] for poets like Chaucer and Gower of being accorded any kind of specific professional status in a society in which all gentlemen were expected to be amateur poets was compensated for by the reception of their works by a discriminating audience able to appreciate the technical problems of poetic composition on their own account. A vignette in Froissart's *Prison Amoureuse* 1001–9 intimates the kind of reception a poem, even that of a 'professional' like Froissart, might expect. Froissart describes how he composes and polishes a well-proportioned lay, reading it over in order to revise and correct it so as to avoid the reproach of Adam or Roger and 'all the others who involve themselves with criticism'.

In sum, the dominion of the God of Love is a portmanteau concept which incorporates within its dimensions ideas which can appear mutually antagonistic. The God of Love portrayed as the patron of gentle behaviour seems to bear little relation to the Cupid of the scholarly moralisations. There is, however, an intermediate position, stated usually with tolerance and mild amusement, which sees the God of Love as the natural lord of young people, who are at the period in their lives when their passions are likely to dominate over their rational natures. It is an easy step from here to personify the God of Love as sexual passion, as *cupiditas*. But other qualities of the young (their emotional warmth and generosity of spirit, for example) surely feed the concept of love as the quintessence of noble living, where interest in the opposite sex is seen as a refinement which finds expression in beautiful

---

[15] E.g. D. Poirion, *Le Poète et le Prince: L'Evolution du Lyrisme Courtois de Guillaume de Machaut à Charles d'Orléans* (Paris: Presses Universitaires de France, 1965), pp. 152–6; K. B. McFarlane, *Lancastrian Kings and Lollard Knights* (London: Oxford University Press, 1972), p. 182.

[16] Green, '*Familia Regis*', pp. 94 ff.

[17] *Poets and Princepleasers*, pp. 127 ff.

language. Besides the praise of women and the preoccupation with poetry-making, therefore, the other feature of the service of the God of Love which we find in much of the work of, for example, Meun, Machaut, Froissart, Gower and Charles d'Orléans, is the association with youthfulness.[18]

The ambiguities which the God of Love bears within himself do not always go unnoticed by medieval writers. For example, the God of Love in Christine de Pizan's *Epistre au Dieu d'Amours* is the promulgator of courtly *louange des dames* and the enemy of all those who defame women. When Hoccleve translated Christine's poem into English soon after, however, he humorously inserted some extra stanzas, so that the God of Love in the English version interrupts his praise of St Margaret's 'loving heart' to point out that he cannot admire her virginity, for it is his nature to war against chastity.[19] It is as if Hoccleve cannot resist making Christine's extremely virtuous God of Love remind himself of that other rather amoral quality which he was thought to embody, the element of erotic passion which was at war with the virtues that Christine admired. Such ambiguity is not commonly foregrounded (as it is not, I think, in the *Legend of Good Women*), even though the inconsistencies often disrupt the internal logic of works which feature the God of Love.[20] Clearly the ambiguities were more readily accommodated by those readers and writers who *lived* the service of the God of Love than they can be by us cultural outsiders and time travellers, critics who try to provide a neat analysis of what the trope meant. In a sense it is true that the narrative sequence concerning the God of Love in the *Legend* only works if we shut our eyes to the inconsistency embodied in its central figure, if we do not try to reconcile too closely what 'love' means for the God of Love, what it means to Alceste, what it means in the poet's self-defence. I touch on each of these variations of the notion of 'love' in my next few chapters.

---

[18] Cf. Poirion, *Poète et Prince*, p. 149.

[19] Hoccleve, *Letter of Cupid* 427–34, in Thelma S. Fenster and Mary Carpenter Erler, eds. and trans., *Poems of Cupid, God of Love: Christine de Pizan's Epistre au Dieu d'Amours and Dit de la Rose, Thomas Hoccleve's Letter of Cupid* (Leiden: Brill, 1990), p. 198.

[20] Cf. Minnis' discussion of Gower's logical problems in *Confessio Amantis*, Minnis, *Shorter Poems*, p. 393.

Chaucer's portrait of the God of Love in the *Legend* is a product of all the positions I have identified in this section. Love is indubitably the youthful 'son of Venus' (F 338/G 313). He is imperious and under suspicion of exercising tyranny over his servants. He is unmoved by rational argument – 'for Love ne wol nat counterleted be/ In ryght ne wrong' (F 476–7/G 466–7), and in the G Prologue he attributes Chaucer's opposition to him to the fact that the poet is one of those 'olde foles [whose] spiryt fayleth' (G 262). On the other hand he is the patron of love poetry, choosing the matter but allowing Chaucer the licence of choosing his own metrical form (F 562), and the queen who accompanies him is an idealisation of virtuous human love and the feminine perfections of humility, meekness and wifely obedience; whether Alceste is to be seen as his wife or not,[21] there can be no doubt that there is an intimate connection being postulated between what the God of Love and Alceste respectively represent. When Chaucer presents himself as dreaming of 'the god of Love, and in his hand a quene' (F 213/G 142–5), who preside over a debate on the poetic propriety of Chaucer's 'defamation of women' in *Troilus and Criseyde*, the audience would recognise the scene as an analogue of a familiar social situation and well-known literary topos.

We have also, I think, a model in which the poet cooperates with a noble patron or aristocratic ideal in the production of a work of art – in earlier chapters I pointed out how the poet-figure in the F Prologue to the *Legend* presents himself as the harp on which the daisy lady makes her music; and again, how he augments the God of Love's formulation of the myth of the daisy/Alceste and gives it poetic form. I have been dealing up till now with the poet's *subservience* to the ideal; the remainder of my study deals with his resistance to its dangerous tyranny. The resistance of the antifeminist man of letters or the courtly

---

[21] The text gives no strong warrant to the view that Alceste and the God of Love are married: Alceste's line 'I, youre Alceste, whilom quene of Trace' (F 432/G 422) draws attention not only to her relationship with the God of Love, but also to her essential characteristic as wife of another man. Older scholars (e.g., Skeat, *Oxford Chaucer*, III, p. xxiv) sometimes assume Love and Alceste were man and wife, a position recently resurrected by D. Wallace in '"Whan she translated was": a Chaucerian Critique of the Petrarchan Academy', in L. Patterson, ed., *Literary Practice and Social Change in Britain, 1380–1530* (Berkeley: University of California Press, 1990), pp. 156–215, esp. p. 210.

'rebellious lover' to the worship of ideal woman, although the major trope in the *Legend*, is only one item in a repeating pattern of heresy and political dissent in the poem. The oppositional pattern dramatised here can be read in many ways: by Lee Patterson, importantly, as resistance to the tyranny of the uncritical celebration of a monolithic court ideology;[22] by Elaine Hansen as a protest against the feminisation of men inevitably required by the service of love;[23] by Robert Frank as Chaucer's demand that his poetry be opened to a wider choice of mode and subject matter.[24] In my reading, the challenge made by the English vernacular writer to the hegemony of old books and Latinate culture is an aspect of the poet's attempt at self-definition. Yet the profound debt which Chaucer also demonstrates towards the inspiration of the courtly and aristocratic ethos as expressed in fourteenth-century French love poetry should never be underestimated. The stance of the clerkly narrator in the G Prologue, however, who, 'lenynge faste by a bente', observes the apparition of the God of Love and the Daisy Queen, exhibits somewhat more detachment from the service of the God of Love than does that of the courtly F Prologue's subservient narrator, who kneels all day before the daisy.

The God of Love and the virtuous Queen Alceste together represent the ideological power and attractiveness of aristocratic culture but also the restrictive demands and limitations of orthodox courtly conventions of writing; it is in this framework that one must consider the question of whether these figures, in the F Prologue at least, also bear any resemblance to Richard II and Anne of Bohemia. With regard to the queen there should be no problem, as I have already pointed out, for there is nothing written of her in the Prologue to the *Legend* that is not extremely flattering and could not have been accepted as a graceful compliment by a lady who came from a family well known for its literary patronage (her grandfather, King Jean of Bohemia, her uncle, Wenceslas of Brabant, and aunt, Bonne of Luxembourg, achieved an idealised representation in the works of Chaucer's French contemporaries). It was once a common suggestion that Alceste was to be

---

[22] L. Patterson, *Chaucer and the Subject of History* (Madison: University of Wisconsin Press, 1991), pp. 58–9.
[23] Hansen, *Fictions of Gender*, p. 3.
[24] Frank, *Chaucer and the Legend*, pp. 11–36.

allegorically identified with Anne, but critics like Kittredge and Lowes felt that this would have involved Chaucer in grave impropriety.[25] Such an opinion may be discarded, as it seems to rest on the outdated notion that Chaucer's use of the terminology of 'courtly love' in his homage to a social superior like the queen inevitably suggested a sincere passion which was, of course, adulterous in intent! Moreover, any notion of an allegorical substitution is unnecessary, especially since Alceste is not associated with Queen Anne in the G version. All that can be said for certain is that in the F Prologue the poem is dedicated to the Queen, and I have suggested that when the poet mistakes the Daisy Queen of his vision for his 'lady sovereyne' a complimentary reference to Queen Anne is implied insofar as all the attributes of the daisy and the virtues of Queen Alceste could equally be praised in Anne. The question of Richard's relation to the God of Love is more difficult, I think. Critics often see the God of Love in the *Legend* as a figure of fun, of limited vision and infantile literary judgement; it is certainly suggested that he is a tyrant, ruled by passion rather than reason. Yet, as I have been pointing out, these features are part of the traditionally ambivalent concept of love, and could have been readily accommodated by the more positive aspects of his character, particularly as developed in the love visions of contemporary French poetry, where the God of Love is fully implicated in the collaboration of poet and patron in the production of courtly poetry. The advice to a king, sometimes thought to be insulting if Richard were meant, is a not unusual feature of fourteenth-century French narrative love poetry, as in Machaut's *Voir Dit*, and indeed it is known that a manuscript was compiled for Richard containing the same kind of material as makes up the *de regimine* speech in the *Legend*.[26] It can hardly be doubted, moreover, that Chaucer's description of the God of Love is a beautiful and dramatic one.

The transformation of the classical Cupid into the medieval God of Love is reflected in iconography – instead of a naked boy, medieval manuscript illustrations usually depict a fully robed young man with

25 Lowes, 'French *Marguerite* Poems', pp. 666–76; G. L. Kittredge, 'Chaucer's Alceste', *MP* 6 (1909): 435–9.
26 See J-Ph. Genet, *Four English Political Tracts of the Later Middle Ages* (London: Royal Historical Society, Camden Fourth Series, 18, 1977).

wings like an angel and a crown on his curling hair. He frequently bears a bow and arrows, but is rarely blind.[27] Chaucer's description of the figure in his vision who accompanies the lady dressed like a daisy conforms to this pattern:

> Yclothed was this myghty god of Love
> In silk, enbrouded ful of grene greves,
> In-with a fret of rede rose-leves . . .
> His gilte heer was corowned with a sonne,
> Instede of gold, for hevynesse and wyghte.
> Therwith me thoghte his face shoon so bryghte
> That wel unnethes myghte I him beholde;
> And in his hand me thoghte I saugh him holde
> Twoo firy dartes, as the gledes rede,
> And aungelyke hys wynges saugh I sprede.
> F 226–36

That the God of Love in this description includes the Amors of *Roman de la Rose* among the most important of his ancestors is clear. Guillaume de Lorris, however, had said that the God of Love was *not* clad in silk, but in a robe cunningly wrought of all the ebullient fertility and teeming plenitude of the earth, flowers, birds, animals, suggesting the God of Love's dominion over the natural world. The robe of Chaucer's God of Love, which is merely of silk heavily embroidered in a trellis pattern of red roses and sprays of greenery,[28] speaks of courtly display rather than mythological dimension, although the description of his sun-crown and radiant face restore to Chaucer's Love a new element of the supernatural.

The detail of the sun-crown is unique to Chaucer's description of the God of Love in the F Prologue. It is a brilliant conception. Along with his green robes, Love's shining face and crown suggest his sun-like domination of the Spring season, burgeoning with new growth, and his affinity with the heliotropic daisy in particular. The only manuscript illustration I have seen which gives a visual impression anything like

---

[27] See Panofsky, 'Blind Cupid', pp. 103–4.
[28] The embroidered robe is typical of the kind of richly elaborate costume which was adopted by men of the English court under the aegis of Richard, according to Mathew, *Court of Richard II*, pp. 25–7. The several portraits of the king depict him wearing garments heavily embroidered with heraldic devices and badges.

that implied by the line, 'his gilte heer was corowned with a sonne', comes from an *Ovide Moralisé* manuscript[29] and depicts Apollo sitting on one of the peaks of Mount Helicon. Apollo in this picture has a young man's face with a crown on his curling hair just like the medieval God of Love is usually drawn, but, because he is the God of the Sun, from behind his head there radiates a crown-like sunburst similar to a heraldic sunburst (rays of the sun emerging from behind a cloud); because he is the God of Poetry, he is playing a harp. Insofar as the service of the God of Love involved the writing of love-poetry, it is attractive to theorise that Chaucer conflated the iconography of Apollo with that of the God of Love. I have already remarked how the Ovidian account of Clytie's devotion to Apollo, as a result of which she was turned into a flower which followed the sun, may have contributed to Chaucer's vision of the daisy and the God of Love. (As a matter of interest we might note that Richard II was famous for his long curling golden hair and was conscious of his physical beauty – contemporary chroniclers remark on it and call him an 'Absalom'.[30] He appears to have cultivated an ideal of clean-shaven adolescent beauty[31] which accords with many manuscript illustrations of the God of Love.) It is rather surprising that in place of a symbol of such visual drama and fertile allusiveness as the sun-crown, Love in the G version is described wearing a simple garland of roses and lilies, and has no 'gilte' hair.

If Chaucer's God of Love wears a conventional robe, he is also not blindfolded, which enables him to turn a stern look on the hapless poet. When Chaucer says he suspects that the God of Love was not blind, in spite of his reputation, because of the imperious stare which freezes the poet's heart (F 237–40), I suspect the intention was to recreate a recognisable social situation, a gathering, perhaps, of some 'court of love' with its elected arbiters of poetic prowess, rather than to relieve Love of the moral stigma of blindness – for, in the *Legend*, Love's vision is not conspicuously more clearsighted or less partial than that normally

---

29 MS Bibl. Nat. 871, fo. 116ᵛ, illustration [72] in R. S. Loomis, *Mirror of Chaucer's World* (Princeton University Press, 1965).

30 E.g. Adam of Usk cites eyewitnesses to Richard's coronation who said he was 'fair among men as another Absalom'. Quoted in S. Armitage-Smith, *John of Gaunt* (London: Constable, 1904; rpt. 1964), p. 190.

31 Mathew, *Court of Richard II*, p. 21.

attributed to 'blind Cupid'. (Richard favoured a formal and elaborate ceremonial in his court, and desired that the distance between himself and others be marked,[32] so that Love's stern look is not out of harmony with what we know of Richard's court.)

This confrontation between Chaucer and the God of Love constitutes the conceptual centre of the *Legend of Good Women*. The unearthly silence lasting 'the mountaunce of a furlong wey of space' (F 306–7/G 232–3) clearly presages some momentous happening, but Chaucer presents himself (still on his knees beside the daisy) awaiting in all innocence a revelation of what the personages in his dream signify, and with no suspicion of the charge of antifeminist writing about to be levelled against him by the God of Love (cf. F 308). Before Chaucer can speak a word in his own defence, the mysterious lady 'clothed al in grene' takes it upon herself to assuage the divine wrath and beg mercy for the poet. In this she imitates the female role of intercessor and peacemaker most often associated with the Virgin Mary, and one which many noble ladies of Chaucer's time thought it fitting to adopt in times of national crisis. The tone which the lady in green adopts to the God of Love is not the one of frenzied emotion so often associated with the appeals of women – we may recall the ladies in the *Knight's Tale* who 'for verray wommanhede' wept and prostrated themselves, persuading Theseus to leave his righteous anger and show pity on Palamoun and Arcite by remitting the death penalty their crime deserved (*KnT* 1742 ff.) – but one of reasoned argument. It has more in common with the advice to rulers offered by men of learning, who were wont to point out that pity (in the sense of mercy) is the virtue which marks out a true king from a tyrant and is conduct which it is often more expedient to pursue than strict justice.

This long speech in the *Legend*, perhaps too long, attracted much attention from the critics of the past. It is not that the humour of addressing a *de regimine principum* to the God of Love was not perceived, but rather that the dramatic appropriateness of large stretches of the speech was not readily apparent. This was what fuelled the critics' speculation that Chaucer was covertly advising Richard II that his behaviour was growing perilously close to tyranny. Certainly

---

[32] Ibid, pp. 14–15.

Queen Alceste's advice addresses aspects of concern in the political life of England towards the end of the fourteenth century, and it has been easy to find parallels of a general nature between Alceste's speech and some speeches which were actually addressed to Richard, as they were recorded by contemporary historians. And, more than that of most Englishmen of the time, Chaucer's career had afforded him ample opportunity to contemplate the terrifying realities of life under the 'tyraunts of Lumbardye' (F 374/G 354).[33] Nevertheless, the details of Chaucer's text are commonplace, perhaps carefully commonplace. Alceste's admonition may be particularly relevant to Richard II but it is also relevant to the fictional God of Love, already conceived of as a tyrant in the *Parliament of Fowls*. We may be virtually certain, however, that Chaucer did not consider the long speech irrelevant, since he appears to have lavished some care on its revision; the G version, moreover, is even longer than that in F.

It is difficult to be sure, then, whether the F Prologue's God of Love and Alceste would have been seen as having reference to Richard and Anne. It seems likely to me that speculation about Richard would never have arisen if we only had the G Prologue, although the *de regimine* speech would have remained puzzling. One suspects it is only the clear reference to the queen in the F Prologue that led critics to see allusions to Richard in the remarks about tyranny and the description of his sun-crown. (Richard had adopted the sunburst as one of his badges, and it is depicted on the robe of the effigy on his tomb in Westminster Abbey, along with white harts.[34] The substitution in G of the much blander crown of roses and lilies for the distinctive and dramatically appropriate sun-crown of F may indicate the deliberate removal of an identifying symbol.) On the other hand, although Chaucer retained the *de regimine*

---

[33] See D. Wallace, 'Writing the Tyrant's Death: Chaucer, Bernabò Visconti and Richard II', in P. Boitani and Anna Torti, eds., *Poetics: Theory and Practice in Medieval English Literature* (Perugia: J. A. W. Bennett Memorial Lectures, Seventh Series, 1990), pp. 117–30.

[34] There is a photograph of the effigies of Richard and his queen (ordinarily difficult to see because of the height of the tomb) labelled [21] in Loomis, *Chaucer's World*. The effigy is stamped all over with an intricate pattern which clearly represents embroidery. A line drawing of the pattern showing the white hart alternating with the sunburst within a trellis design may be found in Mary G. Houston, *Medieval Costume in England and France* (London: Black, 1965), p. 115.

speech in G and even expanded it, thus giving it a significance which is not tied to a specific historical situation, he may never have developed the scene in the way he did if he had not originally had the king in mind.

It is important to summarise the putative relationship of the God of Love to Richard II before we move further. First, it cannot be assumed in the state of current scholarship that there is a definite reference to Richard in Prologue F of the *Legend of Good Women*. It cannot be assumed either that there is no such allusion. The question, so intriguing to scholars at the turn of the century, could profitably be reopened, particularly by those with competence in the disciplines of history or iconography and heraldry. In my own reading, I see no compelling reason why the connection with Richard is impossible, in the ludic context of Prologue F. But, if Chaucer seeded Prologue F with hints that would have enabled Richard to see himself figuring as lord of youthful love, defender of women and poetic arbiter, then the poet proceeded with remarkable caution and, in case the king should have objected to the portrayal of the God of Love as a tyrant, provided himself with plenty of escape routes involving fictional characters making fictional speeches. If the God of Love's sun-crown is to be identified with the heraldic sunburst, and this in itself is a big 'if', then it can be stated securely that Richard did adopt the sunburst as his badge, but that it was not exclusively connected with him, as the white hart was. My observations about Richard's appearance and behaviour lend support to the identification, but are hardly conclusive without other much stronger evidence; moreover, a medieval writer was not likely to suggest that his lord was anything other than fair and virtuous, whatever he was like in reality. The intellectual position the God of Love adopts, that the import of literature should be unambiguously straightforward (if one wishes to discuss virtue in love then one should choose to write about a virtuous lover) may be simpleminded, but was similar to that adopted by Christine de Pizan and the other critics of the *Roman de la Rose*, and could be well defended. (The God of Love's humorous recommendation that Chaucer find examples of good women in the works of writers known for their antifeminism occurs only in the G Prologue, and is of a piece with other characteristics of that version which exhibit a much stronger sense of detachment from the courtly service of love, such as the move away from the dreamer's kneeling posture and the absence of elaborate references to the religion of love.) Moreover, the fairly pointed condemnation of tyranny addressed to Love was nevertheless commonplace ethical material that all men were expected to take to heart. If Chaucer had any intention of alluding to Richard II, I think the motif must have worked something like this: the narrator recognises the personage in his dream immediately as the God of Love, wearing a sun instead of a normal crown and with a supernaturally shining face and angel-like wings. Perhaps coincidentally, the narrator's dreaming consciousness envisages Love with the personal appearance, clothing and demeanour which Richard II might have adopted if he had chosen to preside over a 'court of love' as God or Prince of Love, inspiring not only a vernacular *de regimine* in miniature but also the imaginative poetic act which results in the myth of the daisy's origin, and leading his courtiers in a debate on the virtue of women, and aspects of poetic meaning and decorum.

As I move now to a detailed discussion of the accusation against Chaucer and his defence, I will be concentrating on the way the motif is worked out in the G Prologue, the version whose courtly connections are minimal and where the God of Love operates simply as a spokesman for a particular literary position, initiating and articulating the essential theme of the *Legend of Good Women*. As most readers consider the two Prologues in tandem, however, it has seemed important to analyse the role that Richard possibly played in the original conception of Chaucer's God of Love.

5

The accusation

One of the great puzzles of the *Legend of Good Women* concerns why Chaucer should have embedded a major poetic manifesto in a speech embodying the characteristic concepts and terms of serious medieval political writing. For the purposes of my exposition it is expedient to abstract the discussion of the material of princely advice from that of the matter of poetry, but we should not ignore Chaucer's insistent implication of the one with the other.

Alceste's appeal for mercy to be shown to the poet wavers between viewing Love as a god and as a king, but the emphasis is heavily with the latter. The long speech reveals a close familiarity with the major types of writing favoured in late medieval England in the mode of a *de regimine principum*, that genre in which a man of learning presented his king with traditional advice on how to rule himself and his kingdom wisely. Treatises of this type abounded from antiquity, with a resurgence of new such works in the twelfth and thirteenth centuries after the rediscovery of Aristotle. Many medieval kings owned their own copy of the *Secretum Secretorum* or some other *de regimine*, or had their own vernacular translation made. These kinds of works were also enjoyed by other men and not only rulers, for it was believed that all men should know how to rule their own passions; moreover, as Giles of Rome said in his *De Regimine Principum*, even ordinary men needed to know how to exercise lordship over their children, wives and households. These serious works of political philosophy may seem unduly abstract to the modern eye and display little evidence of realistic political analysis,[1] but they are

---

[1] Margaret Schlauch, 'Chaucer's Doctrine of Kings and Tyrants', *Speculum* 20 (1945): 133–56, esp. pp. 140–1. In my next chapter I will give the bibliographic references for works mentioned in these introductory paragraphs.

invariably introduced by prefaces that tie them to actual historical situations, and ones whose emotional import moved medieval readers, as when Seneca admonishes Nero or Aristotle advises Alexander the Great. A work contemporary with the *Legend of Good Women*, Gower's *Confessio Amantis*, which contains a *de regimine* in Book VII, is pointedly directed to Richard II and, in a later version, to Henry of Derby.

It is interesting that Lydgate's *Secretum Secretorum* and Hoccleve's *Regement of Princes* both borrow phrases from Alceste's speech in their own translations, suggesting that these later poets looked to the speech in the *Legend* as a genuine piece of *de regimine* writing. Gower, like Chaucer in the *Legend* and Machaut in *Voir Dit*, inserts his *de regimine principum* into a work which purports to be about love, Hoccleve's *Regement* and Yonge's *Governaunce of Prynces* insert a great deal of material about love into works which are unashamedly devoted to advising their princes, so that one suspects that the collocation of love and politics had an ethical congruence for the medieval audience not immediately obvious to modern readers. The audience Chaucer envisaged included career servants of the king,[2] who in their hours of gentlemanly entertainment in pursuit of the cultivated life understood what it was to be also servants of the God of Love.

All protestations to the contrary, the *de regimine* form was a polite but not particularly humble genre, and drew attention above all to the learned man's status as custodian of the wisdom of the past. As a literary type whose natural home is in the language of learning, it claimed a new prestige for any vernacular language deemed a worthy vehicle of translation. Leaving on one side for a time the possible references to Richard II, as the G Prologue's lack of reference to the queen and evocation of a specific social occasion gives us licence to do, we may see the mode of Alceste's speech as in some sense as important a marker of the vernacular translator's claim for social relevance as is the detailed discussion of poetic procedure and responsibility. In the arguments brought to bear on the discussion of Chaucer's position in the Kingdom of Love the poet persistently aligns himself with learning and reason in contrast to Love's passionate and limited vision. In the poem's fiction

---

[2] See P. Strohm, *Social Chaucer* (Cambridge, Mass.: Harvard University Press, 1989), pp. 25–46.

the poet occupies the role of the lowliest of outsiders – 'a worm' (F 318/ G 244); nevertheless, in this scene, with its slightly uneasy claim to the wisdom which marks a serious 'poet', Chaucer makes gesture after gesture in the direction of inscribing his vernacular 'makyng' with the marks of *auctoritas*.

THE CHARGE AGAINST THE POET

From the beginning of the God of Love's attack on the poet this alignment with the concerns of learned writing in the vernacular and its relevance to courtly society is evident. Love condemns the poet for his presumption in entering his presence in the first place (G 241–4/ F 315–18). The crime is apparently as much a literary as a social one: it is Chaucer's translations which have encouraged rebellion in those who should have worshipped Love faithfully. The central significance of this speech by the God of Love to the conception of the *Legend* is always admitted but the specifics of the charge are puzzling:

> For in pleyn text, it nedeth nat to glose,
> Thow hast translated the Romauns of the Rose,
> That is an heresye ageyns my lawe,
> And makest wise folk from me withdrawe . . .
> Hast thow nat mad in Englysh ek the bok
> How that Crisseyde Troylus forsok,
> In shewynge how that wemen han don mis?
> G 255–66/F 328–33

The citing of Chaucer's translation of the *Roman de la Rose* as a heresy against courtly law immediately attracts attention. The only part of the Middle English *Romaunt* thought to be by Chaucer gives little justification for the God's remarks. It is less difficult to see how *Troilus and Criseyde* could be put forward as an excuse for a 'recantation' in praise of faithful women, although here again Love's comments are often felt to be misguided. It is frequently too easily assumed that women in the audience really had complained about the choice of Criseyde as heroine of a poem.[3]

---

[3] E.g., in the introduction to the *Legend of Good Women* in Robinson's *Works of Chaucer*, 2nd edn, pp. 482–3, and note to F 329, p. 844. This is a topic I take up in my chapter, 'Palinode'.

Leaving aside such modern assumptions about this passage, several observations may be made. First, Chaucer owns to having translated the *Roman de la Rose*, but whether wholly or in part we do not know. Like other fourteenth-century readers and writers, however, he thinks of the *Roman* as a completed work in the form given it by Jean de Meun.[4] Specifically, from the point of view of the God of Love, the *Roman* is seen as 'heresy'; its prime aim is to hinder the 'devotion' of people who wish to serve Love, by teaching them the folly of trusting him if they have any pretensions to wisdom (F 324–7/G 251–4). Since the God of Love is a character in the *Roman*, we may conclude he is complaining that his glamorous portrayal there was ironically overstated praise and enthusiastic endorsement designed to blame. By translating the *Roman*, the god says, Chaucer, like other impotent old men, shows himself to be the 'mortal foe' of Love and all his servants (G 248–53, 258–63; F 322–7 lacks the reference to 'olde foles') – it is, of course, the God of Love's traditionally biased opinion that those not in the grip of passionate love are not so much wise as old and worn-out, and tells us nothing about Chaucer's actual age or sexual status. Reference to the old age of the poet's persona is thus an important marker which Chaucer has added to the G Prologue at several points (in place of other motifs in F which I discuss later), and indicates to a wider readership than a narrowly courtly one the (jocular) dimensions of the referential field within which the *Legend* is to be interpreted. As part of this same traditional schema, the patronage of the God of Love extends as much towards women as towards the passions of youth, as twin temptations for mature masculine rationality. Love's patronage of women is one crucial source of his ambiguous role in the *Legend*: he is patron both of the untrustworthy Criseyde and the good and faithful Alceste. (In an even more unlikely fashion, he later also claims patronage of widows and virgins.) To tell the story of the faithless Criseyde, as Chaucer has done, is again to warn men not to put their trust in women (G 265–6/ F 333), and thus can be considered a sin against the God of Love.

The line 'For in pleyn text, it nedeth nat to glose' (G 254/F 328) closely translates a line from the passage in the *Roman de la Rose* where

---

[4] See P-Y. Badel, *Le Roman de la Rose au XIVᵉ Siècle: Etude de la Réception de l'Œuvre* (Geneva: Droz, 1980), p. 62.

the Lover, as a clean-speaking servant of Amors, disapproves of Reason's uncourtly use of the 'proper' terms for the genitals (see *RR* 6928–78). The Lover objects to the use of explicit names for these and demands they be 'glossed' with euphemisms suited to the lips of noble ladies, in obedience to Amors' requirement that his servants avoid ribaldry. In connecting Chaucer's translation of the *Roman* with accurate naming, the *Legend*'s God of Love appears to suspect that the refusal to 'gloss' threatens to demystify the ethos of the courtly service of love, revealing, for example, the naked cupidity which underlies the pursuit of the Rose and encouraging wise men to avoid such love. This important section of the *Roman* dealing both with sexuality and signification is one that attracted a great deal of notice both in Chaucer's time and at present;[5] we need not concern ourselves with its ramifications – sufficient to say that the God of Love quotes the line in order to associate Chaucer with the voice of Reason rather than with that of a committed servant of Love. In similar fashion official ecclesiastical culture was suspicious of the consequences of wider accessibility and the liability to heterodox opinion encouraged by a vernacular 'pleyn text' of the Scriptures, when liberated from the interpretative constraints of orthodox glosses.[6] The phrase 'naked text' (a synonym for 'pleyn' or 'bare' text) is also used in the G Prologue's revised version of Chaucer's stated purpose for the *Legend of Good Women*. In G 81–8 the poet/narrator, in his own voice, tells us his 'entent' is to declare 'the naked text in English . . . of many a story', hinting strongly that his audience may not want to believe what 'autours seyn', presumably about the goodness of women, where 'ther lyth non other assay by preve'. The humorously provocative tone of this passage implies that Chaucer will be making available the ancient stories of women to anybody who understands English, to interpret each how he wills according to his own experience, and not simply that the poet is making a translation into English, relatively unadorned in

---

[5] For some recent discussions of this passage, see J. V. Fleming, *Reason and the Lover* (Princeton University Press, 1984), pp. 97 ff.; R. H. Bloch, *Etymologies and Genealogies: a Literary Anthropology of the French Middle Ages* (University of Chicago Press, 1991), pp. 137–41.

[6] Cf. Margaret Deanesly, *The Lollard Bible and Other Medieval Biblical Versions* (Cambridge University Press, 1920), pp. 227–40. For the view that the phrase 'naked text' indicates Wycliffite influence, see Delany, *Naked Text*, pp. 41–2, 120.

style. There is an edge of heterodoxy to the cheeky statement, albeit in an amatory framework, as if Chaucer is quite willing to own, and encourage in others, the charge of heresy that the God of Love brings against him.

The reference to the *Roman* in the God of Love's accusation is probably little more than a signal of the type of discussion to be expected; the topic, that is, will concern the proper interpretation of poetic language as much as the nature of love depicted in some of Chaucer's earlier work. It is fruitful to seek a context for the accusation about the *Roman de la Rose* not in Chaucer's own translation but in that debate about the *Roman* which erupted in written form in France about the time of Chaucer's death, for there is a remarkable similarity between the debating points adduced by the protagonists of the historical debate and the accusations and counter-arguments brought forward in this scene in the *Legend*. Scholars of this well-documented controversy have suggested that the bounds of the celebrated *querelle de la Rose* were not limited to those documents that are extant: it is known that the affair was widely discussed and perhaps even arose from a conversation, and there are other letters and treatises which are referred to by the disputants but are now lost. There are also in existence sermons and poems (like Christine de Pizan's *Epistre au Dieu d'Amours* of 1399 and Hoccleve's *Letter of Cupid* of 1402) which have a somewhat more than tenuous connection with the debate, but are not always considered part of the *querelle* as such.[7] Moreover, the debate has strong affiliations with other literary debates conducted by the French humanists who defended the *Roman*, whereby they sharpened their rhetorical and argumentative skills and perfected their Latin style, concerns germane to their professional lives.[8] There can be little doubt that the arguments adduced on both sides of this debate would have been easily understood by Chaucer and his audience, and it may well be that the kind of

---

[7] An account of the current opinion on the documents convenient for the English reader will be found in Baird and Kane, *Querelle de la Rose*, pp. 14–15. See also Badel, *Roman*, pp. 411–89; K. Brownlee, 'Discourses of the Self: Christine de Pisan and the Rose', *Romanic Review* 78 (1988): 213–21; Fenster and Erler, *Poems of Cupid*, pp. 3–7.

[8] G. C. Furr's contention, 'The Quarrel of the "Roman de la Rose" and Fourteenth-Century Humanism', Dissertation, Princeton, 1979; cf. Badel, *Roman*, pp. 462–82.

conflict postulated by Chaucer in this scene dramatised the way the *Roman* was actually discussed in circles known to the poet.[9]

The participants in the historical debate, intelligent and educated, both lay and cleric, used their understanding of the literary analysis of classical and Biblical texts to discuss the work of a modern and vernacular 'author'; they considered how Jean de Meun dealt with his chosen subject matter to achieve his (debatably) moral purpose, a moral purpose which Chaucer's God of Love objects to and characterises as heresy. It is clear from the *Legend* and from the *querelle de la Rose* that the *Roman de la Rose* stimulated debate on two traditional topics: the ongoing questions about the moral value of poetic discourse and about the virtue of women. These are both aspects of the poem that Jean de Meun evidently expects to be provocative, for he himself draws attention to them in *RR* 15135–302 – the first when he apologises for his use of words which are 'bawdy' or 'silly' in the interest of chronicling the truth, for words are 'cousins of the deeds'; the second when he excuses himself for seeming to satirise women, for he is only following old authorities and they had written from experience.

It is not easy to analyse the nature of the *querelle*, insofar as both sides appear to be at cross purposes, and neither side really answers the other's points in spite of all the clever argumentation. Both attackers and defenders share the assumptions that literature ought to have a moral purpose and, moreover, that misogyny and pornography are bad things.[10] The opponents of the *Roman*, apparently, and paradoxically,[11] of the same opinion as Chaucer's God of Love (cf. G 270), write as if the choice of subject matter is in itself enough to reveal the poet's real intention. Thus Jean Gerson, one of those who were critical of the French poem, condemns Jean de Meun because he writes in the *Roman* 'like a Foolish Lover' (Gerson means that Jean appears to be recommending 'foolish love'). The defenders thought this was the point, but

---

[9]   See Ruth M. Ames, 'The Feminist Connections of Chaucer's *Legend of Good Women*', in Wasserman and Blanch, eds., *Chaucer in the Eighties*, pp. 57–74.

[10]   See Helen Fletcher Moody, 'The Debate of the Rose: the "Querelle des Femmes" as Court Poetry', Dissertation, University of California, Berkeley, 1981, p. 193.

[11]   I say 'paradoxically' because the opponents of the *Roman*, like Christine de Pizan, disapproved of what they saw as Jean de Meun's endorsement of love as naked sensuality, whereas Chaucer's God of Love disapproved of what he considered as Jean's satirising of such a view.

the 'Foolish Lover' was the butt of Jean's satire; to identify the author's opinions with those expressed by various of his characters was naive in the extreme. We could posit an analogous question about Chaucer's poem: because Chaucer chose to write about a 'fals lovere', Criseyde, did this automatically mean that his powerful poetic rendering of Troilus and Criseyde's love affair was to be read as endorsement of the heroine's infidelity? The defenders of the *Roman* in the historical *querelle* would have agreed that it was as likely that Criseyde's story was put forward as an 'ensaumple' of how to 'ben war fro falsnesse and fro vice' (cf. F 466–74/G 456–64). It is easy to suggest a modern analogue, because the same kind of debate erupts today every time there is an outcry against books or films of which the subject matter is known to deal with, for example, violence or sex. Defenders of such works, like the defenders of the *Roman*, are likely to argue that the ultimate effect will depend upon the treatment of the topic, and may work as well as a critique as a defence of the subject in question. Those who disapprove may well respond, like the opponents of the *Roman*, that a powerful depiction of murder or rape may encourage similar behaviour in disturbed people, and so on. A study of the historical *querelle de la Rose* suggests that medieval audiences were able to debate such points with subtlety and sophistication.[12] Although there is humour in the God of Love's condemnation of the poet, I do not think it automatically makes Chaucer's God of Love a figure of fun and his position is likely to be one that Chaucer and other medieval writers were forced to consider squarely.

The coupling of *Criseyde* with the *Rose* is also not only or primarily a comment on the actual nature of Chaucer's major work up till this period – beyond indicating to thoughtful members of the audience that the meaning of a work is not coextensive with its choice of subject matter. Rather it is another signal about the present work. The mention here of the archetypally unfaithful woman, Criseyde, flags Chaucer's entry into the literary game of maligning or defending women, which entertained men of learning for centuries. In the classical era men warned against women and marriage because they were distractions

---

[12] Cf. A. J. Minnis, 'Theorizing the Rose: Commentary Tradition in the *Querelle de la Rose*', in Boitani and Torti, *Poetics: Theory and Practice*, pp. 13–36, 22.

from a life of scholarly study. In patristic times men were warned against women as a threat to male chastity and Christian devotion. Their medieval heirs saw women and marriage as a hindrance to ecclesiastical advancement. No matter the ultimate purpose, the amount of enjoyment derived from the inherited stock of exempla against women and the simple mocking of their foibles remained constant, newly embraced with evident delight by each succeeding generation. The store of antifeminist fable frequently provided subject matter in the study of which young men learned their Latin,[13] so that any man of some education was likely to be well acquainted with it. The G Prologue makes this aspect of the context of the *Legend of Good Women* abundantly clear. Its God of Love formulates his accusation against Chaucer specifically in terms which equate Criseyde's forsaking of Troilus with the evil inherent in women:

> Hast thow nat mad in Englysh ek the bok
> How that Crisseyde Troylus forsok,
> In shewynge how that wemen han don mis?
> G 264–6

Later, in almost his concluding words, the God of Love of the G Prologue locates his charge against the harassed poet in the old metaphysical matrix within which the essence of being woman was identified with the changeability of matter, with 'doublenesse' and 'unstedfastnesse', as an intrinsic characteristic of her nature:

> Thanne seyde Love, 'A ful gret neglygence
> Was it to the, to write unstedefastnesse
> Of women . . .
> Why noldest thow han writen of Alceste,
> And laten Criseide ben aslepe and reste?'
> G 525–31[14]

The God of Love of the G Prologue concludes his accusation against Chaucer by repeating his slur that, in choosing such antifeminist topics

---

[13] Blamires, *Woman Defamed*, pp. 17, 99, 280. Christine frequently points to the role of learned clerks in the dissemination of slander against women, particularly in the education of schoolboys, *Dieu d'Amours* 259 ff.

[14] In F, Chaucer is only accused of the specific 'necligence' of forgetting to put Alceste in his balade *Hyd Absolon* (F 537–40).

as the Rose and Criseyde, Chaucer's jaundiced view shows clearly enough that he has grown too old to present a sympathetic treatment of passionate love: he is an old fool whose 'spirit' fails and whose wit grows cold, the conventional criticism aimed at old clerics who blame youthful lovers (G 258–63), as I have said a traditional and widely recognised biased stance. This idea was so commonly presented as the reason why men choose to slander women and love that further supporting evidence is hardly necessary. The Wife of Bath's remarks on the subject are well known:

> The clerk, whan he is oold, and may noght do
> Of Venus werkes worth his olde sho,
> Thanne sit he doun, and writ in his dotage
> That wommen kan nat kepe hir mariage!
> *WBPr* 707–10

The Wife's other objections to the biased attitude of 'clerks' are also familiar: it is impossible for clerks to speak well of women, but if women wrote the stories there would be as many about bad men (*WBPr* 688–96). Similar ideas appear in the debate surrounding the *Roman*. In 1399 Christine de Pizan put the same reasons for literary bias in the mouth of her own God of Love in *Epistre au Dieu d'Amours* 409–10, 417–18: *les livres ne firent pas les femmes*. Christine's deity also suggests that those who defame women had formerly been caught in his snares, but were now too old, tired or impotent to love. He sees himself and women as equally the victims of such slander: his former wicked and rebellious servants *blasment moy et mon fait, et les femmes diffament* (*Epistre* 493–503). Outrageous bias, usually but not invariably gender-linked, was an accepted part of this literary game, as Christine's God of Love says: 'For well do women know . . . the strongest take the largest cut' (see *Epistre* 419–22, trans. Fenster).

It seems likely that the formulation of the God of Love's accusation against Chaucer in the G Prologue evokes a topos becoming popular towards the end of the century, a systematic literary Defence of Women, to which several major works including the *Legend* and the writings of Christine in the early fifteenth century bear witness. The novelty value of this group was acknowledged and enjoyed within the frame of the patriarchal norm of orthodox literary culture. About 1360

Boccaccio's *De Claris Mulieribus* (*Concerning Famous Women*)[15] had appeared – a scholarly and encyclopedic compilation of biographies of women, showing a slightly more favourable attitude to women than was common in Boccaccio's scholarly work in Latin, and trading on its readers' knowledge of other versions. It was strongly exemplary and didactic, but witty, often parodying accepted ways of lauding women such as the saint's life. Another important analogue is the work of a minor fourteenth-century French writer named Jean Le Fèvre, the translator of a famous Latin antifeminist work which had been originally written about the same period as the *Roman de la Rose*, the *Liber Lamentationum Matheoluli*. Besides translating 'Matheolus', Le Fèvre also composed a companion palinode in defence of women, the book of *Leesce*.[16] Neither Chaucer nor Christine mentions Le Fèvre, but it has been plausibly suggested that Chaucer knew his work,[17] and many of Christine's most compelling arguments in favour of women, particularly those that appear to derive from ordinary observation, seem indubitably to derive from Le Fèvre's *Leesce*. Le Fèvre wrote in the early 1370s, and his two works are to be found in manuscripts of English provenance that date from before the fifteenth century. Le Fèvre is probably to be credited with a crucial formulation of the debate about women, especially the defence, as there was no lack of traditional material on the condemnation of women. Particularly important on both sides of this palinode are the analysis of misogynist logic and its biases, the anti-masculine charges, and the discussion of the flaws in the exemplary technique as a mode of proof. I am not suggesting Le Fèvre's writing as a source for the *Legend*, although even if we possessed only the F Prologue it should be considered at least as significant an analogue as Boccaccio's *De Claris*. But it may well have been as important a

---

[15] G. A. Guarino, trans., *Concerning Famous Women, by Giovanni Boccaccio* (New Brunswick: Rutgers University Press, 1963). For a good account of *De Claris* in relation to the *Legend* see Ann McMillan, trans., *The Legend of Good Women by Geoffrey Chaucer* (Houston: Rice University Press, 1987), pp. 21–5. Cf. also Carol M. Meale, 'Legends of Good Women in the European Middle Ages', *Archiv* 144 (1992): 55–70.

[16] See A. G. Van Hamel, ed., *Les Lamentations de Matheolus et Le Livre de Leesce de Jehan Le Fèvre de Ressons* (Paris: Bouillon, 1892). See also Helen Phillips, 'Chaucer and Jean Le Fèvre, *Archiv* 232 (1995): 23–36.

[17] See Z. P. Thundy, 'Matheolus, Chaucer, and the Wife of Bath', in E. Vasta and Z. P. Thundy, eds., *Chaucerian Problems and Perspectives* (University of Notre Dame Press, 1979), pp. 24–58.

contribution to the reformulation of the G Prologue, probably in the 1390s, as it was to the Tales of the Wife and the Merchant in the *Canterbury Tales*. I am suggesting the possibility that Chaucer, by introducing references to traditional antifeminism, remodelled the G Prologue's frame for the Legends in accordance with the more codified debate about women which became influential towards the end of the century in French and English. In the F Prologue, by contrast, the mixture of sympathy for and jokes about women is much more informal and rooted in popular courtly game-playing.

At the beginning of 1401, Christine de Pizan bundled up most of the documents in the *querelle de la Rose* which had appeared up to that time and sent them off to the queen of France, presumably for arbitration, and also to Guillaume de Tignonville, provost of Paris. The letter she wrote to accompany de Tignonville's dossier refers to this 'good-humored debate stimulated by a difference of opinion among worthy persons'.[18] While the amount of good humour is debatable, the *querelle* was to some extent an exercise in rhetoric for the participants. No one can doubt how carefully each letter has been penned, the loving attention devoted to style (to aspects of which the authors are always drawing their correspondents' notice), the witty arguments, the ubiquitous classical quotations. There was an awareness of how many other eyes would observe these less than private documents. The politeness degenerates somewhat towards the end when Jean de Montreuil, one of the defenders of the *Rose*, writes about Christine's 'feminine limitations' and suggests that his other opponent Gerson disapproves of the *Rose* because of his religious vocation and because 'perhaps he is simply the kind of man who is rendered useless for the propagation of the species, which is, after all, the purpose of this book'.[19] It would be readily understood that the fictional Alceste, like the historical Christine, was a natural defender of women, by virtue of her gender, while the male writers Chaucer or Gerson, presented as old, clerkly and impotent, were their natural opponents.

Christine, however, benefited professionally a great deal from the *querelle*, as she no doubt intended. She had not been invited to the *cour*

18 Hicks, *Débat sur le Roman*, p. 7; Baird and Kane, *Querelle de la Rose*, p. 67.
19 Hicks, *Débat sur le Roman*, pp. 42, 44; Baird and Kane, *Querelle de la Rose*, pp. 153, 154.

amoureuse of Charles VI, a major literary event, where men of letters wrote poems in honour of ladies but were not particularly interested in the views of actual women.[20] Christine's *Epistre au Dieu d'Amours*, a poem exactly contemporaneous with the founding of the *cour* and dealing with the same issues which it debated, is sometimes thought to be the first shot fired in the *querelle de la Rose*. Her distribution of the documents in the *querelle* coincided with the publication of a major manuscript of her poetry.[21] After the *querelle*, Christine's career burgeoned. Her self-dramatisation as the champion of women not only provided her with an entrée into the male world of professional letters, as a participant in a debate whose outlines had long been determined, but remained one of the staples of her prodigious output. Incidentally, Jean de Montreuil and Pierre and Gautier Col, those intrepid defenders of the antifeminist *Roman*, were all enrolled as members of the *cour amoureuse*, formed ostensibly to *praise* women, as were the antifeminist participants of *Les Cent Ballades*.[22] In short, the debate about women and the debate about the *Roman* were largely excuses to display scholarly competence and wit, and thus Chaucer, in presenting himself as one who knows how to handle the matter of women, is claiming a certain scholarly cachet which coincides happily with his other role as advisor to princes.

It must be stressed, therefore, that in the G Prologue the God of Love sees Chaucer's narrative persona as reproducing the point of view not just of old men but of old *clerks*[23] – Matheolus was a 'clerk' and his sorrows resulted from his marrying and forgoing the delights of learning, as I have said, a well-marked literary topos which is important in the misogynous or misogamous writing of such as Jerome, Abelard, Walter Map, John of Salisbury. The God of Love now directs Chaucer to just such writers as sources of stories about good women:

---

[20] See Moody, 'Debate of the Rose', p. 191.

[21] Ibid., p. 190. For Christine's role in converting a private literary interchange into a public event, cf. Badel, *Roman*, pp. 435–7; for her transformation of the dossier on the *Rose* into a '"book" of which she is the author', see Brownlee, 'Discourses of the Self', p. 213.

[22] See A. Piaget, 'La Cour Amoureuse, dite de Charles VI', *Romania* 20 (1891): 417–54, esp. pp. 429, 430, 443.

[23] Cf. Badel, *Roman*, pp. 477–8.

Why noldest thow as wel han seyd goodnesse
Of wemen, as thow hast seyd wikednesse?
Was there no good matere in thy mynde,
Ne in alle thy bokes ne coudest thow nat fynde
Som story of wemen that were goode and trewe?
Yis, God wot, sixty bokes olde and newe
Hast thow thyself, alle ful of storyes grete,
That bothe Romayns and ek Grekes trete
Of sundry wemen, which lyf that they ladde,
And evere an hundred goode ageyn oon badde.
This knoweth God, and alle clerkes eke,
That usen swiche materes for to seke.
G 268–79

Love is here repeating his error that it is the simple choice of 'matere' that determines the writer's 'entente' and therefore advises Chaucer to search his mind and his books for 'good matere' (G 270), that is, for stories about 'good women' in contrast to stories about bad women like Criseyde. The validity of such an assumption bears very little scrutiny; that the assumption was current in Chaucer's time is evidenced by the *querelle de la Rose*. Ironically enough, of course, the great weight of medieval books speak against bad women rather than praise good women, for this is what 'all clerks know'. Love advances his argument with a series of questions which, in spite of the hagiographic style, are as ambivalent in effect as the possible answers:

What seith Valerye, Titus, or Claudyan?
What seith Jerome agayns Jovynyan?
How clene maydenes, and how trewe wyves,
How stedefaste widewes durynge alle here lyves,
Telleth Jerome, and that nat of a fewe,
But, I dar seyn, an hundred on a rewe;
That it is pite for to rede, and routhe,
The wo that they endure for here trouthe.
G 280–7

It is impossible for a critic of any persuasion to avoid the fact that the God of Love here recommends as the best literary sources for stories of good women the two most famous antifeminist works of the Middle Ages, Walter Map's *Epistola Valerii ad Ruffinum ne uxorem ducat* ('Valerye') and Jerome's *Adversus Jovinianum*. Chaucer's editor F. N.

Robinson who, like most older critics, denied any humour in the *Legend*, solved the problem caused by the citing of these indubitably antifeminist writings by pointing out that Jerome also mentioned many good women in *Against Jovinian*, and indeed he did so – 'and that nat of a fewe', as Chaucer here remarks. And Map commended Penelope and Lucretia, although he regrets that there were no longer any such to be found on earth. But although it is true that Jerome and Map tell stories of good women, their names only invoke what was perceived as these writers' true 'entente', the condemnation of women in general. The God of Love continues by recalling the terrible sufferings – burning, beheading, drowning – which Jerome's heroines underwent in order to be true to their love and to preserve their virtue. Indeed, the heroism of women of the past is something which men could hardly attain to (G 302–4). But these are not Christian martyrs, as the speaker says disparagingly, for 'yit they were hethene, al the pak', and Love's praise of good women is in the end ambivalent:

> For alle keped they here maydenhede,
> Or elles wedlok, or here widewehede.
> And this thing was nat kept for holynesse,
> But al for verray vertu and clennesse,
> And for men schulde sette on hem no lak;
> And yit they were hethene, al the pak,
> That were so sore adrad of alle shame.
> G 294–300

While it was traditional to admonish women to emulate the chastity of famous heroines of antiquity, who did not even have the benefit of 'holynesse' – in itself this is an odd virtue for the God of Love to admire – yet, because their motivation was that 'men schulde sette on hem no lak' (G 301), these heroines can also be criticised for loving their own reputations too much, at least in a society who had learned from Augustine that this was the failing of the virtuous but unchristian Lucretia (cf. G 296–9 with *Lucrece* 1812–14). Then again, if we ignore the humour inherent in the fact that it is the God of Love speaking, his words could be seen as an encomium of what the Middle Ages did genuinely value in a good woman, as exemplified in the quotation from *The Book of the Knight of La Tour-Landry* CXIX which I cited earlier because it uses the figure of the *margarita* to stand for traditional feminine virtue:

> [Oure Lorde] spake vpon the mater of women that liueden in clennesse, he likened suche a woman vnto a precious margarite, the whiche is . . . a stone so clere and faire that there is no tache therein, nor spotte of vnclennes; and this is saide be a woman that is not wedded, and she lyuithe in uirginite, clennesse, and chastite; or ellys bi a woman that is wedded, and she kepithe truly and honestly the sacrement of mariage, & also by them that worshipfully and perfitly kepe thaire wedwhode, that lyuen in chastite and in sobriete. These be the .iij. manere of women the whiche God praisithe, and likenith hem vnto the precious margarite, that is all faire, withoute ani foule tache or ani foulenesse.

This account of the 'verray vertu and clennesse' appropriate to the three orders of women, virgins, wives and widows, corresponds almost word for word with that of Chaucer's God of Love, and the Knight of the Tower in the same place also warns his daughters of the supreme importance of not 'losing their name' (cf. G 301). Yet, lest we should miss the possible ironies in his words, Chaucer gives Love some more questions:

> What seyth also the epistel of Ovyde
> Of trewe wyves and of here labour?
> What Vincent in his Estoryal Myrour?
> G 305–7

While it was possible to sympathise with Ovid's heroines, the medieval glosses to the texts of 'the epistel of Ovyde' almost invariably informed readers that the heroines' behaviour resulted from foolish delusion. Vincent de Beauvais's encyclopedic *Speculum Historiale*, his *Estoryal Myrour* which was almost certainly Chaucer's source for *Cleopatra*, contained a compilation of the most abusive phrases against women from Jerome's *Against Jovinian* in a highly concentrated form, but was also a source for details of the story of the Virgin Mary. The questions above all instigate debate; rather than offering certainty, Love's speech in the G Prologue underlines the fact that the praise of women can hardly be contemplated without the counterpoint of the primordial discourse of misogyny, which in a sense spawns the form which the

tenets of medieval feminism take. Love ends with a threat: 'Thow shalt
repente it, so that it shal be sene!' (G 313–16). It is in the end a comic
speech. The God of Love's twin roles as defender of women and patron
of courtly poetry are in conflict.

As defender of women Love announces that the 'corn' of stories will
always be the praise of women, while the 'draf' may in consequence
become that aspect of a writer's work which might otherwise have been
thought to express his true intention of condemning women (cf. G
311–12). The patron of poetry seems lamentably ignorant of those
virtues and procedures of poetic discourse which many readers of the
time held dear. Unlike the defenders of the *Roman de la Rose* he believes
that the 'entente' of poetry can be identified with its 'matere', and, harsh
lord that he is, rigorously stipulates what 'matere' Chaucer should be
using. This will inevitably involve Chaucer in writing a palinode, the
genre which above all demands poetic virtuosity in transforming into
its opposite the sense of any given 'matere'. For such an enterprise there
existed ancient precedent, particularly if the subject concerned was the
faithfulness of Woman.

The God of Love, then, has condemned the poet's earlier work
because it was not written from the standpoint of a committed servant
of love, but rather from that of a clerk, a man of education. When the
Daisy Queen comes immediately to his defence, her long speech to
Love is located just as securely in the learned tradition, as if she were a
trusted advisor to the king, a role appropriate to a writer with pretensions to scholarship (with access, that is, to the Latin language within
which such traditions of advice were normally housed). In the next
chapters we will deal with this speech which in many places seems to
have more political than poetic ramifications.

6

The defence: tyrants of Lombardy

Wallace has recently characterised Alceste's plea for mercy on the poet's behalf as 'the first sustained attempt in English to represent the delicate art of addressing a lord who is imagined to embody (or imagines himself as embodying) absolute power'.[1] Although made up of medieval political commonplace, the speech gives evidence of Chaucer's broad familiarity with the different strands of the tradition of the *de regimine principum*.[2] There are at least three significant groups of texts which influence late medieval English writing in a political vein. One of the most popular was the *Secretum Secretorum*,[3] a pseudo-Aristotelian work ultimately of Arabic origin and much enjoyed in England; this is a brief work, rather gnomic in character, which deals with matters of science and hygiene as well as political advice. Secondly, there were the medieval works that genuinely derive from Aristotle's political thinking, of which the most influential was the *De Regimine Principum* of Giles of Rome (Aegidius Romanus);[4] it was long, dry, schematic, repetitive,

---

[1] Wallace, 'Writing the Tyrant's Death', p. 157.
[2] See J-Ph. Genet's judicious remarks on the problems of classification in this enormous corpus of literature purporting to advise rulers; on the national characteristics which distinguish political writing as consumed in France and England respectively; on the scant attention paid so far to the specific historical conditions in which various texts were produced, *Four English Political Tracts*, pp. ix–xix.
[3] There are numerous late medieval English translations of the *Secretum Secretorum*. See R. Steele, ed., *Three Prose Versions of the Secreta Secretorum* (London: EETS ES 74, 1898); M. A. Manzalaoui, ed., *Secretum Secretorum: Nine English Versions* (Oxford: EETS 276, 1977); R. Steele, ed., *Lydgate and Burgh's Secrees of Old Philisoffres: a Version of the 'Secreta Secretorum'* (London: EETS ES 66, 1894).
[4] I have made use of the French translation of Giles in S. P. Molenaer, ed., *Li Livres du Gouvernement des Rois: a XIIIth Century French Version of Egidio Colonna's Treatise De Regimine Principum* (1899; rpt. New York: AMS, 1966).

short on imaginative appeal, but highly prestigious. There was, thirdly, an older tradition of literature advising rulers, such as the *Policraticus* of John of Salisbury, which called on a hoard of exemplary material drawn from classical and Biblical sources. Hoccleve confesses to using just these three types in his early fifteenth-century *Regement of Princes*[5] and, broadly speaking, Gower compiles Book VII of *Confessio Amantis* from the same strands of *de regimine* writing.[6]

Chaucer's speech is made up of similar material to that which Gower and Hoccleve drew on. Alceste quotes no source except 'the philosopher', but when she implores Love to act like a good king and not a tyrant by showing mercy, her use of phrases like 'kyng or lord naturel' or 'half-goddes' inevitably calls to mind the distinctive turn of phrase of Giles of Rome; at another time she reminds Love that his subjects are his treasure, an idea found in all of the many versions of *Secretum Secretorum*; still later she enjoins him to take note of the nobility of the lion, a story found in Seneca's *De Clementia*.[7] These phrases and images are as recognisably distinctive of the various types of *de regimine* writing as they are imprecise, and suggest that Chaucer is drawing on a mind well read in the tradition rather than on any particular source text – in this respect the composition of the *de regimine principum* speech in the *Legend* is similar to that of the marguerite poetry earlier. In my discussion of the speech I have chosen to allude to the broadly contemporaneous (within a time-period of some thirty-five years) English compilations of Gower, Hoccleve and James Yonge[8] as points of comparison. I also refer to the *De Regimine Principum* of Giles of

---

[5] F. J. Furnivall, ed., *Hoccleve's Works: III, The Regement of Princes and Fourteen of Hoccleve's Minor Poems* (London: EETS ES 72, 1897).

[6] Several of the works I have mentioned might often have been found bound together in a single manuscript, a fact which explains both the character of new compilations and the high level of contamination in works of the *de regimine* type; often material originally belonging to one strand will be found incorporated into a work of different origin. Such is the Anglo-Irish *Gouernaunce of Prynces* by James Yonge, an adaptation of a French work which is clearly a *Secretum Secretorum*, but which has had much other traditional exemplary and didactic material incorporated into it. Cf. introduction to Manzalaoui's edition, pp. xix–xx. See n.3 above.

[7] J. W. Basore, trans., *Seneca: Moral Essays* (London: Heinemann, 1932–5; rpt. 1975); *On Clemency*, in M. Hadas, trans., *The Stoic Philosophy of Seneca* (New York: Norton, 1968).

[8] Yonge's *Gouernaunce of Prynces* (c. 1422) is the third text in Steele, *Three Prose Versions*. See n.3, above.

Rome, and, from among works of the classical period, I mention Seneca's *De Clementia*.

The God of Love ends his accusation of Chaucer by threatening to revenge himself on the poet for his heresy and lèse-majesté (F 335–40/G 313–15). Taken out of context and ignoring the specifically literary crime, Alceste's speech for the defence reads quite straightforwardly as a serious example of the admonitory tradition of a *de regimine principum*. On the one hand, the speech operates consistently, to take the *Secretum Secretorum* as an example, in the spirit of pseudo-Aristotle's attempt by reasonable argument to curb the youthful ruler Alexander's instinctive desire to revenge all personal slights with the death penalty. (The young Richard II was also perceived to overvalue his personal prerogatives.) On the other hand, the God of Love, to whom the speech is ostensibly addressed, was the very personification of just such youthful volatility, passion and capriciousness and could never, by definition, benefit from such reasonable advice. The conflict of registers is apparent from Alceste's first words:

> God, ryght of your curtesye,
> Ye moten herken yf he can replye
> Agayns al this that ye have to him meved.
> A god ne sholde nat thus be agreved,
> But of hys deitee he shal be stable,
> And therto gracious and merciable.
> F 342–7/G 318–23

It is not surprising, perhaps, that Love's courtesy, very much this god's domain, is the first virtue invoked in the plea for mercy. Almost immediately, however, Alceste slips into a *de regimine* register[9] with the demand that gods be 'stable'. But, according to the mythographers, one of the God of Love's distinguishing characteristics was the instability of his passions. As I pointed out in a previous section, Boccaccio stated that Cupid 'is called "winged" to show the instability of the impassioned man'.

There is a delicate irony playing here and throughout the passage: in much *de regimine* writing the king is told that, when he tempers

---

[9] J. D. Burnley concurs with this understanding of Alceste's speech, in *Chaucer's Language and the Philosophers' Tradition* (Cambridge: Brewer, 1979), p. 32.

judgement with mercy, he is imitating God, but here it is a god who is being advised to behave like a good king and not a tyrant, in the very words normally used to advise a king to model himself upon God. Implicit in most versions of the *de regimine* tradition is the notion that if a king is just and merciful, he is like God. James Yonge, for example, is convinced that 'princes' who rule their subjects justly are 'lyke to god the Souerayne gouernoure'.[10] Even Seneca had maintained that a ruler is like the immortal gods when he is 'beneficent and generous'.[11] The orthodox Christian view of Aquinas emphasises both justice and mercy: if the king understands that his position in the kingdom is like God's in the world, he will desire to be just and to treat his subjects with gentleness and mercy like his own members.[12] The requisite conjunction of mercy and justice is made explicit in the G version of the Prologue at this point, where Alceste says that a god must be 'ryghtful, and ek merciable./ He shal nat ryghtfully his yre wreke,/ Or he have herd the tother party speke' (G 323–5). The God of Love, however, has to be taught what deity actually means: 'A god ne sholde nat thus be agreved,/ But of his deitee he shal be stable.' Indeed, Alceste expresses doubt as to whether Love has a right to be called a god at all, when she questions his omniscience and wisdom:

> And yf ye nere a god, that knowen al,
> Thanne myght yt be as I yow tellen shal. . .
> F 348–9

The problem with the speech is that gods are by nature omniscient and wise, just and merciful, and hardly require the offices of a good advisor like Alceste. A king, however, needs to be continually prodded in the direction of good governance and the avoidance of abuse of power, particularly if he is young, with the passions and inexperience of the young. As the speech progresses Alceste therefore soon drops the pretence that she is addressing Love as a god and treats him merely as a king. There is, I think, a bias in her words which leans towards the concerns which are emphasised in English exponents of this kind of

---

[10] Steele, *Three Prose Versions*, p. 207.
[11] See *On Clemency* 19; trans. Hadas, p. 159.
[12] See G. B. Phelan, trans. *On Kingship: To the King of Cyprus* (Toronto: Pontifical Institute of Mediaeval Studies, 1949; rpt. 1982), p. 54.

writing, and it has not been difficult for critics to find similarities between the points she makes (commonplaces as they are) and addresses actually made to or about Richard II.

The lady in green, like a true royal mentor, reminds Love not to be hasty in his judgement because Chaucer may be a victim of false accusation and the lies of deceitful 'losengeours' or flatterers:

> This man to yow may falsly ben accused
> That as by right him oughte ben excused.
> For in youre court ys many a losengeour,
> And many a queynte totelere accusour,
> That tabouren in your eres many a sown,
> Ryght after hire ymagynacioun,
> To have youre daliance, and for envie.
> F 350–6

Most English writings in the *de regimine* tradition, such as the versions and adaptations by Gower, Hoccleve and James Yonge, extensively denounce the evils that the presence of flatterers brings to a court. It is a quite pervasive theme in Hoccleve's *Regement* and Gower devotes some five hundred lines to the subject. They say it is necessary for a king to follow wisdom and not believe the deceitful picture of himself and the world that court flatterers tend to give. (A God, as Alceste intimated, would be wise, by definition.) That kings must be 'stable' (F 346/G 322) in order to penetrate to the truth beneath appearances is stated by Yonge also.[13] Indeed, the essential meaning of 'flattery' in these contexts is one of deceit and distortion of the truth (cf. 'ymagynacioun' [F 355], see *MED* 3 d), a course pursued by flatterers for their own advantage using 'soft' or honeyed words, as Gower says (*CA* VII 2491–7). Flattery, according to Gower, may be contrasted with the perhaps painful, but honest and learned advice of the true mentor of the ruler, the 'Philosophre' or 'Sothseier' who does not spare the truth but speaks with 'wordes pleine and bare' (*CA* VII 2349–51). Englishmen of the late fourteenth century suspected that many who had the ear of Richard II fitted the stereotype of the court flatterer.

Condemnation of flattery is thus a staple of English *de regimine* writing, and indeed Lydgate and Hoccleve quote from this Chaucerian

---

[13] Steele, *Three Prose Versions*, pp. 156–7.

passage in their serious translations of political works.[14] The linguistic echoes in Alceste's words, however, hark back to Guillaume de Lorris, Jean de Meun and Dante, and the pattern of connotation thus brought to the passage indicates the nature of the 'false accusation' which Chaucer conceives himself enduring. Many details of Alceste's description of flatterers derive from Guillaume de Lorris's account of the court of Richesse, the most disreputable of the God of Love's companions in his dance of love:

> Hir court hath many a losenger,
> And many a traytour envyous,
> That ben ful besy and curyous
> For to dispreisen and to blame
> That best deserven love and name . . .
> *Romaunt* 1050–4

The poet Chaucer, presumably, is to be thought of as one of the many 'that best deserven love and name' and 'that worthy be and wyse', who are slandered at Love's court. The commitment of the wise counsellor to seeing and saying truly does not ensure material gain, that is, he is no flattering servant of Richesse. In the same way that this description in the *Romaunt* concludes with an imprecation, 'Wel yvel mote they thryve . . . these losengers, ful of envye' (1067–9), so the passage in the *Legend* is capped with two couplets which execrate Envy as the laundress of the court – the one who washes all the dirty linen – who is never absent from the court and who never suffers want:

> Envie ys lavendere of the court alway,
> For she ne parteth, neither nyght ne day,
> Out of the house of Cesar; thus seith Dante;
> Whoso that gooth, algate she wol nat wante.
> F 358–61

Dante refers to Envy as the harlot (*meretrice*) who inhabits Caesar's house in *Inferno* XIII 64 ff., where Pier delle Vigne, the once-powerful minister of Frederick II, but also a poet, bemoans the unjust accusations of treachery which finally drove him to death. Similarly Gower says that

---

[14] Cf. F 358–61/G 333–7 with Hoccleve, *Regement* 2941–3 and F 354/G 330 with Lydgate, *Secrees of Old Philisoffres* 883. Neither Hoccleve nor Lydgate was writing metaphorically about the court of Love.

Envy 'is of the Court the comun wenche' (*CA* II 3095–7). Although Chaucer has substituted 'lavender' for Dante's *meretrice*, he clearly regarded – and Gower, Hoccleve and Lydgate would have agreed with him – the inevitable presence of envy and flattery at the court as the most meretricious aspect of its ethos.

Particularly intriguing is the verbal allusion in F 352/G 328 to one of Jean de Meun's most striking metaphors in the line, 'That tabouren in your eres many a sown' (F 354/G 330), with its sense that flatterers prevail through the insidious and insistent drum-beat of their words. Jean had written of those who seduce women with false vows, agonised sighs and flattery (whom he calls *flajoleurs* or flageolet-players) that they *aus oreilles leur tabourent* (*RR* 21480). Jean also calls these flatterers and seducers *fleuteurs*, a word similar in sound to 'flater', meaning flatter, in French and Middle English. In Gower and Lydgate a flatterer is often called a 'flatour'. The use of such musical terms suggests the practices of the despised breed of jongleurs or minstrels who in earlier periods haunted the courts but in later medieval times began to be displaced by the more learned court poets and musicians like Machaut. It has often been pointed out how, in the fourteenth century, 'a new breed of amateur household poet' more and more came to displace the professional minstrel in the provision of courtly diversion. The term 'minstrel' had begun to lose its literary connotations and become synonymous with a mere popular entertainer, generally a musician, renowned for unscrupulous flattery and avarice. The new court poets had pretensions to learning and good breeding, and wrote as if they differed from their audience only in terms of their technical facility.[15]

It may well be, then, that the professional terms associated with minstrelsy, particularly those concerning the playing of wind instruments and drums (*fleuteurs* and *taboureurs*), had come to stand for the evils of flattery and avarice, the typical vices of a despised social class. Some modern semantic equivalents come to mind: 'fiddle', in particular, has several senses connoting deceit or triviality, and 'trumpet' and

---

[15] Green, *Poets and Princepleasers*, pp. 103–7. Moreover, according to Poirion, the new *clercs musiciens* who composed for the church as well as the court also wished to separate themselves from other minstrels, jongleurs and entertainers, by often using musical terminology appropriate to the description of minstrels, like *taboureur*, to deprecate court flatterers, *Poète et Prince*, pp. 157–8, 166 (*taboureurs*).

'drum' may each be thought to have a subordinate sense suggesting a certain specious ostentatiousness. In Chaucer's case, we have no way of knowing whether he is referring to actual slander which he has suffered, but his slighting reference to the 'many a losengeour . . . that tabouren in your eres many a sown' has a direct application to his professional reputation as a court poet. Alceste's words dissociate the poet's work totally from that of the lowly strolling entertainers, the productions of whom spring from lying distortion, whose motive is 'envie' and hate, and whose aim is 'daliance'. The register of the *de regimine* which Alceste has adopted here works to present Chaucer in the traditional role of a faithful adviser moved only by truth and wisdom, poorly rewarded, and not affected by fear or favour.

If Alceste's scornful condemnation of court flatterers as flute and drum players is a subtle reminder that the dimensions of this *de regimine* speech are in the end directed to the status of the poet Chaucer as a man of honour and learning whose writing has a serious intention in spite of its surface pleasure, then in the next section of her speech she fixes firmly on matters of literary responsibility and poetic intention. As these are of central importance to the *Legend of Good Women*, I will devote the next chapter to Alceste's discussion of the poet's 'entente'. If he cannot be held responsible for *Troilus and Criseyde* and the *Romaunt of the Rose*, Alceste concludes that the severity of Chaucer's 'crime' may be mitigated and should be kept in mind by a just ruler. She then proceeds to add weight to her argument in favour of mercy by appealing to those more generalised tenets of medieval political philosophy which stress the moral necessity and expediency of being a legitimate king rather than a tyrant:

> This shulde a ryghtwys lord han in his thought,
> And not ben lyk tyraunts of Lumbardye,
> That usen wilfulhed and tyrannye.
> For he that kyng or lord is naturel,
> Hym oughte nat be tyraunt and crewel
> As is a fermour, to don the harm he can.
> G 353–8/F 373–8

These lines signal a return to the traditional language of the *de regimine principum* genre, and Chaucer now almost exclusively imitates such works as the *Secretum Secretorum*, Giles of Rome's *De Regimine*

Principum and Seneca's *De Clementia* (itself a kind of *de regimine*). There may also be echoes of Dante's political writing.

J. D. Burnley has demonstrated that already in the *Parliament of Fowls* Chaucer had wittily characterised the God of Love as a tyrant, and irreverently treated him, with an unmistakable tone of mock-awe, as a *would-be* lord and master, of rather trivial status.[16] Here in the *Legend* Chaucer alludes to the tyranny of the God of Love three times in the space of three lines. The topos of the tyrant had been a significant one in Western thought since ancient times, and had ramifications for moral as well as political philosophy. Medieval political thought which derived from Aristotle stated that monarchy, the rule by a single man, was the best form of government known to man, and consequently its opposite, tyranny, or the corruption of monarchy, was the worst. All government was designed for the common good (*bonum commune* is a key phrase), was subject to the law (Gower makes much of this aspect), and depended on the consent of the governed. The tyrant corrupted good government essentially to serve his own will and pleasure. In the eyes of many writers (John of Salisbury, Aquinas, Giles, and most English works in the genre) a tyrant was prone to seduction by flatterers. There is a great unanimity of terminology among the political writers. Quite representative is Giles of Rome's distinction between a king who has regard to the common good and the tyrant who seeks his own good: *rex respicit bonum commune tirannus uero bonum proprium.*[17] Similar quotations could be multiplied. As Schlauch points out, the contemporary criticisms of Richard II (for example, the statements of the Parliament of 1386 and the articles of deposition of 1399) make heavy use of this familiar terminology, as in the repeated accusation that Richard desired to follow *sue inepte & illicite voluntatis arbitrium*, rather than the laws and customs of England. Chaucer, Schlauch says, 'must have heard the resentment against King Richard formulated in terms already familiar to him'.[18]

Whether he was thinking of Richard II or not, the semantic content of Chaucer's term 'tyrant' is clear, and the subject was indeed a topical one. Allowing for humour, the allusion to 'tyraunts of Lumbardye'

---

[16] Burnley, *Chaucer's Language*, pp. 29–30.
[17] See Schlauch, 'Doctrine of Kings', p. 139.   [18] Ibid., pp. 154–5.

makes the latter point certain. But what connection could there be between the 'tyraunts of Lumbardye' and the God of Love? Chaucer was a fourteenth-century Englishman well placed to have first-hand knowledge of the political situation in Italy and the new application of the old political theories about good government which was provoked by the absolute rule of the emerging city tyrants.[19] In the *Monk's Tale*, which includes several accounts of tyranny, the Monk refers to Bernabò Visconti as 'God of delit, and scourge of Lumbardye' (*MT* 2400). One of the defining characteristics of a tyrant, according to Giles of Rome and Aquinas, was his pursuit of his own pleasure (*delectabilia*), and many English versions of the *de regimine* type have frequent warnings about lechery. Michael Hanrahan has noted an intimate association of sexual seduction and treachery in contemporary history writing about Richard II.[20] It is not hard to see how the term 'God of delit' could as well describe the God of Love, in one of his traditional aspects.

Where moral philosophy overlapped with political philosophy, the epithet attaching most strongly to tyranny was 'cruel', signifying, among other things, the absence of mercy, but capricious behaviour or 'wilfulhede' was also commonly attributed to tyrants. A tyrant was often described as seeking personal vengeance and acting from 'ire'. These terms are all used in Alceste's speech, most specifically in Prologue G (cf. G 323, 355). Such analyses of tyrannical behaviour have their foundation in classical formulations. Thus Seneca wrote in *De Clementia* 11–12:

> What difference is there between tyrant and king, their symbols and prerogatives being the same, except that the wrath of tyrants is capricious whereas the wrath of kings is grounded in cause and necessity. 'What does this imply? Is it not the practice of kings, too, to put men to death upon occasion?' Only when public interest dictates; a tyrant's cruelty is wilful . . . it is clemency which constitutes the great distinction between king and tyrant. trans. Hadas, pp. 151–2

The last sentence is quoted by Gower, Hoccleve and James Yonge. Seneca also remarked how Augustus regretted in his old age, by then a

---

[19] Ibid., pp. 145–48, 154; Wallace, 'Whan she translated was', pp. 161–71; 'Writing the Tyrant's Death', pp. 117–30.

[20] See 'Seduction and Betrayal: Treason in the Prologue to *The Legend of Good Women*', *ChauR* 30 (1996): 229–40, esp. 235–6.

'good prince', how his *ira* used to flare up in his *adulescentia*, that is, he believed he had behaved like a tyrant when he was young, in medieval times the age when one is dominated by the God of Love. Richard II was known to have a blazing temper.

In the context of medieval discussions of tyranny it is often not necessary to attach the modifier 'good' or 'true' to the concept of kingship, when an opposite term to 'tyrant' is being sought. 'Tyrant' is the antonym simply to 'king'. Seneca suggests that the lordship of a king (that is to say, a true or good king), is something belonging to nature (that is, tyranny is unnatural) – 'It was Nature that devised the institution of kingship, as we may learn from bees and other creatures.'[21] Aquinas' formulation of Aristotelian politics sees the rule of a king as something in accordance with nature: 'Again, whatever is in accord with nature is best . . . Now, every natural governance is governance by one . . . Wherefore . . . it follows that it is best for a human multitude to be ruled by one person.'[22] In the same way Alceste says that cruelty and tyranny are not appropriate to him 'that kyng or lord is naturel' (this sounds like the phrase about lordship which Giles of Rome, following Aquinas, uses over and over again),[23] and that such a one should not behave towards his subjects as a 'fermour' or tax-gatherer. While Burnley may be right in suggesting that the allusion, in F 378/G 358, to the tyrant's habit of extorting money from his subjects is a purely metaphorical reference to the harshness of the God of Love,[24] nevertheless its applicability is not immediately obvious. The fact remains that by the time that Alceste starts to warn Love against tyrannous cupidity, her speech reads most naturally as a genuine rebuke to a medieval king and less and less clearly as an address to the mythical God of Love. The lines, 'For he that kyng or lord is naturel/ Hym oughte nat be tyraunt and crewel/ As is a fermour, to don the harm he can' (G 356–8), may be compared to remarks such as this one of Yonge's: 'Sum Pryncis ther bene, that for thar owyn Synguler auauntage

---

[21] *De Clementia* 19; trans. Hadas, p. 158.
[22] *On Kingship*, trans. Phelan, pp. 12–13.
[23] Giles' interest in government which is 'natural' is evident from almost his first words: '*Mes cil est* gouverneur naturel, *qui n'establist ne ne commande for cen que loy et reson enseignent*. . .' (Molenaer, p. 2, emphasis mine).
[24] Burnley, *Chaucer's Language*, p. 32.

. . . takyn atte har talent trew men goodis.'[25] Indeed, condemnations of any ruler who could be described as an 'oppressoure and an extorcionere of vertues men, and a crowel Tyraunt ontollerabill, vpon the grete lordis of his londe' (which was typified for Yonge in 1420 by Richard II) are a marked feature of that writer's *Secretum*, and it is well known how bitterly resented was the heavy taxation of Richard's reign, and the extravagances of his court. Chaucer's own balade, *Lak of Stedfastnesse*, ends with a *Lenvoy to King Richard*, where the poet begs the king to 'hate extorcioun'!

The reasoning with which Alceste proceeds to substantiate her argument in the next thirty lines owes something to the idea of the mutuality of relationship between lord and liege, and something to the conventional political notion that a king must judge his people in accordance with law, but the dominant image of the following lines, particularly in F, derives from the *Secretum Secretorum*. According to its putative author Aristotle, 'the Philospher', a king must realise that it is his subjects, particularly the nobility, who constitute his treasure and deserve to be cherished:

> He moste thinke yt is his lige man,
> And is his tresour and his gold in cofre.
> This is the sentence of the Philosophre,
> A kyng to kepe his liges in justice;
> Withouten doute, that is his office.
> F 379–83

All versions of the *Secretum* of which I am aware, no matter how many variations they incorporate, include the section which visualises the king's subjects as his treasure, for they are the ultimate defence of the realm. A minority among the English versions of the *Secretum* make the same association that Chaucer does between this statement and an exhortation that the king accord the members of his nobility good government and the honour they deserve, or in Chaucer's words, 'kepe his liges in justice . . . [and] kepe his lordes hire degree' (F 382, 384ff./G 366, 370ff.). I quote from a fifteenth-century English translation of a French *Secretum*, where the king is advised:

[25] Steele, *Three Prose Versions*, p. 132.

I trowe þat þou hauys now vnderstandyd, þat þy subgitȝ er þe hauynge of þi hous[26] and þi tresour, wherof þi kyngdom is confermed . . . Now it nedys þanne þat þou gouerne hem wel, and þat þou gyf good entent to here nedys, so þat þou remowe fro hem all þaire wronges . . . Barouns er helpe and multiplicacion of þe kyngdome, by hem ys þe court honourd and gouerned, & ordeyned yn here degreeȝ.[27]

Alceste goes on to insist that justice be done to poor and rich alike, which is a common sentiment in English political writing as in Gower and James Yonge, less so in other versions.[28] Her plea on behalf of the poor (by implication, poor poets?) allows somewhat humorously that the king's righteous and reasonable duty is to honour and enhance his lords (F 384–90/G 370–6) – 'for they ben half-goddes in this worlde here'. This comic momentary return to the fiction that Alceste is addressing the God of Love whose lords might be thought of as demigods[29] is possibly ironic (particularly in F), implying that this is how they evaluate their own status.[30] Giles of Rome's *de regimine* has several striking references to demigods,[31] not in the same context as here, but nevertheless a possible significant nod in the direction of Giles's prestigious work.

But what has all this to do with the rule of the God of Love, except in the most extended metaphorical sense? Its applicability to Richard II in the mid-1380s may have been, however, glaringly obvious. Indeed, when J. L. Lowes pointed out the similarities between Alceste's speech and Knighton's account of the message sent to Richard II by the parliament of 1386, of which Chaucer was a member, he noted that the historical document mentions that both *pauperes et divites* were seeking justice (as well as that the king was acting according to *propriam*

[26] Cf. 'hauynge of þi hous' with Chaucer's 'gold in cofre' and 'the hous of the mooney' of MS Ashmole in Manzalaoui, *Nine English Versions*, p. 84.

[27] MS Lambeth 501, VII 107 – VIII 109 in Steele, *Three Prose Versions*, p. 108.

[28] For Yonge, see Steele, *Three Prose Versions*, pp. 127–8, 168 (sentiments quite unlike other versions of the *Secretum*). Cf. Gower, *CA* VII 2740–5.

[29] Chaucer elsewhere refers to 'satiry and fawny more and lesse/ That halve goddes ben of wildernesse' (*TC* IV 1543–4).

[30] See P. G. Ruggiers, 'Tyrants of Lombardy in Dante and Chaucer', *PQ* 29 (1950): 445–8.

[31] E.g. *De Regimine Principum* I. I. IIII (Molenaer, p. 11); II. II. VIII (Molenaer, p. 202).

voluntatem suam singularem, the traditional attribute of the tyrant).[32]
Moreover, there was a wide-spread feeling at the time that the legitimate
counsellors of the king were being ignored in favour of the worthless
'favourites' on whom Richard was squandering the wealth of England.
There is a measure of correspondence between Alceste's sentiments here
(particularly the rather odd emphasis, given the context, on a king's
attitude to his people's wealth and to his nobles), and those expressed by
Gower many years later, after the deposition of Richard II: 'R[ichard]
brings destruction and merciful H[enry IV] pardons death;/ R. taxes
the people and merciful H. remits taxes;/ R. hates the nobles and
purloins their wealth . . .'[33]

The G version of this section (G 359–69) is rewritten and expanded
in a manner that enhances the sense that Alceste's words have closer
affinities with genuine examples of the tradition of advising rulers than
with the lighthearted parody which often characterises courtly accounts
of the God of Love's dealings with his servants. The demand that a king
be willing to hear his people's complaints and petitions (G 362) has
parliamentary overtones and appears in some versions of the *Secretum*,
as in the passage from MS Lambeth 501 quoted above. It is a tradition
which is also enshrined in accounts of kingship in the literature of
England, so that we find Malory's King Arthur setting himself to hear
his subjects' 'complayntes . . . of grete wronges' immediately after his
coronation when he was 'sworne unto his lordes and the comyns for to
be a true kyng, to stand with true justyce fro thens forth the dayes of
this lyf'.[34] Again there is a striking agreement here with Chaucer's lines
in the G version stating that a king is 'ful depe ysworn . . . to kepe his
lyges in justice' (G 366–8). The historical accounts of the Ricardian
period forcefully remind us what deep significance attached to the
swearing of the coronation oath to rule in accordance with the laws and
customs of England[35] (and indeed Alceste comments that kings have
sworn such oaths 'ful many a hundred wynter herebeforn'). It is
noteworthy that two English versions of the *Secretum* (that of Hoccleve

[32] Lowes, 'Chronological Relations', p. 778.
[33] *Chronica Tripertita* 466–71. Quoted and translated in Green, *Poets and Prince-pleasers*, p. 181.
[34] Vinaver, *Malory*, p. 10.
[35] May McKisack, *The Fourteenth Century*, pp. 390, 497.

and the sixteenth-century version by William Forrest) make mention of the coronation oath, and that Manzalaoui remarks that there is a group of English *Secretum* manuscripts which have treatises on the coronation of kings bound with them;[36] again this seems to be a particularly English bias in this kind of literature.

The climax of Alceste's argument appeals to the gentle nature of the lion, as an exemplum of how refusing mercy is below the dignity of a king:

> For loo, the gentil kynde of the lyoun:
> For whan a flye offendeth him or biteth,
> He with his tayl awey the flye smyteth
> Al esely; for, of hys genterye,
> Hym deyneth not to wreke hym on a flye,
> As dooth a curre, or elles another best.
> In noble corage ought ben arest,
> And weyen every thing by equytee,
> And ever have reward to his owen degree.
>
> F 391–9/G 377–85

The *Secretum* of James Yonge and Gower's Book VII use what is apparently the same story about the Nobility of the Lion who will not take vengeance on a man who has harmed him grievously if the man 'falle doun to the Erthe, as he wolde crye hym mercy'.[37] Chaucer's lines about the lion and the fly do not match this story exactly, indeed, they have no known parallel, although their ultimate import is similar. However, the section in Yonge begins with a quotation from the *De Clementia* of Seneca, and Chaucer's lines are reminiscent of a passage in *De Clementia* 5–7:

> Elephants and lions pass by those they have struck down, relentless-ness is a trait of ignoble animals. Savage and inexorable anger is not becoming to a king, for then he loses his superiority; anger reduces him to his victim's level. But if he grants life, if he grants their dignities to persons in jeopardy who have deserved to lose them, he does what none but a sovereign could do . . . for a king even a raised voice and intemperate language are a degradation of majesty.
>
> trans. Hadas, pp. 144–5

---

[36] Manzalaoui, *Nine English Versions*, p. xx.
[37] Yonge, in Steele, *Three Prose Versions*, p. 181; cf. Gower, *CA* VII 3387–99.

Seneca's view that a king should refrain from executing his wrath from a lofty disregard of insult and because it is below his own dignity is a quite precise equivalent to the sense of the Chaucerian passage.

It is evident that the *de regimine* section of Alceste's speech was executed with care, and if it at times seems to bear a disproportionate weight in the speech as a whole, the conclusion of this section of the speech brings us back to the poet's fictional plight:

> For, syr, yt is no maistrye for a lord
> To dampne a man without answere of word,
> And for a lord that is ful foul to use.
> And if so be he may hym nat excuse,
> But asketh mercy with a dredeful herte,
> And profereth him, ryght in his bare sherte,
> To ben ryght at your owen jugement,
> Than oght a god, by short avysement,
> Consydre his owne honour and hys trespas.
> For, syth no cause of deth lyeth in this caas,
> Yow oghte to ben the lyghter merciable;
> Leteth youre ire, and beth sumwhat tretable.
> F 400–11/G 386–97

There is something here of the medieval penitent grieving for his sin and 'in his bare sherte'; something of the man throwing himself before the noble lion to gain mercy; something of Seneca's edict that a king should pay heed to his own dignity; something of pseudo-Aristotle's advice in the *Secretum* that a king should weigh up how bad a man's crime actually is before venting his 'ire' and demanding the death penalty for trivial offences. Moreover, towards the middle of this passage, Alceste is again addressing Love as a god, and not merely a king.

It would seem impossible to answer with certainty the question of whether the *de regimine* passage is so out of proportion to the ostensible theme as to suggest that Chaucer had his own king in mind behind the fiction of the God of Love. Is its exaggerated length, on the other hand, simply a joke on the preposterous claims of Love to a legitimate reign over men? One can perhaps do no better than to quote an old answer to an old question. Samuel Moore once said sensibly of Alceste's speech:

Now this is excellent advice for the God of Love, but it is as good or better advice for Richard . . . And the language of the passage is so general that it applies to all kings, not merely the God of Love. If Richard failed to see its applicability to himself he must have been singularly deficient in self-knowledge; and if Chaucer failed to foresee its applicability to his sovereign he was considerably more naive than we have hitherto supposed him to have been.[38]

Yet one reason we should be cautious about applying the speech to Richard II lies in the fact that the (probably) revised version of the lengthy speech in the G Prologue is even longer and more politically explicit than in F. The G version lacks F's references to Queen Anne and courtly pastime, and appears designed for a more general audience. This suggests that Chaucer thought a *de regimine* speech in English had wide appeal, and means that we have to find in it some significance beyond the putative reference to Richard II in version F. My suggestion is that its mode acts as another marker of the learning and sense of social responsibility of the poet who composed it, and acts as a counterpoint to the interpolated account of Chaucer as a simple-minded scribe with which Alceste attempts to exculpate him. In the next chapter I turn to the specifically literary dimensions of Alceste's speech.

---

[38] Moore, 'The Prologue to Chaucer's "Legend of Good Women"', p. 493.

7

The defence: matere and entente

Alceste has a list of excuses to offer the God of Love which may be applicable to Chaucer's crime:

> Or elles, sire, for that this man is nyce,
> He may translate a thyng in no malyce,
> But for he useth bokes for to make,
> And taketh non hed of what matere he take,
> Therfore he wrote the Rose and ek Crisseyde
> Of innocence, and nyste what he seyde . . .
> He ne hath not don so grevously amys
> To translate that olde clerkes wryte,
> As thogh that he of maleys wolde endyte
> Despit of love, and hadde hymself ywrought.
> G 340–52/F 362–72

In spite of Alceste's concern for justice, she expresses no high regard for Chaucer's abilities and in fact believes him guilty of the crime of enditing 'despit of love'. Having put the notion of wrongful accusation to one side she broaches the possibility of mitigating circumstances or diminished responsibility. It is not easy to gauge how seriously the audience might have regarded a defence which depends on Chaucer's mental capacity or lack of it. Was he, as Alceste says, too 'nyce' (ignorant or foolish) to know what he was doing, and therefore 'innocent' of the implications of what his translations were saying? In this context, being innocent and thus free of 'malice' or evil intent has no very flattering connotation. It is simply a consequence of being 'nyce', and similarly denotes ignorance or incompetence. Indeed, *MED* cites G 345 to illustrate this meaning of 'innocence'.

Writing, making, enditing, translating, meaning – the whole

accusation and defence scene is peppered with the lexis of literary craft. The scene makes use of the technical terms of scholarly literary analysis such as 'matere', 'entente', 'trete'.[1] The connotations of these terms are almost as important as their content. Indeed Rita Copeland has maintained that Chaucer's very self-assured exploitation of the academic discourse usually applied to authoritative Latin texts, in order to define his own poetic achievement and thus to claim 'the prestige of canonical literary authority', is one of the most notable features of the *Legend of Good Women*,[2] as it is in his contemporary Gower's *Confessio Amantis*. It is as if that, by implication, to apply to Chaucer's own past and future works the language of the schools is to suggest that these English works deserve the same kind of learned attention as the authoritative texts of the classical past, or as such prestigious vernacular works as the *Divine Comedy* or the *Roman de la Rose*.

In alluding yet again to Chaucer as a translator Alceste makes the vernacularity of his work the point at issue, and the status of English as a vehicle for serious courtly writing. With this scene the Prologue to the *Legend of Good Women* gains many of the marks of a scholarly translator's prologue or an *accessus ad auctorem*, using the same terms as might appear, for example, in a typical introduction to Ovid's *Heroides*. Specifically, the identification of *intentio auctoris* was one of the cardinal features of scholarly literary criticism of the set texts and it is the question of intentionality which is implicit in this passage in the *Legend*, and will become explicit. The notion of intention has of course been dismissed in modern literary criticism, but has to be discussed here because the term 'entente' appears central to Chaucer's idea of the *Legend of Good Women*.

Several assumptions lie behind the position adopted by Queen

---

[1] The twelfth- and thirteenth-century teachers of both *artes* and theology produced scholarly prologues to prescribed texts in which students were taught how to analyse authoritative texts by making use of the critical terms *intentio*, *materia* and *modus agendi* or *tractandi*. See A. J. Minnis, 'The Influence of Academic Prologues and Literary Attitudes of Late-Medieval English Writers', *MS* 43 (1981): 342–83; also, at more length, his *Medieval Theory of Authorship*, pp. 20–22 and passim.

[2] See Rita Copeland, *Rhetoric, Hermeneutics, and Translation in the Middle Ages: Academic Traditions and Vernacular Texts* (Cambridge University Press, 1991), pp. 186–202.

Alceste: she does not dispute, for example, the antifeminist bias of the writing of 'olde clerkes' – whether the writers of antiquity or the works of aging scholars – tacitly confirming the view that their only intention in writing about love was to condemn it. Secondly, when Alceste says that to translate 'that olde clerkes writen' is not so bad an action as to invent 'despit of love' out of one's own head, so to speak, and out of 'malice' or a deliberate evil intent, and when she suggests Chaucer may have taken no notice of what he was writing about, she implies the work of translation was as automatic as the mental activity of a hired scribe. Lydgate uses the same image as a modesty topos when he wants to explain why he is so 'dull of wit', and how unable to 'know felyngly' the pain of lovers: 'But euen-like as doth a skryuener/ That can no more what that he shal write/ But as his maister beside dothe endyte/ Ryght so fare I.'[3] But we are dealing in the *Legend* not with a simple affectation of modesty, such as that frequently made by the medieval 'compiler' who typically claimed merely to report others' words, but the reverse, a reminder rather of potency than of passivity. The assertion by Alceste of the poet's extreme subservience in the face of the texts which contain his subject matter only draws attention to the indubitable fact of the poet's conscious activity, to the likelihood that, whatever his work means, that meaning is something he has 'hymself ywrought' (F 372/G 352).

The profession of incompetence recalls a familiar stance which Chaucer adopts in his poetry, but it is significant that these are Alceste's words and nowhere in the *Legend* does Chaucer endorse them himself. Indeed, in his only remarks in his own defence, at the very end of the scene, Chaucer maintains his conscious intention has been misinterpreted. He claims for himself a high ethical intent which may or may not have been the same as his *auctour's*, he does not avoid responsibility for his versions of *Criseyde* or the *Rose*, but leaves it to his readers to perceive and apply to their own lives his exempla's moral *utilitas* of encouraging the avoidance of falseness and vice:

> But trewely I wende, as in this cas,
> Naught have agilt, ne don to love trespas . . .

---

[3] *The Complaint of the Black Knight (Complaynte of a Loueres Lyfe)* 194–7, MacCracken, *Lydgate's Minor Poems*, II, pp. 390–1.

Ne a trewe lovere oghte me nat to blame
Thogh that I speke a fals lovere som shame.
They oughte rathere with me for to holde
For that I of Criseyde wrot or tolde,
Or of the Rose; what so myn auctour mente,
Algate, God wot, it was myn entente
To forthere trouthe in love and it cheryce,
And to be war fro falsnesse and fro vice
By swich ensaumple; this was my menynge.
G 452–64 (identical in F)

It is my feeling that Chaucer briefly speaks here in his own voice, offering a sincere if inadequate explanation for the composition of *Troilus and Criseyde* (his major work up to this time), by declaring his virtuous intent, his desire to commend fidelity in love, in spite of the poem's unpromising subject matter. To my mind all the 'I's' and 'my's' and calling God to witness give the impression of a significant declaration of Chaucer's understanding of his poetic vocation. This is a contention impossible to prove, but the conclusion to *Troilus* lends weight to it. No doubt, however, we would be on safer ground to see it as yet another stance adopted by the narrator/poet's persona in a shifting spectrum of roles: at one moment, for example, he presents himself as the subservient worshipper of the daisy, the one who in the presence of French lyric poetry 'comes after, gleaning . . .', and at another place he is the flirtatious sexual adventurer, complicit (in his poetic dealings with his matter) with the villainous seducers of women in his Legends – we will meet this figure when we turn at last to the *Legend*'s tale collection. Both of these versions of the narrator's persona deal with his role as a literary artist, a 'maker', and the last at least is playful, but here he draws around himself the mantle of the poet of high ethical seriousness, and implies that that 'trouthe in love' which he wishes to further and cherish has little in common with loving 'paramours to harde and hote' (G 260).

The formulation of Chaucer's own defence conforms to the notion that a true author has always, by definition, the intention to encourage virtue and discourage vice in his audience.[4] Further, the distinction he

---

[4] See Minnis, *Medieval Authorship*, pp. 55–8, 190–209.

draws between his own intention and that of his 'auctour' ('what so myn auctour mente . . . it was *myn* entente') is an astounding claim for his competing *auctoritas*, and in marked contrast to Alceste's portrayal of him as mindless scribe. Behind Chaucer's 'authorial' remarks – polite, low-key, reasonable, rather self-effacing – lies the commonplace dictum, often invoked in the poetry of secular love, of the poem as a 'Mirror for Lovers', the reflection of truth, in which one could either look and admire, or look and avoid. While such platitudinous sentiments are not invalid, and no less valid when readers had to apply some effort to distinguish the ultimate moral purpose, one has the impression that, in secular literature at least, this sanction – follow good examples, avoid evil ones– tended to be invoked more often when the exemplary value of an otherwise popular work was morally debatable. Witness Boccaccio's Conclusion to the *Decameron* or Caxton's Preface to *Le Morte Darthur*. It was, not surprisingly, invoked in the *querelle de la Rose*. Christine de Pizan was sharply impatient of the use of this argument by the defenders of the *Rose* to prove that Jean de Meun's intention was after all supremely moral, and was convinced that the only people who defended that work in such a manner were those who derived wicked enjoyment from reading it.[5] In associating such arguments with *Troilus and Criseyde* Chaucer seems to be claiming that his work deserves the same kind of serious engagement and active interpretation on the part of his audience as did the great *Roman de la Rose*.

Significantly, the momentary seriousness and audacity of Chaucer's pretensions to *auctoritas* are quickly and humorously defused when Alceste reminds the poet of the futility of engaging in rational discussion with that well-known autocrat, the God of Love:

> And she answerde, 'Lat be thyn arguynge,
> For Love ne wol nat counterpleytyd be
> In ryght ne wrong; and lerne this at me!'
> G 465–7/F 475–7

Alceste's brusque dismissal of Chaucer's defence is similar to Christine

---

[5] Hicks, *Débat sur le Roman*, pp. 53, 56; Baird and Kane, *Querelle de la Rose*, pp. 51, 54, 55.

de Pizan's equally brusque demand, in the face of similar arguments put
in the historical *querelle*, that literature should be unambiguously
moral, given the fact that not all readers had the capacity, the education
or the will to seek out a virtuous intention behind a superficially or
ironically immoral surface. The *querelle de la Rose* makes it quite certain
that claims of authorial virtue like Chaucer's were known to provoke
vigorous debate at this period.

It has often been noted that whenever Chaucer approaches the idea
of his own *auctoritas*, he almost invariably withdraws from the full
implications of this posture. So here his authorial claims to virtuous
intention are countered with Alceste's sharp rejoinder; the humorous
return to the fictional dimension of his conflict with the tyrannical God
of Love effects a temporary closure of his potentially subversive stance
towards the authority of 'olde bokes' and his heresy in the face of the
demands of courtly literature always to praise and honour the virtue of
ladies. The transparent attempt to mask his manifest poetic mastery of
his matter under the humble guise of a mere translator is yet another
way of dealing with the almost unthinkable concept of a vernacular
auctoritas. In order to put Alceste's excuses on Chaucer's behalf in
context, let us consider some medieval opinions on the responsibility of
the vernacular translator.

The derogatory assessment of the translator/poet's craft which lies
behind Alceste's kindly attempt to defend Chaucer has a specious
quality which is not readily apparent to a casual modern reading since
we no longer value translation highly; paradoxically, just because we
expect a translation to be a faithful attempt to convey the original
author's purpose, with as little acknowledgement of the presence of the
translator as possible. But everything we can deduce from Chaucer's
composition of *Troilus and Criseyde* (the antecedent to this debate), and
the work of translation evident in the *Legend of Good Women* (the result
of it), confirms that it is the poet's ability to produce his own meaning
in the face of the apparent controlling authority of his source material
which is the point at issue. The force of this is as evident to the modern
audience as to the medieval; to modern readers, because for them
Chaucer's *Troilus and Criseyde* has so completely supplanted its 'translated' source that the latter is normally only consulted as a supplement
to the Chaucerian poem. The medieval reader of *Troilus and Criseyde*

could be no less aware of the poet's skill in extracting a new significance out of inherited matter, in light of the potent challenge Chaucer's version offered to the traditional understanding of the archetypal story of woman's infidelity.[6] In the major work of translation from the classics which the *Legend of Good Women* represents, Chaucer is far from being subservient, as will be seen, but playfully questions the veracity of what 'autours seyn' in the face of the everyday experience and understanding of the ordinary English reader (G 85–8).

Medieval translation theory has received a great deal of critical attention in the last decade,[7] and only brief mention of this complex subject needs to be made here. Translation was valued as a type of autonomous discourse in the Middle Ages, and Deschamps's description of Chaucer as *grand translateur* was high praise indeed. The English term is related to the concept of *translatio*, whose root meaning had much wider connotations than are borne by the modern English word, as Chaucer's usage to describe his varying procedures in the *Romaunt de la Rose* on the one hand and *Troilus and Criseyde* on the other might suggest. *Translatio* could describe any transference of meaning, whether at the micro level in the use of figurative language (*translatio* as metaphor) or at the macro level of *translatio studii*, the transfer of the learning of past cultures into a new time, a new context, and (only secondarily) into a new language.[8] In a time when people did not look for new subject matter, it was inevitable that much that was worth talking about had already been treated by the venerable Latin authors, and further mediated in vernaculars more prestigious than English. It was thus almost inevitable that an English writer would be a translator and that he would have to struggle with a sense of the inferiority of his own tongue; many in his audience may have considered a profession of humility more than appropriate.

Medieval people did differentiate between free and close translation,

---

[6] See Gretchen Mieszowski, *The Reputation of Criseyde: 1155–1500* (Transactions of the Connecticut Academy of Arts and Sciences: Archon, 1971).

[7] See the notable and comprehensive contribution of Copeland in *Rhetoric, Hermeneutics, and Translation*, esp. her bibliography and references.

[8] D. Kelly, '*Translatio Studii*: Translation, Adaptation and Allegory in Medieval French Literature', *PQ* 57 (1978): 287–310.

and discussion on the topic was energetic and sophisticated.[9] However, in the province of rhetoric to which medieval literary translation has most affinity, the notion of linguistic fidelity in translation was not a desideratum, but instead the discovery and production of new and appropriate garb for old matter. It has been suggested that Chaucer did not distinguish rigidly between the terms 'translate' and 'endite' (G 350, 351)[10] – for a poet the compositional procedures and creative activity suggested by 'endite' amounted to much the same thing as the recontextualising of his matter in English suggested by 'translate'. In the Prologue to the *Second Nun's Tale*, Chaucer contrasts what he has done in merely 'following' the 'words and sentence' of his story (that is, something approaching a close or faithful translation) with the possible 'subtle inditing' of the saint's legend which would have required more 'diligence' (*SNT* 79–83).

The free rendering which marks so much medieval translation is to some extent the end product of the way students mastered the Latin language and its literature. Vernacular translation ultimately derived from the desire to conserve and pass on the textual heritage of the past by means of the tradition of meticulous commentary and exposition, for translation could only begin once the source text had been interpreted accurately. Even in his attempts to perfect his linguistic skills in Latin (*exercitatio*) or in his interpretation of the set authors (*enarratio poetarum*), the student was warned against the infelicities of literal translation. Commentary on the text may have included passages of close translation but was more likely to proceed by amplifying paraphrase because that encouraged the student to go beyond the literal and convey the structure of connotation and figurative meaning of the original. By these practices the student mastered or domesticated his subject matter and 'made it his own', and provided the necessary

---

9 Forms of Cicero's dictum on translation, *non verbum pro verbo*, were reinterpreted again and again over the centuries, according to the theoretical demands of the translator, as Rita Copeland has traced in 'The Fortunes of "Non Verbum Pro Verbo": Or, Why Jerome is not a Ciceronian', in R. Ellis, ed., *The Medieval Translator: the Theory and Practice of Translation in the Middle Ages* (Cambridge: Brewer, 1989), pp. 15–35.

10 J. D. Burnley, 'Late Medieval English Translation: Types and Reflections', in Ellis, *Medieval Translator*, p. 39; T. W. Machan, 'Chaucer as Translator', in Ellis, *Medieval Translator*, pp. 62–3.

substratum on which his own independent literary composition could be built.[11]

If one wished to 'serve' a text which was to be translated, then, one had first to 'master' it, and translation theorists were well aware of the entangled relationships of 'service'and 'mastery', some of which are enacted in the *Legend of Good Women*. Chaucer's villainous seducers, for example, frequently profess humble service towards women, while they aspire to mastery. In *Dido*, as another example, the poet himself offers 'glory and honour' to Vergil and states that he intends to 'follow his lantern', then almost immediately flouts the authority of the great Latin master: he comments that he could have followed Vergil 'word for word', but it would have taken too long and his own purpose dictated otherwise (cf. *Dido* 924–6, 1002–3, 953–7). In another permutation of the notion that 'mastering' one's matter is paradoxically related to the idea of 'serving' it, Jerome once noted that one mastered the text which one was translating only to find one's own writing mastered by the original.[12] This paradox can also be demonstrated at many points in the *Legend*, where some of the most effective 'Englishing' derives from Chaucer's close imitation of Ovid's text, as in Medea's lament on Jason's defection:

> Whi lykede me thy yelwe her to se
> More than the boundes of myn honeste?
> Why lykede me thy youthe and thy fayrnesse,
> And of thy tonge, the infynyt graciousnesse?
> 1672–5[13]

Indeed, translation had acquired many traditional formulations in the centuries-old discussion of the merits of word-for-word translation versus sense-for-sense, and many paradoxes. The theorising of the relation of meaning, linguistic form and the speaker's motivation is so complex that it inevitably calls into play a number of metaphorical strategies. Given the theme of the *Legend*, one of the most interesting of these semantic fields is the concept of fidelity or betrayal represented by

[11] See Rita Copeland, 'Rhetoric and Vernacular Translation in the Middle Ages', *SAC* 9 (1987): 47–8.

[12] Copeland, 'Non Verbum Pro Verbo', p. 29.

[13] Well treated in Frank, *Chaucer and the Legend*, passim.

the notion of the *fidus interpres*, and the paradox that, for the translator to be most faithful at the level of meaning, he had to betray at the level of the word. Horace in his *Ars Poetica* had suggested that one of the greatest perils for the would-be poet was to show himself a *fidus interpres*, a faithful or unduly literal translator. This phrase had a long life in translation theory as a pejorative term. The sanction against the *fidus interpres* was so strong that several significant translators of philo-sophical writing like Boethius and John Scotus Eriugina apologised when they made literal translations, fearing that they had 'incurred the blame' of the *fidus interpres*! The medieval arts of poetry, like those of Mathew of Vendôme and Geoffrey of Vinsauf, taught the skills required by a poet to develop a topic differently from its source. They enthusias-tically endorsed the Horatian dictum *nec verbo verbum curabis reddere fidus interpres* ('do not try to render word for word like a faithful translator', *Ars Poetica* 133–4) and saw a challenge to poetic ingenuity in Horace's earlier line remarking how difficult it was to make common material one's own (*Ars Poetica* 128). Very well-known material should not be avoided, the arts of poetry advised; on the contrary, the poet should welcome the difficult task of creating a new work from material already frequently treated by earlier poets.[14] To be truly a poet one could not avoid being an unfaithful translator. In Old French, interest-ingly, forms of the verb *traire*, to treat, draw out, translate, are homonyms of forms of *trahir*, to betray, deceive, so that the ear could not distinguish between descriptions of the act of writing or translating and the act of betrayal.[15] It is hard to think of any other medieval context where the ideal of fidelity was not a virtue to be enshrined, but in the ludic context of the *Legend* the conception of translation as a sanctioned transgressive rather than a passive activity allows Chaucer to identify with the traitors in the stories he is about to tell.

In sum, then, a close translation from one language to another was rarely recommended since it was as likely to hinder the clear transfer-ence of meaning as to facilitate it, the idiomatic structure of each language being frequently untransferable, as Jerome and many other

14 Extensively discussed by Copeland, 'Non Verbum Pro Verbo', pp. 24–31; and *Rhetoric, Hermeneutics, and Translation*, pp. 29 ff., 166–78.
15 See R. H. Bloch, *Medieval Misogyny and the Invention of Western Romantic Thought* (University of Chicago Press, 1991), pp. 134–8.

practising translators had maintained. Nevertheless, in some contexts
(the translation of Scripture, for example) slavish translation, free from
the distracting or corrupting influence of rhetorical embellishment and
the potentiality for inaccuracy in sense-for-sense translation, could
connote the most faithful possible attempt to convey the sense of the
original work;[16] in Alceste's speech the plausible concept of translation
as transparent transference of meaning is deliberately confused with the
ideals of rhetorical translation in which the poet puts his own stamp
upon the recreated meaning of the original text. The humble reference
Chaucer makes to his 'gleaning' the odd goodly word left behind by
other 'makers' (F 73–7/G 61–5) in fact disguises a vigorous activity of
high skill and creative endeavour and not one that needed apology.
Indeed, when she speaks of the poet's possible repentance, 'Or him
repenteth outrely of this' (F 368), Alceste tacitly concedes his guilt as
charged and the excuses as worthless.

It is possible, however, that Alceste's other contention that Chaucer may
have only been obeying orders when he slandered Love – 'Or him was
boden maken thilke tweye/ Of som persone, and durste yt nat withseye'
(F 366–7/G 346–7) – would have borne more weight in his audience's
opinion than that he was too stupid to know what he was doing. R. F.
Green has drawn attention to the personal authority wielded by the
head of the household over his *familia*, and the intimacy of the relationship, as well as the absolute loyalty and total commitment demanded of
its members.[17] The demand for translations, moreover, was one
frequently made by persons of importance upon their subordinates
with literary talents. The significance of the accusation scene is not that
it tells us anything about the historical genesis of the *Romaunt* and
Troilus, or even of the *Legend of Good Women*, but that the references to
them are a preparation for the potent effect of the fictional literary
command which the Prologue to the *Legend* purports to reproduce.
When the God of Love and Queen Alceste order Chaucer to spend the
rest of his life writing a 'glorious legende/ Of goode wymmen . . . /

---

[16] See W. Schwarz, 'The Meaning of *Fidus Interpres* in Medieval Translation', *Journal of
Theological Studies* 45 (1944): 73–8. In practice such 'faithful' translations verged on
unintelligibility and certainly inelegance.
[17] *Poets and Princepleasers*, pp. 13–37.

That weren trewe in lovyng al hire lyves' (F 483–5/G 473–5), it is a command the poet 'dare not withsay'. This does not mean, however, that he can be expected to be in personal agreement with the ostensible purpose of the work so produced, any more than he is responsible for the choice of 'matere'. It is a convenient fiction, and the dramatisation of his slightly reluctant acquiescence to the proposition that women are faithful and men are false – a proposition to be found in 'olde bokes' though not often proved by experience – is the source of much of the humour and flirtatious sparkle of the Legends of good women.

It is not unlikely that Chaucer designed the *Legend* as a playful exercise in literary bias. In the composition of the Legends of good women, Chaucer deliberately exposed the strains involved in fitting recalcitrant material to a predetermined intention,[18] the God of Love's contention that the poet's only (honourable or virtuous) course was to to write about 'wemen . . . good and trewe' rather than unfaithful women like Criseyde (G 267–72). But, if it is true that the poet only chose 'bad matter' like Criseyde's unfaithfulness (cf. G 270, 'good matere') in order to warn people against such behaviour, then the project of the *Legend* seems designed to reverse the point ironically: in the *Legend* the subject matter of the commendation of virtuous women may be unimpeachable, nevertheless, Chaucer will show how any expectation of virtuous intention can be subverted by the poet's treatment. Chaucer suggests what happens when 'art becomes propaganda', in Fyler's avowedly anachronistic phrase.[19]

I have been contending that works with a distinctly feminist or antifeminist bias were quite visible as such in the Middle Ages, and that, in a very broad sense, such a tradition is very much a part of the context of the *Legend of Good Women*. More than this, the *Legend* dramatises the viewpoint which the reluctant male poet brings to the attempt to write with a feminine bias – 'For it is deynte to us men to fynde/ A man that can in love be trewe and kynde' (*Tisbe* 920–1). In presenting himself as a poet writing under compulsion Chaucer aligns himself again with the motivation of Ovid as understood by medieval scholars. As in the *accessus Ovidiani*, he creates for his persona an

---

18 Cf. J. M. Fyler, *Chaucer and Ovid* (New Haven: Yale University Press, 1979), pp. 96–115.
19 Ibid., p. 115.

experience which elucidates the meaning of his work by showing how and why he came to write it, a *vita auctoris* or *causa operis*.[20] The fiction that he has been accused by a powerful personage of a crime for which he must make amends strongly parallels those aspects of the life of Ovid which the commentators brought forth as an explanation for the *Heroides*. Thus one twelfth-century *accessus* on the *Heroides* comments that Ovid's *intentio* was to make recompense to Caesar for misleading Roman matrons with erotic poetry, as well as to encourage virtue and to discourage vice, by offering them an example of which women to imitate and which not.[21]

Alceste, moroever, has some additional arguments. A lord, she says, must remember the past good service of the wrongdoer. For the poet Chaucer, this means an enumeration of his poetic works up to this time – a transparent enough indication that the practice of poetry is to be equated with one kind of service of the God of Love – and indeed, with the mention of the 'hymns' the poet has composed for Love's holy-days and those works that Chaucer has written to further Love's divine law and to bring ignorant men to serve and praise him with delight, the linguistic register of religious worship reasserts itself:

> The man hath served yow of his kunnynge,
> And furthred wel youre lawe in his makynge.
> Al be hit that he kan nat wel endite,
> Yet hath he maked lewed folk delyte
> To serve yow, in preysinge of your name . . .
> F 412–15/G 398–404

The ensuing list of poems, taking up some twenty lines, is a valuable passage for Chaucerian scholarship in general, but, superficially at least, appears quite unrelated to the narrative process in the *Legend of Good Women*. It is priceless testimony that along with the *Parliament of Fowls* Chaucer claimed authorship of the *Book of the Duchess* and the *House of Fame* (F 417–19/G 405–7), works which are not so attested in any manuscript. It is useful in the matter of dating the prose translation of Boethius, the *Knight's Tale* and *Second Nun's Tale* (F 420, 425–6/ G 409, 413, 416). There appears to be an updating of the list in the

---

[20] See Copeland, *Rhetoric, Hermeneutics, and Translation*, pp. 187, 193, 199.
[21] Ibid., p. 188.

G version (G 414–15), which includes a translation of Pope Innocent's *Of the Wreched Engendrynge of Mankynde*, now lost, but usually thought to be the Latin prose treatise by Innocent III, *De Contemptu Mundi sive De Miseria Conditionis Humanae*, material from which seems to have been used in the *Man of Law's Prologue and Tale*. Since it is likely that Chaucer was working on this material about 1390, this offers more evidence of a minor type that the G version is a later revision of F. And insofar as the poet has seen fit to make a register of the body of his work as a whole, it bears witness to Chaucer's own acknowledgement of the evidential value of such a corpus, and aligns him with other fourteenth-century poets; like Machaut or Gower who organised and supervised the manuscripts containing their respective 'Complete Works', or like Froissart who, in *Le Joli Buisson de Jonece* 443–52, made a list of his poems like Chaucer's. Most significant of all, the Prologue's list of the poet's other works associates it with the *accessus* to the curricular authors, the list of works occurring frequently as a subgenre of the *vita auctoris*, especially that of Ovid. It has been considered another claim to *auctoritas* on behalf of the vernacular writer.[22]

The inclusion of the religious and philosophical works underlines Chaucer's desire to state his contribution to the intellectual life of society as a whole,[23] although he points out with humour – 'and, for to speke of *other holynesse*' (or in G 412, 'besynesse') – that such works do not fit neatly the fiction of service to the God of Love. No such difficulty attaches to the many balades, roundels and virelayes (F 423/G 411), a totally clichéd collocation in both French and English, which refers to the kind of collection of lyrics that any young man of gentle birth would have felt his mandatory service to the ladies and the God of Love. The observation that the few lyrics of Chaucer's that remain today do not accord well with the description in the *Legend*, either in form or content, is in a sense immaterial, for it is very probable that Chaucer's earliest youthful experiments with poetry would have taken

---

[22] Ibid., pp. 194–5.
[23] According to Green, all the historical evidence points to the fact that works of instruction were far more highly valued in the courts of the late Middle Ages than the works that we are pleased to call 'courtly literature', *Poets and Princepleasers*, pp. 135 ff.

the approved form of balades, roundels and virelayes, and those more than likely in French.[24]

Yet one may be excused for a sense of confusion. While the works cited here do not slight women in the same way that the God of Love has asserted that *Troilus and Criseyde* does, and contemporary opinion believed that the *Roman de la Rose* did, nevertheless several passages in these earlier poems treated the God of Love himself with scorn. I have already mentioned how the opening of the *Parliament of Fowls* derides Love as a tyrant who rewards his servants with 'crewel yre'; moreover, the description of his companions in the body of the poem is less than flattering. And if we assume that the *Knight's Tale* is identical with *Palamon and Arcite* (F 420/G 408), then we might have expected the God of Love to have objected to Theseus' meditation on the plight of the two lovers in lines 1785 ff.: 'Now looketh, is nat that an heigh folye?/ Who may been a fool, but if he love?' and so on. Clearly, Chaucer's slights against the God of Love are not the point at issue, nor the real reason behind this elaborate fiction of 'heresy'. There is an additional couplet, moreover, in the G version of Alceste's speech, which emphasises yet again that the audience is expected to recognise the traditional dichotomy of attitude between the young who serve the God of Love with enthusiasm, and the old who criticise the folly of love-service: 'Whil he was yong, he kepte youre estat;/ I not wher he be now a renegat' (G 400–1). It is a totally inadequate explanation of *Troilus and Criseyde*, of course. We, as Chaucer's audience, however, should be wary of the trap now being set in the *Legend of Good Women*, as far as 'good women' are concerned.

The scene concludes with the God of Love graciously and readily – his amenability is surprising if he were really a tyrant – acceding to Alceste's request to forgive the poet who will perform the appropriate penance (F 442 ff./G 432 ff.). The concluding of this narrative motif makes possible the resolution of the motif of the poet's recognition of the daisy/Alceste figure, as I discussed in earlier chapters. The literary tyranny against which Alceste argues is never precisely theorised, although the general

---

[24] See R. H. Robbins, 'Geoffroi Chaucier, Poète Français, Father of English Poetry', *ChauR* 13 (1978): 93–115.

tenor is clear enough. It is a plea perhaps for a feminine bias in storytelling rather than a masculine, or for literary works to be given a sympathetic and engaged hearing rather than to have harshly inflexible literary judgement imposed upon them, but may be no more than the major example in the Prologue's series of oppositional patterns (the little birds' resistance of the cruel fowler would be another, one which also includes a humorous reference to mercy overcoming judgement), dialogues which stimulate debate and lead finally to the 'acord' of love (F 168).

The scene's paradoxes are not limited to the irony surrounding the status of the God of Love. Alceste, for example, requests in two places that the poem's author be allowed to speak ('Ye moten herken yf he can replye/ Agayns al this . . .' [F 343 f./G 319 f.]; 'yt is no maistrye for a lord/ To dampne a man without answere of word' [F 400 f./G 386 f.]), but when Chaucer attempts to speak in his own defence, Alceste stops him abruptly and apparently comprehensively (F 475–7/G 465–7). Alceste may recommend rational clemency in a spirit both of gentleness and of learning, but she is no more percipient a reader than the God of Love himself, and in fact agrees with him at every point. In my opinion any attempt to make her a model of some particularly feminine mode of reading raises as many problems as it solves.

But the *modus loquendi* of Alceste's speech is enormously significant. In sum, in the scene where Chaucer is arraigned before the God of Love at least three important arguments have been put forward. They are arguments that have proceeded by very indirect means, hidden behind a medieval literary commonplace in which a 'translator' disclaims responsibility for what he writes. These arguments can often only be reconstructed by asserting that the opposite position from that taken by Alceste is the true one, and must be derived from an understanding of the broader context. Chaucer first aligns himself with the search for status of the other court poets and musicians of the late fourteenth century who had pretensions to learning and fine feeling, in opposition to the mere entertainers, the 'jongleurs' and the 'taboureurs', deceitful and malicious flatterers whose only aim was remuneration.[25] In the

---

25 I would not wish to deny, however, that Alceste's demand that a king have compassion on poor folk, and so on, may cloak the poet's hope for some kind of monetary reward. Cf. also F 492 ff./G 482 ff.

second place, he presents himself as *grand translateur*, who by means of his talent, skill and effort has translated into English the treasures of the past and of a foreign culture. Thirdly, both the stance of an adviser to princes and the recording of the poet's whole literary corpus underline a rudimentary self-consciousness that the avocation of poetry had some kind of social worth, if only in the sense that the poet's product validated the system of courtly culture, conceived in the widest possible sense. I say 'rudimentary', because while it is likely that poems like the *Legend of Good Women* and *Confessio Amantis* brought some lustre to the court of Richard II and Anne of Bohemia, there is no other evidence that men of literature were valued for their propaganda value in England at this time. The situation was different on the continent, and would soon change in England.[26] Hoccleve and Lydgate often wrote as overt 'court apologists' in a way Chaucer never did. It cannot be proved that Chaucer received any particular favour because he was a poet.

Many of the phrases which are used in Chaucer's defence are replicated in the later *querelle de la Rose*, further indication that the accusation scene signals to the audience, or some of them, notice that the same issues are at stake as the ones which arose during debates on the *Roman de la Rose*. For example, as in the *querelle*, it is suggested that the problem is not one of theme but treatment – to say that the *Rose* is about a 'Foolish Lover' or that *Troilus and Criseyde* is about a faithless woman is to say very little. In the passages of antifeminist tenor in the *Rose*, Jean de Meun asserts that no blame should belong to him as he is only translating what others have said before. The defenders in the *querelle* repeat this admittedly rather specious argument, as does Alceste in her defence of Chaucer in the *Legend*. As in the *querelle* the poet's intention is debated, and Chaucer asserts strongly that whatever his 'auctor' meant, it was *his* virtuous intention to 'forthren trouthe in love and yt cheryce'. And, as it is stated over and over again by the defenders of the *Rose* that Meun simply desired that the vices he portrayed be shunned and the virtues pursued, so Chaucer says that his intention in writing 'of Criseyde . . . or of the Rose' was that people 'ben war fro falsnesse and fro vice/ By swich ensample'. Just as a defender of the *Rose* believes that criticism of Jean de Meun can only be the result of envy

---

[26] Green, *Poets and Princepleasers*, pp. 172–3, 179–82.

for, 'no genius escapes such barking dogs or the bites of enviers',[27] so Alceste suggests that in this matter the God of Love should beware of the likelihood of envious detractors in his court. Finally, in Chaucer's self-dramatisation of himself as an ordinary man compelled by his liege lord to espouse a cause he perhaps would not have chosen freely, there is a probable allusion to the well-known medieval critical dictum, having its roots in classical theory of literary decorum, that a character must be understood as speaking in accordance with his own nature, biases and situation.

There is a sense, then, in which the question of the infamy of women, or their virtue, is only a side issue, or a representative issue, while the main end in the *Legend* is the further exploration of the techniques and responsibilities of 'poetic feigning'. Not that the woman question was not a topic perennially attractive, and the genre of the palinode which Chaucer is about to introduce connected with it from earliest times. Chaucer stands condemned in the court of Love as a translator into English of material which dishonours women. I will be suggesting that this posture parallels a certain disrespect for the classical authors, encapsulated in the G Prologue by the cheerful and cheeky announcement by the poet that his audience may have trouble believing the 'autoritees' he is about to translate (F 97–102/G 81–8). In the *Legend of Good Women* Chaucer dramatises the ability of the vernacular poet to impose his will on ancient stories in a humorous and even carnivalesque mode. In the *Legend* the ladies of classical story, often queens of their own domains, self-sufficient and wealthy, fall ready prey to the wiles and persuasive speech of the prisoner in the dungeon or the ship-wrecked mariner – the confrère, apparently, of the humble English translator of these same classical stories. The potency, the virility, of the seducer or rapist, it will be seen, informs the linguistic and metaphoric structure of the Legends. The simple charge of antifeminism which makes up the God of Love's charge in the G version does not make the parallel so clear as does the more allusive account of the F Prologue, where the wording of the God of Love's accusation against Chaucer that he has *said* of Criseyde 'as [hym] lyste' (F 332) is matched in the Legends

---

27 Hicks, *Débat sur le Roman*, p. 44; cf. pp. 10, 109; Baird and Kane, *Querelle de la Rose*, pp. 154, 57, 112.

by the narrator's oft-repeated comment that the villain of each story has *done* with his victim 'what so that hym leste' (for example, *LGW* 2469). The challenge offered to the prestige of Latinate literary culture by the vigour of emerging vernacularity is not, however, without some accompanying anxiety which finds expression in the exaggerated abuse, but barely concealed enjoyment, of the exploits of the villains which inhabit the *Legend.* An intriguing and unsourced passage in the *Legend of Hypsipyle* (1524 ff.) shows Hercules furthering Jason's seduction of Hypsipyle by disguising the hero's intentions under the fiction of his shyness and unwillingness to pursue his own cause, a patent untruth. Alceste's defence of Chaucer as a passive and simpleminded scribe enacts a similar strategy, as transparent to Chaucer's worldly wise audience (cf. 1554–6) as was the feigning of the *Legend*'s villains.

This brings to an end for the time being my discussion of the Prologue to the *Legend of Good Women*, in which the poet presents himself as the humble literary servant of women, a worshipper of the transcendendent marguerite, but also as one condemned, paradoxically, for the literary traduction of women's reputation. He must make amends with a retraction in kind. Before I turn to the stories that comprise Chaucer's 'legendary' written in recompense for his earlier 'sin', I wish to take some time to consider the late medieval vogue for the genre of the literary retraction. As the tonality of the Legends is so problematic, perhaps for audiences of the period, certainly for our own time, it is important to appreciate the climate of anticipation which the promise of a palinode would have generated in its audience. I will be suggesting that its association with poetic virtuosity and skill in pleading a case, along with an element of gender-biased humour, are likely to have predisposed its audience to viewing the virtue of the heroines of this palinodal project with a degree of scepticism that the Prologue to the *Legend* will have already fostered.

PART III

The Palinode

8

The Palinode

The palinode is defined as a poem in which the poet retracts something said in an earlier poem (the derivation of the Greek word παλινωδια 'recantation', from παλιν 'back again' or 'over again', and ωδη 'song', shows its origin in a literary or rhetorical game). The theme commonly treated in a palinode was the slander or praise of Woman, or Love, and in this topic it had its origin, if the Greeks are to be believed. *OED* says a palinode (under the obsolete form 'palinody') is 'a name first given to an ode by Stesichorus, in which he recants his attack upon Helen', and cites Puttenham's *Arte of English Poesie* (1589): 'So did the Poet Stesichorus . . . in his Pallinodie vpon the disprayse of Helena, and recouered his eye sight.' That the ancients clearly recognised that the topos of the 'dispraise of women' only very partially conveyed truth is demonstrated in this story by the punishment of blindness inflicted on the poets who indulged in it, and the restoration of sight when the poets recanted.[1]

The *Legend of Good Women* conforms neatly to the palinode form. It is frequently surmised that Chaucer decided to write the *Legend* because *Troilus and Criseyde* had offended the women at court. This is most unlikely. Many medieval writers wrote apologies to women, but the stories which tell how they were upbraided by women and forced to recant are probably myths. Brantôme's account of seeing a tapestry which described Jean de Meun's contretemps with the women of the court is certainly apocryphal. Brantôme says that his own *Les Dames Galantes* was intended to give the lie to Jean's implication in the *Roman* that all women were harlots at heart. Because of the feminine anger this

---

[1] Both Stesichorus and Homer are said to have received this punishment.

aroused, the story goes, Jean was stripped naked, but avoided a beating by inviting the lady who was the greatest whore to strike the first blow.[2] Whether authentic or not, the story hardly redounds to the honour of feminine virtue.

The great stir caused in the 1420s by Alain Chartier's *La Belle Dame sans Mercy*, a work which, as Piaget says, had no great originality in theme,[3] was undeniably manufactured by a certain Pierre de Nesson for whom the anger of the ladies of the court was only a front, a practical joke organised by a rival poet.[4] In *La Belle Dame* Chartier had described how he overheard the laments of a man about to die because a lady had cruelly rejected his suit. A letter then appeared demanding that Chartier come to court to have his case examined which was signed by ladies whose love-lives were 'scandalous even by the standards of the corrupt and cynical court of the king of Bourges',[5] demonstrating how spurious the concern for female virtue was in actuality. Chartier duly composed an *Excusation de Dames*,[6] which displays many of the conventions typical of the literary retraction: the God of Love appears to the poet and accuses him of writing a work against love and women. Chartier claims he has never defamed women's virtue or honour and protests that it is unfair to blame him for simply reporting another's words. The ladies, however, did not find the *Excusation* an acceptable recompense for Chartier's original slur on women's reputation for pity. A *Response des Dames* then followed which treated Chartier even more harshly and threatened him with death if he did not seek pardon and amend his book. Poems for and against the lady without mercy, of varying wit and originality of point of view and narrative situation, continued to appear throughout the fifteenth century. They make fascinating reading. The element of debate is paramount, each new poem answering point by point the contentions of the previous poem. All the while, according to this elaborate game, that Alain Chartier was supposed to be banned

---

[2] The story is cited in Green, '*Familia Regis*', p. 97.

[3] A. Piaget, 'La *Belle Dame sans Merci* et ses Imitations', *Romania* 30 (1901), p. 26. Piaget pursues this group of poems in a series of articles with the same title: *Romania* 30 (1901): 22–48, 317–51; 31 (1902): 315–49; 33 (1904): 179–208; 34 (1905): 375–428.

[4] See Green, '*Familia Regis*', p. 100.

[5] Ibid., pp. 100–1. Cf. Poirion, *Poète et Prince*, p. 47.

[6] See E. J. Hoffman, *Alain Chartier: his Work and Reputation* (New York: Wittes, 1942), pp. 61–2.

from the court, history shows that this secretary of the king and archdeacon of Paris was pursuing his normal important diplomatic duties.[7] Indeed Piaget, as a patriotic Frenchman, was thoroughly dismayed at such frivolous *préoccupations poétiques des courtisans*, who were devoting so much attention to *cette querelle ridicule*, at a time when France was in such a parlous state.[8]

In his *Dialogue with a Friend*,[9] another late medieval palinode, Hoccleve gives as a reason for writing the long tale of Jereslaus' wife (a good woman) the need to make amends to the ladies, in writing, for speaking ill of them in his *Letter of Cupid*. This appeal to the wrath of the ladies seems a patent and probably humorous excuse for the new work, for the *Letter of Cupid* had appeared many years previously and was a translation of one of the most avowedly feminist works of the Middle Ages, Christine de Pizan's *Epistre au Dieu d'Amours*. The *Letter of Cupid* 148–54 does indeed quote many of the traditional antifeminist dicta of the Middle Age, but only so they can be refuted, and their male and clerkly bias pointed out. This is typical of the feminist side of the debate, and women may have been justifiably irritated that, in this 'game', the male side of the argument never missed out on a hearing, no matter which side was ostensibly espoused. The introductory passage to the Tale section of Hoccleve's poem shows the strong literary influence of Chaucer: the Wife of Bath is given as the authority for the view that women do not like being slandered (694 ff.); it is stated that, although holy writ testifies that men should have domination over women, yet it is the reverse in 'probacioun' (729 ff.); and, like Jean de Meun, Jean Le Fèvre, Chaucer and Alain Chartier, Hoccleve says he was not responsible for the bad things said against women, he was only a 'reportour/ Of folkes tales, and that they seide I wroot:/ I nat affermed it on hem, god woot!' (761–3). Hoccleve adds that women are so powerful that there is no point in trying to resist. His friend points out that not only will the new work please women but also Hoccleve's lord, Duke

---

[7] Piaget, '*Belle Dame*', pp. 36–7.

[8] Ibid., pp. 23, 35. The purely literary nature of such debates is confirmed by Piaget's citation (ibid., pp. 35–6) of another quarrel similar in nature: Pierre de Nesson also composed a *Lai de Guerre* which is an explicit answer to Chartier's *Lai de Paix*.

[9] F. J. Furnivall, ed., *Hoccleve's Works: I, The Minor Poems* (London: EETS ES 61, 1892), pp. 133–9.

Humfrey of Gloucester, who will probably show it to the ladies with whom it is his 'desport and mirthe' to have honest 'daliaunce' (703 ff.). This would seem striking confirmation of Green's suggestion that the *querelle des femmes*, while paying lip-service to the honour of women, was ultimately a source of male literary enjoyment.[10] That is, it was Humfrey, rather than the ladies, who was interested in Hoccleve's recantation.

If the ladies at the court of Richard II really complained about *Troilus and Criseyde*, it is because they knew what was expected of them. For it is essential to realise that the palinode is above all a rhetorical ploy. It displays the writer's skill and wit to advantage, but tells us nothing about his genuine opinions on the subject. Recent accounts of such extreme palinodal forms as the 'arts of love' emphasise that the juxtaposition of opposing literary strategies exposes the nature of fiction itself.[11] Chaucer's palinode in the *Legend*, moreover, conforms to conventions so ancient as to be mentioned by Socrates in *Phaedrus*, to which, therefore, it is worthwhile devoting some attention.

The main topic which Socrates addresses in *Phaedrus* is rhetoric, and the proper service which rhetoric owes to truth. Socrates admits, however, that most practitioners of the art believe that skill in persuasive speech is everything, and the ultimate end of little importance. The dialogue begins with Socrates' own involvement in just such a rhetorical competition, when he caps a famous orator's speech condemning love with his own extempore, but brilliantly argued, speech on the same subject. In the full flight of his eloquence he suddenly stops, con-science-struck, 'as if I had committed some sin against deity . . . But now I have seen my error.' Love is the son of Aphrodite and a god, Socrates says, and thus can be sinned against. Recalling Stesichorus' and Homer's ancient sin in defaming Helen of Troy, he vows that he will make a similar purification and recantation (παλινωδια). Socrates then proceeds to speak on behalf of love as enthusiastically as he had denounced it previously. The three discourses on love thus stand witness to the ability of rhetoric to espouse any position, to lie or speak truth with equal effect. Only after this sparkling rhetorical display, and

[10] Green, '*Familia Regis*', passim.
[11] See P. L. Allen, '*Ars Amandi, Ars Legendi*: Love Poetry and Literary Theory in Ovid, Andreas Capellanus, and Jean de Meun', *Exemplaria* I (1989): 181–206.

Socrates elsewhere in the dialogue acknowledges the sportiveness of the convention, does the philosopher turn to analyse the nature of love and the true use of rhetorical and dialectical skill.[12]

It is not necessary to assert that Chaucer knew this dialogue of Plato's to see how well-marked the convention was from early times. There is the *sin* of writing ill of women, the *displeasure* of the god, Love, the *recantation* or palinode performed in atonement. As Winsor points out, there is the usefulness of the convention in displaying the poet's literary skill in juxtaposing divergent points of view and directing his material towards a goal which he had intended from the beginning.[13] I have suggested that Hoccleve used the palinode as an excuse for a new work and it is likely that Chaucer had already something like the *Legend of Good Women* in mind at the end of *Troilus*:

> Bysechyng every lady bright of hewe,
> And every gentil womman, what she be,
> That al be that Criseyde was untrewe,
> That for that gilt she be nat wroth with me.
> Ye may hire gilt in other bokes se;
> And gladlier I wol write, yif yow leste,
> Penelopeës trouthe and good Alceste.
> *TC* V 1772–8

There are many other examples of palinodes which, while not exactly sources of the *Legend*, Chaucer undoubtedly knew and appreciated.

Ovid's *Ars Amatoria* and *Remedia Amoris*[14] afford examples. These were work of Ovid's middle age, published about 1 AD. These were a comic imitation of the versified technical manuals, very much in vogue at the time, which treated such activities as viticulture or bee-keeping. (In the *Ars*, women are considered as a genus of animal whose habits

---

[12] H. N. Fowler, trans., *Plato: Euthyphro, Apology, Crito, Phaedo, Phaedrus* (London: Heinemann, 1917), pp. 461–3. Isocrates and other ancient authorities also looked to Stesichorus as the originator of the palinode form, and said that the gods themselves demanded this poetic apology, see Winsor, 'Study', p. 1.

[13] Ibid., pp. 2–3.

[14] See J. H. Mozley, trans., *Ovid: The Art of Love, and Other Poems*, 2nd edn, (London: Heinemann, 1979), from which all translations of the *Ars* are taken. My discussion of the *Ars* and *Remedia* is influenced by L. P. Wilkinson, *Ovid Surveyed* (Cambridge University Press, 1962), pp. 49–62; and A. S. Hollis, 'The *Ars Amatoria* and *Remedia Amoris*', in J. W. Binns, ed., *Ovid* (London: Routledge, 1973), pp. 84–115.

and habitat must be understood if they are to be caught, or farmed; thus the favourable seasons for the hunt, and so on, must be examined.) Its audacious humour derives from elevating the trivial occupation of finding a mistress – Ovid is adamant that he speaks neither to nor about honest matrons – to the status of a utilitarian skill gained with some arduousness at the feet of a master. The didactic manual was a pompous and pedantic genre, given to scholarly display, poetic circumlocutions, and mythological digressions. Ovid burlesques the various characteristics of the type, but the technique most relevant to the current purpose is his skill at drawing exemplary material from mythology. With a lively imagination Ovid enjoys entering into the thoughts and feelings of the great tragic heroines in their unlikely predicaments, often treating them as simple every-day Roman *puellae*, unfortunately deprived of having studied under Ovid, the master himself. Here, as elsewhere, Ovid treats women cynically, but not unsympathetically.

Not unnaturally, Books I and II of the *Ars* treat the pursuit of love from the point of view of men. Book III, however, is a palinode purporting to take the side of women and its opening lines parallel Chaucer's attitude towards the heroines at many points, ending with an allusion to Stesichorus' palinode in praise of Helen of Troy. In the first two books of the *Ars*, Ovid had twitted Roman sensibilities by equating love with the serious duties of military service; in his palinode the theme of warfare is resumed. The easy victories of men, trained by Ovid, lack honour, since the opposing side is defenceless and unskilled. Ovid therefore must arm the Amazons, the protegées of Diana and Cupid (*Ars* III 1–6). The modern term 'war of the sexes' thus describes quite accurately a key theme of the *Ars*, and indeed connotes that aspect of pleasant skirmishing which Ovid has in mind, for the tone of bitter hostility against women which marks so many later antifeminist writers is quite foreign to Ovid's spirit, as it is to Chaucer's. Nevertheless, he pretends to listen to the chauvinist questions of his male readers, 'Some one or other may say to me, "Why do you add gall to serpents, and betray the sheepfold to the mad she-wolf?"' (*Ars* III 7–8). As medieval antifeminists would have heartily concurred with such descriptions of women, so Ovid's remonstrances on behalf of women become part of the stock in trade of the small band of medieval writers who espouse a feminist position: Jean Le Fèvre and Christine de Pizan also ask why, because some were bad, is it fair to blame the whole sex,[15] for, as Ovid says, 'yet Penelope is chaste' and Alceste died in her husband's place (*Ars* III 9–20). Palinodes commonly exploit the deficiencies of the exempla technique as a mode of proof, as will be seen. (In *Remedia* 461, moreover, Ovid suddenly pretends to be weary of his lists of examples – 'Why do I waste time on cases whose number wearies me?' – a stance Chaucer was also to adopt in the *Legend*.) Ovid's argument that women do not often hurt men by wielding flames or savage bows, nor are men so often deceived by women as the reverse (*Ars* III 29–31), may also be read in Christine's *Dieu d'Amours* 645–51.

But Ovid's attitude to the famous seducers of mythology, perfidious Jason, Theseus, Demophoon, Aeneas, has an edge that Chaucer clearly recognises. As Chaucer's good women are 'innocent', 'sely', too liable to pity and trust in the promises of men, so Ovid describes the ancient heroines, in the light-hearted context of his palinode, as simply lacking in skill (*Ars* III 41–2). His presentation of a Medea pregnant and displaced by another in Jason's affections, Phyllis running up the hill *only* nine times to see if Demophoon was returning,[16] while purporting to sympathise with women, does not show the ladies at their heroic and tragic best. Ariadne and Dido, he says, simply did not know how to keep their men (*Ars* III 33–43). This opening passage of *Ars* III suggests other common components of the palinode. There is, for example, the obligatory command of a deity – here Venus defending her own and demanding a new poem which will right the wrongs perpetrated in Ovid's two earlier books (*Ars* III 43 ff.). There are other examples of special pleading and visible partiality – as Virtue is herself female, Ovid says, it is 'no wonder if she please her own folk' (*Ars* III 23–4). Several times in the course of his project of writing Legends to champion the female sex Chaucer will allude humorously to his difficulties in overcoming the inevitable chauvinistic bias involved in being a man. The mock horror that Chaucer expresses in *Phyllis* towards Theseus' and Demophon's persistent and hereditary deceitfulness also reflects Ovid's amused tolerance of men's natural tendency to be oath-breaking villains:

---

[15] Cf. Christine de Pizan, *Dieu d'Amours* 193–200.

[16] The implication is that Phyllis foolishly killed herself too soon, for Demophoon was unavoidably delayed – more clearly stated in *Remedia* 55–6.

There are, too, certain villains of ill fame unquestionable; but thousands are guilty of deserting their sweethearts. Learn from the complaints of another to fear this prospect for yourselves; nor let your door be open to a false lover. Ye maids of Athens, believe not Theseus' oaths: the gods he will call to witness, he has called upon before, and thou too, Demophoon, heir of Theseus' reproach, art no longer trusted since thou didst play Phyllis false. *Ars* III 453–60

There is also something of Chaucer's conclusion to *Phyllis*, where, after warning women that all men are treacherous, he adds, 'And trusteth, as in love, no man but me' (*LGW* 2561), in Ovid's advice (in a similar context), that poets are more fitted than other men to love, and alone may be trusted (see *Ars* III 533–4, 539–40).

The *Remedia Amoris* formed a kind of double palinode with the *Ars*. But here again Ovid is inventive. It is not love itself that is recanted, although Ovid knows Cupid is worrying about his title (*Remedia* 1–2), and suspects his poet of some crime or betrayal (*Remedia* 3–4). Ovid placates Cupid by informing him that he does not write for happy lovers, like himself (*Remedia* 13–14), nor would he wish to unwrite his earlier books teaching how to love (*Remedia* 11–12), he only desires that the unhappy in love need not perish (*Remedia* 15 ff.). As Nicander had written a treatise on poisonous reptiles and then another about antidotes,[17] so Ovid writes a poem describing cures for the wounds that love causes. Thus the *Remedia* is not simply a palinode, but a burlesque of 'antidote' poems. The rhetorical ingenuity required to re-use the old precepts in yet new ways is at a premium, and, as L.P. Wilkinson observes, 'the poet is at least as much intent on amusing the reader as on curing the unhappy lover'.[18] In the *Remedia*, the tragic heroines receive attention similar to that in Book III of the *Ars*. Ovid now claims that the mythological horror stories would simply not have occurred at all if the participants could have taken his advice. Poor silly Phyllis would have lived, Dido would not have died, Medea would not have killed her children, Tereus would not have been a rapist, Troy would not have fallen because Paris would not have abducted Helen, Scylla would not have betrayed her father and country for love of Minos (*Remedia* 55–68). At several other points in the *Remedia* Ovid offers unusual

---

[17] See Hollis, *Ars*, p. 110. [18] Wilkinson, *Ovid*, p. 58.

The Palinode

slants on the familiar stories of the heroines. Phyllis is cited at length as an example of the fatal results of loneliness (*Remedia* 591–608). If Ariadne had been poor, Ovid writes in *Remedia* 745–6, she would have loved more wisely. (Several of Chaucer's men in the *Legend* are clearly attracted by their ladies' wealth.) Tereus' infatuation with his sister-in-law Procne is presented as a case in point demonstrating how it is safer to keep two women on a string than to be enthralled with one (*Remedia* 459–60). There is a clear precedent for Chaucer not to view pathos as the only possible response to these traditional stories.

It is easy to see how Chaucer may have found in the *Ars* and the *Remedia* a model displaying the rhetorical possibilities and entertainment value inherent in the palinode genre; moreover, Ovid's texts suggest specific strategies which could be adopted in a not wholly serious treatment of women. An example closer to home lay in Machaut's two *Jugement* poems. The enormously popular *Jugement dou Roy de Behaingne* was written in the 1330s, *Le Jugement dou Roy de Navarre contre le Jugement dou Roy de Behaingne* not until about 1350. That the latter was meant to be read in relation to the earlier is evident from the title, and also from the fact that, when Machaut supervised the manuscripts containing his collected works, he ignored his normal chronological arrangement and had *Navarre* placed next to *Behaingne*. This time lapse should be one reason to adopt with caution the suggestion of Ernest Hœpffner, Machaut's early editor, that *Navarre* was written because of the anger it caused among the ladies, but as is usual with such stories, the evidence for this rests solely on the accusation, made by a lady within the poem, that Machaut had defamed ladies in *Behaingne*.[19]

It is difficult for a modern reader to judge whether *Le Jugement dou Roy de Behaingne*, or *Troilus and Criseyde* for that matter, would at first glance have appeared antifeminist documents requiring recantations, for they do not do so to us. Chaucer's original audience, however, would have come to *Troilus and Criseyde* with preconceptions about the

[19] Hœpffner, *Machaut: Œuvres*, I, p. lxix. See also R. B. Palmer, ed. and trans., *Guillaume de Machaut: The Judgment of the King of Bohemia (Le Jugement dou Roy de Behaingne)* (New York: Garland, 1984) and his *Guillaume de Machaut: The Judgment of the King of Navarre* (New York: Garland, 1988). There is a translation of *Behaingne* and part of *Navarre* in Windeatt, *Chaucer's Dream Poetry*.

heroine's intrinsic unfaithfulness different from those of modern readers. The debate in *Behaingne* concerns who suffers the most, a lady whose lover had died or a knight whose lover was unfaithful. No doubt the arguments adduced to prove that the lady who lost her love through death suffered least – arguments stating that since love is carnal and sinful, and dependent on the presence of the lover's body, the lady will soon forget both her grief and her lover when he is no longer there (see Reason's speech in *Behaingne* 1665–1723) – were mildly shocking, in a humorous way, but it was a fairly traditional topic. William Calin quotes several relevant examples of topics for jeux-partis, for example: 'You have a lady dwelling at Abbeville . . . When you go to see her, would you prefer to find her dead or that she had deceived you with a man of wealth and repented of it?'; 'Suppose you love a young noble woman, which would cause you more sorrow – if she married or if she died?'[20] Nevertheless, once the poet himself indicates the need for a palinode, it is easy enough to see antifeminism in the aforementioned provocative undervaluing of the suffering of the lady who grieves for the death of her beloved, along with such matters as the knight's unkind equation of his unfaithful lady with Fortune and intrinsic changeableness (*Behaingne* 684 ff., 695 ff.). The knight's speech is in fact a condemnation of the essential nature of Woman. Something similar might be detected in *Troilus and Criseyde*, if one were to look for it – Criseyde is associated, for example, with imagery of the moon and, of course, is described explicitly as 'slydynge of corage'.

But there is no explicit antifeminism in *Behaingne*, and indeed all the characters are unfailingly courteous to the grieving lady. The knight wins because he makes the better case; this is only another way of saying that Machaut has devoted much more space, and thus rhetorical display, to the knight's side of the argument. As the accusing lady in *Navarre* implies, it is Machaut, as writer of the poem and manipulator of the arguments, and not the king of Bohemia, as the so-called judge, who is rightly responsible for what has been said. The lady makes several comments on Guillaume as a writer which might be related to the question of Chaucer's conscious 'entente' in writing *Criseyde* and

---

[20] W. Calin, *A Poet at the Fountain* (Lexington: University Press of Kentucky, 1974), p. 40.

the *Rose*; she says she knows that Guillaume is not drunk when he writes, and knows very well whether he is doing well or committing wrongs in his works, for they are written with great effort (865–76). This emphasis on a written poem was evident even within *Le Jugement dou Roy de Behaingne*, where the knight points the king of Bohemia to the account of the debate which had been 'written down more fully above' (*Behaingne* 1595–6), presumably by the narrator/observer/participant/clerk, Guillume de Machaut. Hœpffner points out that in *Navarre* Machaut departs from his usual habit of signing poems with an acronym, and instead gives the narrating voice his own name.[21] Gone is the self-effacing diffidence of the narrator of *Behaingne*, to be replaced by self-confidence and a consciousness that it is his role as poet of courtesy and 'fine amour' that is on trial.

Le Jugement dou Roy de Behaingne is well known to Chaucer scholars; unfortunately, for students of the *Legend of Good Women*, the same may not be said of *Le Jugement dou Roy de Navarre*. Critics have acknowledged the relevance of the opening section of *Navarre* dealing with that part of the poem's narrative situation which is similar to the accusation scene in the *Legend*. But they have ignored the progress of the actual palinode which describes how Machaut loses the case but sticks to his original point of view, becoming more vigorously antifeminist in the process. For there is a sense in which Machaut in *Navarre*, supposedly a retraction of *Behaingne*, slanders ladies far more vigorously than was ever done in the earlier poem. *Navarre* is a lengthy poem of some subtlety, and clearly required an alert audience or readership. The best that can be attempted in my account here is to make some comments on those techniques of Machaut's which have relevance to the *Legend of Good Women*.

The similarities of basic situation between *Navarre* and the *Legend of Good Women* have indeed been noted, most effectively by Robert M. Estrich.[22] The poem begins with a narrator – as in the *Legend* there is little to be gained in dissociating the narrator from the poet – who is deeply affected by melancholy and fear of the plague and the evil of the times. Hearing that the survivors of the plague are again beginning to

---

21 Hœpffner, *Machaut: Œuvres*, I, p. lxix.
22 R. M. Estrich, 'Chaucer's Prologue to the *Legend of Good Women* and Machaut's *Le Jugement dou Roy de Navarre*', *SP* 36 (1939): 20–39.

marry and otherwise enjoy themselves, Machaut also ventures out from his self-imposed 'prison' in order to hunt hares. So engrossed is he that he ignores the greeting of a *dame de grant noblesse*, in much the same way that the grieving lady in *Behaingne* was unaware of the presence of the knight whose lady was faithless. Guillaume is summoned before this lady who accuses him of deliberately slighting her, as he had also deliberately wronged ladies in one of his books. She demands an admission of guilt. Guillaume is astonished and afraid:

> Not for the sake of any misdeed
> That I had committed myself,
> But rather because I feared the gossip-mongers
> Who are at all times harmful,
> Through falseness and envy,
> To the good people who lead decent lives.
> But I was certain that I had done
> No harm in my entire life
> To any lady whomsoever.
> *Navarre* 829–37[23]

It is of course the same excuse made by and on behalf of the Chaucerian persona in the *Legend*. The lady in *Navarre* restates the argument of both sides in *Behaingne*, concluding that Machaut must recant, since he had stated decisively and written in his book that the man whose lady was false suffered more than the lady whose beloved had died. How dare he? She demands that he affirm 'the opposite view, that's the correct one' (1027–38). Guillaume refuses to retract his judgement, but is quite prepared to have the case reheard. He and the lady agree that the King of Navarre (whose virtues in love and arms are effusively praised) would be a worthy judge. Once in the presence of the king, Machaut becomes uncomfortably aware that the lady who accuses him is very much at home there, and that he, a lone male, must defend his case before a formidable court consisting of the powerful lady and her twelve attendants. These are realistically (and somewhat maliciously) portrayed as a group of vigorously articulate noble ladies, and are no less formidable when they are revealed to be a collection of allegorical virtues – Congnoissance, Raisons, Attemprance, Pais, Constance, Foy,

---

[23] Trans. Palmer, as in the succeeding quotations from *Navarre*.

Charité, Honnestez, Prudence, Souffisance, Largesse, Doubtance de Meffaire.

Guillaume and the ladies take turns to speak and, while the hapless poet doggedly holds to his original position, the ladies all agree that Guillaume is wrong and that death is the supreme sorrow. Every argument adduced is carefully weighed by the other speakers and extensive use of supporting exempla is made by each side; the ladies favour 'olde appreved stories', like those of Dido, Medea, Ariadne, Thisbe and Hero, while Guillaume likes to cite contemporary experience. The grounds of the debate tend to shift in the course of the argument. At the beginning there is a new examination into which of the two protagonists of *Behaingne* suffered the most, but before long it is clear that the real point at issue is the relative merits of the male and female sexes. The disputants argue about whether men or women suffer the most, then which are capable of most suffering, and thence which sex is capable of most love or most loyalty. Guillaume delights to point out when a lady has wandered from the point or when the exemplum she has told supports his case better. The ladies, moreover, fall into a rather specious trap when they move from arguing that death is the greatest sorrow (a tenet which would have wide acceptance) to putting forward as examples of supreme love the rather questionable suicides of some of the ancient heroines, who are portrayed as having crossed the dividing line of *mesure* in love. Even some of the other ladies believe that women like Dido loved foolishly and out of measure. *Le Jugement dou Roy de Navarre*, in sum, is a veritable Bible on how the case for and against such a topic might be argued.

Advised by Mesure and Raison, the judge finally finds Guillaume guilty on three counts. There is the original crime of the judgement made in *Behaingne*; the second is the discourtesy he showed in ignoring the lady and being extremely rude to her attendants in the court case; thirdly, he argued his case badly (the flaws in his reasoning are pointed out minutely). Guillaume repents, Reason reveals that the name of the noble lady is Bonneürté, and Guillaume kneels to receive his sentence from the king. He is to make *trois amendes*, three poems, a lay, a chanson and a balade – and unlike Chaucer's God of Love, the King of Navarre carefully prescribes the metres of each (4173–94). Guillaume confesses his misdeed and, like Chaucer in the *Legend*, vows he will begin his *amoureus lay* without delay, and will make a present of the whole book to his lady, begging for pardon (4195–212). The motifs which *Navarre* has in common with the *Legend of Good Women* are many, motifs such as the literary sin and literary repentance and restitution (commenced without delay), as well as the revelation of the noble lady's name and the poet's intention to present her with his book. In the naming of his own name in 4199–200 (*Je, Guillaumes dessus nommez,/ Qui de Machau sui seurnommez*), together with the review and high valuation put upon his poetic works earlier in the poem (for example, 862 ff.), there is also the self-conscious presentation of himself as poet.

But, because Guillaume's female opponents greatly outnumber him and although he was indeed extremely discourteous, it does not necessarily mean he was wrong, and he never admits this in so many words. The debate dramatises entertainingly the lack of objective validity in the arguments of opponents whose very nature and essential interests are at stake – the ladies speak in the character of the virtues they represent, but Guillaume himself is no more objective. As Calin points out, Guillaume's persona is marked by the vices thought to be character-istic of the male clerk: melancholia, cowardice and antifeminism.[24]

As for the ladies' speeches, the line which their arguments take often undercuts the virtues they represent and the force of the case they are presenting. It is hardly surprising, for example, that Prudence castigates the hero of one of Guillaume's stories for stupidity, because he cut off his ringed finger to send to his lady who wanted her ring back. On the other hand, one does not expect Foy to launch into a learned discussion on the true grounds of faith, and then criticise the *gullibility* of another of Guillaume's heroes who too readily believes that a letter saying his lady is married comes from the lady concerned (Foy does not believe it herself).[25] It is likely that Machaut envisages that his poem will instigate an active partisanship in his male and female listeners, so that even if the male side loses, there are many jokes to be made against the female advocates, in their arguments and interruptions of each other,

[24] Calin, *Poet at the Fountain*, p. 117.
[25] Cf. Calin's remark, 'It is no accident that *Raison* rambles on about meteorological phenomena and the rules of scholastic debate and that *Mesure* praises herself in so unrestrained a manner,' ibid., p. 120.

for example. For good measure there is also a statement of the full male chauvinist position, which, however, Guillaume only presents himself making when finally intolerably provoked by the arguments of the ladies.

Something of Machaut's methods may be indicated by the following summary of a brilliant sequence towards the end of the debate proper when Franchise attempts to prove that women are more loyal in love than men. (The segment affords some insight into the attitudes which Chaucer might have expected his audience to bring to the *Legend of Good Women*.) Franchise begins:

> It has been generally observed
> About true loving in all ages
> That women have done better with it
> And have remained more loyal
> Than men in every way.
> I intend to prove this – and it's right I do so –
> With some exempla that I wish to relate
> Because they are relevant to this argument.
> *Navarre* 2699–706

The examples which Franchise chooses are the betrayal of Ariadne by Theseus and Medea by Jason. The stories are told with very much the same points of emphasis that Chaucer employs in the *Legend*. The women helped the heroes in their hour of need (and incidentally handed over their virginity), and the men in turn swore eternal love, but abandoned their benefactresses for other women when the need was over. Franchise pronounces a humorous curse on faithless men similar to those invoked by Chaucer in the *Legend*:

> Theseus, perjuring himself,
> Swore to her by his gods and law
> That he would never prove false
> And that he would always be faithful to her.
> He lied, the traitor.
> Why wasn't he drowned in the sea?
> *Navarre* 2755–60

In her enthusiasm to convey the intensity of their 'loyalty', Franchise does not neglect to enumerate the traditional list of follies and even crimes into which Medea and Ariadne were led by love. Even worse, she caps her argument about superior female loyalty by describing how each of these betrayed heroines afterwards soon married someone else:

> For Aegeus, the king of Athens,
> Was beguiled by Medea;
> Bacchus honored Ariadne
> Greatly, for he dearly loved her.
> These two married the women
> In their own countries and crowned them.
> *Navarre* 2803–8

This is a strangely happy ending to two tales of supposed woe. Moreover, apart from implying *disloyalty* to their first lovers, little lustre is added to the female cause by recalling Ariadne's marriage to Bacchus (suggesting as it does that Ariadne gave herself over to drunkenness), or by associating Medea's marriage to Aegeus with deception. Franchise's argument about superior feminine loyalty is so severely undermined by these details that her further point that the greater capability for suffering on the part of women proves greater love is correspondingly weakened (2811–18). Guillaume's patience with his feminine adversaries is wearing thin. With scant courtesy, he tells Franchise that her supporting exempla are irrelevant to the issue, that women can behave as badly in love as men, and that in any case exempla can always be found to 'prove' any position:

> Damsel, the treason
> Of either Theseus or Jason
> Has nothing to do with the issue we're arguing,
> And this is hardly the first,
> Nor will it be the last betrayal
> To be discovered among lovers,
> Both women and men.
> I wouldn't give two apples
> For proving your point
> By the introduction of exempla such as these.
> For if I intended to argue my case
> With examples, I could find more than
> Ten, truly more than twenty of them.
> *Navarre* 2823–35

It is well to realise that not all the audience of the *Legend of Good*

Women would have been naive enough to regard the extensive citing of exempla as valid proof, although Machaut is here dramatising the tendency to do so. Guillaume proceeds to call up examples of his own – the lover of the Chateleinne de Vergi, and Lancelot and Tristan suffered far more than women ever could, he says. He adds the story in which the man, whose lady wants her ring back, sends her the ring attached to his finger, which he has cut off because he had promised her he would never remove the ring. Prudence then points out the foolishness inherent in the behaviour of these lovers, and adds the intersting point that Lancelot and Tristan at least earned glory, honour and riches from their travails (and nothing worthwhile can be gained without suffering), while their ladies had only the suffering and the slander (2977–86). Guillaume is finally so incensed that the thin veneer of courtesy towards ladies falls away, and after accusing Franchise again of wandering from the point, he launches into a lengthy and gratuitously antifeminist diatribe of some seventy lines. Since the heart of woman contains nothing strong, nothing sure, nothing stable, he says, it is impossible that she could suffer for long any great joy or torment and she certainly forgets easily what she does not see. But:

> In contrast, a man's heart is firm, secure,
> Wise, experienced and mature,
> Virtuous and strong enough to endure,
> But humble in suffering adversity.
> *Navarre* 3047–50

He asserts that *everyone* says these things and approves of what Guillaume said in his earlier poem. Largesse and Doubtance de Meffaire are scandalised at the poet's evil speech against women, and remonstrate with him, pointing out, incidentally, that *everyone* does not think like him, a clerk. Guillaume is somewhat aggrieved that he should be punished simply because he speaks the truth. Finally the ladies are all muttering. Guillaume sarcastically suggests to the judge that the whole case might be expedited if the ladies be permitted to put their case in unison. As the women all speak at once even the judge is smiling, and order is only reimposed with difficulty.

   This narrative sequence is a brief pointer to the skill and verve with which Machaut exposes the weaknesses of the opposing sides. It is likely that his audience delighted in the unexpected turns which the familiar topic gave rise to in the procedure of the debate. It is a poem which must have provoked much further discussion among its listeners, and behind the ostensible subject there are several other points at issue. On reflection one realises, for example, that it is courtesy itself that is under trial as much as the relative merits of men and women. Machaut is tried and sentenced for discourtesy, as much as for being wrong. There is also a sense in which the concept of always praising ladies is being tested.[26] The whole debate appears to result from the pretended feminine pique which Bonneürté feels towards Machaut because he is inadvertently discourteous to her; at the very least, it is an excuse to twit him. (Machaut is actually extremely courteous once he realises she is there.) Like the discourtesy shown to the knight by the lady at the beginning of *Behaingne*, there is nothing malicious nor premeditated in Machaut's not acknowledging her greeting – he is simply preoccupied. Moreover, Machaut is condemned for discourtesy because he dared to argue at all against ladies, although the cause was one he conscientiously believed to be right. The practice of the courteous life and not defaming ladies seems an almost unattainable ideal.

Still further reflection suggests, however, that the real significance of the poem lies in the revelation of the noble lady's name as Bonneürté, which seems to signify that kind of happiness or serenity which is immune to the blows of Fortune (3852 ff.), and was possibly originally a complimentary pun on the name of Bonne of Luxembourg, as I noted earlier. The conflict is essentially between Melancholy and Bonneürté. At the beginning of the poem Guillaume has not really rid himself of the melancholy induced by the plague and its attendant ills when he refuses to acknowledge Bonneürté's greeting. Every reader must observe the very high number of references to laughter and smiling in *Navarre*, as a fact requiring interpretation. Calin remarks on the laughter, but thinks this implies that one cannot be expected to take such a trial seriously.[27] On the contrary, however, all this jollity implies the positive value of the general good humour which marks such a debate. The contrast with the horrors of the plague, and Guillaume's melancholy and fear, and the bright courtly scene where the lively debate takes place

---

[26] Calin makes this point well, ibid., p. 113.   [27] Ibid., pp. 120–1.

is marked indeed. (This is one aspect of the compliment being paid to the King of Navarre, to present him as lord of such a court.) Guillaume's sin lies in not responding readily enough to the *bonneürté* now offered him, of which he (and presumably many of his audience) were bereft during the plague and as they contemplated the other evils of the times.

This perception is interestingly confirmed in Glending Olson's study of the medieval medical view of the recreative value of literature. He documents the belief that the pursuit of cheerfulness was an invaluable aid to health in the face of the inevitable destructive effects of melancholy and anxiety induced in people by such disasters as the Black Death. Standard aids to such medicinal good spirits were music, songs and stories. These went along with the enjoyment of moderate pleasure from dancing, good clothes and conversation with proper persons.[28] Like the story-telling in the *Decameron*, the love-debate in *Le Jugement dou Roy de Navarre* seems to have been independently conceived as a health-giving response to the fear caused by the plague:

> The judge's 'ordenance' (3755), which he arrives at with the help of Raison and Mesure, among others, clearly suggests a mode of secular behaviour meant to be seen as admirable, one that would be a corrective to the moral pestilence that has led to the Black Death. Toward the end of the poem Raison delivers a long panegyric to Bonneürtez, and it entails . . . an affirmation of the validity of well-ordered living, secular or sacred, one that implicitly offers a range of human experience that stands against the irrationality and destructiveness which the introduction portrays.

Properly motivated recreations (*esbanois*), apparently, belong as much to the world of Raison and Mesure as true friendship and learning.[29] Olson notes that the creation of the *cour amoreuse* of Charles VI, often mentioned in these pages as having concerns related to those in the *Legend of Good Women*, also appears to be a therapeutic response to the plague.[30] One might further guess, *pace* Piaget, that the game of alternately slandering and defending women which the controversy about *La Belle Dame sans Mercy* exploits, as does the *Legend*, far from being merely frivolous, may have been seen to have serious recreative value in hard times. Even at the best of times such courtly playfulness

---

[28] Olson, *Literature as Recreation*, p. 172.   [29] Ibid., p. 187.   [30] Ibid., p. 195.

acted as 'an important marker of social identity, declaring the nobility to be, as a class, released from the penance of both labor and prayer' while the linguistic facility and mental nimbleness such poetry required in its composition and appreciation were probably perceived to have utilitarian value in the education of the courtier.[31]

It is clear that *Navarre* provided Chaucer with a dazzling antecedent, a near contemporary example of the palinode genre, in its way as technically inventive as Ovid's *Ars* and *Remedia*. As in those works, it draws attention quite consciously to the poet's skill, and this is as much true of the literary 'sin' which occasioned the present work as the palinode itself. The implication is that only a work which has made some impact requires a palinode,[32] and the palinode itself draws attention to its author's deft manipulation of the narrative voice or voices. *Le Jugement dou Roy de Navarre* would have suggested, if such were necessary, the perennial interest of the traditional topic of the palinode, the 'defence' of women, and offered the challenge of inventing a fresh treatment. Like the narrator of *Navarre*, Chaucer presents himself compelled by some powerful personages to maintain courtesy towards women in the face of all the promptings of male good sense. In *Navarre* Machaut had undermined the women's side by showing them pushing too far the argument that death is the ultimate test of faithfulness. Chaucer goes one step further in the *Legend* by putting this manifest *reductio ad absurdum* into his own male mouth, and likewise draws attention to the other absurdities inherent in the method of 'proof' by exempla. It is time at last to turn, in the chapters of my next section, to the specific strategies which make up Chaucer's contribution to the traditional game of the palinodic praise of women.

[31] Patterson, *Chaucer and the Subject of History*, pp. 53, 55.
[32] See Winsor, 'Study', p. 4.

PART IV

The Legends of good women

9

Ariadne: the ladies and the critics

Chaucer's 'good women', and their stories, have troubled readers of the
Legend of Good Women. The strange fluctuations in tone between
mockery and pathos, the provocative choice of heroine, the sameness of
their stories, the boredom which the poet professes for their tragic
plights, all have left readers unsure of the response demanded of them.
Positivist scholars at the turn of the twentieth century had found the
Legend of Good Women one of Chaucer's most interesting poems. But
once the question of the relationship of the two Prologues was argued
out and the sources of the Legends thoroughly investigated there was
for a time little left to say. It was felt that if one ignored Chaucer's many
'blunders' and lapses of tone in the Legends one could respond to the
'genuine pathos' of the heroines' tragic plights. It was the easy assumption that the *Legend of Good Women* could be taken at face value, that it
combined a 'fresh' delight in nature and daisies with a 'naive' appreciation of the goodness (and hence, suffering) of 'noble womanhood',[1]
which led to the belief that the poem was in the end boring, and that
Chaucer was as bored as his readers. Indeed the notion of Chaucer's
boredom with the *Legend of Good Women* was a convenient fiction
allowing scholars to dismiss a puzzle for which they could provide no
adequate interpretative framework. When in 1908–9 Goddard questioned Chaucer's choice of candidates for the list of exemplary good
women and said that the 'real significance of the poem' was that the
Legend incorporated 'a most unmerciful satire upon women',[2] the small

[1] For a representative early twentieth-century account of the *Legend* which uses phraseology such as this, see R. K. Root, *The Poetry of Chaucer: a Guide to Its Study and
Appreciation*, rev. edn (1921; rpt. Gloucester, Mass.: Smith, 1957), pp. 135–50.
[2] Goddard, *Legend of Good Women* (1908), p. 101.

scholarly community interested in the *Legend* was horrified. Critical orthodoxy pronounced that the heroines of the *Legend* were good and faithful in the only way that mattered to a medieval audience.

The ultimate source of Chaucer's collection of tales about 'Cupid's saints' has always been acknowledged to be Ovid, and particularly his *Heroides*,[3] cited in the G Prologue as the 'epistel of Ovyde/ Of trewe wyves' (G 305–6). The stories of all but one of Chaucer's heroines are found in Ovid, and all but four in the *Heroides*. Yet, while it is true that Chaucer's Legends are pervaded with an Heroidean ethos, nevertheless, direct translation of the letters makes up a quite small proportion of the Chaucerian texts. Ovid's collection of letters from women to their (usually unfaithful) lovers has affinities with the art of rhetorical declamation, of pleading a case, of persuasive presentation of a point of view; in this case Ovid plays the advocate for (and gives a voice to) those minor characters in the stories of the 'heroes' – the ladies they loved and left. Indeed, the *Heroides* in medieval times were often seen as a palinodal response to Ovid's arguably antifeminist *Ars Amatoria*. In the *Heroides* Ovid, like Chaucer, was faced with the problem of variation on a theme, of again and again making something new out of similar and potentially monotonous tales. The *Heroides* were profoundly intertextual, and exploited the audience's knowledge of other literary versions of the stories. This in itself caused difficulties for medieval readers because the narrative aspect of each Heroidean letter was frequently deficient, and one of the functions of the medieval *accessus* or introductions which accompanied Latin texts of the *Heroides* was to supply elements of the story needed to understand Ovid's witty allusions. Chaucer's desire to construct narratives to which a fragment of Heroidean complaint could be attached involved him in extensive compilation of material from different sources.

Many of the problems of interpretation in the Legends, therefore, are bound up with the question of how the Chaucerian text relates to the medieval matrix of Ovidian commentary. As well as providing narrative detail, the various medieval *accessus* to Ovidian texts[4] agreed in stressing

---

3 See G. Showerman, ed. and trans., *Ovid: Heroides and Amores*, 2nd edn (Cambridge, Mass.: Heinemann, 1977).

4 Minnis discusses medieval *accessus* to the Heroides in *Medieval Authorship*, e.g., pp. 55–6, 182–3, 226–7. A number of *accessus* relevant to the *Legend* are quoted in

the moral import inherent in their author's writings, for such works were studied because they pertained to 'Ethics',[5] the study of behaviour. Making use of traditional schema[6] the *accessus* to the *Heroides* again and again pointed out that Ovid's *materia* was good and bad kinds of love; his *intentio* was to commend chaste and lawful love like that of Penelope for her husband Ulysses, and to condemn illicit love like Phaedra's love for her stepson Hippolytus, and infatuated love like that of Phyllis who fell in love with a stranger; the *utilitas* in reading this kind of book lay in drawing attention to such cautionary tales.[7] Each epistle had its own introduction as well, indicating how Ovid's *intentio* in the specific tale contributed to his general moral schema. Thus heroines like Medea and Ariadne are castigated in the introductions to their particular letters. Occasionally the infidelity of the men such as Jason and Theseus was reprehended also, and Hypermnestra was one of the few whom Ovid was thought to have commended for her *pietas et amor legitimus et castus*.[8] After making the choice of heroine for his *Legend of Good Women* Chaucer could not have turned to a Latin text of Ovid without encountering commentary including very severe moral criticism of the ladies' virtue, something insisted upon despite Ovid's advocacy of the women's side of the story. An occasional commentary conceded that part of Ovid's 'intention' was 'to delight and be for the general good'.[9]

I intend now to look in detail at aspects of Chaucer's praise of women in a handful of the Legends. First there is the *Legend of Ariadne*, whose many paradoxes drew attention to it from the earliest years of scholarly

Shaner, 'An Interpretive Study'. Minnis extensively cites Shaner's earlier B.Lit. thesis: M. C. Edwards, 'A Study of Six Characters in Chaucer's *Legend of Good Women* with Reference to Medieval Scholia on Ovid's *Heroides*' (Oxford, 1970).

5 Minnis, *Medieval Authorship*, pp. 25, 56, 182.
6 Exhaustively discussed by Minnis, ibid., pp. 18–28, and passim.
7 See the example from MS Bern, Burgerbibliothek 411, quoted from Edwards in A. J. Minnis, 'John Gower, *Sapiens* in Ethics and Politics', *MÆ* 49 (1980): 207–8. Cf. the *accessus* to the *Heroides* in F. Ghisalberti, 'Medieval Biographies of Ovid', *JWCI* 9 (1946): 11, 44–5; R. B. C. Huygens, *Accessus ad auctores; Bernard d'Utrecht; Conrad d'Hirsau* (Leiden: Brill, 1970), pp. 29–33; R. J. Hexter, *Ovid and Medieval Schooling: Studies in Medieval School Commentaries on Ovid's Ars Amatoria, Epistulae ex Ponto and Epistulae Heroidum* (Munich, 1986), pp. 137–204. See also A. J. Minnis and A. B. Scott, eds., *Medieval Literary Theory and Criticism c.1100–c.1375: the Commentary Tradition* (Oxford: Clarendon, 1988), for translations of three *accessus* to the *Heroides*, pp. 20–22.
8 MS Bern, Burgerbibliothek 512, fo. 74ʳ, quoted in Shaner, 'An Interpretive Study', p. 110.
9 See Minnis, *Medieval Authorship*, p. 55.

interest in the *Legend* – witness the fact that modern editions devote more notes to *Ariadne* than to any other Legend – to demonstrate the nature of the interpretative problems offered by the *Legend*, its humour and its pathos, particularly as they are revealed by the conflicting responses of critics over the years. Next I will use the literary reputation of Medea, a bad woman if ever there was one, to investigate the effect of expurgation on a well-known story and to see how the choice of such a story contributes to the ethos of Chaucer's tale collection as a whole. In a further attempt to weigh Chaucer's intention either of straightforward praise or of satire, I will examine the doubtful credentials for virtue of the Chaucerian Cleopatra, the first of his 'good women'. I then use the *Legend of Dido* to demonstrate the ancient lineage of the topos of the 'matter of Woman', and the place of the classical heroines within it, and draw the inference that the so-called monotony of the Legends of good women should rather be seen as the literary craftsman at work on variations on a theme. I conclude my discussion of *Dido* with some observations on the nature and function of pathos in the Legends, a topic further examined when I turn to the *Legend of Lucrece*. With this Legend, moreover, whose heroine has perhaps the most irreproachable reputation for virtue of all the *Legend*'s heroines, we must face squarely the oversimplified notion that Chaucer approaches the idea of feminine goodness in an ironic mode, but cannot escape the conclusion that even in Lucrece's case the virtue of women is a topic for debate. My discussion of the *Legend of Phyllis*, the second last of the Legends, will suggest that Chaucer the poet identifies himself profoundly but humorously with the 'bad men' of the Legends, the seducers and rapists who impose their will on their passive female victims.

ARIADNE

For some of the Legends (especially *Tisbe* and *Lucrece*) Chaucer draws on an already fully worked out narrative in Ovid, and follows its outline quite closely. Other heroines like Dido and Medea had received extensive literary treatment in the medieval period. With Legends like *Ariadne* the situation is quite different. The story of how Ariadne eloped with Theseus, after helping him kill the Minotaur and escape from the labyrinth, does not appear commonly in medieval vernacular poetry until the fourteenth century (and probably after the appearance of the *Ovide Moralisé*),[10] and Chaucer's Ovidian sources offered little in the way of a well-rounded story. *Heroides* X tells of Ariadne's anguish on finding that Theseus has abandoned her on a deserted island. The Theseus/Ariadne story in Book VIII of Ovid's *Metamorphoses* is but a tiny appendage to the Scylla/Minos story (serving as a transition from the subject of Minos to the subject of Daedalus), and even there Ariadne figures only in a side comment. Many pages in the *Metamorphoses* are devoted to the course of Scylla's unnatural passion for her father's enemy, while all that Ovid says of Theseus and the killing of the Minotaur is:

> There [in the labyrinth constructed by Daedalus] Minos imprisoned the monster, half-bull, half-man, and twice feasted him on Athenian blood; but when . . . a third band of victims was demanded, this brought about the creature's downfall. For thanks to the help of the princess Ariadne, Theseus rewound the thread he had laid, retraced his steps, and found the elusive gateway as none of his predecessors had managed to do. Immediately he set sail for Dia, carrying with him the daughter of Minos; but on the shore of that island he cruelly abandoned his companion. Ariadne, left all alone, was sadly lamenting her fate, when Bacchus put his arms around her, and brought her his aid. He took the crown from her forehead and set it as a constellation in the sky, to bring her eternal glory.[11]

The *Legend of Ariadne* puzzled the older Chaucerian scholars of good classical education because it presented a version of the story known to no ancient text. The Theseus of Chaucer's story eloped not only with Ariadne but also with her sister Phaedra, and deserted the former for the latter. The stories of Theseus' relations with the two Cretan princesses were not linked in this way in classical texts. As source studies progressed, it was shown that medieval glosses and *accessus* to the

---

[10] The *Ovide Moralisé* was a fourteenth-century translation of Ovid's *Metamorphoses* into French poetry. After the translation of each story a 'moralisation' was attached. Many readers like Machaut and Chaucer appear to have appreciated the translation, while ignoring the moralisation. See C. de Boer, ed., *Ovide Moralisé*, 5 vols. (Amsterdam: Verhandelingen der Koninklijke Akademie van Wetenschappen te Amsterdam: Afdeeling Letterkunde, 1915–38).

[11] Mary M. Innes, trans. *The Metamorphoses of Ovid* (Harmondsworth: Penguin, 1955), pp. 183–4.

Heroides, the *Ovide Moralisé*, and other vernacular versions such as the ones in *Le Jugement dou Roy de Navarre* and *Confessio Amantis* recorded the same story.[12] Indeed most of the early part of Theseus' story in *Ariadne* was the same as the one recounted in the *Ovide* and *Navarre*. The establishment of the fact that this was the common medieval version of the story and that Chaucer's 'Ovid' was frequently mediated to him through associated commentaries and vernacular translations was one of the achievements of the early critical work on the *Legend*. No great significance, then, attaches to the fact that Chaucer has Theseus abandon Ariadne for Phaedra.

Notwithstanding this, Chaucer's *Ariadne* story is developed with quite peculiar emphases. Gower, in contrast, tells the traditional medieval version of the story of Theseus, Ariadne and Phaedra quite straightforwardly, with plausible, if trite, motivation. Gower's exemplum in *Confessio Amantis* V 5231–495 sensibly indicates the evil of ingratitude, and it must be stated that the morality of Theseus' behaviour in abandoning Ariadne had a problematic quality even in ancient times. In Chaucer's version, Phaedra is not only more beautiful than Ariadne, but more quick-witted as well. She, and not Ariadne, devises the whole plan to save Theseus, and expounds it in a lengthy speech (1985–2024).[13] It is she who decides that they will make Theseus some 'balles . . . of wex and tow' which he can throw down the monster's throat to 'encombre his teth' (2003–6); it is Phaedra, too, who devises the 'clew of twyn' by means of which Theseus can find his way out of the labyrinth which is 'krinkeled to and fro' (2012–18). In Chaucer's version, for some reason, Phaedra usurps much of Ariadne's role, and when the narrator apostrophises Theseus on the matter of the gratitude owed to any woman who saved him 'from cares colde', it is Phaedra who deserves just as much gratitude as Ariadne, the ostensible heroine, if not more (1952–8). But why? What was Chaucer implying by these strange distortions of the better known versions? It seems clear

[12] The main studies were J. L. Lowes, 'Chaucer and the *Ovide Moralisé*', *PMLA* 33 (1918): 302–25; S. B. Meech, 'Chaucer and the *Ovide Moralisé* – A Further Study', *PMLA* 46 (1931): 182–204; S. B. Meech, 'Chaucer and an Italian Translation of the *Heroides*', *PMLA* 45 (1930): 110–28. For the possible influence of the Italian translation, see also Janet M. Cowen, 'Chaucer's *Legend of Good Women*, Lines 2501–3', *N&Q* n.s. 31 (1984): 298–9.

[13] See Frank, *Chaucer and the 'Legend'*, p. 120.

that he was provoked by the rather unpromising source material available to him to invent a complex and richly parodic *Ariadne* which almost reverses the import of, for example, Gower's simple story of an innocent but deserted Ariadne and a callous and ungrateful Theseus.

Indeed, the 'gratitude' motif, and the concept, so dear to romance, of earning love as a kind of *quid pro quo*, is pushed to its limit in Chaucer's version of the Theseus and Ariadne story.[14] Even allowing for the general medieval respect for rank, there is an inordinate amount of attention paid in *Ariadne* to the desirability of rescuing a 'kinges sone' (1953, 1975, 2055, 2080, 2130; 1979 and 2023 ['lordes sone']), and the material rewards likely to result from such a rescue. Ariadne and Phaedra believe that it is particularly appropriate for them to take pity on a 'kinges sone'; that people surely will not condemn their behaviour since it is 'evere of gentil women . . . the wone/ To save a gentyl man' (2131–2). Good courtly sentiments. Moreover, a 'kinges sone' is a particularly valuable prize, and his value as a marriage partner more than that of the service he offers as a mere page, a hint Theseus is not above planting in the princesses' minds (2054–9). Ariadne takes the hint, moved as much by his youth and good looks, as by his suffering (2074–7). Ariadne's proposal of marriage in return for saving him (2080–93) is quite blatant,[15] and makes rather cruel commentary on the fact that it is the thought of (socially advantageous) marriage which motivates many of the ladies in the *Legend*, and is the promise by which they are most easily seduced (see the stories of Dido, Hypsipyle, Medea, Phyllis). The vow the villainous 'heroes' are so constantly accused of betraying is the promise of a wedding. For this the ladies of the *Legend* will hazard their virginity and their reputation. Several critics have made much of the heroines' interest in marriage as signifying the virtue of their love.[16] But it is not so much love and marriage which is the theme in the *Legend*, as it is the comic presentation of the promise of

---

[14] Ibid., pp. 118–28.

[15] Since at least the time of Goddard critics have been noticing that Ariadne asks to be abducted. Yet, like the presence of Phaedra, this is not totally the invention of Chaucer, and he would have found the barest hint of Ariadne's marriage proposal in the *Ovide Moralisé*.

[16] E.g., D. S. Brewer, 'Love and Marriage in Chaucer's Poetry', *MLR* 49 (1954): 461–4; H. A. Kelly, *Love and Marriage in the Age of Chaucer* (Ithaca: Cornell University Press, 1975), esp. chapter 4; Minnis, *Shorter Poems*, pp. 416–20.

marriage as a cheap and effective bargaining counter for heroes engaged in higher enterprises. For example, the significance of marriage to such as Jason is neatly indexed by the bathetic two-line dismissal of his marriage to Hypsipyle, and joined as in several other places with the despoiling of her wealth:

> The somme is this: that Jason wedded was
> Unto this queen and tok of her substaunce
> What so hym leste unto his purveyaunce;
> And upon hire begat he children two,
> And drogh his sayl, and saw hir nevere mo.
>
> 1559–63

This then is one paradigm in the Chaucerian Legends of the *desertae*: Dido, Hypsipyle, Medea and Phyllis all similarly fall in love with men who are not only 'semely' and smooth-tongued but, above all, of high rank, and who use their gentility to deceive their female victims.

If Ariadne's aggressive wooing makes explicit the kind of bargain which underlies the 'love' between hero and lady, then it is also true that Theseus' vows of lifelong service and undying gratitude may be regarded as invalid because made under duress – from the 'masculine' perspective on the Legends, this is another paradigmatic aspect of the desertion of the heroines. Indeed by means of his powerful analogy with Nysus' daughter Chaucer shows just how insubstantial the obligations of 'gratitude' to a 'good woman' may be. At the beginning of *Ariadne* Chaucer upbraids both Minos (the king of Crete and Ariadne's father) and Theseus for their 'grete untrouthe of love'. He then tells us how the Athenian Theseus came to be a prisoner in Crete, about to be devoured by the Minotaur. The story of the enmity between Crete and Athens includes the story of how Minos besieged the city of Alcathoe and how the city was betrayed to him by Scylla, the daughter of Alcathoe's king, that is, 'Nysus doughter' (1908). As I have noted above, there is the same connection of the Ariadne/Theseus story with the Scylla/Minos story in the *Metamorphoses*. Standing upon the wall of her city, Scylla sees Minos and because of his 'beaute and his chyvalrye' is immediately consumed with love for him, 'so sore that she wende for to dye' (1908–13). Chaucer does not elaborate how she cuts off her father's magic lock of hair, murders him, and hands over the city to Minos, who is horrified at her unnatural crime and spurns her. She throws herself into the sea but the gods turn her into a bird (in Chaucer's words, 'the goddes hadde of hire pite'). This was a well-known story and Scylla received universal condemnation, even from Ovid, for her unnatural passion. Yet Chaucer refers to this same passion as her 'kyndenesse' (1918) and, as has occasionally been noted, makes Scylla into a 'good woman', insofar as, like Ariadne, Dido, Hypsipyle, Medea and Phyllis, she has been repudiated by a man to whom she had shown favour. Chaucer says of Minos with mock-severity:

> But wikkedly he quitte hire kyndenesse,
> And let hire drenche in sorwe and distresse,
> Nere that the goddes hadde of hire pite;
> But that tale were to long as now for me.
> 1918–21

That the concept of ingratitude towards Scylla is not the most appropriate moral of this story should be clear. And in case it is not clear, Chaucer draws an explicit parallel between Nysus' daughter and Ariadne, who similarly betrayed her father, with a preemptive castigation of Theseus' impending 'ingratitude' (1952–8). However, the obligation of gratitude is not always binding, as is very clear in Ovid's account of Scylla and Minos in the *Metamorphoses*. Chaucer draws another parallel between Ariadne and Scylla in the similar words he uses to describe how the gods took pity on them, and his consequent *occupatio* declining to speak further on the matter. With the lines about Scylla (1920–1, quoted above) compare these lines about Ariadne:

> But shortly to the ende I telle shal.
> The goddes han hire holpen for pite,
> And in the signe of Taurus men may se
> The stones of hire corone shyne clere.
> I wol no more speke of this mateere . . .
> 2221–5

The story of Ariadne's crown actually recalls a story which adds no lustre to Ariadne's faithfulness, for it conceals and recalls how she was soon comforted by Bacchus in her grief over Theseus' desertion. The Ariadne story in Machaut's *Jugement dou Roy de Navarre* 2805–6 similarly praises Ariadne for faithfulness while drawing attention to her rapid consolation by Bacchus. Boccaccio, who shows little interest in

Ariadne, takes this episode to mean that she got drunk.[17] In no medieval version I know is the Ariadne/Bacchus story flattering to Ariadne. It is not impossible that the astrological reference to Taurus (otherwise difficult to explain) is a hint about the sexual predilection for bulls common to the female members of Ariadne's family,[18] and Chaucer's *occupatio* in both the Scylla story and Ariadne's is ostentatiously necessary censorship.

The wooing of Theseus and Ariadne in this Legend is still further elaborated, in another of the paradigmatic accounts of how the loves of the good women are conducted. Theseus in *Ariadne* is shown to be a master of the effective techniques of courtly seduction. His immediate response to the unexpected offer of rescue by the daughters of Minos is to vow eternal faithfulness, and he continues to protest at extravagant length throughout his two long speeches that he is no liar or traitor (2029–73, 2103–22). Theseus takes care to use the correct courtly forms from the first moment he is brought before the sisters: 'Adoun sit Theseus upon his kne –/ "The ryghte lady of my lyf," quod he' (2028–9). But the full opportunism of his pose of courtly lover is comically exposed when he caps his protestations of undying love with the announcement that he has loved the unseen Ariadne from afar for seven years (2114–22). Rarely has the medieval maiden been shown to express such relish at the mercenary consequences and enhanced social position of her bargain, as does Ariadne, more than pleased at this last token of Theseus' long-standing faithfulness:

> This lady smyleth at his stedefastnesse,
> And at his hertely wordes and his chere,
> And to hyre sister seyde in this manere,
> Al softely: 'Now, syster myn', quod she,
> 'Now be we duchesses, bothe I and ye,
> And sekered to the regals of Athenes,
> And bothe hereafter likly to ben quenes . . .'
> 2123–9

---

[17] Boccaccio's only mention of the Ariadne story in *De Casibus* says, 'When Theseus returned victorious from Crete and had left Ariadne drunk (*vinolentus*) and asleep on the isle of Naxos, he married Phaedra, whom he originally brought back for his son, Hippolytus', L. B. Hall, trans., *The Fates of Illustrious Men* (New York: Ungar, 1965), p. 21.

[18] Ariadne's grandmother Europa fell in love with a bull who was actually Jupiter, and her mother Pasiphae made love to a real bull, by whom she conceived the Minotaur.

Almost every critic has noted that Ariadne is more than usually gullible here. Indeed the sense that Ariadne and Phaedra fit rather uneasily the model of the innocent medieval heroine is signalled from their first appearance, of which we read (remember Nysus' daughter standing on the wall [1908]):

> they stode on the wal
> And lokeden upon the bryghte mone.
> Hem leste nat to go to bed so sone . . .
> 1971–3

This last off-hand remark leaves the ever so slight impression that these two girls are at a loose end and ripe for amorous adventure. They are more than ready to respond with 'gret pite' to Theseus' 'compleynynge', which they overhear, and to have 'compassioun' on his 'wo' (1971–6). If the audience does not already feel that the behaviour of the two sisters is less than ladylike, then Ariadne will suggest it to them:

> As evere of gentil women is the wone
> To save a gentyl man, emforth hire myght,
> In honest cause, and namely in his ryght.
> Me thynketh no wight oughte us herof blame,
> Ne beren us therfore an evil name.
> 2131–5

Ariadne is rich with such implications, but the early critics ignored most of them unless there was also a puzzling error of fact or self-contradiction. *Ariadne* contains a number of these: for example, the confusion of Minos, king of Crete, and Mynos, judge of the underworld, in the first line of the Legend, and the mistranslation of the details pertaining to the human tribute which the Athenians had to send to Minos. Yet again, Theseus' prison in exile cannot possibly face 'the mayster-strete of Athenes' (his home town), although all but two manuscripts give this reading for line 1966, and it is almost certainly Chaucer's own.[19] The early scholars were interested in this kind of question, which could be dealt with in an apparently objective and properly learned fashion, and could ultimately be attributed to Chaucer's carelessness or limitations in knowledge and available

---

[19] See *Riverside Chaucer*'s notes to *LGW* 1886, 1932, 1933 and 1966.

material. But we must ask if this is all that may be gleaned from *Ariadne's* enigmas.

One puzzle that attracts the notice of all readers of *Ariadne*, whether they have a good classical education or not, relates to Ariadne's request to Theseus to marry Phaedra to his son on their return to Athens (2096–100). Theseus is only twenty-three years old (2075), and even allowing for the difference in medieval marriage customs, it is hard to imagine that he could have had a son of marriageable age, especially since he had been in love with Ariadne from afar for the past seven years (2120). But to attribute details such as these to Chaucer's 'carelessness' is such a desperate measure that alternative explanations must be sought, even if they lead away from the older view that we are dealing here with a slipshod version of the Ariadne story. Firstly, it seems undeniable that the mention of Theseus' son and Phaedra in tandem inevitably recalls the story which made Phaedra's name almost a medieval household word for illicit passion. This story, recounted in *Heroides* IV, concerned Phaedra's incestuous love for her stepson Hippolytus and her destruction of him when repulsed.[20] Reference to this taints to some extent the thesis of the *Legend* that for the most part women are good, a thesis already under question from the first lines of *Ariadne*, where Chaucer attempts to conform the story of Scylla (a woman of notoriously evil passions) to the pattern of the poor innocent, betrayed by an evil man (1900–21). Secondly, one of the effects of stating that Theseus is 'semely' and 'yong' and 'twenty yer and three' is to emphasise that this is a young man's escapade, one of the several amorous adventures of the great hero's youth, and one that was often treated as a minor incident in the major adventure of killing the Minotaur. It is Theseus' quick wit that is being demonstrated when, by assuring her of his seven years' love, he seeks to consolidate his unexpected good fortune in finding Ariadne so willing to rescue him. Surely designed as a humorous climax pointing up the expediency of Theseus' wooing speech, the seven years

[20] The *accessus* cited at the beginning of this chapter mentions Phaedra's illicit love for her stepson, Hippolytus; Filippo's double preface to his Italian translation of the Epistles of Ariadne and Phaedra specifically names Hippolytus as the son of Theseus to whom Phaedra was betrothed, see Meech, 'Italian Translation', p. 116. So does Boccaccio in *De Casibus* (see n.17, above). Gower notes this evil consequence of Theseus' abandonment of Ariadne for Phaedra.

do not represent an objective fact, one which somehow has to be reconciled with the fact that he is only twenty-three.

There is another problem with Theseus' age, here and in the *Knight's Tale*. The Theseus of the *Knight's Tale* seems a man of mature wisdom, whose latest adventure involved 'winning . . . the regne of Femenye'. When he speaks slightingly of the domination of love, in the course of which he confesses, 'I woot it by myself ful yore agon/ For in my tyme a servant was I oon . . .' (*KnT* 1785 ff.), it seems reasonable to assume that he might have been referring to his youthful adventure with Ariadne and Phaedra. Unfortunately for this theory, however, Hippolyta, whom Theseus is engaged in marrying in the *Knight's Tale*, was the mother of Hippolytus, Phaedra's stepson, whom Phaedra falls in love with when she is Theseus' wife. The events of the *Knight's Tale* then would have to have occurred before those of the *Legend of Ariadne*. It seems possible that Chaucer had not thought these things out, which would not be surprising, as Theseus' love life was inordinately complex and included an early abduction of Helen of Troy (which Chaucer could have read about in Guido del Colonne's *Historia*). Otherwise Chaucer must have wished to characterise the whole affair as a youthful peccadillo more than he wished to be accurate or consistent. Boccaccio's *De Casibus Virorum Illustrium* and Lydgate's *Fall of Princes* get the sequence of events correct.[21]

Certainly, it has proved difficult for critics to separate the two apparently inconsistent portraits of Theseus, and, as there is some indication that Chaucer composed the two tales fairly close in time, it would seem unwise to do so. There are a number of verbal echoes between the *Legend of Good Women* and the *Knight's Tale*, and there is every reason to suppose that *Palamon and Arcite*, mentioned in the Prologue to the *Legend* (F 420/G 408) and probably an early version of the *Knight's Tale*, did not precede it by any length of time. One of the most interesting early pieces of criticism of the *Legend of Good Women* was the observation by J. L. Lowes that several events in the *Legend of Ariadne* could be found in no other version of the story, either classical or medieval, but paralleled events in the *Knight's Tale*.[22] Chaucer, he

---

[21] See Hall, *Illustrious Men*, pp. 19–23; Bergen, *Fall of Princes* I 118–26.

[22] Lowes, 'Chronological Relations', pp. 804–10.

felt, faced by gaps in the narrative of Ariadne in his sources, used suggestions from Boccaccio's *Teseida*, the major source of the *Knight's Tale*, to fill these gaps. According to Lowes, Boccaccio's story provided Chaucer with a way of introducing Ariadne to Theseus, by allowing her to overhear his complaints. Chaucer places the prison of Theseus in a tower (as was that of Palamon and Arcite). In the *Knight's Tale* the tower was 'evene joynant to the garden wal/ Ther as this Emelye hadde hir pleyynge' (*KnT* 1060–1); there the prisoners see her, and in the *Teseida* she overhears their groans. In *Ariadne*, Theseus' prison was 'joynynge in the wal to a foreyne' (1962); this was the 'foreyne' or privy to the princesses' chamber above, and was apparently the conduit by means of which they can hear 'al his compleynynge'. There would appear to be little similarity between an 'amorous garden' and a privy, but in fact both 'garden' and 'foreyne' translate Boccaccio's word *giardino (amoroso)*.

As well as this, Theseus offers to serve Ariadne and Phaedra as a page performing menial labour, in the same way that Arcite serves in Theseus' house in the *Knight's Tale*, and who, 'sith his face was so disfigured/ Of maladye . . . He myghte wel, if that he bar hym lowe/ Lyve in Atthenes everemoore unknowe' (*KnT* 1403–6). In *Ariadne*, Theseus says he will disguise himself so well and 'me so wel disfigure and so lowe,/ That in this worlde ther shal no man me knowe' (2046–7). (In the *Teseida*, Arcite through his grief *sì era del tutto trasmuto/ Che nullo non l'avia* raffigurato.)[23] Moreover, if Chaucer was using the *Teseida* at this point to flesh out the story of Theseus and Ariadne, there is at least an explanation for his strange slip in writing that Minos' prison and his daughters' chamber faced the 'maysterstrete/ Of Athenes' (1965–6), the setting of the *Teseida* and the *Knight's Tale*.

Although these parallels are compelling, they are also mystifying, or so scholars like Lowes thought. In particular, the portrayal of Theseus as a callous villain and his imprisonment in a privy led Lowes to posit that *Ariadne* must have been written earlier than the *Knight's Tale*:

> If the *Ariadne* followed the *Knight's Tale*, what we have is a decidedly inferior and rather sketchy replica of two motives already fully and

[23] *Teseida* IV 28, quoted ibid., p. 807.

artistically worked out. That is, to say the least, inherently improbable. More specifically, while the substitution of the 'foreyne' of the *Legend* for the lovely picture of the garden in Boccaccio is on any theory puzzling enough . . . the view that just that substitution of all others should be deliberately made for Chaucer's own exquisite rendering of the picture in the *Knight's Tale* is almost inconceivable. And finally, that after he had created the very noble and stately figure of Theseus in the *Knight's Tale* Chaucer should, once more deliberately, superimpose upon it in his reader's (*sic*) minds the despicable traitor of the *Legend of Ariadne*, only the most convincing external evidence could lead one to believe. On the other hand, that the crude and not particularly meritorious sketch should precede the more finished and elaborate development is merely in the natural order of things.[24]

Of course, it is not obvious to every reader, particularly today, that it was 'inherently improbable' and 'almost inconceivable' that *Ariadne* should follow the *Knight's Tale*, nor that the reverse position was 'merely in the natural order of things'. The early students of the *Legend* had a tremendous drive to read the Legends seriously and pathetically. So much so, that Skeat and Tatlock denied that 'foreyne' meant privy,[25] apparently because the anti-romantic effect on a love begun in such an inauspicious place was in conflict with the tone they believed to dominate the Legends. R. W. Frank, however, was not reluctant to provide a reading of *Ariadne* which takes full account of Chaucer's decision to translate *giardino* as 'foreyne' – 'It is a word outrageously inappropriate in a love narrative, and yet it is there.'[26] Frank saw in *Ariadne* an early exploration of attitudes to love later expressed in the *Merchant's Tale* and had no need of the older scholars' desperate remedies, such as changing the meaning of 'foreyne'. For Frank in the 1970s it was within the bounds of possibility that *Ariadne* was conceived quite deliberately as some kind of parodic or uncourtly version of the *Knight's Tale*. Frank goes on to point out the very unromantic context in which Chaucer would have found Ariadne's story in the *Metamorphoses*

---

[24] Lowes, 'Chronological Relations', pp. 809–10.
[25] See note to *LGW* 1962 in Skeat's edition, where it is stated that 'foreyne' could not mean 'privy', but rather 'outer chamber; belonging to the *chambres grete*, or set of larger rooms occupied by the daughters of the king'.
[26] Frank, *Chaucer and the 'Legend'*, p. 115.

and the *Ovide Moralisé*, where it concludes a series describing the aggressively unnatural desires of Scylla for Ariadne's father, Minos, and of her mother, Pasiphae, for the bull, which resulted in the birth of the Minotaur. In an even more stringent recent critical judgement, again contrasting strongly with the idea of the older Chaucerian scholars that *Ariadne* was an exercise in sometimes bungled courtliness, Lee Patterson finds that, in turning such a sardonic eye on the pretensions of 'gentillesse', Chaucer exposes the lack of principle and naked expediency which are masked by the aristocratic ethos to which the *Legend*'s heroes conform and which was valorised in the *Knight's Tale*.[27]

Readings of *Ariadne* such as that of Frank are enhanced by the recent contention that the *Legend of Good Women* is marked by a strong element of sexual word-play and innuendo. Sheila Delany has pointed to the potential for a sexual interpretation which many passages in the *Legend* yield.[28] Scholars are often and rightly sceptical of the too ready assigning of sexual connotations to individual words in writers such as Chaucer, but Delany concentrates on clusters of words and passages where the possible examples of double entendre amount to quite a high number. In my observation, such clusters occur in passages in the *Legend* which, on other grounds entirely, attract attention for the peculiar contribution they make to the ethos of the Legend in question and which Chaucer has interpolated into his source material – such are the sea-battle in *Cleopatra*, the hunting scene in *Dido*, Thisbe's concluding speech in *Tisbe*, and, most particularly, Phaedra's speech in *Ariadne*, where the heroine concocts in great detail the plan by which Theseus might kill the Minotaur. According to Delany, in this speech of some forty lines (1985–2024), Phaedra conceives of Theseus' project of entering the labyrinth, killing the monster, and escaping safely, in terms of sexual penetration of the female body. The place where the monster

---

[27] Patterson, *Chaucer and the Subject of History*, pp. 238–9.

[28] Sheila Delany, 'The Logic of Obscenity in Chaucer's *Legend of Good Women*', *Florilegium* 7 (1985): 189–205, slightly expanded in chapter 3 of Delany, *Naked Text*. A. J. Minnis, for one, is unpersuaded by Delany's evidence, particularly in light of the kind of courtly audience usually postulated for the *Legend*, see Minnis, *Shorter Poems*, pp. 343–4. For a strong warning against the modern critic's too ready identification of obscenity in Chaucer, see L. D. Benson, 'The "Queynte" Punnings of Chaucer's Critics', in *Studies in the Age of Chaucer: Proceedings* I (Knoxville: New Chaucer Society, 1984), pp. 23–47.

lurks is described as 'krynkeled to and fro/ And hath so queynte weyes for to go' (2012–13), seen by Delany as a clear reference to female genitalia, while in many medieval registers the notion of woman as monster (1928, 1991) or fiend (1996) is common.[29] Phaedra, a representative in the Middle Ages of just such a monster of female sexuality, graphically maps out what Theseus needs to do in language redolent of the testing of his virility:

> Lat us wel taste hym at his herte-rote,
> That if so be that he a wepen have,
> Wher that he dar, hys lyf to kepe and save,
> Fyghten with the fend . . .
> 1993–6

and runs through a comprehensive catalogue of penile euphemisms to match her allusions to female genitalia:

> For in the prysoun ther he shal descende,
> Ye wote wel that the beste is in a place
> That nys nat derke, and hath roum eek and space
> To welde an ax, or swerd, or staf, or knyf;
> If that he be a man, he shal do so.
> And we shul make hym balles ek also . . .
> 1997–2003[30]

Many readers will have reservations about accepting this interpretation of Phaedra's speech, but disquiet with such interpretations often reveals underlying assumptions about the kind of writing *likely* to be found in the *Legend of Good Women*. An interesting demonstration of this can be found in Thomas W. Ross's *Chaucer's Bawdy*, the most comprehensive study of the erotic dimensions of Chaucer's linguistic practice.[31] Ross

---

[29] Cf. Dinshaw, *Chaucer's Sexual Poetics*, pp. 78–80. For woman as monster, see quotation from Le Fèvre, in Blamires, *Woman Defamed*, pp. 195–6; for woman's association with the devil, see Blamires' index entry under 'devil'. In his scatological *Corbaccio*, a parodic and palinodic work designed to vituperate women and love, Boccaccio calls the hellish place where he finds himself in his dream the 'Labyrinth of Love', see A. K. Cassell, ed. and trans., *The Corbaccio: Giovanni Boccaccio* (Urbana: University of Illinois Press, 1975), p. 10.

[30] For further detail and documentation see Delany, 'Logic of Obscenity', pp. 196–7.

[31] T. W. Ross, *Chaucer's Bawdy* (New York: Dutton, 1972). I will not usually give page numbers in future reference to words discussed by Ross, as they are arranged alphabetically in dictionary fashion, and can be conveniently so consulted.

categorically denies the likelihood of sexual connotation in several of the words in Phaedra's speech ('queynte', 'balles'), even though such connotation is well attested in *MED* and elsewhere,[32] since he thinks the *Legend of Good Women* a 'sodden failure', partly because of its lack of sexual detail (see p. 147). This is a very circular argument: from Ross's point of view the *Legend* is a failure because of its lack of specifically sexual material, therefore he asserts that words which frequently have a sexual connotation do not have such a connotation when they appear in the *Legend*. The exception that proves the rule is the *Legend of Dido* which Ross considers 'bawdy' in its entirety (p. 188), and thus a place where he finds many erotic references. Ross, in his valuable introduction, admits the likelihood that bawdiness will be found or not found according to the reader's expectation and apprehension of context (cf. p. 20); as, up till recently, scholarly presuppositions about the *Legend* have not included the notion that the activities of its female martyrs could have sexual overtones, such have not been found.

Charles Muscatine gives an interesting account of normative medieval sexuality as it appears in the French fabliaux (a form of tale-telling with which Chaucer and many of his audience may be thought to have had some familiarity), and the linguistic register, particularly of sexual euphemism, which accompanies it.[33] (If Phaedra's speech has sexual overtones at all, then we are not dealing with direct obscene puns, or even dirty language, but with lexis which in some contexts appears as sexual euphemism.) Muscatine says the language of the fabliaux is dominated by male sexuality, describing the sexual act, for instance, as 'to be a man' (cf. *LGW* 2002) and in terms of military aggression. There is a large range of euphemisms for the penis including weaponry (pp. 110–12) – *LGW*'s 'wepen' (1994), 'ax', 'swerd', 'staf', 'knyf' (2000) are very much in this mould, and are associated with 'thyng' (the most

---

[32] *MED*'s earliest reference to 'bal' meaning testicle is from the *Proverbs of Hending* (before 1325): 'The maide that gevit hirsilf alle/ Othir to freman othir to thralle . . . / And pleiit with the croke and with the balle,/ And makit gret that erst was smalle' – 'croke' (*MED* attested for penis) also occurs in the *Cleopatra* sea-battle passage. In 1972 the relevant volumes of *MED* had not appeared for some words on which Ross wished to comment, e.g. 'queynte' or 'staf', but the question in the case of these words was not one of attestation, but the *likelihood* of vulgar connotation in the context of the *Legend*.

[33] C. Muscatine, *The Old French Fabliaux* (New Haven: Yale University Press, 1986).

common euphemism for penis in French) and 'clewe' in *LGW* 2140. Muscatine says that, in the fabliaux, testicles are not only balls, but among much else, 'balls of yarn' (p. 113) with which we may compare Chaucer's 'clewe' or ball of twine. The fabliaux take as axiomatic conventional notions of insatiable female appetite (pp. 121–2), have a large range of terms for the vagina, the shape of which 'prompts some crude jokes on the theme of its creation by means of a spade or an axe' (p. 118) – again we may note Phaedra's comment that Theseus will have room to wield an axe in the labyrinth (*LGW* 2000). For all this coincidence, Phaedra is not, superficially, describing a sexual encounter.

It may also be asked whether Queen Anne and her ladies would have responded favourably to the vulgar implications of Phaedra's speech which Delany perceives. This is a slippery area of critical speculation, and many earlier confident guesses about what Anne would have approved or disapproved of are now discounted. In practice we have little concrete information as to what was enjoyed by audiences of mixed company in the court of Richard II, if such was the *Legend's* destination,[34] beyond the texts associated with it and analogous situations. Of French audiences of a somewhat earlier period Muscatine comments that 'we must . . . visualize a mixed audience, which, in the mood to hear fabliaux, expected to hear plain language, along with a rich array of metaphorical variations, without embarrassment' (p. 132), although the situation was changing under the 'spread of the ethic of courtliness or gentility' (p. 133). It is true that medieval male writers frequently drew attention to passages with an erotic orientation by apologies to the ladies, but how often are these anything more than rhetorical ploys, underlining the effect of the naughtiness rather than ameliorating it? Against Christine de Pizan's strong disapproval of the sexual explicitness and innuendo of the *Roman de la Rose* (in which she was supported by a male writer, indicating that such distaste was not necessarily gender-specific), we may set, for example, Boccaccio's comment that he wrote the *Decameron* for the enjoyment of women. In

---

[34] Michael Bennett, however, notes in passing the occasional association of debauchery with the court of Richard II, see 'The Court of Richard II and the Promotion of Literature', in Barbara Hanawalt, ed., *Chaucer's England: Literature in Historical Context* (Medieval Studies at Minnesota, 4, Minneapolis: University of Minnesota Press, 1992), p. 8.

the frame story of the *Decameron* Boccaccio depicts noble ladies, who are wise and virtuous and careful of their reputations, but, in the stories they listen to and recite for recreation, women characters who are as sensual and devious as women are commonly portrayed in the general run of misogynist discourse. Boccaccio describes the noble ladies in his frame story as sometimes, because of their modesty, trying not to smile at a risqué story, sometimes giggling, sometimes laughing so that their jaws ached,[35] and it does not seem unreasonable speculation that real women in mixed audiences, even allowing for the differences between noble English ladies and those that Boccaccio describes, if the occasion was appropriate, behaved just like this. Boccaccio's description of the behaviour of ladies is of course not reportage, but as much a literary construct (a description of how a male writer thought women might react) as are the familiar 'apologies to women'.

Moreover, we cannot escape so easily from the possibilty of sexual innuendo in the *Legend* by arguing that it would have offended feminine sensibilities, since so many other aspects of the poem show women scant respect, as I shall examine in later chapters. As the poet in turn pities, taunts and flirts with the women of his implied audience, one wonders how much pleasure female listeners took in stories in which women were portrayed as willing dupes of the superior wiles of men (as in *Dido*), as tender chicken dinners for wily foxes (as in *Medea*), as victims of male violence in rape (as in *Philomela* or *Lucrece*),[36] or ones in which the seriousness of the heroine's plight was callously dismissed (as in *Phyllis*), if they were not obliged to accept it all as good fun – I leave it to others to discuss the element of gender asymmetry in this, for the fun is clearly more funny to men than to women. If Chaucer indulges here in a lapse of taste by flouting the courtly dictum of clean speech, then this in itself is an indication of the kind of social

---

[35] M. Musa and P. Bondanella, trans., *The Decameron* (New York: Mentor, 1982), response to First Day, Fourth Story, p. 42; to Second Day, Second Story, p. 73; to Second Day, Tenth Story, p. 159. Chaucer portrayed the mixed company of the Canterbury pilgrimage laughing, or mostly laughing, at the *Miller's Tale* (*RPr* 3855–8).

[36] The writings of Christine de Pizan afford historical evidence that some medieval women at least did not enjoy seeing themselves portrayed as the dupes of male seducers, see *Dieu d'Amours* 519–32, or as the covertly compliant victims of rape, see E. J. Richards, trans. *Christine de Pizan: The Book of the City of Ladies* (New York: Persea, 1982), II 44. 1, pp. 160 ff.

situation for which the *Legend* was originally designed, those festive and recreational events whose literary productions tilted irreverently at the normal conventions of politeness and were marked by the audience's enthusiastic partisanship according to gender. Indeed the hints of antifeminism in the *Legend* may be designed to provoke women listeners into defending their sex,[37] and it is easy to see how *Ariadne* could elicit the same type of gender-biased debate among the members of a mixed audience that we see dramatised in the *Jugement* poems of Machaut, for Chaucer gives us plenty of material which could be used in conversation to defend or condemn both Theseus and Ariadne, as I have shown.

It must be acknowledged that the sexual innuendo in *Ariadne* is not so compelling that it is unable to be denied, and it may always have been conceived as a kind of optional extra, something which could be emphasised in certain performances but allowed to remain in abeyance in others.[38] In my opinion, we cannot escape the issue by contending that such was the case at a performance designed for Queen Anne. It seems quite unlikely that Chaucer would include covert obscenity in a work which would insult the person to whom it was dedicated if it was overt. If obscenity is there at all, the most likely possibility is that Chaucer composed such material with an initial mixed audience in mind, one whom he conceived would cooperate with its subversive gestures towards the orthodox courtly representation of women. An element of vulgar speech does not sit oddly with the tradition of the subversive palinode, discussed in the last chapter, whereby Chaucer ostensibly performs penance for his sin, at the same time doing exactly what he was originally condemned for. Is it not possible, then, that for the amusement of his gentle audience he is dramatising himself as the uncourtly 'worm' that the God of Love says he is, since he speaks disrespectfully of women and indulges in sexually-oriented word-play in the manner of the *Roman* ('in pleyn text it nedeth nat to glose')? We

---

37 For a similar observation that antifeminist material in French Romance may have invited resistance on the part of a feminine audience, see Roberta L. Krueger, *Women Readers and the Ideology of Gender in Old French Verse* (Cambridge University Press, 1993), esp. chapter 3, 'Playing to the Ladies'.

38 Cf. Beryl Rowland, '*Pronuntiatio* and its Effect on Chaucer's Audience', *SAC* 4 (1982): 33–51.

might speculate that women in the audience may have castigated Chaucer for using impolite language, as in this game they were in a sense required to do, and that he might have replied disingenuously that the obscene ideas were not in his words but in the minds of his audience ('Blame nat me'), or that he was only making his fictional personage Phaedra, one who had a reputation for sexual obsession, speak in character.

Some observations that few would argue with may be made in regard to this question of how Phaedra's speech should be interpreted. Most will acknowledge that the interpolation of the speech is very peculiar; for example, although Phaedra with this egregious speech displaces Ariadne as the one who instigates and devises the plan to save Theseus, nevertheless, in spite of its length and detail, her speech has no immediate narrative consequences. That is to say, as soon as Phaedra stops speaking, the narrator takes up the story again as if Ariadne is its undisputed heroine, according to her traditional role, and Phaedra ceases to be mentioned. Moreover, on even the most literal reading of the speech, there can be no doubt that Phaedra desires to test Theseus' manhood ('Lat us wel taste hym at his herte-rote . . .', 'If that he be a man . . .'), and a recent feminist reading contends that the establishing of masculinity, particularly vis-à-vis femininity, is one of the major themes in the *Legend of Good Women*.[39] In this view, in almost every Legend the hero has to contend with the dangerous power of women: perhaps an actual woman able to help him escape from his position of humiliating powerlessness (Theseus' case here, cf. *Dido, Hypsipyle and Medea, Phyllis*); or he is implicated in behaviour considered the preserve of women, such as wiliness, deceit and infidelity (see the same Legends); or he vitiates his male nature and duty by succumbing to sensuality and pleasure either in the person of a woman, Cleopatra, or because of his own lower nature whose animal vices of sensuality and irrationality were thought to be tinged with the feminine (see *Cleopatra, Philomena, Lucrece*); or he fails in his masculine duty of protecting women as a father or husband (*Tisbe, Hypermnestra*, as well as the rape stories). As I have said, the testing of virility is verbally explicit in

---

[39] See Hansen, *Fictions of Gender*, pp. 1–15.

Phaedra's potentially taunting speech – the only question is whether Phaedra elaborates the idea with an explicitly sexual colouration.

In sum, the notion of Woman intimated here and the overtones of sexual conquest which mark Theseus' victory are very far from the idea of 'fair womanhood' which most of the older scholars believed Chaucer was celebrating in the *Legend of Good Women*. The women of the *Legend of Ariadne*, Scylla, Phaedra, Ariadne, are no distant objects of veneration and inspiration, aloofly virtuous like the Daisy Queen Alceste; rather they are passionate and desiring subjects, fully sexual beings. Such a concept of women is rarely considered complimentary in medieval times. The telling of this Legend may well have something in common with Reason's sexual explicitness which the Lover finds so offensive in the *Roman de la Rose* and which appears to lead the God of Love to condemn Chaucer's translation of the French poem into English, for its possible sexual innuendo would subvert Love's requirements that his servants use fine language and always speak politely of women. Not surprisingly, so long as the majority of critics interpreted the *Legend* as straightforward praise of a notion of 'ideal womanhood', the possibility of the poem containing obscenity was unthinkable.

Peculiar conglomerate that *Ariadne* is, it is not difficult to see how it might have been put together. Ariadne's story seems to have been little known before the appearance of the *Ovide Moralisé* in the fourteenth century, and Chaucer's sources offered little in the way of a well-rounded story. His first view of Ariadne may well have been the flippant treatment in *Le Jugement dou Roy de Navarre*, which appears to lie behind the story in the *House of Fame*. When Chaucer consulted the *Heroides*, it is pertinent to remember that the scholarly apparatus to his copy of Ovid probably told him that *intentio auctoris* was to display the effects of *amor stultus*, and that Ariadne was too ready to trust a stranger and reprehensibly betrayed her family and homeland.[40] The location of the Ariadne/Theseus story in the *Metamorphoses* in near proximity to the story of Scylla, and his Italian translation of the *Heroides* as well as the *Ovide Moralisé* informing him that both Phaedra and Ariadne were involved, perhaps led him to conform Ariadne's story to these other

---

40 These matters are mentioned in *Heroides* X, although only a medieval moralist would have picked them out as *intentio auctoris*.

stories thought to indicate rapacious female sexuality. In turn the presence of the two sisters may have suggested a comic role reversal of the *Teseida*, now with two predatory females in love with one relatively helpless male, and where the one who appears to win the prize is supplanted by the other (possibly more deserving) sister. Phaedra's reputation for sexual obsession enticed him into the witty tour de force in which the plan to save Theseus is couched in erotic double entendre. The brief remark in the *Ovide* to the effect that Ariadne proposed marriage probably completed his unique conception of 'what really happened' when Theseus went to Crete to kill the Minotaur.

It would seem difficult to deny that Chaucer was amused by his account of how Ariadne came to be a deserted 'good woman'. Yet the comic features are not the end of *Ariadne*. For, as in all the Legends of the deserted ladies, Chaucer appends to his narrative section a quotation from the appropriate Heroidean epistle. There have been many critics who have found Ariadne's lament after her desertion genuinely moving:

> 'Allas,' quod she, 'that evere I was wrought!
> I am betrayed!' and hire her torente,
> And to the stronde barefot faste she wente,
> And cryed, 'Theseus! myn herte swete!
> Where be ye, that I may nat with yow mete,
> And myghte thus with bestes ben yslayn?'
> The holwe rokkes answerde hire agayn.
> No man she saw, and yit shyned the mone,
> And hye upon a rokke she wente sone,
> And saw his barge saylynge in the se,
> Cold wex hire herte . . .
> 2187–97

Frank notes that it is often difficult for readers who see humour in the first part of *Ariadne* to believe that the lament can be anything but comic as well. Nevertheless, he opts 'for the possibly more dangerous choice and [reads] the last section seriously'.[41] On both counts he is probably right. While presumably one could read in a mocking tone of voice the passage where Ariadne kisses all the places where Theseus had

---

[41] Frank, *Chaucer and the 'Legend'*, pp. 128–9.

set his feet (2208–9), for example, there is little in the text that demands sarcasm. Chaucer does in fact play down the exaggerated gestures which display Ariadne's grief in *Heroides* X; she does not pull *all* her hair out,[42] nor does she address the empty bed quite so often. Like so much in the *Legend*, however, one's response becomes more ambivalent as the passage proceeds. Her closing lament that she cannot go home to her country, even if there were a boat, adds to the pathos of Ariadne's plight (2215–16), but it also reminds the audience of her betrayal of family and country, which, it will be remembered, medieval glossators insisted was Ovid's intention to convey.[43]

In terms of the history of the myth Chaucer was right to present Ariadne as a pathetic heroine, for she was the archetypal *deserta* of classical times; alone on a rocky isle she had no need to threaten suicide, as death was only too inevitable. There are fifty-six pictures of Ariadne at Pompei, mainly portraying her abandonment on Dia, which was always conceived as the central scene in her life and the turning point in her story. In her desertion and as the object of Bacchus' desire she was the quintessential pathetic and erotic symbol.[44] In Roman times the romantic pathos of her situation was potently attractive, and Vergil borrowed from it in creating his tragic picture of Dido. Lipking chooses to open his book devoted to the poetic theme of abandoned women – abandoned in the twin senses of deserted and given over to passion – with a discussion on Ariadne.[45] The older Chaucerian scholars had a tendency to ignore the humour of the large part of *Ariadne* in order to appreciate the pathos of its end. Modern readers in general find no difficulty with the irony of this tale, which then seems to impose a requirement to downplay its pathos. Yet both are there, in *Ariadne*, and in the complex medieval response to women in general.

My historical survey of changing critical responses to *Ariadne* suggests strongly that the crucial enigma in *Ariadne*, and the *Legend* as a

---

[42] Cf. *Heroides* X 147.
[43] Cf. *Heroides* X 65–70.
[44] See Winsor, 'Study', pp. 411–15.
[45] L. Lipking, *Abandoned Women and Poetic Tradition* (University of Chicago Press, 1988); see also Florence Verducci's chapter on Ariadne in *Ovid's Toyshop of the Heart: Epistulae Heroidum* (Princeton University Press, 1985).

whole, is just this juxtaposition of humour and pathos[46] and the accurate weighting of each in any interpretation (many of the other problems which bothered scholars over the years can be explained). It has also underlined the fact that the elements of the pathetic and the humorous have had a genuine appeal to different audiences at different periods, and it may be true that various medieval audiences also differed in their responses, some downplaying the ironic in favour of the pathetic in a way similar to the early modern Chaucerian scholars, others perhaps responding vigorously to the poet's dramatisation of his problem in finding a truly virtuous woman out of which to make an exemplary story. I think Chaucer might have hoped for an audience which would have debated the problems he offered it in the *Legend of Good Women* in a spirit of game, an audience that would have sympathised with the pathos of Ariadne's desertion but noted that she brought her troubles on herself, that would have condemned Theseus' treachery but observed how cleverly he extricated himself from prison, certain death, and an importunate woman.

This dialectic between humour and pathos, this yoking of a slightly disrespectful attitude to woman's virtue with sympathy for her suffering, will subtend my discussion of other Legends. I will leave to one side for a time a fuller treatment of the pathos of the heroines' stories, while I consider in the next chapters whether it is possible that Chaucer could seriously have desired to construct Good Women out of the multi-murderer and child killer, Medea, and the man-hungry Cleopatra.

---

[46] Cf. Verducci's discussion of the very similar problem of assessing the tonality of Ovid's *Heroides*, *Ovid's Toyshop*, esp. pp. 81–5. John Kerrigan has noted how in general a certain 'unfocused comic air' seems to bedevil the most serious attempts to portray the pathos of female lament, see J. Kerrigan, ed., *Motives of Woe, Shakespeare and 'Female Complaint': a Critical Anthology* (Oxford: Clarendon, 1991), p. 65.

Medea: the ladies and their reputations

Ovid's *Heroides*, the classical text purporting to sympathise with women on which Chaucer draws heavily in the *Legend*, depended for its appreciation on its audience's knowledge of the treatment of the heroines in other texts.[1] A weakness in one of the most important modern studies of the *Legend*, Frank's *Chaucer and the Legend of Good Women*, is that it takes very little account of what Chaucer's audience might have known and thought of the subjects of his Legends. Frank's procedure of taking the Legends at their face value reveals many of their very real virtues, but the suspicion of many modern readers that Chaucer had an overriding ironic purpose in treating as 'good' heroines who were frequently considered 'bad' is not allayed, indeed is often enhanced by Frank's analysis.

For a very long time the *Legend* was read as a faintly boring collection of naive eulogies of classical ladies whom medieval people alone could have considered 'good'. 'The rubric "explicit Legenda Cleopataras Martiris"', said the editor F. N. Robinson, 'has a humor for us that it could not have had for the readers at the court of Richard II.' But, he noted disapprovingly, the suggestion that Chaucer had a 'satirical purpose' and the 'attempt to find unrecognized humor in the *Legend* . . . is ill-advised'.[2] Presumably following J. L. Lowes,[3] he pronounced what became the authoritative judgement on the *Legend* for a good part of this century: 'There can be no doubt that in the mind of Chaucer

---

[1] See H. Jacobson, *Ovid's 'Heroides'* (Princeton University Press, 1974) and Verducci, *Ovid's Toyshop*. For extensive discussion of the relationship of the *Heroides* with its sources, and the *Legend of Good Women* with the *Heroides*, see Winsor, 'Study'.

[2] *Works of Chaucer*, p. 482.

[3] See Lowes, 'Travesty', pp. 513–69.

and his contemporaries the heroines he celebrates were good in the only sense that counted for the purpose in hand – they were faithful followers of the God of Love.' Lowes had addressed this question in 1909, in answer to some of the first published suspicions that the *Legend* had an ironic purpose. He pointed out that the same heroines whom Chaucer praised were endlessly cited in medieval literature, and said this proved that they were 'stock exempla of fidelity in love'.[4] Lowes' evidence is in fact quite suspect. When Chaucer refers to Medea, Phyllis and Dido in the *Book of the Duchess* 724–34, it is only to condemn the foolishness of their behaviour. Or to take another of Lowes' examples, the list of suffering women in Book VII of Boccaccio's clearly satirical *Elegia di Madonna Fiammetta*. The ladies cited there are almost identical to Chaucer's list in the *Legend*, including Cleopatra, and their sufferings are indeed admired, yet the narrating voice is a severely compromised one. The lovelorn Fiammetta is foolish and self-deluded, a prime example of an unreliable narrator.[5] Her opinion is not one which can easily be identified with any objective view of what is good. That is, the fact that the Chaucerian heroines are cited by other writers only demonstrates the medieval popularity of the topos of cataloguing female heroines, and provides no evidence that Chaucer intended straightforwardly to praise them. Lowes has in fact ignored the very point that Chaucer was at pains to stress in the Prologue to the *Legend*, that the meaning of a work of literature cannot be identified with its subject matter, that the writer's 'entente' is revealed much more clearly by treatment and context.

Is it possible to tell if Chaucer were really defending women, treating them as 'good in the only sense that counted', by comparing the stories in the *Legend of Good Women* with commonly received opinions about them? Were their often questionable histories well known in Chaucer's time, and would his treatment of them as a consequence have been considered ironic or humorous? This is not a problem that is relevant in *Ariadne*, whose heroine was not especially bad or well known; but

---

[4] Ibid., p. 546.
[5] E. Hutton, *Boccaccio's Amorous Fiammetta*, modernised from the English translation of Bartholemew Yong (London: Navarre Society, 1942), esp. pp. 318–44. Also R. Hollander, *Boccaccio's Two Venuses* (New York: Columbia University Press, 1977), pp. 40–9.

other ladies like Medea or Cleopatra were more likely to evoke notions of bad women, and it would seem possible in such cases to establish a norm against which one could test whether any particular account was likely to be ironic or not, although there are many pitfalls along the way. It is a dangerous procedure, for example, to speak as if an exact equivalence for the symbolic value of each of the Ovidian ladies can be established. It is tempting to say simply that Medea was known as a witch and then that Chaucer's portrayal of her as a good woman suggests an ironic purpose. But it was perfectly possible for a medieval writer to ignore a high proportion of the facts of any biography in order to pick out, emphasise and make exemplary just one of its subject's features, as will be seen, and as has been recently reemphasised by Minnis.[6] It is in fact the feature of medieval thinking on which Lowes and Robinson based their arguments about the goodness of Chaucer's good women.

The topos of the exemplary catalogue of ladies[7] could be, and was, put to different purposes in different works, but it is obvious that the effect of the catalogue is likely to be less precise, less complex, in the simple decorative list of exotic names (as in Chaucer's balade, *Hyd Absolon*) than in the collection devoted to fully worked out narratives. In the latter, of the nature of things, the author could not avoid imposing a point of view on his story by all the compositional processes of selection and emphasis, something indicated much less readily in the simple allusion; in other medieval tale collections about women, such as Boccaccio's *De Claris Mulieribus* and Christine's *Cité des Dames*, one is rarely at a loss as to what the author intends in any individual story.

Along with the literary reputation of the individual heroine, the context in which any tale occurs is usually a significant indicator. The catalogue of extended narrative pieces concerning women such as the *Legend of Good Women* exhibits is likely to have several traditions or contexts which must be taken into account. On the one hand the effect of any catalogue is a product of the choice of its individual components. On the other hand the force of the whole grouping can delimit the effect of each story in the catalogue (particularly apparent in the *Cité des*

---

[6] Minnis, *Shorter Poems*, pp. 338–9.
[7] For a good account of the topos of the catalogue of ladies in relation to the *Legend*, see McMillan, *The Legend of Good Women*, pp. 11–26.

Dames). Thus the interplay between the power of the group and the contribution of the individual component to the group must constantly be kept in mind. Some names are so well known that their very presence indicates the context in which the catalogue is to be interpreted. For example, the citing of Criseyde is enough to suggest that the catalogue will be dealing with feminine unfaithfulness, but the appearance of the Virgin Mary in a list tends to preclude an ironic interpretation. The Prologue to the *Legend of Good Women* informs us that the poem is to be seen in relationship to *Troilus and Criseyde* and the *Roman de la Rose*, one dealing with the unsteadfastness and wrong-doing of women and the other dealing with the foolishness of love (see G 255–66). The points which Chaucer is making through his exemplary stories about women are likely to refer to these broad topics of debate, yet, as my discussion of critical responses to *Ariadne* has shown, it is not at all easy to be sure whether Chaucer is espousing or burlesquing the concept of the virtue of womankind.

Finally, it is worth underlining that the 'normal' or 'commonly received opinion' cannot by itself determine any specific text, any more than can a work's sources. In the same way that many early studies saw no humour in the Legends because of a conviction that in their context they were designed to be seriously pathetic, so some modern commentators imply that simply because other medieval writers disapproved of the heroines then so also did Chaucer. This is as true of modern criticism of Ovid's *Heroides* as of Chaucer's *Legend of Good Women*.[8] Although Ovid's work was persistently engaged in some kind of dialogue with that of his literary predecessors or contemporaries and knowledge of this enhances one's appreciation of his poetry immensely, nevertheless it is possible to work out from the texts themselves where the poem is leading. Similarly with Chaucer it seems a good principle only to accept the evidence of source material and analogues which confirm what the text suggests of itself. In order to investigate further the context in which the *Legend of Good Women* addresses the topos of the Catalogue in Defence of Women it will be necessary to examine the traditional accounts of several more of its heroines.

---

[8] Jacobson, *Ovid's 'Heroides'*, p. 9.

MEDEA

If the mere name of Medea is mentioned, as in fact happens only rarely, it is more than likely to have a pejorative significance. Augustine speaks of 'the Medeas, the Phaedras, the Clytemnestras' to signify people exemplifying the most nefarious aspects of pagan culture.[9] Walter Map, in *Valerius ad Ruffinum* (Dist. IV c 4), concludes his warning to his young friend about to marry: 'But, to give support to my argument from the testimony of ancient writers, read . . . Ovid's Medea, and you will find that almost nothing is impossible to a woman.'[10] Geoffrey of Vinsauf says: 'One [mode of Emphasis occurs] when we call the thing itself by the name of its property . . . thus: "Medea is wickedness itself"'.[11] These remarks by authoritative writers are at least suggestive of the idea against which other adaptations of the Medea story play. The qualities that lie behind the bald mention of Medea are likely to include insatiable lust and unnatural and inhumane cruelty. She was known as a murderess, necromancer and sorceress.

As far as Chaucer is concerned it is unnecessary to trace her reputation back any further than Ovid. In Book VII of the *Metamorphoses* Ovid describes how when Medea first saw Jason she 'was seized by an overwhelming passion of love and, though she long fought against it, her reason could not subdue her mad desire'. Some hundred lines are required to trace the tumultuous battle that ensues within Medea's breast, until at last Cupid overcomes 'filial affection and modesty' – with the help of Jason's good looks and smooth tongue – and she promises to help him gain the golden fleece by means of her sorcery.[12] The Epistles of Hypsipyle and Medea in the *Heroides* supplement the *Metamorphoses* account of Medea's later career: her flight with Jason and her attempt to delay her pursuing father by the murder and dismemberment of her brother, Absyrtus, and the scattering of his remains so that her father would have to stop and pick

---

[9] *De Consensu Evangelistarum, PL* XXXIV (1848), 1191, quoted in Shaner, 'An Interpretive Study', pp. 57–8.

[10] James, *Courtiers' Trifles*, p. 310. Translation from Blamires, *Woman Defamed*, p. 114.

[11] *Documentum de Arte Versificandi* II 2 32–4, quoted in E. Gallo, *The 'Poetria Nova' and its Sources in Early Rhetorical Doctrine* (The Hague: Mouton, 1971), p. 192.

[12] Trans. Innes, pp. 155–7.

them up; her rejuvenation of Jason's aged father, Æetes, by sorcery, and her engineering of the death of Jason's uncle, Pelleas, by his own daughters – all this she did for love. The *Heroides* also allude to her revenge on Jason for abandoning her for Creusa, whereby she slaughtered her two sons by Jason, and burnt and poisoned Creusa to death; her flight and remarriage to Aegeas and her attempt to poison Aegeas' son, Theseus. Medieval glosses on the *Heroides* conform her story to the pattern of Ariadne and Phyllis: in addition to *stultus*, however, Medea's love was also called *nepharius*: *stultus*, because she trusted a stranger and betrayed and deserted her father and fatherland, *nepharius*, because she killed her brother and children.[13]

Chaucer would have known other accounts. Almost certainly he read Benoît de Saint-Maure's account of the Jason and Medea story in the *Roman de Troie*.[14] Indeed, this was a significant source for Gower's parallel account in *Confessio Amantis*, and was relatively sympathetic towards Medea. Chaucer's avowed main source in the *Legend* besides Ovid, however, was Guido del Colonne's *Historia Destructionis Troiae*, the Latin adaptation of Benoît. In contrast to Benoît, Guido's every mention of Medea spawns a gratuitously virulent antifeminist outburst, suggesting that Medea is the personification of every vice that female nature is heir to – intrinsic changeableness, vanity, insatiable lust, and so on.[15] In itself it is an extraordinary choice of source material for one whose ostensible aim is to portray the virtue of women. It is remotely possible that other versions which Chaucer knew included the *Argonauticon* of Apollonius of Rhodes or Valerius Flaccus (probably the latter), because he cites the Greek word correctly in *LGW* 1457 as a place where a complete list of the Argonauts could be found. These works are usually thought to portray a relatively gentle 'young Medea' and deal with Jason's relationship with Hypsipyle as well. (Medea and Hypsipyle are linked together in the same Legend in Chaucer, as two casualties of Jason's career of seduction.) It has never been firmly established whence

[13] See MS Bodleian, Canon Class. Lat. 1 fo. 15ʳ. Quoted in Shaner, 'An Interpretive Study', p. 56.

[14] L. Constans, ed., *Benoît de Sainte-Maure: Roman de Troie*, 6 vols. (Paris: SATF, 1904–12), I, 715–2078, pp. 38–105.

[15] N. E. Griffin, ed., *Guido de Columnis: Historia Destructionis Troiae* (Cambridge, Mass.: Mediaeval Academy of America, 1936), pp. 15–27.

Chaucer derived his account of Hypsipyle, but Dante and Boccaccio each comment briefly on the fact that Hypsipyle and Medea were both Jason's victims.[16]

Boccaccio's account of Medea in *De Claris Mulieribus* is not unfairly representative of the bitterly pejorative medieval view of Medea, making explicit what was implicit in Ovid's humorously non-committal version:

> Medea [was] the most cruel example of ancient wickedness . . . she was quite beautiful and by far the best trained woman in evil-doing . . . By intoning enchantments, she knew perfectly how to disturb the sky, gather the winds from their dens, cause tempests, hold back rivers, brew poisons, make artificial fires for all kinds of conflagrations, and all other things of that sort. Far worse, her soul was not in discord with her arts, for, if those failed, she thought it very easy to use steel.[17]

The Heroidean Epistle, however, spawned some versions of her story that suggested that she deserved sympathy for the ingratitude she suffered at Jason's hand, so that there are in effect two Medeas. Lydgate, for example, talks in *A Wicked Tunge wille Sey Amys* 115 of the 'kyndenesse of Mede',[18] although in the *Fall of Princes* he vigorously follows Boccaccio's account of the evil Medea, and in his *Troy Book* expatiates at enormous length on Guido's severely antifeminist account. Medea, it has recently been suggested, offers a prime example of the argumentative potential[19] of what I am calling the 'matter of Woman'; dominated by love as she is, Medea may readily be made to demonstrate either its inspirational or its destructive power.

Nevertheless, the obvious question suggested by the material I have cited is how would it be possible for Chaucer to turn a lady of such reputation into a 'good woman', even in the limited sense that the God of Love might give to such a term? In order to make her an exemplum

---

16 Shaner, 'An Interpretive Study', pp. 47–8. Shaner notes that brief accounts of Hypsipyle are found in Hyginus' *Fabulae*, Statius' *Thebaid*, the First and Second Vatican Mythographers, Walsingham and the *Ovide Moralisé*, ibid., pp. 45 ff.

17 Guarino, *Famous Women*, p. 35.

18 MacCracken, *Lydgate's Minor Poems*, II, p. 843.

19 Janet Cowen, 'Women as Exempla in Fifteenth-Century Verse of the Chaucerian Tradition', in Julia Boffey and Janet Cowen, eds., *Chaucer and Fifteenth-Century Poetry* (King's College London Medieval Studies, 1991), pp. 51–65.

of betrayed womanhood Chaucer in fact denudes of almost all detail a story which normally lends itself to rich embroidery (almost all the individuating detail of the double *Legend of Hypsipyle and Medea* focuses on Jason's plight and exploits). Is such a highly censored version of *Medea* then ironic? Some critics such as Frank and Kolve feel that the Legend should be taken at face value, just because the censoring is so thoroughgoing.

Certain medieval conceptual habits lend credence to the notion that an ironic intention is not necessarily implied if Chaucer's *Legend of Medea* appears to be at odds with most other accounts. One is exemplified by the ingenious religious allegories of classical stories, where it sometimes seems that the less obvious the connection, the more elegant the comparison was considered. The writers of such moralisations could indeed produce a Medea *in bono* as well as her more usual *in malo* signification, although the modern reader is likely to consider particularly far-fetched such interpretations as that of the *Ovide Moralisé*, which presents Medea as Christ's grace and wisdom, winning mankind's salvation (the golden fleece). Bersuire in *Ovidius Moralizatus* VII at one point says she symbolises the Blessed Virgin who helps Jason (the wise young priest) achieve the tests set for him by Æetes (God the Father). At another point he equates her with the intellect, and at another suggests that Jason is Christ and Medea is human nature, to which he weds himself for the overcoming of the devil. Needless to say, less violence to the literal implications of the story is done in Bersuire's *in malo* interpretations, which equate Medea's sorceries with the evil wiles that women use to enchant men, and her chariot pulled by flying dragons with female instability, while the murder of her brother is an example of the extremes to which evil women are led through lust, and so on.[20] This kind of allegorisation seems to be totally ignored in the secular courtly literature of the fourteenth century which makes frequent use of classical myth. Nevertheless a similar habit of mind is at work when Christine de Pizan has Reason in the *Cité des Dames* praise Medea, along with Circe, the other well-known sorceress, as exempla of learned women. In isolation from all other relevant facts of their histories, and seen from the figure of

---

[20] See Shaner, 'An Interpretive Study', pp. 53–4.

Reason's limited point of view that women are capable of education and have as clever minds as men, it is in fact true that Medea and Circe must have exerted some considerable intelligence in mastering the lore of magic. (Elsewhere in the same book, when her immediate purpose is different, Christine asserts that sorcery and enchantment are evil.) To reach her end, Christine simply omits the references to Medea's cruelty and wickedness in the first sentence of the paragraph which I quoted above from Boccaccio and instead commends her knowledge.[21] She then follows the rest of the paragraph unchanged, leaving out the last sentence about Medea's murderous tendencies, of course, to present us with an out of context, witty, but presumably unironic, thumbnail sketch of a learned lady.

Medieval readers sometimes objected to the exemplary technique, however, if the exemplum conflicted too disconcertingly with other known facts in the story. This is demonstrated in a debate that arose in the fourteenth century over why Dante placed Julius Caesar in the highest region of hell and Brutus and Cassius in the lowest. The assessment of Caesar's career was controversial, and Dante was clearly taking sides when he decided that the good that Caesar had brought to Rome outweighed the evils of his tyranny. At least, this was Coluccio Salutati's argument in defence of Dante. Boccaccio, who did not approve of Caesar, was forced to confront the issue we are considering, in *Il Comento alla Divina Commedia* II 87, where he links Caesar, 'who . . . was incestuous, basely deflowered many women, robbed and emptied the Roman public treasure and, what is more, tyrannically seized the government of the state and held it while he lived', with one of the treacherous 'heroes' of the *Legend of Good Women*, 'Aeneas, who, according to Virgil's testimony, lived for some time with Dido with little honor, and who besides, in the opinion of most people, plotted with Antenor the betrayal of Ilion, his city (a deed not only foul but most sinful)'. Boccaccio's conclusion was that 'Dante chose these famous figures because they were known to all men as having certain definite virtues. The poet placed them where he did to symbolize these virtues and *for artistic purposes he forgot the vices of which they were guilty*'

---

[21] Richards, *City of Ladies*, I 32. I, p. 69.

(emphasis mine).[22] The point I am making is that a medieval audience no more accepted without question a story severely distorted from the straightforward implication of its known facts than do we. They may have understood the purpose of the distorting process, but they still experienced the shock of the collision between the author's shaping purpose and the story's common-sense connotations.

An example of a version of the Medea story which is censored but not noticeably ironic is Gower's rather sympathetic account in *Confessio Amantis*. Gower devotes almost 1000 lines to Jason and Medea as an exemplum against perjury:

> Thus miht thou se what sorwe it doth
> To swere an oth which is noght soth,
> In loves cause namely.
> *CA* V 4223–5

Gower portrays the love that arises between Jason and Medea as a gently romantic business, genuine enough on both sides, although the passage is not without its own mild humour. But in order to make a complete history of Medea[23] at all sympathetic, it has to undergo some censoring. Gower retains the murders for which can be generated some kind of psychologically plausible explanation, that is, the revenge killing of Jason's third wife, Creusa, and of Medea's own two children by Jason. But the gratuitously ferocious murders of her brother, Absyrtus, and Pelleus (Jason's uncle) are omitted, and in their place Gower substitutes quite innocuous remarks – for the one, he says that Medea's father pursued her and Jason but could not catch up (*CA* V 3910–26), without mentioning that Medea had dismembered her brother to distract her father from the pursuit; for the other, he simply writes that King Pelleus was dead (*CA* V 4187–9), without mentioning that Medea killed him. Gower devotes a quite inordinate amount of space to the details of Medea's sorcery, apparently because he felt his readers would find it interesting (as they probably did), and does not

---

[22] Quoted in R. G. Witt, *Hercules at the Crossroads: the Life, Works and Thought of Coluccio Salutati* (Durham: Duke University Press, 1983), pp. 370–1.

[23] Benoît's version, which Gower largely follows, treats Medea with a measure of sympathy because he only deals with the young Medea, before she has committed most of her famous crimes.

stress its evil nature: 'Bot yit for the novellerie/ I thinke tellen a partie' (*CA* V 3955–6). The intention was evidently to soften his portrait of Medea somewhat, while not at the same time depriving it of everything quintessentially Medean. It is of course no part of Gower's brief to make her a 'good woman', but only to show that she was justified in resenting Jason's ingratitude and perjury. Gower claims neither too much nor too little for Medea.

On the other hand Jean de Meun and Machaut's ostensibly sympa- thetic portraits of Medea include references to many of Medea's worst features, as did Ovid's Epistle. In all these three, part of the authorial intent is to display a biased and unreliable narrator. Jean's La Vieille in the *Roman de la Rose* cites Medea's treatment by an ungrateful Jason as good reason for a woman not to confine herself to loving one man only – Medea in fact moved quite quickly into the arms of Aegeas after the defection of Jason. She then describes how Medea *estrangla par dueil et par raige* her two children, eschewing a mother's pity (*RR* 13632–4). Machaut's Franchise, in *Le Jugement dou Roy de Navarre* 2781–98, mentions Medea to exemplify the generosity of women in love, in lines even more damaging to Medea's reputation for virtue:

> She deserted her country and her father,
> And had her dear brother cut up.
> She killed Pelia in great madness,
> And all this in order to make Jason king . . .
> She was so desperate,
> So out of her mind, so crazed,
> That to spite Jason she killed
> The two infants which were hers
> Because they resembled him,
> And afterwards put her own house to the torch!
> trans. Palmer

The series of devastating one-liners, and the innocent simplicity with which it is suggested that Medea's madness is no more than might be expected of a betrayed woman, effectively damns her, for the reader knows that however common the experience of betrayal may be, not every such woman resorts to killing her husband's children and setting fire to the house into the bargain. The fervour of her love and the intensity of her grief are both indexed by inhuman and even criminal behaviour. Jean de Meun, Machaut, and Gower all tell the Jason and Medea story from Medea's point of view, and all give an original twist to its exemplary value, varying in some way the theme of Jason's ingratitude on which Gower dilates. But, following Ovid, they make sure we remember her crimes as well. It becomes difficult to sympathise with a victim who has so many victims of her own; as Ovid makes Hypsipyle say: '*Medeae Medea forem*',[24] 'I would have been Medea to Medea', where 'Medea' stands for something like 'ferocious vengeance'. Even Christine, in spite of her brief to defend women at all costs, and whom we can hardly accuse of irony, must have been aware that to describe Medea and Circe simply as learned women was, if not humorous, then certainly piquant.

Chaucer, alone of all these writers, censored his Legend of all the detail which makes Medea's story interesting or even worth telling – there is almost nothing about her extensive magic powers, nothing about the procedures she devised to win the golden fleece, nothing about her revenge, to mention only a few of the features that authors usually commented on. Is Medea's betrayal of itself enough to make her a 'good woman', especially since a reader might speculate that it was only common sense for Jason to get as far away from such a woman as possible? That is, in order for the narrator to have Medea stand as a falsely betrayed woman, he has had to prune so much questionable detail from the story that there is literally nothing of Medea left. Are we to assume that, of all the contemporary writers who treated Medea, Chaucer alone was naive enough to think he could present a Medea whom it was possible to accept literally as a 'good woman'? Neither Gower's nor Christine's versions of the story, it will be remembered, had this as their aim. Gower's tale, Chaucer's other references to Medea, to her cruelty and her murders (*MLT* 72–3; *BD* 726–9) and to her sorcery (*KnT* 1944), the popularity in courtly circles of the *Roman de la Rose* and *Jugement dou Roy de Navarre*, suggest that even those members of his audience with the most limited extra knowledge of Medea would have had sufficient to make possible an ironic perspective on the severely censored version in the *Legend of Good Women*. That is to say, no audience of which we can conceive for the *Legend*, learned or

---

[24] *Heroides* VI 151.

courtly, can have approached *Medea* with a blank mind, particularly given Chaucer's promptings, which I shall discuss later and which suggest that Chaucer's version has more in common with those of Jean de Meun and Machaut than of Gower and Christine. The probability is high that people in the Middle Ages were more than able to recognise the kind of expurgation that may have been necessary to produce a picture designed to praise, blame or excuse a personage.

Here we see another feature of medieval thinking which is relevant to our question. Judicious selection of material in order to present a sympathetic or hostile perception of one's client might be said to be one of the first principles of the art of rhetoric. A comparison here with the practice of history writing in the Middle Ages is instructive. Beryl Smalley attests that partiality was built into any attempt at contemporary or near contemporary history and provides several entertaining examples of the judicious selection of material sometimes needed to produce a flattering biography.[25] We must assume, I think, that hearers as well as writers understood the necessity laid upon authors to shape the facts in accordance with the desires of, say, a patron. We can be sure that most of Chaucer's original listeners knew how to discount an unduly favourable account, to decode the flattery, so to speak. The same study by Smalley notes that it was normal for historians to analyse what motives may have lain behind an ostensible motive, and that they tended, if anything, to suspect the worst. This should alert us to the fact that the capacity to read between the lines was well developed in an educated medieval audience. In Christine's collection of stories flattering to women, the *Cité des Dames*, there appears to be very little difference between the procedure which enables Christine to enrol both Medea and her own contemporary, the notorious Isabeau of Bavaria, among the virtuous ladies considered worthy of dwelling in the City of Ladies. Descriptions of Isabeau's way of life from other sources suggest that her morality was quite contrary to that usually espoused by Christine, and Blanche Dow noted many years ago that contemporaries must have been rather surprised to read the praise of

---

[25] Beryl Smalley, *Historians in the Middle Ages* (London: Hudson, 1974), pp. 15, 74–5, 185, 190 and passim.

Isabeau as most virtuous of women given by Christine's character Lady Rectitude.[26]

That Christine has a vested interest in praising women, whether alive or legendary, is obvious. Chaucer's situation is rather different. Medea was neither a live contemporary of his, nor, if he seriously wished to write favourably about women, did he even need to choose her as a subject. Why produce the carefully expurgated version at all? Chaucer makes use of the accepted procedures of laudatory biography, but since the conditions which make such procedures necessary only apply in a real life situation, Chaucer's use of them here in a totally fictional context is probably designed as a humorous contribution to his characterisation of the narratorial voice. Chaucer's narrator is pictured as one compelled to praise the protegée of a powerful, if fictional, overlord, the God of Love, manfully selecting the few respectable details of her life which he feels can bear further scrutiny. We have noted that the academic traditions on how to interpret a text advised readers to take into account the author's life or situation as part of his purpose. When the topic is the highly charged one of woman's virtue, then both a female author and a male writing reluctantly and under compulsion are factors which contribute entertainingly to one's understanding of the texts' distortions. Sheila Delany has noted the similarities in procedure in Chaucer and Christine, and their differences in apparent intention – the one objecting to the distortion to reality caused by the 'unambiguous praise of woman' which he subverts by irony, the other objecting to the distortions of clerical misogyny which she rectifies by restoring the balance with her own one-sided pictures.[27]

Further to this, when the narratives are as brief as here, in contrast to the Chaucerian treatment of Criseyde which is expansive enough as to be self-referential, the clues to the writer's intention are usually to be found in the context. The large number of other stories in the *Cité des*

---

[26] Richards, *City of Ladies*, II 68. 1, p. 212. See Blanche Hinman Dow, *The Varying Attitude Towards Women in French Literature of the Fifteenth Century* (New York: Institute of French Studies, 1936), pp. 250–1.

[27] Sheila Delany, 'Rewriting Woman Good: Gender and the Anxiety of Influence in Two Late-Medieval Texts', in *Medieval Literary Politics: Shapes of Ideology* (Manchester University Press, 1990), p. 85.

Dames confirms the seriousness of Christine's desire to uphold women, which is not to deny other aspects of her project, such as to portray herself before patrons such as Isabeau of Bavaria as a learned and witty writer, skilled as Medea was skilled in sorcery. But the context provided by the whole tale collection in the *Legend of Good Women* is profoundly ambivalent in effect. Indeed, I have embarked on this discussion of Chaucer's choice of the Medea story precisely in order to investigate what it contributes to the whole collection, rather than the reverse procedure of using the context created by the whole catalogue to determine the meaning of one of its components. Moreover, as Chaucer's project has so narrow a focus – good women, not famous women or competent women, and as there are so few candidates treated – ten (in the text of *LGW* as we have it), rather than a hundred or so, then the status of Medea as a Chaucerian Good Woman is not of minor importance. The significance of Medea is not diluted by the proximity of many other exempla, nor, when the subject is goodness, can one's attention be easily diverted from the characteristics of one who normally represents badness.

Some further observations, however, suggest that Chaucer had little expectation that his audience would invest much sorrow in Medea's plight. Chaucer's version is not like other 'favourable' accounts of the Medea story, because the more than thorough expurgation is a merely negative procedure marked by few corresponding moves to engage our sympathy or admiration. Moreover, while Chaucer's *Medea* conforms to the old pattern of the innocent maiden who falls in love with an attractive stranger, who is seduced, betrays her parents and is in turn betrayed, Chaucer follows Jean de Meun and Machaut in not removing quite all the incriminating references, as, in a similar situation, Gower or Christine would have done. For example, while there is no mention in *Medea* of her vengeance on her children and on Jason's new wife, Chaucer does not remove from the companion Legend *Hypsipyle* her predecessor's curse on Medea, 'that she moste bothe hire chyldren spylle,/ And alle tho that sufferede hym his wille' (1574–5), a reference which depends for its point, as in Ovid, on knowledge of the whole story of Medea's vengeance taking. This same *Legend of Hypsipyle and Medea*, incidentally, is the one where Chaucer says, 'Ye gete namore of me, but ye wole rede/ Th'origynal, that telleth al the cas' (1557–8), which I read as a humorous prompt to the audience that there is more to this story than meets the eye, not a solemn direction to look up the original text, which was by no means readily available. Several mentions are made within the Legend of the actions which most medieval commentators on Ovid categorised as betrayal of her father and homeland (1653 ff., 1666). Similarly Medea's concluding lines (1672–5), powerfully translated from Ovid, emphasise the gullibility and infatuation the commentators also condemned. Perhaps even more damaging is Chaucer's reference to his source in Guido del Colonne (1396, 1464), part of the learned Latin tradition which condemned Medea so comprehensively, in contrast to the milder vernacular versions like that of Benoît. Chaucer quotes several of Guido's most dramatic similes from one of his particularly antifeminist passages concerning women's insatiable lust and constant desire for new men, of which Medea is an outstanding representative. Among much else in a similar vein, Guido castigates Medea's father for seating her next to Jason, as he must have known how the concupiscence of women compels them to seek men in endless succession, as matter must 'appetite' form:

> For we know the heart of woman always seeks a husband, just as matter always seeks form [*sicut appetit materia semper formam*]. Oh, would that matter, passing once into form, could be said to be content with the form it has received. But just as it is known that matter proceeds from form to form, so the dissolute desire of women proceeds from man to man, so that it may be believed without limit, since it is of an unfathomable depth [*cum sit profunditas sine fundo*].[28]

This appears to be a reference to the theory of 'hylomorphism' (originating with Aristotle but generally accepted by scholastic philosophers) which contends that everything is composed of passive matter, and of an active principle of form. Matter is to be thought of as constantly mobile and never at rest in its search for form which alone will give it actuality.[29] Perhaps Guido was repeating a common

---

[28] Griffin, *Historia*, p. 17; trans., Margaret Elizabeth Meek, quoted in Blamires, *Woman Defamed*, p. 48.

[29] Cf. Knowles, *Medieval Thought* (London: Longman, 1962), pp. 13, 245; J. A. Bryant, 'Another Appetite for Form', *MLN* 58 (1943): 195–6.

scholastic joke on woman's inherent changeableness.[30] There can be no doubt that in the opening lines to *Medea*, Chaucer has Guido's witty metaphor in mind, except that he has wrenched it from its 'natural' connection with women and transferred it to Jason:

> To Colcos comen is this duc Jasoun,
> That is of love devourer and dragoun.
> As mater apetiteth forme alwey,
> And from forme into forme it passen may,
> Or as a welle that were botomles,
> Ryght so can false Jason have no pes.
> For to desyren thourgh his apetit
> To don with gentil women his delyt,
> This is his lust and his felicite.
> 1580–8

Chaucer's collocation of 'apetiten', 'desyren' and 'devouren' cleverly develops Guido's image. The words connote both the philosophical idea of matter's 'privation' and desire for form, and the notion of the greedy eating associated with the deadly sin of Gluttony. Jason is a 'sly devourere . . . of gentil wemen, tendre creatures' (1369–70), and the narrator describes Jason's consumption of women as being like the fox's enjoyment of the birds he steals by night (1389–93). Jason gobbles up tender women as the fox eats 'tendre capouns'. Nevertheless, the context from which Chaucer drew this memorable image of matter 'appetiting' form is that of vigorous philosophical antifeminism, and it is not unlikely that some of his audience would have recognised it as such.

The *Legend*'s Medea story, that is to say, does come to us in a frame in miniature, a frame whose interest is almost entirely in Jason and which inevitably and designedly affects our response to Medea. This frame story not only cynically designates Jason's amorous adventures as belonging to the amoral world of the fox, but makes the powerful sorceress just one term in a demeaning series of abandoned women. The 'marriages' of the two chief victims of Jason's trail of seduction are

---

[30] Lydgate's translation of Guido expands gleefully on the 'insaciate change and mutabilite of women', then condemns *Guido*'s antifeminism, see H. Bergen, ed., *Lydgate's Troy Book*, 4 vols. (London: EETS ES 97, 103, 106, 126: 1906–35), I, 1836–1904, 2097 ff., pp. 66–74.

each treated in a couplet whose bathos effectively demolishes the women's claim to be tragic heroines. Thus of Hypsipyle the narrator says, 'And upon hire begat he children two,/ And drogh his sayl, and saw hir nevere mo' (1562–3), and of Medea, '[He] doth his oth, and goth with hire to bedde;/ And on the morwe upward he hym spedde' (1644–5). His desertion of Medea and marriage to Creusa ('the doughter of the kyng Creon') are treated with similarly devastating cursoriness (1656–61).

The seriousness of Chaucer's ostensible aim to defend women is compromised by the choice and treatment of the Medea story, the more so as the seductive power of the male betrayer Jason is valorised, as well as his success in exploiting and containing the most dangerous of enchantresses. If *Hypsipyle and Medea* makes any attempt to engage our sympathy, then it is for Jason's undeserved suffering at the hands of his uncle. It has often been noted that Jason receives far more attention from Chaucer than do either of his chief female victims. Jason's career as a seducer was no more ideologically sound in Chaucer's time than today and yet rarely has the exaggerated abuse the narrator directs at him been seen as anything but comic. The story has been transposed from the context of orthodox morality, where good people earn a just reward, to the ludic realm of the world of the night where all the prizes go to the undeserving fox:

> For [false lovers] shal have wel betere love and chere
> Than he that hath abought his love ful dere,
> Or hadde in armes many a blody box,
> For evere as tendre a capoun et the fox,
> Thow he be fals and hath the foul betrayed,
> As shal the good-man that therfore hath payed.
> Al have he to the capoun skille and ryght,
> The false fox wol have his part at nyght.
> 1386–93

A tacit assumption that women, or their virginity, are normally paid for (1391), bought (1387), owned (1392), or, alternatively, stolen (1393)? Probably Chaucer only means to contrast Jason's barnyard morality with the orthodoxies of courtly wooing; it is an iconoclastic gesture towards the ideal forms of official culture, indicating the register within which we are to interpret Medea's story. It clearly reduces women to the status of sexual and economic prey. In the egregious choice of Medea as a 'good woman' one might have expected Chaucer at least to have aligned her with the other predatory heroines who from a position of power initiate sexual contact with the heroes – Nysus' daughter/ Phaedra/Ariadne, Cleopatra, Dido – and from involvement with whom men have a right to extricate themselves. In choosing instead to tokenise Medea, Chaucer like Jason plunders her of all that is properly her own.

On the one hand we are invited to interpret the Jason and Medea story as if it were an episode in the courtly game of seducing women that Alceste had deplored so severely in the Prologue to the *Legend*, but which, Chaucer's tone implies, the audience will judge less gravely:

> As wolde God I leyser hadde and tyme
> By proces al his wowyng for to ryme!
> But in this hous if any fals lovere be,
> Ryght as hymself now doth, ryght so dide he,
> With feynynge, and with every subtil dede.
> Ye gete namore of me, but ye wole rede
> Th'origynal, that telleth al the cas.
> 1552–8

The last two lines, however, recall that other aspect of the *Legend*'s context, the element of learned *jeu d'esprit* drawn from the matter of scholarly antifeminism, as found in the Latin books which educated men enjoyed. I have already noted the reference to Guido's opinion about women and matter. Walter Map, in *Valerius ad Ruffinum* (Dist. IV c 3), also jokingly recommends dissolute behaviour like Jason's over the fidelity of marriage, since 'a number of threads form an easier bond than a single chain' and 'many fits of sickness with intervals of health are less injurious than a single ailment which never ceases to vex with pain that cannot be cured'.[31] From the perspective of men either of the court or of the school, particularly in their leisure reading, the importance of the female victim of male predatoriness is debased.

---

[31] James, *Courtiers' Trifles*, pp. 300–3. R. F. Green comments on similar attitudes displayed by a minority of the participants in the *Cent Ballades* (c. 1389), 'Chaucer's Victimized Women', *SAC* 10 (1988): 5–7. I differ from Green in that I see such passages as visibly ludic, counter-orthodox, outrageous.

When Jason, in order to 'bedote' Hypsipyle, acts 'as coy as is a mayde [and] loketh pitously, but nought he sayde . . .' (1548–9), he shows he knows how to exploit and to protect himself from women, in a manner Map would have approved of. The adoption of false but appealing appearances and other forms of deceit might well appear a 'feminine' mode of behaviour,[32] but from the point of view of the Ovidian lover are to be thought of as stratagems appropriate to warfare, and indicate the literary and social context in which the *Legend of Good Women* is to be understood. Dissimulation and infidelity like Jason's could be, and frequently were, blamed as simply morally wrong, particularly in serious didactic writing, but in other contexts were reacted to as mere peccadilloes which enhanced male power and virility rather than detracted from it – Chaucer in the *Legend* pretends to the one but invites the second. In short, Jason is showing himself an apt pupil of Master Ovid who advised men to 'deceive the deceivers', betray the betrayers – a precept which was enthusiastically endorsed by Jean de Meun in the *Roman de la Rose*, and a concept of Woman to which Christine de Pizan strenuously objected in her debate about the *Rose*. Chaucer's Jason is able to beat women at their own game, and even the appropriation to Jason of Guido del Colonne's antifeminist dictum that women seek men in endless succession, as matter appetites form, is worn by Jason as a badge of honour. Indeed Chaucer is introducing to English the cynical attitude to the heroines of the classical love stories typical of the clerical wit with which Jean de Meun in the *Rose* and Guillaume de Machaut in *Navarre* ornamented courtly vernacular literature:

---

[32] For a different viewpoint see Hansen, *Fictions of Gender*, pp. 1–15. Hansen suggests that the position of powerlessness in which so many of the heroes initially find themselves and the 'feminine' wiliness by which they extricate themselves are an aspect of their 'feminisation'. I find it hard to detect evidence that Chaucer experienced, or incited in the male members of his audience, a high level of masculine anxiety when faced with the femininised position in which Jason's tribulations placed him, and the deceit and sexual adventurism which he used to escape them. In short, I do not agree with Hansen that Chaucer is serious in his condemnation of men, but I do agree with her contention that Chaucer in the *Legend* is no protofeminist and offers no genuine analysis of or sympathy with the position of women beyond what was characteristic of his age.

Yif that I live, thy name shal be shove
In English that thy sekte shal be knowe!
Have at thee, Jason! Now thyn horn is blowe!
1381–3

Given that the comic abuse of Jason's deceit only enhances his
wonderful natural powers of seduction (1603–8), I doubt that Chaucer's
picture of Medea offered much satisfaction to women members of the
audience. The substitution of Medea, dupe of Jason, for Medea,
powerful sorceress, hardly invites empathy from women, even medieval
women, particularly as the heroine admits that the only defence her
victimisation admits was that she valued Jason's yellow hair more than
her reputation.

I have written at length about Chaucer's use of the famous Medea
story, not because it is a very significant Legend in itself, but because
it is another paradigm of the interpretative problems associated with
the *Legend* as a whole. Like many of the other Legends *Medea* does
not offer unequivocal directions as to its interpretation; nevertheless, a
reading which accepts a portrayal of Medea as an innocently betrayed
victim leaves one with a sense of unease. Unlike many of the other
Legends, however, we know precisely Chaucer's sources for his
version: his powerful evocation of the context of clerical antifeminism
achieved when he locates his source material in the work of Guido del
Colonne, accompanied as it is by the invitation to trivialise his
heroine's suffering at the hands of the sexual adventurer, Jason,
produces a concept of Medea contrasting markedly, and thus ironically, with the idea of Medea, the Innocent, which the *Legend of Good
Women* ostensibly depicts. My examination of other medieval versions
of the Medea story suggests that expurgation, of itself, is not enough
to prove an ironic intention, although one suspects that Chaucer saw
his cleaning up of Medea's reputation as humorous. However, the
active shaping of the Medea story in all the versions we have examined
(including the moralisations of Bersuire and the *Ovide Moralisé*),
frequently involving gross distortions of well-known 'facts' as they do,
demonstrates how well adapted were the stories of the classical heroines
to draw attention to the writer's power to make of his matter what he
willed.

Although it seems likely that Chaucer viewed many of his heroines as less than 'good', the question is not so easy to examine when our circumstantial evidence is not so strong as in the case of Medea. It is unlikely, for example, that Chaucer thought Hypsipyle, Medea's co-victim of Jason's seduction, as quite the 'innocent' he calls her in *LGW* 1546, but probably she was not so famous that her name could raise the same set of expectations as could that of the nefarious Medea. That she was not very well-known is most likely,[33] and thus her story is not so baldly developed as in *Medea*, where the impact must come almost entirely from audience expectation of a dramatic tale, and from the humiliating bathos which the story derives when made simply a sequel to *Hypsipyle*.

In the next chapter we will turn to a heroine whose modern reputation, at least, is as bad as Medea's, but who is not portrayed as the victim of a male seducer, that commonest of the *Legend*'s paradigms. Cleopatra's reputation did not accompany her as powerfully as did Medea's in medieval times, but she is presented as ambivalently as her fellow heroines. The ambivalence of her tale, however, centres on whether love for her is an inspiration or a temptation to its hero Antony.

[33] For a wider discussion of Hypsipyle, see Minnis, *Shorter Poems*, pp. 367 ff.

II

Cleopatra: legend of Cupid's saint

Because its heroine has as unsavoury a reputation as Medea, we might expect to be able to interpret the *Legend of Cleopatra* in a similar fashion, in essence, by a simple comparison of Chaucer's version with other accounts. But this is not the case – since we are not entirely sure what Chaucer's source was, and since we are much less certain what his audience would have known about the subject. It is important to look at this Legend, as it begins the series of 'good' women, and as in both Prologues the God of Love stipulates that Cleopatra is what he means by a good woman (F 560, 566/G 542), and what he means by a saint or martyr of love. In addition, in *Cleopatra* the poet appears to be following closely the God of Love's command to be brief, because there are many stories to be treated:

> At Cleopatre I wol that thou begynne . . .
> Suffiseth me thou make in this manere:
> That thou reherce of al hir lyf the grete,
> After thise olde auctours lysten for to trete.
> For whoso shal so many a storye telle,
> Sey shortly, or he shal to longe dwelle.
> F 566–77

Here is another example of the familiar ambiguity of the *Legend*. Is this, as it appears, a simple exhortation to brevity, or is it an open invitation to expurgation, spoken as it is by the God of Love in connection with Cleopatra, who has been called the 'greatest courtesan in history', or, in the words of John of Salisbury and Boccaccio, the 'poisonous whore' (*meretrix venena*)? In fact, in the brief compass of the *Legend of Cleopatra* there is a relatively extended *occupatio* recalling the poet's commission to 'sey shortly', on the occasion of Cleopatra's wedding, or non-wedding, to Antony:

> The weddynge and the feste to devyse,
> To me, that have ytake swich empryse
> Of so many a story for to make,
> It were to longe, lest that I shulde slake . . .
> And forthy to th'effect thanne wol I skyppe,
> And al the remenaunt, I wol lete it slippe.
> 616–23

Does this simply mean what it says, or does it conceal the fact that there is a large 'remenaunt' in Cleopatra's story that needs to be skipped over? Or is Chaucer simply padding a story about which he can find little detail? All these possibilities could be true.

Although the manifest contradiction between the Cleopatra of most historical accounts and Chaucer's presentation of her as a good woman has frequently led to the view that *Cleopatra* is ironic, in recent times this type of contradiction in the poem has been accounted for by Kolve[1] as essentially serious in intent. As this response has been put forward as the fundamental paradigm of the Legends, I will later give it more consideration. Frank, whose discussion of the *Legend of Cleopatra* is perhaps his least effective, believes that Chaucer and his audience knew nothing of Cleopatra because there is no known reference to the Egyptian queen in medieval English before Chaucer's own reference to her in the *Parliament of Fowls*. This position has been disputed by several more recent critics. Beverly Taylor, in particular, has documented the fact that Cleopatra had been celebrated since soon after her death, by pagan and Christian alike, as a significant figure in world history,[2] even though it is likely that the shape her story received at the hands of Augustan propagandists may have borne little resemblance to the 'real' Cleopatra.[3] The judgement of the historians known by medieval readers was frequently critical of her lust and ambition. It is

---

[1] See Kolve, 'Cleopatra to Alceste', pp. 130–78.

[2] Beverly Taylor, 'The Medieval Cleopatra: the Classical and Medieval Tradition of Chaucer's *Legend of Cleopatra*', *Journal of Medieval and Renaissance Studies* 7 (1977): 249–69.

[3] See Lucy Hughes-Hallett, *Cleopatra: Histories, Dreams and Distortions* (London: Bloomsbury, 1990), passim.

not necessary to maintain that a medieval audience had at its fingertips the huge corpus of material on Cleopatra cited by Taylor, in noting that it fed into what knowledge there was of Cleopatra in medieval times. While it is true that mention of Cleopatra is not common in the vernacular languages before Chaucer's time, except in Italian, this in no way implies that her career was not known to many of Chaucer's audience. Boccaccio alluded to her in several of his Italian works, and treated her and Antony's history extensively, and with intense hostility, in his Latin works, *De Casibus Virorum Illustrium* and *De Claris Mulieribus*.

We know that Chaucer knew the first of these works. Boccaccio's account of 'Mark Antony, the Triumvir, and Cleopatra, Queen of Egypt' in *De Casibus* is highly pejorative, obsessively dwelling on their lust and the sensuality and luxury which marked their life together. Boccaccio recounts Antony's early history, including his marriage to Octavia, the sister of Octavian who became the Emperor Augustus. He describes Cleopatra's incestuous marriage to her brother, her attempt to gain the throne by poisoning him, and her seduction of Julius Caesar. He writes of the success Antony enjoyed with Octavian until 'Fortune was now invited to make way for his downfall', whereupon, after enduring some military disasters, Antony was

> seized by the beauty of the lascivious Egyptian, Cleopatra. Under the spell of her attraction, he was feverish and ran around as if he were about to put in her lap all the titles he had received for his victories and the rewards of his triumphs . . . He laid down his arms as if all the prestige of Roman honor rested with her charms and gave himself over to indolence and sloth. He wasted his time in never-ending sensuality and gluttony . . . He ordered it proclaimed that he had divorced Octavia and married Cleopatra.

Cleopatra entices Antony to declare war on Rome, and a 'fleet was prepared which you would have thought carried the perfumes of Saba, Arabia, Syria, and other countries, as well as the robes and pomp of kings, rather than the arms of conflict'. The disastrous naval Battle of Actium ensues and Antony and Cleopatra are defeated. Boccaccio continues: 'The Egyptians began to turn their ships about. Their leader was the famous Cleopatra, the woman who had begged and wished for the Roman Empire, the woman with golden ships and purple sails. And immediately, Antony, her proud sponsor followed her.' Unable to obtain terms of peace, Antony commits suicide. Cleopatra surrenders, and 'with the charm of her eyes and figure she tried in vain to lure the young Octavian into desiring her'. Rather than be led in triumph she puts serpents to her breasts and dies beside Antony.[4]

The account in *De Claris Mulieribus* is similar, although it pays less attention to Antony, and concentrates more on Cleopatra's 'crimes' and her 'greed, cruelty and lustfulness'.[5] I am not presenting these stories as sources of the Legend, as such, although the similarities between the two works by Boccaccio and Chaucer's *Cleopatra* were strong enough to be considered so in many editions of the *Legend*. The brief account by Vincent de Beauvais in his *Speculum Historiale*[6] is a more likely source, as I shall discuss below.

I think it possible that Chaucer could have known several accounts like these of Boccaccio. If Chaucer did not, then many men who heard his tales would have done so – it needed no particular erudition – and Frank's contention that he took a fancy to the unusual name in Dante, used it in the *Parliament of Fowls*, and tried to pad out the story as best he could for the *Legend of Good Women* does not bear scrutiny. It demands an astonishing amount of naivety on Chaucer' part, and is belied by the focal position given to Cleopatra in the Prologues. It seems unlikely that he would have concentrated there on a suspicious character over whose story he had little control through lack of knowledge.

When we turn to Chaucer's text, we find that the poet has acceded to the God of Love's desire for brevity with a vengeance. He brings Antony and Cleopatra together swiftly and to the crucial point of their rebellion against Rome in sixteen lines (580–95). The opening lines of the Legend conceal the manner in which Cleopatra, 'his queene', came to

---

[4] Hall, *Illustrious Men*, pp. 170–4.

[5] Guarino, *Famous Women*, p. 192.

[6] See W. K. Wimsatt, 'Vincent of Beauvais and Chaucer's Cleopatra and Croesus', *Speculum* 12 (1937): 375–81; Pauline Aiken, 'Chaucer's *Legend of Cleopatra* and the *Speculum Historiale*', *Speculum* 13 (1938): 232–6. The older scholars, Bech and after him Skeat, suggested as a source the *Epitome Rerum Romana* by Florus. Vincent's version of Antony and Cleopatra is clearly a condensed version of Florus', and his particular compression of the events is closer to Chaucer's. Frank agrees that Vincent's story is Chaucer's most likely source.

rule Egypt by engineering the death of Tholome 'the kyng' (580–2). (By carefully starting the story at the beginning of Cleopatra's reign one avoids the telling of a fair portion of her crimes.) There are, however, faint echoes of Boccaccio's attitude in *De Casibus* with the allusion to Fortune owing Antony 'a shame' in lines 589–90. These echoes grow even stronger as the narrative proceeds to elaborate on the death and dishonour which befell him through his love for Cleopatra. The reference to the 'rage' into which love has brought Antony and love's 'snare' in which he is so tightly enmeshed is derisive, and leaves no doubt that a tale of sexual passion is envisaged, rather than one of idealised courtly devotion (599–600). If Ross's observations in *Chaucer's Bawdy* are accurate then there is also a strong erotic charge in the lines:

> Hym thoughte ther nas nothyng to hym so due
> As Cleopatras for to love and *serve*;
> Hym roughte nat in *armes* for to *sterve*
> In the defence of hyre and of hire ryght.
> 603–6 (emphasis mine)

This sentence may allude to the courtly service a man offers his lady by taking up arms and even dying in her defence. It may also be read so that the service he offers her is animal-like copulation, the death he dies is orgasmic, and the arms refer to amatory embraces.[7] The stigma of uxoriousness flashes momentarily in line 605 – in the suggestion that Antony no longer cared about the profession of honourable warfare – before the completed sentence transmutes this into the concept, acceptable in chivalric terms, of the defence of his lady's right (606), and the line may be compared to Boccaccio's disapproving remark, in the above quotation from *De Casibus*, 'He laid down his arms . . .', etc. And, while a certain glamour may attach to the notion that, for the sake of Cleopatra's love, 'al the world [Antony] sette at no value' (602), the Middle Ages in general did not approve of a love whose end result was the death or destruction of a 'ful worthy gentil werreyour' (597).

In all the tumble of events depicted in the opening lines of *Cleopatra*,

---

[7] See 'rage', 'serve', 'armes', 'sterve' (die) in *Chaucer's Bawdy*. Ross does not cite these *loci* in the *Legend*, presumably because he does not find it a text in which obscenity is likely to be found.

what is clear is that the hero is a rebel to Rome and a false deserter of his wife (591–4), tightly bound in the chains of the madness of love for another woman. The structure of lexical connotation is such that it is not material whether an audience knows the details of the Cleopatra story or not. Chaucer's lines do not contradict the traditional story if it is known, but even if it is not known, they create a picture of a passionate love affair that destroys its hero, formerly a noble warrior. The narrative in fact suggests that Antony was sent from Rome to subdue Cleopatra who subdued him instead, so that Rome itself was threatened. I am aware that I could have phrased this sentence less pejoratively, and more romantically, yet I am convinced that many of Chaucer's audience would have read the story in this way, since the topos of how Love, Fortune, and/or Woman could bring even the strongest or wisest man to his knees – witness Adam, Samson, David, Solomon, Aristotle or Vergil – is one of the commonplaces in works dealing with the 'matter of Woman'.[8]

After hastening through this litany of robust facts, the narrator suddenly modulates his tone into the mild and gently idealising sentiments suitable to the description of a proper medieval hero ('Worthi to any wyght that liven may') and heroine ('This noble queene'), which culminates in the one-line description of Cleopatra's dark attractiveness with a cliché normally reserved for the fragile beauty of a more conventional heroine: 'And she was fayr as is the rose in May' (607–13). One's misgiving that the description of Antony's behaviour so far given showed little in the way of 'chyvalrye', 'gentillesse' or 'discrecioun' is confirmed with the narrator's suspiciously qualifying, 'As certeynly, but if that bokes lye . . .' Moreover, any idea that Antony and Cleopatra have been converted into conventional medieval lovers is dispelled in the final couplet:

> And, for to make shortly is the beste,
> She wax his wif, and hadde hym as hire leste.
> 614–15

This last line so disrupts normal notions of the 'sovereignty' that should obtain in marriage that the scribes of several of the *LGW* manuscripts evidently believed an emendation was in order, even at the expense of

---

[8] E.g. see James, *Courtiers' Trifles* pp. 290–3.

conventional grammar. Thus, Bodley 638 gives, 'She was his wyf & had hir at his lest'; Arch. Selden B 24, 'Sche wox his wyf and had hir as him lest'; Additional 9832, 'She was his wyffe and did as hym leste'; Trinity College Cambridge 3. 19, 'She was hys wyf and had hir as him lest.'[9] Clearly these scribes felt that the line should have described Antony having Cleopatra as it pleased him, rather than vice versa. This raising of the bogy of female 'maistrie' (by suggesting that Cleopatra does what she wants with Antony once they are married) effectively dispels, in my opinion, any notion that Chaucer was thinking of a soft and sentimental Cleopatra, 'a true and faithful wife', as some critics insist on describing her.[10]

Mention of the marriage brings the narrator to the passage refusing to describe the wedding which I have quoted above (616–23). One's initial reaction may be that this rhetorical stance draws attention to the fact that there was no marriage, according to history. This is not so strong a point as it seems, however, for many medieval versions say that the lovers did marry, and even Boccaccio, in *De Casibus*, says: 'Finally she was first mistress, then wife, to Antony.' One other such account is that of Vincent de Beauvais in his *Speculum Historiale*, who notes that 'lascivious Antony, corrupted by love of Cleopatra', married her after repudiating the sister of Augustus, on whom he then declared war – *Porro cum esset lascivius anthonius correptuus amore cleopatre egipti regine. repudiata augusti sorore ipsam sibi cleopatram matrimonio copulavit. et augusto bellum indixit.*[11] These are of course the essential facts that Chaucer has given in the opening thirty-five lines of *Cleopatra*, and it is likely that this is the account that Chaucer had open before him. That is to say, no matter how much else Chaucer knew of Cleopatra, and the influence of Boccaccio seems indubitable, he probably 'used the

---

9   The passages in which these lines are embedded are not otherwise noticeably corrupt. I cite these scribal variations from F. J. Furnivall, ed., *A Parallel-Text Edition of Chaucer's Minor Poems* (London: Chaucer Society), Part III, xi, 1st series, no. 21; *Supplementary Parallel-Texts to Chaucer's Minor Poems*, Part I, 1st series, no. 22. The Cowen/Kane edition seems to imply that the reading I have cited from Bodley 638 should be that of Pepys 2006.

10 Cf. Frank, *Chaucer and the 'Legend'*, p. 41; Kolve, 'Cleopatra to Alceste', p. 131.

11 Vincent's account of Cleopatra is taken from Wimsatt, 'Vincent of Beauvais', p. 378, cf. Aiken, 'Chaucer's *Legend*', pp. 232–3. A translation of the whole passage from Vincent may be found in Minnis, *Shorter Poems*, pp. 354–5.

great encyclopedia, as we use one today, for the purpose of ready reference, for the sake of brushing up his memory of this or that bit of scientific lore, this or that legend'.[12] If the relatively brief entry in Vincent's encyclopedia were used, the expurgation theory is of course deprived of much of its power, and suggests that Chaucer had to shape this story by adding material, rather than by cutting.

Vincent, like Chaucer, proceeds immediately to the sea-battle of Actium. For one of the most significant naval battles in world history Chaucer substitutes a typical medieval sea-battle – and, with its 'grete gonne', even a late fourteenth-century sea-battle. It has been shown that almost every line in this vigorous passage (634–53) can be paralleled in Froissart's accounts of the crucial battles in which, about the time of the *Legend* and earlier, English ships defeated the nation's enemies at sea.[13] Chaucer's embroidery on Vincent's short notice of Actium produces a wonderfully realistic set-piece, with its strong alliterative phrases describing all the sights and sounds of a contemporary sea-battle, indeed all the 'dirty tricks' with which each side sought to gain the advantage. It is a passage which Chaucerians would not be without, although it seems to have scant relevance to the theme of the betrayal of 'good women'. But there is also a sense in which the violence, emotion and thrusting action of the energetic account suit Antony and Cleopatra's remarkably uncourtly story of passion, rebellion and treachery.

It comes as no surprise that this egregiously lengthy piece of padding to the brief account in the source is one of the places where Delany notes, alongside the primary literal sense, a particularly high concentration of sexual innuendo: 'the ships meet, up goes the trumpet, out comes the big gun, down come the stones, in goes the grapnel with its phallic crooks, the men press in. Finally there is a pouring forth – of peas; then a sticky white substance appears – lime, to be sure – and the

---

[12] Wimsatt, 'Vincent of Beauvais', p. 381.

[13] W. H. Schofield, 'The Sea-battle in Chaucer's "Legend of Cleopatra"', in *Anniversary Papers by Colleagues and Pupils of George Lyman Kittredge* (Boston: Ginn, 1913), pp. 139–52. The passage is frequently linked with the tournament in *KnT* 2605–16, and is another of the similarities between that the *Knight's Tale* and the *Legend*. Cf. also N. F. Blake, 'Chaucer and the Alliterative Romances', *ChauR* 3 (1969): 163–9.

opponents "go together". This last is a common synonym (says *MED*) for copulation.'[14] Whether or not this passage is so full of erotic innuendo will be questioned by many; however, once suggested, it is by no means easy to dispel. *MED*, moreover, attests the meaning of penis and testicles for 'croke' and 'stones' respectively, and, as far as female genitalia are concerned, Ross intimates in *Chaucer's Bawdy* that he would not be surprised to find the word 'cuppe' (647) meaning vagina in Chaucer, although he can be confident of no examples, and certainly none in the *Legend* – the *Riverside Chaucer*, incidentally, has a question mark over the significance for this passage, at the literal level, of bringing the 'cuppe'. Under the heading of what Delany calls 'suggestive images' come the weaponry, the joining of the ships with grappling hooks after they have hurtled together with a tremendous thud, all the frenzied innings and outings. Most surprising is Delany's suggestion that the peas poured out on the deck to make it slippery (648) imply seminal fluid. The meaning of 'He poureth pesen upon the haches slidere' has never been satisfactorily resolved, because it is the one example of the practice of contemporary naval battles for which there is no external corroboration. The line has spawned several articles, some from scholars with sea-faring, and even naval warfare, experience, who suggest that the idea was so odd at the literal level that 'pesen' must surely need emendation.[15]

In sea-battles 'grenades' containing greasy or soapy substances were sometimes hurled onto the opposing vessel, where they smashed and made the decks slippery (in the same way that breakable containers of 'Greek fire' were hurled to set it on fire). But how and why would you 'pour peas'? Dried peas would no doubt impede foothold, but if you poured them rather than hurled them, would you not impede your own progress as much as that of your opponents, unless you were in retreat or trying to repel boarders? 'Pesen' in the sense of pease porridge has seemed unlikely, yet *MED* offers one sense for 'pesen', not noted by Delany, which perhaps lends some colour to her equation of pouring peas and ejaculation: sense 5. a cites Trevisa's use of 'pesen' to describe

---

[14] Delany, 'Logic of Obscenity', p. 192.
[15] See K. G. T. Webster, 'Two Notes on Chaucer's Sea-Fight', *MP* 25 (1927–8): 291–2; F. J. Mather, 'Pesen at Actium: a Chaucer Crux', *JEGP* 43 (1944): 375–9; R. M. Smith, 'Action at Actium – An Alliterative Crux in Chaucer', *JEGP* 44 (1945): 56–61.

the milky look of the spawn of fish or frogs – for example, 'In march watir is nought wel holsom to drynke, for þanne watir is namliche infecte by *schedinge of seed of pesin and mylk of fissch and froggis*' (emphasis mine). *OED* has similar citations, so that this is no more desperate a reading than the never-accepted emendations of our sea-faring scholars.[16] As I have said, there are no known extra-literary references to the practice of pouring peas on decks in naval battles, but W. Todd Furniss thinks that the sixteenth-century poet George Gascoigne's account of the naval battle of Lepanto provides an 'exact analogue' of Chaucer's description of the pouring of (parched) peas and the hurling of pots of (unslaked) lime. Furniss asserts this represents an independent and thus eyewitness account which he contends is certainly not influenced by Chaucer.[17] I cannot concur with this assessment of the Gascoigne passage, which reads to me like a highly rhetorical and very literary set piece, with strong alliteration in each line, as in Chaucer. In my opinion it may well number Chaucer's sea-battle in *Cleopatra* among its ancestors – Gascoigne elswhere compares himself to 'that worthy and famous knight Sir Geffrey Chaucer'.[18]

As in the matter of Phaedra's speech in *Ariadne*, it should be remembered that even the most literal reading of this passage has several questions hanging over it – the meaning of the gun, the cup, the peas, the disproportionate length and general appropriateness, the fact that the passage would read most naturally as favouring the eventual victory of the tale's protagonists (especially if there were no prior knowledge of the story), so that the conclusion, 'Antony is schent' (652), comes as a surprise. If the passage describing Antony and Cleopatra's battle with Octavian also has overtones of their own 'meeting together', then Antony's destruction may be understandable after such frenetic sexual activity. Indeed it has long been noted that the egregious battle scene has displaced a banquet scene, a narrative topos

---

[16] Muscatine cites a number of terms used in the fabliaux for semen such as *la mole des os* (marrow) and *aubon* (egg-white), *Old French Fabliaux*, p. 189.

[17] W. Todd Furniss, 'Gascoigne and Chaucer's *Pesen*', *MLN* 68 (1953): 115–18. The lines referred to are from 'Gascoignes devise of a maske for the right honorable Viscount Mountacute' 192–3. See *George Gascoigne: A Hundryd Sundry Flowers 1573* (Menston: Scolar Press, 1970), p. 388. If peas were ever used as an ad hoc weapon, they would have been carried on board in the ship's stores, not its armoury.

[18] *Flowers*, p. 203.

where more often than not Antony and Cleopatra's lust and conspicuous consumption were emblematised.[19] Perhaps the ancient use of the imagery of naval battle to stand for sexual congress leads the poet to imbue his account of the Battle of Actium with the flamboyant sensuality which traditionally pervades the love story of Antony and Cleopatra, but which flouts dramatically the normal courtly limits of describing the love of a 'ful worthy gentil werreyour' and a 'noble queene . . . fayr as is the rose in May'.

According to most versions of the story, the end comes for Antony when he sees Cleopatra turn and flee 'with al hire purpre sayl' (cf. 654); abandoned by Cleopatra and with Augustus pursuing the remainder of his fleet, Antony takes his own life (654–61). Vincent says, *cleopatra regina cum aurea puppe veloque purpureo prima fugere cepit. et ilico insecutus est eam anthonius. instare vestigiis augustus. Quod cernens anthonius propria se manu interemit.* The order of events is left ambiguous in Chaucer, although in my opinion the traditional order (that is, Cleopatra's flight followed by Antony's suicide) is at least alluded to when in line 656 the narrator ostensibly expresses sympathy for the queen's understandable (feminine) weakness:

> Fleth ek the queen, with al hire purpre sayl,
> For strokes, whiche that wente as thikke as hayl;
> No wonder was she myghte it nat endure.
> 654–6

Vincent goes on with the damaging details concerning Cleopatra's unsuccessful attempt to save herself by seducing Augustus, who spurns her: *regina vero ad pedes augusti provoluta temptavit oculos ejus sed spreta ab eo desperavit.* Rather than be led in triumph to Rome she determines on suicide. This is usually given as her reason rather than her love for Anthony. In a somewhat muted manner – 'His wif, that coude of Cesar have no grace,/ To Egipt is fled for drede and for destresse' (663–4) – Chaucer alludes to Cleopatra's failure to seduce Augustus.

The major section of the Legend, however, that which highlights her 'martyrdom' in the proper fashion of the saint's legend, is introduced

---

[19] Cf. Fyler, *Chaucer and Ovid*, pp. 100–1. For the topos of Cleopatra's banquet, see Hughes-Hallett, *Cleopatra*, pp. 63–7.

with four lines that call upon one of the key motifs in the 'religion' of
courtly love:

> But herkeneth, ye that speken of kyndenesse,
> Ye men that falsly sweren many an oth
> That ye wol deye if that youre love be wroth,
> Here may ye sen of wemen which a trouthe!
> 665–8

Some critics (for example, Kolve) take these lines solemnly at face value
and most others ignore them, but they surely anticipate the increasingly
mock-severe castigation, as the Legends progress, of the age-old male
pastime of seducing women with easy promises – the pastime which
Alceste mourns is considered a 'game' among Chaucer's contemporaries
(F 486–9/G 476–9). It is hardly necessary to document the literary
lover's extravagant plea that he will die if his lady does not treat him
kindly. Death is mentioned in all Chaucer's 'Complaints'. Lydgate's
Complaint, for Lack of Mercy ends: 'I nere but dede, pleynly, tis is no
fable/ Withoute recure, for lacke of mercy.'[20] In French and English in
the fifteenth century there is a multiplication of poems concerning
ladies who are able to resist this plea, who in fact do not believe it – *La
Belle Dame sans Mercy* is the most famous, and caused much mock-
horror and debate till the end of that century. In *Cleopatra*, the
implication is that men have no real intention of dying if their ladies are
'unkynde' or if they lose their loves, but that women actually do it (cf. F
568–9). A similar moral is drawn in the *Legend of Tisbe* (910–11), with
which *Cleopatra* is probably meant to be paired. In these two opening
Legends the heroes are not 'unfaithful men', but the suicide of the
heroine after the loss of her lover is set against the behaviour of those
men who only talk about killing themselves. This is not necessarily a
flattering comparison. The *Book of the Duchess* 724–39 says that those
who die for love are fools and are damned.

The manner of Cleopatra's death in Chaucer differs from all other
accounts except Gower's.[21] She has a wonderful shrine built of rubies
and all the fine stones she could find in Egypt, and, after filling it with
spices, places in it Antony's embalmed body. Then, instead of applying

---

[20] MacCracken, *Lydgate's Minor Poems* II, p. 382.
[21] Cf. *CA* VIII 2573–5.

one serpent, at the most two, to her arm or breast as she lies besides Antony's body, in Chaucer Cleopatra procures all the serpents to be had, puts them in a grave she has had dug next to Antony's tomb, enters the pit of serpents quite naked, and willingly embraces death 'for love of Antony that was hire so dere' (669–80, 696–701). Before her extravagant death, however, she extravagantly affirms her faithfulness to Antony (681–95). D. D. Griffith noted that serpent-pits are common in hagiographical literature, and his is a most useful insight that Chaucer has conformed Cleopatra's death to the ones willingly embraced by Christian martyrs, and has likewise given her a dying speech affirming the 'true faith'.[22] There are certainly many readers who find no irony in Cleopatra's final judgement on herself, that there 'was nevere unto hire love a trewer quene' (695), but that she was an exemplum of a true wife, 'unreprovable unto [her] wifhod ay' (691). Goddard, on the other hand, noted that Cleopatra needed to specify that it was Antony whom she was addressing among the shades of her dead lovers: 'I mene yow, Antonius, my knight' (684).[23] While this at first seems a puerile comment, it again intimates that aspect of the traditional story of Cleopatra in which women of powerful sexuality are inevitably considered promiscuous,[24] and suggests that the best possible view of things was that she has been faithful in turn to a series of lovers.[25] It is instructive that no critic has ever advanced a better explanation of line 684.

Cleopatra's nakedness (696), in Chaucer's version, is as unusual in the medieval period as the highly original pit of serpents where she dies. It is an interesting coincidence, given that Cleopatra's was a story Chaucer was unlikely to have known well, that he makes of her death an erotic tableau which reminds us of how artists in the Renaissance and much later frequently painted her naked, with serpents caressing her

---

[22] D. D. Griffith, 'An Interpretation of Chaucer's *Legend of Good Women*', *Manly Anniversary Studies* (1923), rpt. E. Wagenknecht, ed., *Chaucer: Modern Essays in Criticism* (New York: Oxford University Press, 1959), p. 401.

[23] Goddard, '*Legend of Good Women*', p.62.

[24] Cf. Hughes-Hallett, *Cleopatra*, pp. 52–3.

[25] This motif appears sporadically in courtly poetry, e.g. in Oton de Grandson's *Balade* XLIX of which the refrain is *Je n'ay riens fait qu'Amours ne m'ait fait faire*, where Oton explains how Love himself recommends moving on from one love affair to another. See Piaget, *Grandson*, pp. 342–3.

breast.[26] By contrast, in most medieval textual accounts, and in most of
the manuscript illustrations printed in Kolve's article, 'Cleopatra to
Alceste' (illustrations mainly from the early fifteenth century and
mainly of the French translation of *De Casibus*), Cleopatra is depicted
fully clothed as a queen, with snakes attached to her arms, or naked to
the waist, with snakes attached to her breasts. Chaucer's dying Cleopatra retains her sensual appeal and a certain glamour, as is part and
parcel of her story; indeed Hughes-Hallett has pointed out how the
'mystique of suicide', even though condemned by the Church at least
from the time of Augustine, continued to receive a sneaking admiration
as the ultimate validation of a love true unto death, in story at least.
(This mystique of suicide also confers its glow of secular sainthood on
the majority of Cleopatra's sisters in the *Legend of Good Women*.)
Neither is Chaucer's Cleopatra unheroic; indeed, one of the few positive
elements of her story that Chaucer was likely to come upon praised her
as an exemplum of Fortitude.[27] As in so many later representations of
Cleopatra it is difficult to present her charms as almost irresistable and
at the same time to make a strong case for her repulsiveness; indeed,
Boccaccio became almost hysterically strident in his attempts to do so.
Chaucer's Cleopatra remains dangerously alluring: she represents the
danger that feminine sensuality offers to male rationality and obligation
to family and proper political allegiance, but her danger differs from
that of a figure like Medea who, once crossed, was likely to kill you.

V. A. Kolve wishes to reappraise the whole matter of the iconograph-
ical significance of Cleopatra's death. Even though all Chaucer's likely
sources condemn Cleopatra, he believes Chaucer to have intended to
portray a 'good woman', albeit in a somewhat limited sense. Chaucer's
queen, he points out, builds for Antony's body a magnificent mauso-
leum, built of precious stones and full of spices. She has thus arranged
for him 'what Petrarch might have called the triumph of Fame over
Death'. Next to it she has her own grave dug, fills it with serpents and
enters it naked, into a living death, so to speak. 'Cleopatra in her death
dramatizes, and accepts with a fiercely stoic courage, the medieval

[26] See figs. 1–4 in Kolve, 'Cleopatra to Alceste', pp. 133–6, and Hughes-Hallett, *Cleopatra*, passim.
[27] Hughes-Hallett, *Cleopatra*, particularly chapter 4, 'The Suicide'. For Tertullian's commendation of Cleopatra's fortitude, see ibid., p. 116.

commonplace that man's flesh was eaten by worms and serpents in the grave.' Kolve likens Chaucer's intention here, as he analyses it, to the meaning inherent in the so-called *transi* tombs which were becoming fashionable in the late Middle Ages (not however seen in England at this time). These double tombs depicted an effigy of the person as he was in life, with all his pomp, and below this an effigy of the same person in death, naked and eaten by serpents and toads. Therefore, united in death as the lovers are, 'the splendor of Antony's tomb images their fame, while the horror of Cleopatra's serpent-ridden grave delineates that other truth which Fame can disguise or cover over, but never alter or deny. The two parts of the image are inseparable.' Cleopatra's faithful love, and that of the other 'good women', has intrinsic value, but ends only in death, Kolve suggests, and their deaths are meaningless except in the worldly terms of 'fame, the avoidance of shame, the preservation of good name'. Kolve believes that Chaucer's ultimate intention was to have his *Legend of Good Women* culminate in the Legend of Alceste, a good woman who overcame death, and thereby prefigured the resurrection of Christ.[28]

In spite of its wealth of illustrative material, Kolve's article seems curiously wrong-headed. One wonders, for example, if medieval readers pondering some of the manuscript illustrations of Cleopatra, serpents at her breasts or arms, which are reproduced in the article (figs. 5–11), would not have found them iconographically assimilated to some medieval representations of Luxuria or Lechery,[29] in the same way that Kolve intimates that the illustrations he reproduces of the deaths of Dido and Lucrece are 'imagined . . . in terms of the traditional iconography of despair'. Kolve has himself noted the similarity of these depictions to some twelfth-century French stone carvings of Luxuria (note 14, p. 235), and there certainly exist text-based images which imply this connection, such as the story LXVII in the *Gesta Romanorum* where a woman in hell is represented with serpents hanging from her breasts in token of her previous life of lechery.[30] Kolve seems to recognise that the Chaucerian scene might well signify the grave's

[28] Kolve, 'Cleopatra to Alceste', pp. 146–51 and figs. 17–24.
[29] Cf. ibid., p. 152 and figs. 25–7.
[30] See S. J. H. Herrtage, ed., *The English Versions of the Gesta Romanorum* (London: EETS ES 33, 1879), pp. 383–4.

rebuke to Cleopatra's sins of pride and lechery, but denies that it does, because he is convinced that Chaucer presents Cleopatra 'as Anthony's wife, faithful to him even unto the grave'.[31] Like all critics who see the *Legend* as serious praise of women, albeit limited by their pagan status, Kolve ignores all the evidence which is pulling in another direction. Such a piece of evidence is Chaucer's concluding *moralitas*:

> And this is storyal soth, it is no fable.
> Now, or I fynde a man thus trewe and stable,
> And wol for love his deth so frely take,
> I preye God let oure hedes nevere ake!
> Amen.
>
> 702–5
> *Explicit Legenda Cleopatre, martiris.*

If this flippant prayer is answered, the audience may be assured of no more headaches,[32] for they will never find a man of such fabulous virtue that he would die for love, unless of course it be Pyramus, the hero of the very next Legend. It is necessary in line 702 to emphasise that Cleopatra's heroic faithfulness is an actual fact of history – the phrase, 'storyal soth', is an added indication that Chaucer's source has been Vincent's *Storiale Mirour*, as he calls it in the G Prologue – or his audience might have been inclined to think it was a myth! I have noted how the idea that a good woman was a fabulous beast like a black swan was an old medieval joke, and lies behind the Prologue to the *Legend*'s insistence that one must turn to books when there is no other evidence in experience. Hughes-Hallett comments, not specifically in regard to Chaucer's Cleopatra, that Cleopatra's death made her finally chaste: 'For the only good woman is a chaste woman, and the only chaste woman is a dead one',[33] a comment that was also made in medieval times, as in the poem (Robbins' *Secular Lyrics*, no. 180) which I quoted

---

[31] Kolve, 'Cleopatra to Alceste', p. 150.

[32] Delany interprets this 'cryptic remark' as yet another sexual pun, depending on the medieval medical term, *caput virgae*, for tip of the penis, so that a man could be said to have two heads, both of which could ache, see Delany, *Naked Text*, pp. 143–4. Delany says: 'This usage is amply documented in medical literature' (p. 143), but she does not make it clear whether she is referring to the putative pun or simply the medical meaning. She notes references to heads (plural) aching in *Troilus* II 549–50 and III 1561. I quite concur that the line about headaches is cryptic in any reading.

[33] Hughes-Hallett, *Cleopatra*, p. 131.

in an earlier chapter to the effect that the only good woman was one wearing a marble robe or tomb.

It is not that the aspects of Cleopatra's death that Kolve concentrates on are historically unsound or may not be part of the context of the Legends considered from the broadest possible viewpoint. It is just that they are made so little of by Chaucer, and in addition falsify so much of the *Legend*'s tone. One could agree that, if Chaucer indeed knew of Petrarch's *Triumphs*, one of the few places where Cleopatra had been mentioned in vernacular poetry as Kolve notes, he would have under-stood the triumph of Fame over Death and Love, but I find little indication that this is of the essence of the 'larger idea'[34] of the *Legend*. It is also true that the topos of the catalogue of ancient heroines is sometimes used elegiacally in medieval literature in pursuit of an *ubi sunt* theme. 'Where now are the snows of yesteryear?' Villon said in his *Ballade des Dames du Temps jadis*, and on the same theme Lydgate also wrote:

> Whilome full feyre was Polixene,
>   So was Creseyde; so was Helene
> Dido also of Cartage quene,
>   Whos beaute made many one pleyne;
> But dethe came laste and can dystene
> Their freshenes, and made them ful base,
>   Youre remembraunce let not disdeyne,
> That now is heye some tyme was gras.[35]

In spite of the fact that this stanza from a longer poem and the stanza following it use not only the ladies' names but even the rhymes of Chaucer's balade *Hyd Absolon*, there is not the slightest hint that this theme contributes anything to the *Legend of Good Women*.

Yet *Cleopatra* is indeed a paradigm and what Chaucer does with the story is important for our understanding of the poem as a whole. It is significant that Chaucer chose a woman whose reputation for virtue was questionable by most standards to be the one that the God of Love names specifically as a martyr in his service (cf. F 566–9), for even Christine de Pizan ignores her in the *Cité des Dames*. This provocative

---

34 Kolve's term, 'Cleopatra to Alceste', p. 131.
35 *That now is Hay some-tyme was Grase* 49–56, MacCracken, *Lydgate's Minor Poems* II, p. 810.

choice inevitably points up the bias in the God of Love's vision and underlines his traditional patronage of (female) sensuality and passion. The command of the God to be brief allows the poet to explore the comic potential of only hinting at the truth. Chaucer did not have an Ovidian version of the Cleopatra story to work with, as he did for every other Legend, but, like Ovid, the English writer shows himself here a master of indirection, able to exploit what is not said as much as what is said; not saying directly, for example, that Cleopatra abandoned Antony at the Battle of Actium, but excusing her for doing so. Although Chaucer's source may have been a relatively brief encyclopedic reference, the evidence of the text suggests that he knew the kind of story Cleopatra's normally was and developed his version accordingly; Frank's view that Cleopatra was an unknown quantity when Chaucer naively introduced her is untenable. More than is the case in any other Legend the creation of *Cleopatra* develops out of the concept of a parodied saint's legend, with its dramatic story replete with exotic detail, with its martyr's death of the heroine and her 'confession' of the true faith of the God of Love, although the serpents here are as likely to signify the deadly sin of Lechery to some minds as they are to intensify the audience's sense of the martyr's suffering.

Chaucer may have meant Cleopatra's story to be contrasted with that of Alceste, who also died and went to Hell (which was thought to be inhabited by serpents). This is a firm link between the heroine of the Prologue and the heroines of the Legends (cf. F 549–66/G 530–42). On the other hand its storyline is made similar to the old love-story of Pyramus and Thisbe which follows it, so that in both there is a double suicide for love's sake, a double grave, and a hero at least as virtuous as the heroine, although nothing could be less similar than the characters of the two tales, the one pair so innocent, the other pair so experienced. If Chaucer meant the two opening stories to be linked in their similarities and dissimilarities, then he again would be following the same course as Ovid in the *Heroides*, as I shall suggest in the following chapter on *Dido*. There I shall address the concept of the *Legend of Good Women* as variations on a theme, where the theme is an essentialist view of Woman, canonised in literature in the figures of Dido and Cleopatra.

12

Dido: composite Woman

The fact that Cleopatra was a figure of 'storial sothe' made her less easy
to dismiss than the great witch Medea and the other heroines of
mythology. Cleopatra had a staggering effect on the men of her time,
many of whom were instrumental in forming the minds of the Middle
Ages. She was perceived by her contemporaries as lustful, greedy,
changeable, moving from man to man; she wished to rule Rome itself
and transfer the seat of power to Egypt. The historical Cleopatra
embodied in the most threatening fashion what was then conceived of
as the nature of Woman. That she conformed so neatly to a preexisting
stereotype is no coincidence; even in her own lifetime, as has recently
been suggested, the shape that was being given to her written story was
constructed under the aegis of her and Antony's political enemy, the
emperor Augustus.[1] Chaucer might apply the cachet of 'storial sothe' to
her story, but it was no less a 'fable' than those of the other heroines of
the *Legend of Good Women*.

Cleopatra was a strong motivating force behind her contemporary
Vergil's creation of Dido, another African queen who almost succeeded in
distracting the founder of Rome from his destiny. In addition, however,
Vergil compounded his literary Dido from the archetypal heroines of
Greek literature, the pathos of the deserted Ariadne, the passion, magic
arts and curses of Medea, the power to hinder of Circe and Calypso.[2] So,

---

[1] See Hughes-Hallett, *Cleopatra*, esp. chapter 2, 'The Story According to Octavius',
pp. 36–69.

[2] Götz Schmitz, *The Fall of Women in Early English Narrative Verse* (Cambridge
University Press, 1990), notes, in passing, similarities between the Vergilian Dido and
still other of the Greek heroines, such as the prophetess, Cassandra (pp. 23–4) and the
child murderer, Procne (p. 26).

in addressing the problem of the real-life Cleopatra, there is a sense in which Vergil's literary invention of the figure of Dido presupposed and powerfully transmitted a composite portrait of Woman, or an abstraction 'Womanness', a notion which provoked a remarkably similar response in classical and medieval times, and much later. (Chaucer's tale-collection in the *Legend*, consisting as it does of *Ariadne, Medea, Cleopatra, Dido*, and so on, inevitably draws on many of these ancient concepts of the feminine as a means of addressing the topic of the virtue of women.) It is a concept of Woman as one possessed of a dangerous power of seduction, sometimes troped as enchantment, but one whose position demands acute pity because of her ontological and social inferiority. Even when most sympathetic towards women, it is a totally androcentric concept. Thus Ovid's Heroidean Dido retells the story of her relationship with Aeneas with an emphasis on the woman's point of view; her concerns are pragmatic, non-idealistic, domestic, she is faithful to love in a way that Aeneas is not. Because her story, like that of Ovid's other heroines, is shorn of its true epic context, as Götz Schmitz has recently pointed out, it suffers from the severely limited perspective of the letter writer isolated in private pain and a moment of time.[3] But making Dido represent this traditional paradigm of feminine suffering is no more flattering to the notion of Woman, a fact that is also relevant to the *Legend of Good Women*. That is to say, medieval debates about women may argue (often in palinode form) that women are not flighty and unstable but that old exempla show them faithful to their lovers even to the point of death. This fidelity, however, paradoxically displays their essential irrationality and the triviality of the parameters within which they live. The putative relationship of the *Legend of Good Women* to *Troilus and Criseyde* is obvious: the later work 'proves' that all women are not unfaithful like Criseyde – by showing that many women are foolish enough to take their own lives in the aftermath of an unhappy love affair.

It has often been pointed out that the perceived sameness of the stories in Chaucer's *Legend* imitates the oneness in virtue of the saints who populate genuine collections of saints' lives.[4] But the fact that in

---

[3] Ibid., pp. 24–5.

[4] E.g., Dinshaw, *Sexual Poetics*, pp. 72–4; Cowen, 'Structure and Tone', pp. 417–20; Kiser, *Telling Classical Tales*, pp. 101–11.

successive retellings any story of one of the ancient heroines might have been contaminated by characteristics originally belonging to another also has a bearing on this problem. That is, it is no naive accident that the archetypal accounts of the women whose stories Chaucer told are so similar, but a deliberate strategy indulged in by writers of the high Classical period. Ovid, whose artistic problem of variation on a theme in the *Heroides* was similar to Chaucer's in the *Legend*, had quite deliberately emphasised and created similarities between his heroines' careers, in order to demonstrate his skill in developing the stories differently – Howard Jacobson, for example shows conclusively how Ovid's Phyllis mimics Vergil's Dido, and how his Hypsipyle in turn mimics Phyllis.[5] As in the Vergilian creation of Dido, Ovid's rhetorical project involved a witty dialogue with past literary creations – his Ariadne and Catullus' Ariadne, his Medea and the Medeas of Apollonius and Euripides, his Dido and Vergil's Dido, the last of which conflicts Chaucer could not help being aware of. Thus the so-called monotony of the *Legend* had its roots over a thousand years earlier, and the adaptation and exploitation of literary stereotypes of the feminine by Chaucer's masters Vergil and Ovid must bear some of the blame. The similarities among the heroines of the *Heroides* and among those of Chaucer's Legends have a double importance then; they indicate the essential oneness in the nature of Woman, as then perceived, and they also exalt the skill and worth of the poet as poet, for they afford him a stage on which can be enacted his poetic virtuosity.

The emotive power of the story of the Carthaginian queen is from a historical point of view perhaps the strongest of any of the heroines with which we have to do. The story as Vergil devised it told how Aeneas landed on the shores of Dido's realm of Carthage after he had wandered the seas following the destruction of Troy. Aeneas and Dido fall in love (by divine intervention), but (by the intervention of other gods) he is recalled to his destiny to found Rome, and sails from Carthage. A distraught Dido kills herself, immolating herself on a funeral pyre. Ovid acknowledges that from its first publication Vergil's creation of Dido attracted more interest than any other part of the

---

[5] See Jacobson, *Ovid's 'Heroides'*, pp. 62 ff., 383.

Aeneid.[6] Hundreds of years later St Augustine remembers how in his adolescent and sometimes unwilling studies of literature, he wept for Dido's death.[7] In the fourteenth century some scholars had rediscovered the fact that Vergil's Dido bore little resemblance to another and earlier Dido of legend and perhaps history. Both Petrarch and Boccaccio were inordinately proud of presenting the story of the woman they believed the 'true Dido', one who had lived many hundreds of years before Aeneas, who had died a chaste widow, who chose rather to 'burn than to marry', as Tertullian had written wittily, and who was celebrated as such by Jerome.[8] Chaucer never alludes to this particular conflict between Vergil and history; the literary character as treated by Vergil and Ovid seems always more suitable for his purposes. But perhaps the 'why' of Vergil's literary creation of Dido presented itself to him as Ovid's challenge to Vergil obviously did (the use of the Dido story in the *Hous of Fame* bears witness to this fact). Vergil's Dido and Ovid's Heroidean package also represented for him, as for many another medieval man, a veritable bible on the portrayal of feminine psychology. The question of how the literary Dido came to be, and the concept of essential femininity it incorporated, is therefore not irrelevant to Chaucer's *Legend of Good Women*.

Vergil must be seen as the Roman emulator of Homer – he portrays an Aeneas wandering the world at the same time as the great Greek hero Odysseus. Thus his Dido is contemporaneous with Circe, Calypso and Nausicaa (a lady to whom Odysseus tells his travels but, unlike his other hostesses, to whom he does not succumb, as in the end Aeneas does not succumb to Dido). Vergil's tragic account of the conflict between love and duty, between the passions and rationality, was written at a time when the Hellenistic interest in love was becoming an important literary topic; Catullus' Ariadne was one of his models, and late classical commentators like Servius and Macrobius acknowledge Vergil's debt to

[6] *nec legitur pars ulla magis de corpore toto, Tristia* 23. 535.

[7] R. S. Pine-Coffin, trans., *Saint Augustine: Confessions* (Harmondsworth: Penguin, 1961; rpt. 1974), I 13, pp. 33–4.

[8] Mary Louise Lord, 'Dido as an Example of Chastity: the Influence of Example Literature', *Harvard Library Bulletin* 17 (1969): 22–44, 216–32. This article is useful for the Dido legend as a whole (not only for the 'chaste Dido'). See also Schmitz, *Fall of Women*, chapter 2, 'Dido and Elissa', for his more recent account of the historical, Vergilian, Ovidian and Chaucerian Dido, pp. 17–43.

Apollonius' Medea,[9] a heroine who was helpful to the hero Jason as Dido was to Aeneas, and who was not a hindrance, but a distinct advantage in the achievement of his heroic task.

It is acknowledged that Vergil was in some sense a propagandist,[10] although his references to the Augustan ethos are not simple, but elusive and thought-provoking. Thus there are many parallels but also differences between Aeneas and the emperor Augustus (the 'Cesar' and 'Octovyan' of *Cleopatra* 592 and 624), which are particularly eye-catching if Dido is thought to allude in some sense to Cleopatra. For example, Cleopatra had been the lover of Julius Caesar, and therefore had a connection with the Augustan line; Augustus himself, however, had resisted the African queen, as Julius Caesar and Antony had not, and could therefore be compared with Aeneas as lover of Dido in both positive and negative ways. Moreover, Dido was a queen, and as the Romans did not know of many queens they would have seen her inevitably as a reference to their African contemporary. Cleopatra had come to the throne via the death of a brother, as had Dido.[11] Indeed, antiquity regarded Egypt itself as a threatening place whose people worshipped the female deity Isis, where powerful and competent queens were not unknown even before Cleopatra VII and where women dominated over men in ordinary Egyptian society.[12] Romans feared the threat of Cleopatra to Rome itself, and the transfer of Rome to Alexandria,[13] as Dido wished Aeneas to join forces with her people. Romans would moreover have recognised Dido's curse (as Medea had cursed Jason) as bearing on the antagonistic relations between themselves and the Carthaginians. A huge amount of hostile

---

[9] See Introduction to A. S. Pease, ed., *Publi Vergili Maronis: Aeneidos, Liber Quartus* (Cambridge, Mass.: Harvard University Press, 1935), pp. 12–15.

[10] For an account of the artistic and moral/political problems with which the *Aeneid* presented Vergil, and how he solved them, see K. Quinn, *Virgil's Aeneid: a Critical Description* (London: Routledge, 1968), chapter 1; also Hughes-Hallett, *Cleopatra*, pp. 59–62.

[11] See Pease, *Aeneidos*, pp. 23–7; Quinn, *Virgil's Aeneid*, pp. 135–49; K. Quinn, 'The Fourth Book of the *Aeneid*: a Critical Description', in J. V. Muir and E. R. A. Sewter, *Greece and Rome*, 2nd series, 12 (1965), pp. 16–26; Hughes-Hallett, *Cleopatra*, p. 48.

[12] See R. Mortley, *Womanhood: the Feminine in Ancient Hellenism, Gnosticism, Christianity, and Islam* (Sydney: Delacroix Press, 1981), p. 20; Hughes-Hallett, *Cleopatra*, pp. 50–1.

[13] Pease, *Aeneidos*, p. 28.

propaganda was directed against Cleopatra in her own time; it is not only Vergil who referred to Cleopatra but Ovid and Horace and many others.

Boccaccio mentions all these aspects of the creation of the literary Dido, except the specific relationship to Cleopatra which is generally recognised by modern scholars. In *De Genealogia* Boccaccio acknowledges the fictitiousness of Vergil's Dido and gives reasons for the Roman poet's decision to ignore the historical 'woman of exceptionally high character, who would rather die by her own hand than subdue the vow of chastity fixed deep in her heart to a second marriage'.[14] Boccaccio recognises the imitation of Homer, and the poetic utility of Dido as an auditor of Aeneas' sufferings (this allows Vergil to begin his story *in medias res*). He perceives Vergil's purpose in honouring Augustus by showing Aeneas 'resolutely and scornfully setting his heel upon the wanton and impure promptings of the flesh and the delights of women'. He sees Dido's dying curse as Vergil's means of glorifying Rome 'for they imply the wars between Carthage and Rome'. He gives the traditional moral interpretation of such ancient scholars as Servius:[15]

> [Vergil] represents in Dido the attracting power of the passion of love, prepared for every opportunity, and in Aeneas one who is readily disposed in that way and at length overcome. But after showing the enticements of lust, he points the way of return to virtue by bringing in Mercury, messenger of the gods, to rebuke Aeneas, and call him back from such indulgence to deeds of glory. By Mercury, Vergil means either remorse, or the reproof of some outspoken friend, either of which rouses us from slumber in the mire of turpitude, and calls us back into the fair and even path to glory. Then

---

[14] C. G. Osgood, trans., *Boccaccio on Poetry* (1930; rpt. New York: Liberal Arts Press, 1956), p. 67.

[15] Servius, Latin grammarian of the end of the fourth century, was the author of a large standard commentary on Vergil, which remained widely influential in the Middle Ages and much later. His explanations ranged from the lexical, grammatical and rhetorical, through matters of history, geography and mythology, to the ethical and spiritual. Servian or Servian-based or Servian-type commentary made it possible for the medieval student to master the literal, but not unnuanced or unsophisticated, sense of Vergil's text, along with a sense of its cultural alterity, see C. Baswell, *Virgil in Medieval England: Figuring the Aeneid from the Twelfth Century to Chaucer* (Cambridge University Press: 1995), pp. 49–51.

we burst the bonds of unholy delight, and, armed with new fortitude, we unfalteringly spurn all seductive flattery, and tears, prayers, and such, and abandon them as naught.[16]

It is instructive that Boccaccio writes simultaneously about what is connoted by the literary theme of the feminine, and about Vergil's poetic aims and procedures, a nexus to which I shall return. Although Boccaccio believed Dido was a 'good woman', 'of distinguished family, young, fair, rich, exemplary, famous for her purity, ruler of her city and people, of conspicuous wisdom and eloquence', he had no difficulty in identifying her with the 'enticements of lust', 'wanton and impure promptings of the flesh', 'unholy delight', and so on, particularly since she was a widow and thus 'experienced' and 'more easily disposed to that passion'. It is not unlikely that something like this conception of the Dido and Aeneas story would lie in the minds of many who heard or read Chaucer's *Legenda Didonis martiris, Cartaginis Regine*, whose heroine was in no sense a genuinely 'bad woman', as Cleopatra was usually regarded, but whose feminine attractions made her as dangerous a temptress to male virtue. Christopher Baswell's study shows that, in the England of the late fourteenth century, manuscripts of Vergil were being newly copied or were receiving fresh layers of annotation by intelligent and engaged readers with access to good Servian and other types of commentary.[17] Baswell's account of the 'Norwich commentator' of MS London, British Library Additional 27304, for example, implies a reader, contemporary with Chaucer, with access to a complete manuscript of Vergil, one with an interest not only in the literal meaning of Vergil's text but also in its literary and rhetorical pleasures, a reader as well with a stong ethical bent, who tends to praise Aeneas as a wholly admirable hero, with the concomitant need to figure Dido as 'sin' or 'lechery'.[18]

Vergil had presented both Dido and Aeneas sympathetically; indeed, perhaps his greatest triumph was to make the character of Dido so sympathetic, given her numerous similarities to the Medea of Greek literature and all the hostile reminiscences of Carthage and Cleopatra

---

[16] Osgood, *Boccaccio on Poetry*, pp. 68–9.
[17] Baswell, *Virgil in England*, passim, esp. pp. 68–80, 163–7.
[18] Ibid., pp. 153–4.

that her portrayal must have held for a Roman audience. Both hero and heroine are presented as figures of integrity and honour. Although there is no doubt that Vergil valorises Aeneas' heeding of the call of duty above Dido's pain, he even-handedly exposes the shortcomings and sufferings of both characters. The personal happiness of both Dido and Aeneas is subordinate to the demands of a higher destiny, which Vergil indicates by personifying the Olympian gods and allowing them to interfere in the affairs of the human protagonists.

Chaucer's *Legend of Dido* is in many respects a travesty of Vergil, whom he pretends to follow as *Dido* opens:

> Glorye and honour, Vergil Mantoan,
> Be to thy name! and I shal, as I can,
> Folwe thy lanterne as thow gost byforn,
> How Eneas to Dido was forsworn.
> In thyn Eneyde and Naso wol I take
> The tenor, and the grete effectes make.
>
> 924–9

These lines and the program of the *Legend* encourage a suspicion that Chaucer will actually be following Ovid instead of Vergil, but this is not the case. Although Chaucer is clearly influenced by the perspective taken by Ovid in *Heroides* VII, he only uses it explicitly in the last few lines of *Dido*. Chaucer does in fact follow Vergil's Latin or a close translation quite exactly;[19] however, he takes a pointedly cavalier attitude to his illustrious source and his narrator is openly sceptical of Vergil's veracity. One characteristic of Chaucer's *Dido* which seems most at odds with Vergil is the narrator's attitude to the gods. The Roman audience, as well as the well-educated medieval audience, might have questioned Vergil's use of Olympian *dei ex machina*, but they would nevertheless have understood what he meant by it, as in the

---

[19] Ibid., p. 256 ff. See also Frank, *Chaucer and the 'Legend'*, pp. 57–8. Various aspects of Chaucer's relationship to the 'Medieval Vergil' are discussed in A. C. Friend, 'Chaucer's Version of the Aeneid', *Speculum* 13 (1938): 317–23; E. B. Atwood, 'Two Alterations of Virgil in Chaucer's *Dido*', *Speculum* 13 (1938): 454–7; D. R. Bradley, 'Fals Eneas and Sely Dido', *PQ* 39 (1960): 122–5; L. B. Hall, 'Chaucer and the Dido-and-Aeneas Story', *MS* 25 (1963): 148–59. Baswell notes similarities to the *Ilias* of Simon Aurea Capra in several aspects of Chaucer's *Dido*, *Virgil in England*, pp. 402–4 and n102, pp. 109, 112, 122.

quotation from Boccaccio above or in the late fourteenth-century commentary, described by Baswell, where the pagan gods are credited with an 'implicit metaphorical quality; they are mere fictions, artistic effects'.[20] Chaucer takes every opportunity to ridicule it. Vergil's Dido is understandably and sarcastically disbelieving of Aeneas' protestations that he had been ordered to leave by the gods; Ovid's Dido takes up the same attitude. But even the narrator in Chaucer is a thoroughgoing agnostic. Reluctant to believe that Cupid took the place of Ascanius (Eneas' son) to implant love in Dido or that Eneas was invisible when he first saw Dido, he is sceptical also of Venus appearing to Eneas dressed as a huntress and of the heavenly origin of the storm which drove Eneas and Dido into a cave together and alone.[21] Chaucer's flippant tone – 'as of that scripture,/ Be as be may, I take of it no cure' (1144–5) – suggests that this attitude has nothing to do with a religious problem with pagan divinities, as in some other medievalised Aeneids. The implication in *Dido* is that the whole affair is understandable in simple human terms, and rather disreputable ones at that. Eneas is presented as the very type of the false lover and opportunistic seducer who exploits the inherent pity and gullibility of women:

> O sely wemen, ful of innocence,
> Ful of pite, of trouthe, and conscience,
> What maketh yow to men to truste so?
> Have ye swych routhe upon hyre feyned wo,
> And han swich old ensaumples yow beforn?
> Se ye nat alle how they ben forsworn?
> Where sen ye oon, that he ne hath laft his leef,
> Or ben unkynde, or don hire som myscheef,
> Or piled hire, or bosted of his dede?
> Ye may as wel it sen, as ye may rede . . .
> 1254–63

In lines 1268–75 Eneas' behaviour is described as, from one point of view, conforming to the traditional medieval stereotype of the man in love, but it is also one that draws heavily on the cynical recommendations

---

[20] Baswell, *Virgil in England*, p. 74.
[21] *LGW* 1139–45, 1020–1, 971–1003, 1218–28.

for seduction in the *Ars Amatoria*:[22] Eneas is just an opportunistic ingrate, shallow and callous:

> This Eneas, that hath so depe yswore,
> Is wery of his craft withinne a throwe;
> The hote ernest is al overblowe.
> And pryvely he doth his shipes dyghte,
> And shapeth hym to stele awey by nyghte.
> 1285–9

Given all this, Eneas' protestations that the gods and his father's ghost have called him to resume the task for which he is destined (1295–1300) can seem nothing else but a further ludicrous attempt to gull Dido. Although he makes it clear that the affair was initiated by Dido, and was always to some extent one-sided, Vergil nevertheless intimates that Aeneas loved Dido. In the specious sorrow of Chaucer's Eneas contemplating his departure – 'Therwith his false teres out they sterte,/ And taketh hire withinne his armes two' (1301–2) – there could be no stronger contrast than with Vergil's picture of an Aeneas, deeply moved by his love for Dido and her suffering, yet, true to Stoic ideals, resolved to show no emotion. One wonders whether Augustine would have wept for Chaucer's Dido, a sentimental and pathetic figure as Eneas' dupe, but, shorn of her true context, hardly tragic.[23] In truth Chaucer's mock-serious condemnation of Eneas' treason[24] is only a means of trivialising the pathos of Dido's plight, her betrayal portrayed as the inevitable consequence of her own feminine gullibility and susceptibility (1061–81). Chaucer of course has not been the only commentator to view Dido thus.

Indeed, a number of twentieth-century Vergilian scholars have felt called upon to deemphasise Aeneas' criminality and to minimise Dido's suffering in the context of Aeneas' great destiny. Pease writes, 'A modern

---

22 Ovid in *Ars Amatoria* gives much detailed instruction in the 'feigning' (cf. *LGW* 1266) and false promises (cf. *LGW* 1234 ff.) necessary to gain a mistress, e.g. *Ars* I 631 ff., 645; cf. the description in *LGW* 1268–75 with *Ars* I 229 ff. (banquets give openings); *Ars* I 75 ff. (seek ladies in temples); *Ars* I 733 ff. (let leanness prove your feelings); *Ars* II 273 ff. (advice about poems); *Ars* I 437 ff. and II 261 ff. (usefulness of letters and small, not wastefully large, gifts).

23 Cf. Frank, *Chaucer and the 'Legend'*, p. 77.

24 For a recent account of the significant medieval counter-tradition portraying Aeneas as political and amatory traitour, see Baswell, *Virgil in England*, pp. 18–21.

reader finds Aeneas' sin in his leaving Dido, but the author certainly intended it to lie in his staying so long with her as he did.'[25] Quinn also warns modern readers against a certain 'misplaced sentimentality' in regard to the Dido and Aeneas story: 'What about Aeneas? He has seduced a beautiful queen who was perhaps only too anxious to be seduced. To a Roman, as to an English gentleman of the seventeenth or eighteenth century, if not to us, the act would not have seemed one that need lie heavily on the conscience.'[26] There can be no doubt that Chaucer portrays Dido as 'only too anxious to be seduced', as she slides from excited interest in a 'new' man in her life, through pity and into love and the desire to sleep with him (1075–81, 1150–8).

Indeed, while it eminently suited Ovid to burlesque Vergil's Stoic ideals, I think Chaucer was not untouched by them. Members of his audience who knew anything of the *Aeneid* may have noted that, until the section portraying Eneas as a faithless lover, the love affair of Dido and Eneas in the *Legend of Good Women* is as one-sided as in Vergil. In a memorable and unsourced passage (1114–25) Chaucer's Dido heaps gifts upon Eneas, the niggardliness of whose responding gift can be described in one line.[27] Thoroughly medievalised, Dido's court is as lavish and pleasure-seeking as that of Vergil's Epicurean Dido, a seduction and a temptation from the path of duty (cf. 1100 ff.). Chaucer calls her 'this amorous queene', and 'this lusty freshe queene'. She leads Eneas round with her constantly (1097), and the notion of fire (here associated with desire), like 'new', weaves throughout the poem:

> ther gan to breden swich a fyr
> That sely Dido hath now swich desyr
> With Eneas, hir newe gest, to dele,
> That she hath lost hire hewe and ek hire hele.
> 1156–9

As the *Riverside Chaucer* notes, 'dele' here means 'have sexual inter-course', and the Legend is laced with euphemisms relating to sexuality – 'so priketh hire this newe joly wo' (1192).[28] Indeed many of the words

---

[25] Pease, *Aeneidos*, p. 45.
[26] Quinn, *Virgil's Aeneid*, p. 141.
[27] See Frank, *Chaucer and the 'Legend'*, pp. 68–9.
[28] *MED* gives a number of sexual meanings for the verb 'priken', usually with Chaucer citations, although never from the *Legend of Good Women*.

which cluster around Chaucer's description of Dido had, in Ross's phrase, acquired an 'erotic encrustation' – amorous, lusty, fressh, fyr, daunce, juste, hunt, joly, priken, plesaunce, pleye, refressh, ese, etc.[29] Dido's sleep is tormented with the symptoms of love-sickness in a fully sensual and quite unladylike manner:[30]

> This noble queene unto hire reste wente.
> She siketh sore, and gan hyreself turmente;
> She waketh, walweth, maketh many a breyd,
> As don these lovers, as I have herde seyd.
> 1164–7

Like Vergil's Dido, she appears to have persuaded herself that her affair with Eneas has the status of marriage, a delusion exploded when he decides to leave her (cf. 1238 with 1304–5, 1322). The sea-battle in *Cleopatra* seemed an icon of the mood and action of that poem; in *Dido* there are several such passages which encapsulate the essentially opposite characteristics of hero and heroine in a way that is almost Vergilian. Thus Chaucer medievalises Vergil's hunting scene (1189–1211), but it loses none of its symbolic force, richly sensuous as it is, and redolent of the impending sexual encounter.

In the first part of *Dido*, then, Chaucer seems perfectly aware of the Vergilian ethos, the masculine reserve and resolve of Eneas, the equivocal femininity of Dido – the softness, pity, gullibility, sensuality, the excited interest in anything 'new' and superficially attractive (see especially 1063–81), although, while her 'newfangelness' is stressed, Chaucer's descriptions also imply her emotional generosity, her 'fredom', her 'pity'. The second part of the Legend where the narrator suddenly imposes on his story the inaccurate stereotypes of betrayed lady and false lover draws attention, perhaps unpleasantly, perhaps humorously, to the procedure he intends to adopt with all his stories of the *Legend*'s deserted women. That is to say, he draws attention to an attitude to the seduction of women which sees it as essentially trivial.

Yet, even if Chaucer has suggested in his choice of words that Dido

---

[29] For 'erotic encrustation', see Ross, *Chaucer's Bawdy*, p. 168. *MED* notes some kind of sexual overtone for all these terms, except for 'fresshe', and Ross's comments seem quite reasonable in regard to this word – *MED* cites the Wife of Bath for a sexual sense in 'refressh'.
[30] See *Riverside Chaucer*'s gloss to *LGW* 1156–9.

was to some extent responsible for her betrayal because of her feminine sensuality and weakness, nevertheless her portrayal remains sympathetic. So sympathetic, indeed, that by the following century the Scottish poet Gavin Douglas, in the Prologue to his own translation of the *Aeneid*, takes 'venerabill Chauser' to task quite severely for misrepresenting Vergil's larger meaning in presenting Aeneas as a traitor to Dido ('The Proloug of the First Buke of Eneados' 410–16).[31] The crux of the matter for Douglas is that Aeneas was not 'maynsworn' and showed no 'onkyndnes', as Chaucer had implied, for the hero had made no contract with Dido nor could the command of the gods be lightly dismissed. Dido knew of his destined course for Italy from the beginning (417–44). To present Aeneas otherwise is grievously to slur Vergil (the 'prince of poets') – presumably it is the fact that Chaucer makes so much of following Vergil's lantern (413) that draws Douglas' remonstrances. The only excuse he can offer for this slur on Vergil and Aeneas (410, 415), therefore, is that his 'maister Chauser' was deliberately taking the woman's part when he blamed Aeneas and Vergil, 'For he was evir (God wait) all womanis frend' (445–9).

This is an important observation, for it identifies a crucial aspect of the literary context of the *Legend of Good Women*, in that Douglas perceives it as belonging to the debate about men and women, and thus to a recognisable rhetorical genre. Douglas may also be thinking of courtly social occasions where such partisanship as he perceives in Chaucer's version was actively indulged, 'in lovyng of thir ladeis lylly quhite' (447). Chaucer's early readers may have recognised just such social occasions in Dido's feast, full not only of every luxury but 'of many an amorous lokyng and devys' (*LGW* 1102). Interestingly, in a manuscript of Douglas' own poem the debate is taken up in marginal comments on these lines, disagreeing that Douglas managed to justify Aeneas' treachery to Dido. The Cambridge MS of Douglas' *Eneidos* contains a 'brief series of marginal notes that accompany Prologue I and the first seven chapters of Book I', which is probably composed by Douglas himself. The marginal comment on I Prologue 425, 'This argument excusis nocht the tratory of Eneas na his maynswaring', and

---

[31] D. F. C. Coldwell, ed., *Virgil's Aeneid: Translated into Scottish Verse by Gavin Douglas* (Edinburgh: Blackwood, 1957), p. 12.

on 437, 'Heir he argouis better than befoir', are in the same hand as the rest of the commentary and may possibly indicate Douglas debating within himself, or else represent the one place where the scribe sees fit to interject.[32] These stories about women clearly provoked similar responses over many centuries, even millenia, and a humorous acknowledgement that there was a man's side to each story, and a woman's.

It is worth noting, in this context, that there are several classical and medieval works which rewrite the myths to defend the heroes from the charge of being traitors to women, for, particularly in the Middle Ages, treachery always remains a highly emotive term.[33] For example, Plutarch recounts one attempt to exonerate Theseus: the ship of Theseus and Ariadne is driven off course to Cyprus by a storm, the pregnant and terribly seasick Ariadne is put ashore by herself, and Theseus is swept back out to sea while trying to rescue the ship.[34] Another version of the Theseus and Ariadne story tells how Theseus was ordered by Bacchus in a dream to abandon Ariadne. Servius records how Demophoon did return to Phyllis only to find she had impatiently killed herself.[35] In the fifteenth century Raoul Lefevre wrote a book about Jason which purported to remedy the slander against him by those who said he did not keep his promise to Medea. In it Jason is tricked into his various amours, or bewitched, and is eventually reunited with his first (and fourth) love, Myrrha! Lefevre's work was translated by Caxton and indeed was the first English book printed by him,[36] an indication of the longevity of interest in debating and justifying the behaviour of either sex in these stories of the heroines. In *Dido* Chaucer may condemn Eneas for his 'treachery', but makes it clear at the same time that Dido is betrayed not by any conscious design on Eneas' part but by her own feminine nature.

Vergil's creation of Dido, then, and the subsequent exploitation of this

---

[32] Priscilla Bawcutt, *Gavin Douglas: a Critical Study* (Edinburgh University Press, 1976), pp. 85, 107–8.
[33] See Green, 'Chaucer's Victimized Women', pp. 15–18.
[34] I. Scott-Kilvert, trans., *Plutarch: the Rise and Fall of Athens* (Harmondsworth: Penguin, 1960; rpt. 1985).
[35] Shaner, 'An Interpretive Study', p. 195, notes the previous two examples.
[36] J. Munro, ed., *William Caxton: The History of Jason. Translated from the French of Raoul le Fevre* (London: EETS ES 111, 1913).

figure by later writers including Chaucer, draws our attention to a well-marked literary topos, which I have often referred to as the 'matter of Woman'. In responding to the threat to Rome (or Roman males, according to Hughes-Hallett) of the real-life Cleopatra, Vergil made his Dido incorporate the characteristics of several ancient mythical heroines. This literary construct, moreover, conforms to the philosophical view of the nature of Woman which was current as the first millenium opened and which shaded the work of Jewish and New Testament writers as well as the pagan masters. As is often pointed out, much of the history of Western thought is pervaded by the dichotomy perceived between matter and spirit, exemplified for the Middle Ages in the differentiation between the sexes: woman, because of her physical makeup, is identified with matter and man with spirit (the Latin word for mother, *mater*, was said to be contained within *materia*, matter; but *vir*, man, to be contained within *virtus*, strength, virtue, moral perfection).[37] Aristotle had associated maleness with activity, form and perfection, the feminine with passivity, matter and deprivation.[38] This was not merely symbolic discourse; the differences were thought to have a scientific basis and, from the time of Eve's succumbing to the temptation of the serpent, an evidential basis in history as well. I have noted how in the thirteenth century Guido del Colonne described Medea, in patently philosophical terms, as equivalent to formless matter, searching endlessly for the form which alone could give it existence. But Woman is also the temptress Eve, whose physical beauty 'has the power to seduce man from his purpose, to draw him down from his proper realm of thought to her realm of matter'.[39] The

---

[37] See Joan M. Ferrante, *Woman as Image in Medieval Literature: From the Twelfth Century to Dante* (New York: Columbia University Press, 1975); for *vir, virtus*, p. 6; *mater, materia*, p. 19 (Isidore), p. 104 (Aquinas). Cf. Blamires, *Woman Defamed*, for Isidore, pp. 43–5; Aquinas, p. 47. See also Minnis, *Shorter Poems*, pp. 424 ff.; Mortley, *Womanhood*, passim; Bloch, *Medieval Misogyny*, pp. 25 ff.

[38] See I. Maclean, *The Renaissance Notion of Woman: a Study of Scholasticism and Medical Science in European Intellectual Life* (Cambridge University Press, 1980), p. 8; for Aristotle's citation of the Pythagorean opposites of male/female, limit/unlimited, one/plurality etc., pp. 2–3. For quotation from Aristotle's *De Generatione Animalium*, see Blamires, *Woman Defamed*, pp. 39–41.

[39] Ferrante, *Woman as Image*, p. 17. For the pervasiveness of the ideas which underlay the subordination of women, see the account of their promulgation in theology, civil and canon law, in sermons, didactic poems, courtesy books etc. in Margaret Hallissy, *Clean*

Cleopatra of Augustan propaganda in every way embodies this notion of Woman as temptress in the most pejorative sense possible; the literary Dido is a softer form of an essentially similar figure. Chaucer associates Dido with beauty, luxury, pleasure (1035–8, 1094–1102), and portrays her as one who as a woman is peculiarly liable to be deceived by appearance (1066–77, 1254–63). Even one of the strongest defenders of her chastity, Boccaccio, has no difficulty in assigning Dido the symbolic significance of carnal weakness in the life of Aeneas, simply because she was the female member of the pair of lovers.

There is a sense in which another aspect of the series of unhappy tales which make up the *Legend of Good Women*, that pathos[40] which alienates many modern readers, also has its roots in this philosophical view of Woman. The pathos which Vergil incorporated into his literary construct of Dido is thus also an essential aspect of her femininity in this view. *Pathos* is a complex philosophical term. Its basic meaning is that which happens to a person or thing, an event, experience, emotion or attribute (there is a tendency for the word to connote a *bad* experience). Philosophers found it extremely difficult to work out how *pathos* was related to *pathe*, the passions which the soul undergoes, but the word is connected with the more material aspects of a person's being, the experiences mediated by the senses.[41] Woman, in all her materiality and liability to suffering, is thus the natural vehicle of the pathetic. In addition to the type of the feminine represented by the seduced and abandoned Dido, there are several other narrative permutations on the natural pathos of the feminine state: raped women such as Philomela and Lucretia who are actually treated by Chaucer in the *Legend*, and abducted women like Helen of Troy who could well have been one of Chaucer's heroines, as she was one of Ovid's. She and her beauty are mentioned with the other heroines in the balade *Hyd Absolon*, and I draw attention to her here because her name is so

Maids, True Wives, Steadfast Widows: Chaucer's Women and Medieval Codes of Conduct (Westport, Connecticut: Greenwood Press, 1993), pp. 10–23.

40 For a recent discussion of the varying narrative strategies which Chaucer's pathetic tales employ, see Dorothy Guerin, 'Chaucer's Pathos: Three Variations', *ChauR* 20 (1985): 90–112. Guerin discusses *Lucrece*, *Philomela* and *Hypermnestra*.

41 H. G. Liddell and R. Scott, *A Greek-English Lexicon* (rev. H. S. Jones, 9th edn, 1940; Oxford: Clarendon, 1977); F. E. Peters, *Greek Philosophical Terms: a Historical Lexicon* (New York University Press, 1967).

frequently joined in the various references of other writers and artists to the idea of composite womanhood represented by the heroines who appear in Chaucer's *Legend* – for example, we may find her name linked not only with Cleopatra, but even with Lucretia, as three women who caused the destruction of men by virtue of the irresistibility of their beauty as women. Raoul Mortley, a historian of the thought of the Late Classical and Hellenistic periods, notes the affinity of the story of Helen of Troy with that period's notions and myths of womanhood. Mortley suggests that Helen's state of suffering and her many abductions, rescues, seductions and final miserable death underline the fact that she is always being acted upon and has no autonomous power of acting herself.[42] Many other accounts of her story, however, emphasise the destructive effects of her fabled beauty in the war that was fought for her sake. Baswell notes a twelfth-century Latin poem on Troy which omits all reference to Dido but 'casts the subversive danger of woman onto the earlier figure of Helen, thus producing an Aeneas of uninterrupted imperial intention and marital purity'.[43] It was just such condemnation of Helen that is said to be the origin of the palinode form, a fact which underlines again my observation that many medieval accounts of women are entangled with theoretical comments on the nature of literary representation.

Many of Chaucer's Legends embody this same understanding of the nature of women: the pathos of the abandoned Ariadne, for example, which Vergil incorporated into his picture of Dido alongside her Cleopatra role, is emblematic of the states of desolation and bereftness, of unfulfilled desire, her association with the passions, which were thought of from ancient times as typically feminine. The Dido of both Vergil and Chaucer is subject to all four of the primary passions (*pathe*) – fear, sorrow, entreaty and distress – which Mortley notes are associated with the pathos of being a woman, and for which men pity her,[44] and Chaucer's Dido, in her anguished contemplation of her imminent betrayal and terror at the destruction that will be enacted on her by the surrounding 'lordes' for Eneas' sake, confronts Eneas thus:

---

[42] Mortley, *Womanhood*, pp. 63–4.
[43] Baswell, *Virgil in England*, p. 178.
[44] Mortley, *Womanhood*, pp. 65, 66, 114 .

'Is that in ernest?' quod she; 'Wole ye so?
Have ye nat sworn to wyve me to take?
Allas, what woman wole ye of me make? . . .'
She kneleth, cryeth, that routhe is to devyse;
Conjureth hym, and profereth hym to be
His thral, his servant in the leste degre;
She falleth hym to fote and swouneth ther,
Dischevele, with hire bryghte gilte her,
And seyth, 'Have mercy. . .'
1303–16

Götz Schmitz has made the comment: 'Forsaken women in the *Heroides* tradition are often shown on or near their beds . . . [indicating] their essentially domestic and private outlook.'[45] Thus when Eneas 'as a traytour' steals away from Dido by night ('slepynge he let hire lye'), and sails with his 'companye' for Italy (1326–31), the pathos of Dido's personal tragedy and the hero's commitment to his masculine destiny are underlined simultaneously. Ariadne's bed was the classic pathetic icon, but I suspect that for Chaucer Dido is the ultimate embodiment of the pathos of the feminine.

After Vergil's time, writers perceived in the figure of Dido this potent emotive combination of distraction from male duty and object of profound compassion. In *Confessions* 5. 8, St Augustine describes how he escaped from the dominance of his mother, Monica, by fleeing secretly in the night from Carthage to Rome. In Augustine's meditation on this episode of his life he portrays Monica as Eve 'seeking in sorrow what she had brought into the world';[46] however, it seems to me that there is more than a little of Carthaginian Dido in Monica as well, as she weeps, deceived and forsaken, when the hero sails for Rome. Monica was indisputably a 'good woman': yet Augustine can describe her desire not to be parted from her son as 'carnal affection', her hindrance as Dido-like, and her ensuing intense sorrow as the natural female inheritance of Eve, whose suffering was incurred as punishment for her part in the Fall of Man (Genesis iii 16). The philosophical idea of Woman was powerful enough to override all experiential evidence to

---

[45] Schmitz, *Fall of Women*, p. 248, n. 47.
[46] See Pine-Coffin, *Confessions*, p. 101.

the contrary, as Christine de Pizan might have said. Augustine could portray his mother as 'carnal affection' even though the facts of his own family life suggested the reverse of the accepted philosophico-theological model, with a father dominated by passion and infidelity and a mother who exhibited strength and forbearance, as Mortley notes.[47] An unstated conviction of the natural superiority of masculine concerns contaminates even this most sympathetic literary account of the suffering of women. If the context implies a debate about the virtue of women, if as in the *Legend*'s version of *Dido* the hero's great destiny is noted (as in *Dido* 962) and the heroine's sensuality and passionate nature underlined, then her suffering is liable to appear to follow naturally from her desire to deflect the man from his duty (the humorously exaggerated berating of the hero for his treachery is likely to be seen for what it is, a sop to the 'ladies').

The quality of pathos in the Legends was thus for medieval minds as intrinsic to the nature of Woman as her sensuality and 'unsteadfastness'. In a more positive sense, Woman's susceptibility to pity and her ability to evoke pity were valued inasmuch as the softening effect of pity had power to enoble men: Alceste's intercession before the God of Love in the Prologue is a prime example. Jill Mann has recently explored this aspect of the role of 'womanly pitee' in the Legends,[48] although my weighting of the tonal manipulations in the *Legend* suggests that Chaucer is much less sympathetic to women in this work than Mann believes, and much more exploitative. Many modern readers experience difficulty in valuing the pathetic in works like Chaucer's,[49] but we should accept that for late medieval man the experience of shedding tears for the pathos of the feminine state was an enjoyable one, that such emotional indulgence was not only considered morally uplifting, but had entertainment value. For a few lines at the end of this Legend, as Chaucer gently and expansively tells us about Dido's preparations for her death, there is no reason to doubt his 'so gret routhe' (1345).

---

[47] Mortley, *Womanhood*, pp. 87, 113.

[48] Jill Mann, *Geoffrey Chaucer* (London: Harvester, 1991), esp. pp. 8–16, 39–47.

[49] Cf. Frank, *Chaucer and the 'Legend'*, pp. 94–5, for Chaucerian pathos. See also the allusion to 'that sentimentalization of religious feeling, or "affective piety" . . . which was in full flow in Chaucer's day' in Minnis' note on 'Chaucer's cultivation of the pathetic style in the *Legend*', *Shorter Poems*, p. 344.

Compared with the similar account in the *Hous of Fame*, the longer lines of the *Legend*, the closer imitation of Ovidian detail, produce a Dido story less exemplary and formulaic, which demands a more urgent engagement with the pathos of the betrayed woman.

A further point: Woman's passivity, her state of always being acted upon, as well as her association with matter and the passions, suggest part of the reason why the stories of feminine suffering which Chaucer persistently dealt with were so appropriate a rhetorical subject for poets to exercise their skill upon – for the classical poets as well as Chaucer. In Catullus' Poem 64, one of the earliest and most significant examples of this topos of the betrayed and suffering heroine, the poet describes a coverlet for a marriage bed, on which is depicted the story of Ariadne, abandoned by Theseus and lamenting the untrustworthy promises of lustful man. Catullus' description of this beautifully woven and dyed artefact is the centre piece to his poem, and stands for and celebrates the poet's own intricate craftsmanship.[50] It is unlikely that Chaucer knew Catullus. But the identification of woman and matter/subject matter is quite explicit in the *Ars Amatoria* (a not unlikely source of inspiration for Chaucer's concept of the palinodal praise of women), where Ovid, as master of amatory and poetic matters, advises young men how to treat women, as love objects and as poetic subject, drawing his illustrative material from cynical and humorously biased views of the classical heroines.[51] Indeed, it has been acknowledged in relation to *Anelide and Arcite* that stories about the betrayal of women often work as tropes of the poet's treatment of his subject matter;[52] and we begin to suspect that the straightforward discussion of the translator/poet's 'matere' and 'entente' in the Prologue to the *Legend of Good Women* is

---

[50] See R. A. B. Mynors, ed., *Catullus* (London: Oxford Classical Texts, 1958); R. Jenkyns, *Three Classical Poets: Sappho, Catullus and Juvenal* (London: Duckworth, 1982), 'Catullus and the Idea of a Masterpiece', pp. 85–150. For the motif of the woman's complaint, see Catullus 64, 143–8.

[51] See Molly Myerowitz, *Ovid's Games of Love* (Detroit: Wayne State University Press, 1985), chapter 4, 'The Lover's *Materia*', esp. pp. 109–17. Such a notion of woman/subject matter contrasts with the conventions of Roman love elegy which views woman as inspiration; Chaucer employs a similar dialectic, contrasting the heroines of the Legends with the daisy/Alceste figure who is treated in the Prologue to the *Legend* as the source of his poetic inspiration.

[52] Favier, '*Anelida and Arcite*', pp. 83–92.

being humorously enacted in the Legends. *Dido* offers itself as the story of the betrayal of a trusting, generous and noble woman by a callous seducer, and we are invited to show compassion for her tragic death. But Eneas' career as a traitor to love and women is paralleled by the narrator's brutal treatment of his source material: in the hero's necessary betrayal of Dido in the service of his imperial destiny Chaucer finds a potent exemplar of the imperative laid upon the vernacular translator not to adhere too faithfully to his source material, according to medieval poetic theory.

In *Dido* Chaucer both draws attention to the illustriousness of his classical source, 'Glorye and honour, Vergil Mantoan,/ Be to thy name! and I shal . . . / Folwe thy lanterne,' (924–6) and then proceeds to challenge Vergil's authority at every turn in his translation – 'I coude folwe, word for worde, Virgile,/ But it wolde lasten al to longe while' (1002–3); '[Vergil's account of Aeneas' earlier history] nis nat to purpos for to speke of here,/ For it acordeth nat to my matere' (954–5), and so on – it is the English poet's own purpose, matter and intent, his independent authorial control, which is significant,[53] and is as much a focal point in the Legend as is Eneas' betrayal of Dido, as indeed the opening lines imply (924–9). At the very beginning Chaucer blandly asserts that he will draw his story of 'how Eneas to Dido was forsworn' from the deliberately opposed accounts of Vergil and Ovid, and indeed his consummate mastery of the matter of Dido, his creation of a Dido of his own and of his own time, derives from the contest he promotes between Vergil and Ovid. There is a sense in which Chaucer has 'betrayed' his Vergilian matter by restricting Vergil's story of Aeneas to those elements of its plot which Dido focuses on in the *Heroides*,[54] and he has 'betrayed' Ovid by restoring elements of Vergilian epic context to Dido's private sorrow. And, as if to emphasise the intimate association of female protagonist and poetic subject matter, Dido and *Dido*, Baswell also talks about the Chaucerian narrator's betrayal of his heroine Dido: Dido, he says, is 'left victim of both the narrator and Eneas, tricked out of her regality and power by their fowler's craft', converted from 'this noble quene' of the Vergilian account into an

---

[53] Copeland, *Rhetoric, Hermeneutics, and Translation*, pp. 198–201.
[54] Baswell, *Virgil in England*, p. 257.

Ovidian 'sely Dido'.[55] But before I discuss further the pointed association of the poet/translator and the untrustworthy male in the *Legend of Phyllis*, I will turn to Chaucer's most serious engagement with the pathetic, and his least compromised, in the *Legend of Lucrece*.

[55] Ibid., pp. 268–9, p. 264 and n. 105, p. 402. Cf. n. 4 and n. 5 in my chapter on *Phyllis*.

13

Lucrece: too good to be true?

The technique of pretending to praise what all in fact condemn, or to value highly what all in fact despise, an aspect of Chaucer's ironic technique in mentioning Cleopatra's 'unreprovable wyfhod' and Medea's 'kyndenesse', is not adequate to describe the whole of the *Legend*. There is also *Lucrece* to be considered, the heroine of which Legend few have believed was not a genuinely 'good woman', and the pathos of whose situation Chaucer treats with less ambivalence than that of some of her fellow heroines. The *Legend of Lucrece* is one of the more admired in the *Legend of Good Women*. Part of its success is due to the fact that Chaucer here has to deal with a fully worked out narrative from Ovid's *Fasti*,[1] rather than a fragmentary series of allusions as is the case with those of the Legends derived from the *Heroides*.

But is Chaucer's treatment of Lucrece all that it seems? Hers was the story of a chaste Roman matron who was raped by her husband's friend and kinsman, the king's son, Tarquin. Out of dread for the posthumous ill-fame with which Tarquin threatened her, Lucretia had offered him no physical resistance, but committed suicide after informing her husband and relatives of what had happened. In revenge, the Tarquins were exiled from Rome. The main classical accounts are those of Livy and Ovid, both of whom Chaucer notes, and the latter of whom he follows. Lucretia was generally admired in classical times for her heroic virtue, although Ovid had some mild fun at her expense, in those places where he heavily exaggerated her conformity to the standards of the chaste Augustan matron.[2] Christians, too, generally praised her. She

[1] J. G. Frazer, trans., *Ovid: Fasti* (London: Heinemann, 1876), II 721–852, pp. 108–19.
[2] For the element of specific parody of Livy in Ovid's version of the Lucretia story

was an example of feminine chastity for Tertullian and Jerome, and in the fourteenth century her virtue was extolled by Petrarch, Boccaccio and the Menagier of Paris, while Dante placed her in Limbo with the virtuous heathen rather than in the Hell of the suicides. Walter Map and Jean de Meun's Jaloux took the line that there are nowadays no women as chaste as Lucretia.

But another strand entered the history of the Lucretia legend with the writings of St Augustine, in all his immense authority. Faced with the pastoral care of Christian women who had been raped during Alaric's sack of Rome in 410 AD, Augustine in the *City of God* addressed the effect of Lucretia's example. It appears that women such as these had been criticised for not committing suicide to avoid rape, or after being raped.[3] They 'refused to kill themselves', Augustine writes, 'because they did not want to escape another's criminal act by a misdeed of their own'. That is to say, to kill an innocent person, even oneself, is murder (*City of God* I 17). Purity or pollution is a matter of the mind, and evil acts done to a person's body, such as 'acts involving lust', do not make the sufferer guilty if the will does not give consent, but may nevertheless 'engender a sense of shame'. Augustine argued, however, that 'any man of compassion would be ready to excuse the emotions' which lead women to commit suicide to avoid rape (*City of God* I 16 and 18). Augustine's treatment of the literary exemplum of Lucretia is important because he believed it would bear some weight with the Romans with whom he was arguing.

Augustine clearly thought that Lucretia was as chaste as she was reputed to be. This important premise must be remembered during his closely reasoned but highly rhetorical attack on those who defended Lucretia's suicide. Augustine notes the truth of a paradox in a Declamation he had heard on the subject of Lucretia which stated: 'There were two persons involved, and only one committed adultery.' Why then, Augustine asks, was the adulterer only punished by banishment while

(particularly the heroine's excessive modesty and excessive patriotism), see Winsor, 'Study', pp. 123–5.

3 *De Civitate Dei* I 16; H. Bettenson, trans., *Concerning the City of God against the Pagans* (Harmondsworth: Penguin, 1972), pp. 26–7, all quotations from this edition; cf. G. E. McCracken, trans., *Saint Augustine: The City of God Against the Pagans* (London: Heinemann, 1957), pp. 74–5.

the innocent Lucretia received (by her own hand) the death penalty? If there is no unchastity when a woman is raped, then there is no justice in punishing someone innocent and chaste. But, perhaps, Augustine suggests provocatively, she killed herself because she was not so innocent, but had inwardly consented to the act, 'enticed by her own desire'. That is, she had enjoyed it. This would save her from the stain of murdering an innocent peron, by making her an adulteress because she consented.

> Then her defence is faced with a dilemma. If her homicide is extenuated, her adultery is established; if she is cleared of adultery, the murder is abundantly proved. There is no possible way out: If she is adulterous, why is she praised? If chaste, why was she put to death?
> *City of God* I 19

This epigram – *Si adulterata, cur laudata? si pudica, cur occisa?* – was something of a time-bomb in the history of the Lucretia story, as we shall see. It should be clear that Augustine did not believe that Lucretia was adulterous, so that the second part of the epigram applies: if she was innocent, she should not have been punished by death. Why then did she commit suicide? Augustine's answer is also historically important, as he continues:

> However, in the case of the noble example of that woman, it is enough for us to quote what was said in her praise: 'There were two persons involved, and only one committed adultery.' This suffices to refute those who, because any notion of chastity is alien to them, jeer at Christian women violated in captivity. They believe Lucretia to have been too good to be polluted by giving any consent to adultery. Her killing of herself because, although not adulterous, she had suffered an adulterer's embraces, was due to the weakness of shame, not to the high value she set on chastity. She was ashamed of another's foul deed committed *on* her, even though not *with* her, and as a Roman woman, excessively eager for honour, she was afraid that she should be thought, if she lived, to have willingly endured what, when she lived, she had violently suffered. *City of God* I 19

Lucretia acted from 'the weakness of shame . . . and as a Roman woman, excessively eager for honour' (*pudoris infirmitas . . . et Romana mulier, laudis avida nimium*). In this she was not to be a model for Christian women.

Augustine's account reveals that Lucretia was already a subject for 'declamation'. In other parts of the passage Augustine mentions Lucretia's 'literary defenders' and quotes from Vergil on the topic of suicide, all of which suggests that the legitimacy of her suicide was a topic of debate even among his pagan contemporaries. Indeed, it would be true to say that in the classical accounts themselves certain moral questions were considered relevant to the rape of Lucretia, even leaving aside the significant questions of political debate and the ethical justification of suicide. The virtue of women is specifically posed as problematic. In Livy's version, Lucretia's death puts forward the moral problem of whether there can be guilt without the intention to commit an evil act. In Livy and Ovid, moreover, the story begins with an account of bored Roman soldiers discussing the relative merits of their wives – it is in effect a 'testing-the-faithfulness-of-women' story. Even in Livy, Lucretia's virtue has exemplary status and his Lucretia says she must die though innocent, for 'never shall Lucretia provide a precedent for unchaste women to escape the death they deserve',[4] words which recall Livy's opening discussion on whether women can ever be trusted away from masculine supervision.

In a manner reminiscent of Chaucer's Criseyde bewailing the ruin of her reputation in the ages to come (*TC* V 1054 ff.), so Shakespeare's Lucrece is fearful lest her 'good name, that senseless reputation . . . be made a theme for disputation'.[5] (The practical consequences of ill fame that Dido envisages in the *Hous of Fame* 353–60 – that is, that people will now say that once she has so behaved with Aeneas, so she will continue – also appear in versions of the Lucretia story, from early times, as will be seen.) By Shakespeare's time her reputation had indeed become a theme for disputation. After Augustine there were in effect two Lucretias – Lucretia the 'protomartyr', who was easily assimilated to that part of the Christian value system which esteemed chastity above every other virtue, and another who might loosely be called the 'Augustinian' Lucretia, whose virtues were carefully scrutinised and often condemned. Augustine's view of Lucretia seems to have lain dormant, as far as literature is concerned, for many centuries, but from

---

[4] R. M. Ogilvy, ed., *Titus Livius: Ab Vrbe Condita* (Oxford University Press, 1974), II 58, p. 73.

[5] J. W. Lever, ed., *The Rape of Lucrece* 820–2 (Harmondsworth: Penguin, 1971).

the fourteenth century onwards a vigorous debate on the subject may be identified.[6] The 'dilemma' of Lucretia was actively discussed, particularly in the sixteenth and later centuries: some condemned her suicide; some said her consent to the rape proclaimed her an adulteress; and the reformer Tyndale castigated her for glorying in her chastity and in her pride in the opinion of men, which pride 'God more abhorreth than the whoredom of any whore'.[7] There were also bawdy and burlesqued versions of the Lucretia story, in which there were almost always elements of the debate about women (both attack and defence).[8]

Before turning to the evidence of Chaucer's *Lucrece*, it is worth considering what might have been known about Augustine's views on Lucretia in the England of the fourteenth century. Andrew Galloway has recently given an account of 'the first full considerations of Lucretia's story since Augustine's' in the commentaries on the *City of God* made by the fourteenth-century 'classicising' Oxford friars, Nicholas Trevet, Thomas Waleys and John Ridevall.[9] Galloway says, 'In the early fourteenth century, educational ambitions of many kinds increased, spurring the desire to present full texts of works like Augustine's to the common clergy and even the laity' (p. 816). This chain of commentary on Augustine by Trevet, Waleys and Ridevall, sympathetic on the whole towards Lucretia, according to Galloway, nevertheless wrestles with the problem of her possible consent to the rape and the rightness of her suicide; the English commentators show understanding of her Roman need to preserve her honour, but assume some kind of guilt on her part since Augustine had consigned her to a Vergilian underworld. John Ridevall is the most willing of the three to exonerate her; although he mentions and dismisses the possibility of her consent to pleasure, he sees her guilt residing mainly in her

---

6 For the fascinating history of the Lucrece story see Rachel M. Goldman, 'The Lucretia Legend from Livy to Rojas Zorilla', Dissertation, City University of New York, 1976; I. Donaldson, *The Rapes of Lucrece: a Myth and its Transformations* (Oxford: Clarendon, 1982).

7 Quoted in Donaldson, *Rapes of Lucrece*, p. 34. The whole of Donaldson's chapter 2, 'The Questioning of the Myth', is relevant here, as is Goldman's chapter 3. Both writers devote a separate chapter to Shakespeare, but have little to say about Chaucer.

8 See Goldman, 'Lucretia Legend', chapters 5 (particularly Heywood) and 6; also Donaldson, *Rapes of Lucrece*, chapter 5, 'Joking About Rape: the Myth Inverted.'

9 A. Galloway, 'Chaucer's *Legend of Lucrece* and the Critique of Ideology in Fourteenth-Century England', *ELH* 60 (1993): 813–32.

culturally induced self-murder.[10] Ridevall's commentary (c. 1340) was not well known but his comments on Lucretia appear to have been incorporated into Higden's universal history where they would have received wide dissemination in late fourteenth-century England.[11] Ridevall, followed by Higden, concludes that Lucretia killed herself not 'from virtue but rather the weakness of passion' and 'on account of fear and shame'; her suicide was 'vituperable and unjust' even according to Roman law, but committed 'so that she would not lose fame and human glory, for which she longed most greatly according to the mores of her people'.[12]

I would like now to consider the Latin *Declamatio Lucretiae* by the Italian humanist Coluccio Salutati (Chaucer's contemporary), which was perhaps the first European literary or rhetorical work to exploit Lucretia's story using material influenced by the point of view taken in the *City of God*, and is thus a significant analogue to the Chaucerian version. The *Declamatio* was a work of Salutati's youth and immensely popular;[13] we have absolutely no evidence that Chaucer knew it, but it is not anachronistic to bring it forward as yet another testimony to the resurrection in the fourteenth century of the Augustinian dilemma concerning Lucretia. At the command of his patron Duke Humfrey, who owned a copy of Salutati's Declamation, Lydgate translated it and inserted it into his *Fall of Princes* II 1002–344, although it contradicted Boccaccio's opinion of the virtuous Lucretia given in *De Casibus Virorum Illustrium*, which Lydgate translates in another section of the same poem.

Salutati's brief one-sentence introduction to his debate notes the fact

---

[10] Ibid., pp. 819–22, esp. p. 821.
[11] For Higden, see ibid., pp. 822–3. Galloway states that Higden is 'probably . . . Chaucer's direct source' (p. 826). I am proceeding on the assumption that Chaucer was acquainted with the Augustinian view of Lucretia, but do not stipulate an exact source.
[12] Ibid., pp. 823–4.
[13] B. L. Ullmann mentions 'over fifty manuscripts', many more than of Salutati's other works now more famous, see *The Humanism of Coluccio Salutati* (Padua: Editrice Antenore, 1963), p. 34. According to Ullmann (p. 34) and Goldman ('Lucretia Legend', p. 43), the *Declamatio* was very influential and found its way into English, Italian and German literature. It was the foundation of Matteo Bandello's *Novella* XXI. Stephanie H. Jed prints a transcription of Salutati's *Declamatio Lucretiae*, with a translation, in an appendix to her *Chaste Thinking: the Rape of Lucretia and the Birth of Humanism* (Bloomington: Indiana University Press, 1989), pp. 145–52.

of Lucretia's consent or lack of physical resistance (*ipsa consentiente*), without which fact, presumably, the full effect of the debate would be lost. One half of the *Declamatio* is made up of the arguments of Lucretia's father and husband that she should not kill herself because she is not guilty. They said she had not consented, that her virtue and honour were known to all, as had been proved when Collatinus and Tarquin had come to visit her by night. They will avenge her injury. Though her body was corrupted, her mind was innocent; for 'no blame is contracted without consent' (*nulla sine consensu culpa contrahitur*). Unclothed, asleep, not expecting such an event, how could she have resisted an armed man prepared to murder and commit adultery? All her kinsmen excuse her and warn that people will be inclined to believe her guilty if she kills herself.[14]

The other half of the *Declamatio* is made up of Lucretia's response to her kinsmen. She says they must not forbid her to die, lest people consider that she preferred rather to live in shameful disgrace than to die. She alludes to the shame brought on her father, husband and children. She begs her husband and father to pity her, and confesses a secret crime. She implies that when she recalls the rapist's embrace she is assailed by 'the enticements of [her] disobedient members' and remembers the 'traces of the marital flame' – Lydgate's Lucretia, in *Fall of Princes* II 1275–88, talks obscurely of 'delit' and a 'maner constreyned lust in deede', even though she was 'oppressed against her will'. According to Salutati's Lucretia, that pleasure must be avenged with a sword. She goes on to say that, as the powers of Venus are so great in anyone who has experienced pleasure and that women forget grief so quickly, it is possible that she will now begin to enjoy disgraceful behaviour. She continues that, as she cannot prove her innocence with witnesses, she will prove it with her blood. Since her earthly body with its former beauty was the cause of the adultery, her soul and blood must be poured out. She will provide no example for Roman women to persuade themselves that they should live in unchastity.[15] (Lydgate alludes in similar terms to 'the fairness of her earthly body', in *Fall of Princes* II 1318, indicating that women, simply because they are female

---

14 See Jed's transcription of Salutati, *Chaste Thinking*, pp. 145–6.
15 Ibid., pp. 146–8.

and beautiful, do not have to be active temptresses to be held responsible for men's descent into sensuality.)[16] It will be clear that the self-condemnation of Salutati's Lucretia depends on the assumption that women are by nature irredeemably sensual, and Salutati's defense is often quite salacious – 'Let me pierce with a sword this breast which that violent one loved, feeling first my nipples with his fingers impressed for the purpose of exciting lust.'[17]

Donaldson says that Salutati's Declamation, which he nowhere specifically quotes, 'finally [allows] a victory to the defence'.[18] This is surely incorrect; in my reading of the work, Salutati leaves the debate unresolved and designedly provocative. Donaldson may have been mislead by Bandello's *Novella* XXI (fifteenth century, see note 13 above), which relies heavily on Salutati's arguments, but pronounces on behalf of Lucretia. (In the *Novella*, the narrator listens to two friends debating the rightness of Lucretia's suicide at a dinner party. Castiglione, the Courtier, is then asked for his opinion; in actuality, in the speech Bandello gives to 'Castiglione', Salutati's arguments are being translated word for word, but with the addition of a determination in Lucretia's favour.)[19] It is true that in the late Middle Ages Lucretia would normally have been accepted as a truly good woman, with no questions asked. But it is also true that there is an apparent conflict between Salutati's description of Lucretia as 'consenting' and her kinsmen's argument that there is no sin where there is no 'consent' (the same word). This would seem to demand criticism of Lucretia, for if she consented, she was not without sin. Of course, it could be debated that the word 'consent' denoted something different in each case, and this is probably the point: the Declamation encouraged a debate.

The *Declamatio Lucretiae* is not well known today and indeed a modern printed version has appeared only recently, but its aim would seem consonant with Salutati's later writings. It may well have been a rhetorical exercise,[20] designed above all to train the writer in effective

---

[16] Cf. Hansen's comments on the irrational and seemingly 'gratuitous male lust' with which the two rapists of the *Legend* are afflicted at the sight of their beautiful victims, *Fictions of Gender*, pp. 5–6.
[17] Trans. Jed, *Chaste Thinking*, p. 151.
[18] Donaldson, *Rapes of Lucrece*, p. 38.
[19] Goldman, 'Lucretia Legend', pp. 43–4.   [20] Ibid., p. 42.

argument and the writing of good Latin. Like Salutati's innumerable letters, in which various polemical points of view are taken and vigorously argued, it would have been intended for public scrutiny and comment, particularly that of humanist friends.[21] It was the piquancy of the intellectual debating points which the narrative of sex and violence gave rise to which seems to have made the story of Lucretia so popular from Salutati's time onwards, and the questioning of such matters as Lucretia's consent, guilt and pleasure constitutes a continuing counterpoint in all significant versions. In Shakespeare's *Rape of Lucrece*, the debate is internalised within Lucrece's own psyche.

It would not have been difficult then for Chaucer to have known of the Augustinian notion of Lucretia's enjoyment of the rape as a cause for guilt, as well as her excessive concern for her honour as a cause of her suicide; indeed Higden's *Polychronicon* and Salutati's Declamation indicate that these were ideas which were discussed in the late four-teenth century. When we turn to Chaucer's text, we find he moves swiftly to cite St Augustine's opinion of 'the verray wif, the verray trewe Lucresse', which in light of the history I have just outlined is surely significant:

> Now mot I seyn the exilynge of kynges
> Of Rome, for here horible doinges,
> And of the laste kyng Tarquinius,
> As seyth Ovyde and Titus Lyvius.
> But for that cause telle I nat this storye,
> But for to preyse and drawe to memorye
> The verray wif, the verray trewe Lucresse,
> That, for hyre wifhod and hire stedefastnesse,
> Nat only that these payens hire comende,
> But he that cleped is in oure legende
> The grete Austyn, hath gret compassioun
> Of this Lucresse, that starf at Rome toun.
> 1680–91

In this economical establishment of the context and intimation of the nature of the story, after the citing of the main source-material in Livy

---

[21] Ullmann, *Salutati*, passim. Furr sees such debates as of the same kind and having the same purpose as the *querelle de la Rose*, 'Quarrel of the *Roman*', passim.

and Ovid, there seems little doubt to me that Augustine's compassion for Lucretia occupies a focal position (1690–3). Critics frequently brush the reference aside, saying it has no significance for Chaucer's story. Yet the lines quite accurately sum up Augustine's attitude to Lucretia, who surely is to be included among those victims of rape on whose suicides Augustine had compassion.[22] (It is often forgotten that Augustine only brings up the story of the fabulously chaste Lucretia out of his concern for the welfare and mental health of actual rape victims, and all his command of rhetoric and casuistry is called into play for the purpose of protecting such women from the charge that they had not followed Lucretia's example.) Moreover, much of Augustine's arguments hinges on the 'commendation' that Lucretia received at the hands of contemporary 'pagans' (cf. *LGW* 1690), indeed it was this commendation of Lucretia's suicide which made the fate of Christian rape victims so hard to bear. The last four lines of the Chaucerian passage I have quoted should thus alert us that Chaucer's intent may well have included the insertion of Augustinian and Christian perspectives into the Ovidian and pagan account of the 'verray trewe Lucresse'.

It is generally agreed that Chaucer followed Ovid's account in *Fasti* closely; although he mentions Livy there is not much evidence that he had read him. I will now examine Chaucer's account to see if it gives any other sign that he knew of the 'Augustinian' view of Lucretia. Even in the passage already quoted, it might be true to say that Chaucer derived the name of Lucrece's husband, Colatyn, from Augustine's Collatinus, and his incorrect notion that she died in Rome may have come from Augustine's mention several times of the 'Roman' context – neither of these facts is clear in Ovid; Livy would have given both her husband's name and home (Collatia) correctly, another sign that the Roman historian was not the source of Chaucer's *Lucrece*.

Chaucer's story begins traditionally with the decision of the Roman 'knyghts' to relieve their boredom during the siege of Ardea by praising their wives (presumably a competition). Colatyn says that deeds are more important than words, and as everyone knows the virtue of *his*

---

[22] Schmitz also perceives an Augustinian influence on the *Legend of Lucrece* but talks about Augustine's '*alleged* compassion' (emphasis mine), *Fall of Women*, p. 83. Galloway comments that a 'sympathetic historicist . . . Augustine decidely is not', see 'Chaucer's *Lucrece*', p. 832, n. 47.

wife, he invites Tarquinius to go with him to Rome to prove it (1694–1711). In Livy and Ovid a contrast is drawn between the other wives, who are engaged in merrymaking and drunkenness when their husbands come to check upon them without warning, and the faithful Lucretia, who is spinning wool with her handmaids – a traditional activity of good women (cf. 1721). Chaucer concentrates on the visit of Tarquinius and Colatyn to Lucrece. Chaucer's account of what Colatyn and Tarquinius saw is rather softer, slightly medievalised, compared with Ovid's: Chaucer's Lucrece, for example, expresses anxiety for her husband's safety (1721–32), but her sentiments are far less martial-minded than those of Ovid's, and she is concerned not so much for her servants to finish her husband's war-cloak as to ensure their 'besynesse' (1723), to avoid 'slouthe and idelnesse' (1722), as a good medieval housewife should. Her meekness and downcast eyes are likewise features which many medieval people would consider indicated a good woman, as did her unadorned hair (1720, 1734, cf. 1749). Chaucer concludes his picture of a good woman par excellence by noting that her outward appearance was totally consonant with her inward heart, and 'acorde bothe in dede and sygne' (1739).

Lucrece's wifely chastity, which Chaucer says was 'embellished' by her tears 'full of honesty' (1736–7), her tender fears for her husband's safety (1724 ff.) – Ovid also notes that these features of Lucretia produced a pleasing aesthetic effect – her beauty, of course ('hire yelwe her, hire shap, and hire manere' [1747]), and finally her lack of availability (1754), all have as stirring an effect upon the medieval Tarquinius as her 'artless grace' and 'virtue incorruptible' had on the Roman. In this view of Lucrece seen through the eyes of Tarquinius as well as of her husband – in the intimacy of her bed chamber, 'dischevele, for no malyce she ne thoughte' (1720) – one is reminded of the 'soft porn' effect to which Kerrigan suggests the traditional literary portraits of lamenting women, betrayed and distraught (the Ariadnes and the Didos), are liable to give rise; moreover, Guerin has commented how Chaucer, by slightly changing Ovid's account to lay emphasis on Lucrece's unbound hair and the piteousness of her weeping, has increased the erotic impact of the scene.[23] In spite of the fact that

---

[23] Kerrigan, *Motives of Woe*, p. 64; Guerin, 'Chaucer's Pathos', p. 96.

Tarquinius is given some of the features of a courtly lover, the overall structure of connotation in Chaucer's choice of vocabulary is not courtly. What Lucrece's beauty, innocence and modest behaviour inspire in him is not love but 'coveytynge' and 'blynde lust' (1756). The constant remembrance of the details of her appearance does not inspire in him noble deeds but a sudden 'desyr' which burns like fire and makes him mad (1750–2). The despair of the traditional lover at his lady's inaccessibility is described in cynical terms – 'For wel thoghte he she wolde nat ben geten' (1753). Tarquinius is indeed of noble birth, but, given the lexical pattern of this passage, the introductory line, 'Tarquinius, this proude kynges sone' (1745), may well intimate the same 'sentence' that this story commonly held for other contemporary writers like Boccaccio and Gower; that is, it symbolises the evil pride of kings that lustfully oppress their innocent subjects,[24] and later in this Legend the rape is characterised as 'the horryble dede of [Lucrece's] oppressyoun', for which the Tarquins were exiled (1868–70).

Chaucer understands as essentially sinful Ovid's account of Tarquinius' continuing state of sexual arousal which in the next lines he powerfully translates in terms of the sea continuing to 'quappe' days after a storm has gone (1765–8). He follows Ovid in delineating the growth of Tarquinius' passion, but uses very pejorative terms. He traces the 'blynde lust' ever feeding upon itself and retaining its power, along with the strengthening of the rapist's brutal resolve. Chaucer never uses the word 'love', even when Ovid uses *amor*, but instead qualifies the 'plesaunce' that Tarquinius derives from his memory of Lucrece as 'delit or an unrightful talent':

> And as the se, with tempest al toshake,
> That after, whan the storm is al ago,
> Yit wol the water quappe a day or two,
> Ryght so, thogh that hire forme were absent,
> The plesaunce of hire forme was present;
> But natheles, nat plesaunce but delit,
> Or an unrightful talent, with dispit –

---

[24] In *De Casibus*, Boccaccio appends to his account of the rape of Lucretia a digressionary chapter, 'Against the Prodigious Lust of Princes', see Hall, *Illustrious Men*, pp. 73–81; Gower's Rape of Lucrece is part of the Education of a King in Book VII of the *Confessio*.

'For, maugre hyre, she shal my leman be!
Hap helpeth hardy man alday,' quod he.
1765–73

Significantly, to his 'unrightful talent', presumably Ovid's *iniusti . . .
amoris* (*Fasti* II 779), is added the element of cruelty and probably
humiliation in the words 'with dispit', and the ruthlessness of Tarquinius' concluding words confirm that he knows he would have to, and
fully intends to, rape Lucrece.

Let us pause to consider the effect of this lexical pattern in the
description of Tarquinius' thoughts and words; the irrationality of his
passion – 'desyr/fyr', 'wodly'; its illicitness – 'unrightful talent'; sinful-
ness – 'blinde lust', 'coveytynge'; naked sexuality uncontaminated with
love or courtly refinement – 'nat plesaunce but delit'; cruelty – 'with
dispit'; finally, and noticeably, its coarseness – 'leman', 'shap' (beauty,
but also female genitalia).[25] This is no comic villain as in several other
of the Legends; I would hazard a guess, rather, that the delineation of
Tarquinius' desire for Lucrece is designed to titillate. Given the
voyeuristic, rapist's eye view of Lucrece in her bedchamber and the
powerful account of Tarquinius' sexual arousal, we are being invited, I
think, to empathise with Tarquinius, if not to approve. In light of these
things, if we return to the opening scene in 1694 ff. we become aware of
the verbal hints which may have alerted the original audience to the
likelihood of a tale of rape whose erotic aspects will be given full weight.
Tarquinius is described as 'lyght of tong' (given no doubt to the coarse
language which he later exhibits), and in his 'pleye' begins to 'jape' (the
conjunction of these words in association with Tarquinius' light tongue
strongly suggest that the crudities of sexual adventure bulk large in his
speech).[26] Thus his invitation to 'speke of wyves' (1702) seems an

---

[25] 'Leman' is frequently pejorative in Chaucer's usage. For 'shap', see Ross, *Chaucer's
Bawdy*. He cites *OED* for the connotation 'excellence of form, beauty' (sense I. 4. b)
but also that of 'sexual organs' (sense III. 16 – from before 1000 AD). *MED* records the
same range of senses for 'shap', see senses 2. c and 6. a and b. In several similar *loci*
which describe a man thinking about a woman in whom he is sexually interested,
Chaucer mentions her 'shap' as one of the attributes the man contemplates (cf. *WBPr*
258, *Romaunt* 2566). At the very least 'shap' connotes the woman's physical shape as
distinguished from a male (cf. *MED*, sense 2. b), and in Tarquinius' mind must be
equivalent to the 'plesaunce of hire forme' (1769).
[26] For the sexual orientation of 'lyght', 'pleye', 'jape', see Ross, *Chaucer's Bawdy*.

attempt to initiate a bout of smutty conversation, which culminates in Colatyn's rash invitation to go and spy on *his* wife's virtue. (Many versions of the Lucretia story blame Collatinus for risking his wife's security by exposing her to the rapist.)[27] There may well be a certain complicity here on the part of the narratorial voice itself, when it states of Colatyn that 'the *husbonde* knew the *estris* wel and fyn/ And *prively* into the hous they go' (1715–16): if it seems redundant to point out that the husband knew the ins and outs of his own house,[28] is Chaucer making an obscene reference to Colatyn's knowing the secret recesses of his own wife's body?

But to take up the narrative again. Tarquinius returns to Colatyn's house 'in the nyght ful thefly', enters Lucrece's chamber, and, with his hand at her throat and sword at her breast, threatens to kill her if she cries out (1779–95):

> No word she spak, she hath no myght therto.
> What shal she seyn? hire wit is al ago.
> Ryght as a wolf that fynt a lomb alone,
> To whom shal she compleyne, or make mone?
> What, shal she fyghte with an hardy knyght?
> Wel wot men that a woman hath no myght.
> What! shal she crye, or how shal she asterte
> That hath hire by the throte with swerd at herte?
> She axeth grace, and seyth al that she can.
> 1796–1804

Ovid has a similar series of questions and answers at this point (*Fasti* II 801–4). Some critics feel that these questions are unduly defensive for a situation that should require no such defence. In the brevity of Ovid's three lines the questioning is perhaps meant to convey the possible courses of action that run through Lucretia's mind almost simultaneously. Chaucer's lines are more leisurely, and draw more attention to themselves, even though they are rhetorical questions, or are at least

27 For the duty laid on husbands and fathers to protect their women, see Hallissy, *Clean Maids*, pp. 44–9, 101–11. Cf. Hansen, *Fictions of Gender*, p. 8.
28 Cf. *MED*, 'estre', sense 3. d, 'an apartment, room, hallway or recess in a building' (usually pl.). Cf. Hallissy, *Clean Maids*, pp. 108–9, for the 'vulgar analogy between a house and a woman's body' in Chaucer's *Lucrece*, and specifically her chapter 'Women and Architectural Space', pp. 89–111. For a similar erotic usage of 'estris', cf. *Romaunt* 3626. See Delany, *Logic of Obscenity*, p. 195.

able to be answered adequately. In practice, the effect of this series of questions on some readers has been to suggest answers other than the ones offered by the narrator. Goddard scandalised other Chaucerian scholars in 1909 by suggesting that 'Lucrece had ample opportunity to cry out during Tarquin's preliminary speech . . . [and] Chaucer himself has assigned four or five contradictory reasons for her failure to warn the house.'[29] For the narrator to phrase his comments at this point in question form is a decidedly equivocal device, for which Ovid is ultimately responsible, but one which produces not uninteresting effects. It allows the narrator ostensibly to see the situation from the female point of view, but it also raises the traditional questions about rape (Why didn't she call out? Why didn't she struggle?), which might otherwise never have been asked, at least about Lucrece. The contrasting effect of, say, Boccaccio's account, which simply states that Lucretia was raped, is obvious:

> [Tarquin] went into the room when Lucretia slept. By this adulterer's drawn sword she was threatened not with death but with disgrace, for he forced himself into her embrace against her wishes. After he had gratified his pleasure, he left.[30]

In Chaucer's attention to Lucrece's inner thoughts we perhaps begin to see the Augustinian influence on his version, for Augustine, in his determination to condemn Lucretia's suicide, had questioned her private 'will', 'her hidden consent',[31] which could never be known to anyone other than herself but only inferred from her later actions. In point of fact, I do not think that Chaucer believed Lucrece guilty, but it seems he was not averse, in a discussion of the nature of women, to open up the whole question of female complicity in rape.

Chaucer's Tarquinius has no redeeming features. He wastes no time in persuasion or bribes, as even Ovid's villain had done, and, obdurate to Lucrece's pleas, proceeds at once to the ultimate threat, not only of death, but of death and lasting shame; if she will not cooperate he will kill not only her but her stable boy, lay him in the bed beside her, and

[29] Goddard, 'Chaucer's *Legend*', p. 78.
[30] Hall, *Illustrious Men*, p. 76.
[31] See Galloway, 'Chaucer's *Lucrece*', p. 814, for the views of some twelfth-century canonists on Lucretia's 'will' (*voluntas*) and her 'conditional choice' to be raped, and for the views of the 'Oxford classicists' – particularly Ridevall, p. 820.

claim that he killed them after catching them in adultery (1805–11). Lucrece loses consciousness:

> These Romeyns wyves lovede so here name
> At thilke tyme, and dredde so the shame,
> That, what for fer of sclaunder and drede of deth,
> She loste bothe at ones wit and breth,
> And in a swogh she lay, and wex so ded
> Men myghte smyten of hire arm or hed;
> She feleth no thyng, neyther foul ne fayr.
>
> 1812–18

Why does Lucrece swoon at this point? It is not a regular feature of the story. It is clear from the explanation in lines 1813–14 that it is the 'fer of sclaunder' that weighs more heavily even than the 'drede of deth', although the addition of the second modifies the excessive sensibility to shame attributed to Lucrece, at which point many readers experience an incipient suspicion that Chaucer may be sending up the virtuous Lucrece. Yet, significantly, the same detail occurs in Gower (*CA* VII 4986), where it appears perfectly serious.

Remembering Augustine and Salutati, however, the answer may be that the detail forestalls the question they posed: did Lucrece kill herself because she would not have been able to help taking pleasure in the deed? This emphasis on the pleasure she experienced was the main tenet of the argument Salutati gave Lucretia against herself. As Chaucer and Gower's Lucrece had fainted, 'she feleth no thyng, neyther foul ne fayr', as Chaucer says explicitly, and thus she is redeemed from this charge. But, unfortunately, she is inevitably impaled on the other horn of Augustine's dilemma, as Chaucer also intimates when he comments, 'These Romeyns wyves lovede so here name/ At thilke tyme, and dredde so the shame . . .' Augustine, it will be remembered, did not believe Lucretia guilty of complicity, but he said that she must therefore have succumbed unworthily to 'the weakness of shame', because she was a 'Roman woman, excessively eager for honour'. Lucretia is condemned for her sinful pride in her virtue and spotless reputation. Augustine's specifically Christian view of Lucretia was that her situation, for which he indeed had compassion and for which he demonstrated acute psychological insight, contrasted with that of the raped Christian woman. For the latter, it is enough that she have a clear conscience in the sight of God, making her reputation in the sight of men unimportant. There seems compelling evidence that Chaucer knew what kind of a debate he was inviting when he formed his *Legend of Lucrece*.

Chaucer tells us no more of the rape than this, and moves quickly to the scene of Lucrece's suicide. In Ovid the scene is perilously close to burlesque – Lucrece's modesty is so great that she makes four attempts to tell her assembled kinsmen, and even 'in dying she took care to sink down decently: that was her thought even as she fell'.[32] There is not so much exaggeration in Chaucer, not so much blood to welter in, and, as his Lucrece is less patriotic than Ovid's, her hair does not stir at Brutus' militant speech, nor need she move her lightless eyes in approval. Indeed, if one's heart is not a stone (*LGW* 1841), one is moved by Lucrece's suffering in her shame. Nevertheless, many of Chaucer's readers, including myself, find discomfiting what remains of Lucrece's excessive modesty and love of 'clennesse and trouthe', even in death.[33] In Chaucer's account Lucrece, before killing herself, brings herself with difficulty to tell her husband and kinsmen what has happened, and in the course of her dying pays full attention to the decorous arrangement of her clothing:

> But pryvely she kaughte forth a knyf,
> And therwithal she rafte hirself hir lyf;
> And as she fel adoun, she kaste hir lok,
> And of hir clothes yet she hede tok.
> For in hir fallynge yet she had a care,
> Lest that hir fet or suche thyng lay bare;
> So wel she loved clennesse and eke trouthe.
> 1854–60

Again we cannot be certain that Chaucer expected responses such as mine. Gower's dying Lucrece also took care that 'Hire clothes with hire hand sche rihte,/ That noman dounward fro the kne/ Scholde eny thing of hire se (*CA* VII 5072–4). Gower also includes the detail of her 'dedlich yhe', with which she confirms Brutus' speech – again this

---

[32] *Fasti* II 823–47.
[33] Cf. 'The detail [of Lucrece covering her feet] . . . borders on the sentimental and perhaps slips over the border for some', Frank, *Chaucer and the 'Legend'*, p. 108. Examples of such a response could be multiplied.

appears to be quite serious in Gower, and suggests that, given an audience who revered feminine modesty highly, it is difficult to tell whether such a detail as the covering of her legs while she died would be seen as wholly admirable or an ironic comment on an ostentatious display of virtue.[34] Minnis has pointed out that such details are totally consonant with the hagiographical tradition and the notion of Lucrece as a pre-Christian female 'saint'.[35] Guerin, however, has noted the humour in Lucrece's dying modesty but sees it as a 'vital ingredient in the artlessness Chaucer is trying to convey'.[36] For my own part, the knowledge that Chaucer copies Ovid at this point confirms my instinctive response that Chaucer was here mocking the 'verray trewe Lucresse' ever so slightly. It is not that one feels that Chaucer and Ovid are intimating that Lucrece is not good, but rather that she is too good to be true.

Two other points may be made about this scene. In the first place, some have thought that Lucrece's determined refusal of forgiveness in the face of her kinsmen's insistence that she bore no guilt for something she could not help reveals the spiritual pride of which she has been occasionally accused: 'Be as be may,' quod she, 'of forgyvyng,/ I wol nat have noo forgyft for nothing' (1852–3). Why is forgiveness mentioned at all if Lucrece has done nothing wrong? – Chaucer talks of forgiveness three times in six lines and of guilt twice, as indeed Lucretia's kinsmen talk of 'absolving her from blame/guilt' several times in Salutati's version.[37] Galloway believes that Chaucer's Lucrece kills herself 'because those around her reveal that they think she has in fact already done something wrong'.[38] On the other hand, Chaucer may intend the semantically imprecise but psychologically acute offer of forgiveness to be seen simply as the valiant attempt of Lucrece's kin to assuage her subjective, if illogical and unjustified, experience of contamination. Although so strongly expressed, with three negatives, it is doubtful whether there is a qualitative difference between the lines in which

---

34 Donaldson notes that Addison discussed with approval this detail (presumably from Ovid, not Chaucer) in *Spectator* no. 292, *Rapes of Lucrece*, p. 14.

35 Minnis, *Shorter Poems*, p. 365.

36 Guerin, 'Chaucer's Pathos', p. 94.

37 See Jed's transcription of Salutati, *Chaste Thinking*, p. 146; e.g., '*Te pater te vir culpa absolunt . . . [alii] te culpa absolvunt.*'

38 Galloway, 'Chaucer's *Lucrece*', p. 827.

Lucrece refuses forgiveness and Ovid's '*quam*' dixit '*veniam vos datis, ipsa nego*' (*Fasti* II 830). The passage can not be easily set aside, because it operates as the dramatic and affective highpoint of the concluding part of the narrative section of this Legend – the scene of Lucrece's actual death which follows generates a significantly lower emotional charge, I think. I confess I am finally unable to make up my mind as to what the offer and refusal of forgiveness signifies. This also is characteristic of the *Legend of Lucrece* and of the *Legend of Good Women* as a whole: the text teases, raises questions, but offers no firm direction as to how the questioning should be resolved.

There is a second interesting aspect of the scene involving the exchange between Lucrece and her kinsmen, which is not like anything in Livy or Ovid. The concern that Chaucer's Lucrece feels for the 'foule name' her *husband* will now bear (1844–6) is however similar to that expressed in the Salutati version. In her self-condemnation, Salutati's Lucretia makes obsessive use of words connoting disgrace, defilement, prostitution, adulteration and debasement. The concern of Chaucer's Lucrece for her husband's good name has never struck modern readers as unusual, perhaps because it harmonises with Shakespeare's *Rape of Lucrece*, but it is interesting that it coincides with no other of the earlier versions we have been considering, except that of Salutati in the fourteenth century. The mention of excessive shame is Augustinian, but the saint does not specify family dishonour explicitly, and he condemns any notion that 'blood' or even one's 'name' *could* be 'polluted'.

Chaucer brings the narrative section of the Legend to a conclusion with a brief mention of how Lucrece's rape led to the exiling of kings from Rome, so that the Romans considered her a saint and 'ever hir day yhalwed dere/ As in hir lawe' (1871–2). It has often been noted that such language fits well in a legendary of saints' lives. Chaucer's concluding remarks, however, are fraught with the same kind of ambivalence which has been developing in the course of this Legend:

> I telle hyt for she was of love so trewe,
> Ne in hir wille she chaunged for no newe;
> And for the stable herte, sadde and kynde,
> That in these wymmen men may alday fynde.
> Ther as they kaste hir herte, there it dwelleth.
> 1874–8

Adopting again the mode of 'artless' moralising, the narrator's glowing praise of Lucrece depends on an implicit assumption that most women are by nature false, unstable and always desiring a new man (in which context her resistance to rape is something remarkable). These lines thus offer either a grossly insensitive or a consciously inadequate comment on Lucrece's suffering, although as I have earlier pointed out, this view of the nature of women was a minor part of the frame for the Lucretia story since the time of Livy and was an explicit element in Lucretia's self-condemnation in Salutati. The mention of the status of Lucrece's 'wille' in 1875 may well call up the terms of the Augustinian debate. Nor do the final lines offer any resolution:

> For wel I wot that Crist himselve telleth
> That in Israel, as wyd as is the lond,
> That so gret feyth in al that he ne fond
> As in a woman; and this is no lye.
> 1879–82

It would appear to be the ultimate encomium; Lucrece is accommo-dated almost into the rollcall of Christian saints. Unfortunately, however, the Biblical citation is a misquotation. It was a man, the Roman centurion, of which Christ said he had not seen a faith like his in Israel (Matthew viii 10; Luke vii 9). Of course, Chaucer may have meant the Syro-Phoenician woman, whose faith Jesus commended somewhat differently (Matthew xv 28). It may be a slip on Chaucer's part, and it looks so genuine a quotation that readers frequently accept it as such.[39] If *Lucrece* were straightforwardly a tale of simple pathos, then I believe this would be the most acceptable solution. But as I have shown *Lucrece* to have so many problematic details, none of them perhaps conclusive in themselves, yet in total quite substantial, then it seems wise to accept the misquotation – 'and this is no lye' (1882) – as a final ambivalent gesture. The opening mention of the opinion of him 'that cleped is in oure legende/ The grete Austyn' in fact calls to mind that there is a great difference between Lucrece's standards of virtue and

---

[39] E.g., Donaldson writes, 'Chaucer in the *Legend of Good Women* goes further, presenting Lucretia almost as a Christian figure, whose actions prompt one to think of Christ's words on the steadfastness of women', *Rapes of Lucrece*, p. 26.

the one that obtains 'in oure legende', by which standard she is condemned for her pride in her virtue.

But Chaucer's treatment of *Lucrece* significantly alters the simplistic view of the *Legend of Good Women* which my consideration of those Legends devoted to the group of *desertae* may have given. In many of the other stories it would seem that Chaucer was damning women by purporting to praise them. *Lucrece* is clearly different. Although my study reveals that qualifications must be made, my impression is that Chaucer did respond to Lucrece in the traditional way as a good woman, a 'verray wif', and readers over the years who have taken his character in this way are not seriously misled. Our assessment of Tarquinius' character is not compromised by the kind of mock-serious condemnation that appears in almost every other Legend. The closing *moralitas* has even a certain world-weary sadness in its attitude to the tyranny that women suffer from men, one that contrasts markedly with the flippancy of so many of the conclusions to the Legends:

> And as of men, loke ye which tirannye
> They doon alday; assay hem whoso lyste,
> The trewest ys ful brotel for to triste.
> 1883–5

These lines make a particularly striking contrast with the mood of the narrator's comments which bring to an end the *Legend*'s other rape story, *Philomela*, where women are likewise advised to beware of all men; because of shame, Chaucer says, most men will not murder or rape them, yet they will be faithful for as short a time as the rapist Tereus – unless perhaps there is no other woman around (2387–93).

Yet if the pathos of *Lucrece* is not markedly contaminated by the potential for humour, nevertheless for some audiences it will have been complicated by the significant element of debate. Sympathy with the heroine is not the only response which Chaucer's text elicits: Lucrece is first presented to us as the subject of the crude talk of soldiers and as the object of the rapist's gaze. Such narrative procedures develop a sense of distance from the victim's plight which makes it possible to offer up Lucrece's private tragedy to debate. Like the recipients of Salutati's *Declamatio*, like the dinner party guests of the 'Courtier' in Bandello's *Novella*, there must have been gentlemen in Chaucer's audience who were prepared to 'roll Lucrece on their tongues' (cf. *TC* V 1061). Today's readers may doubt that the notion of female sexual enjoyment would have been considered intrinsic to the question of the rape of Lucretia, but there is plenty of evidence that it was. Christine de Pizan, for example, introduces her story of Lucretia in the *City of Ladies* with remarks which sound very modern, but which in fact demonstrate that some attitudes to rape have an ancient history and were very much alive in Chaucer's time. She tells how troubled she is by men arguing that many women want to be raped even when they verbally protest.[40] It is interesting that male writers like Salutati and Lydgate, as well as some modern critics,[41] had no difficulty in accepting Augustine's surmise that women may experience pleasure in rape. Chaucer and Gower neatly sidestep the question. I would postulate, however, that the *Legend of Lucrece* demonstrates that Chaucer knew of Augustine's 'what ifs', and the famous dilemma in which Lucrece is condemned whatever her motives may have been. By her swoon Chaucer has absolved Lucrece from the stain of complicity in rape, but he has left open the question of too much pride in her reputation for 'goodness', read 'chastity'.

My impression is that Chaucer probably did not care if his story was read straight, for pathos remains a primary ingredient. (This goes for the other Legends as well; for the Legend of one of the worst, *Cleopatra*, as for one of the best, *Lucrece*, and for those other heroines who were not as bad as the one or as good as the other.) Nor do I think that *Lucrece* was a private joke, and the question is similar to that of obscenity in the *Legend*. From what we know of Chaucer's audience and his wider readership, it comprised at least some well-educated people who would have been ready and willing to discuss the pros and cons of Lucrece's virtue, and there were at least some social situations in which the hints of the Augustinian debate about Lucrece could have become operative. Chaucer was probably as disposed as Gower to see the women's side of any story and the frequent irrationality of the men's side, but there were too many literary opportunities to exploit if the

[40] Richards, *City of Ladies* II 44. 1, pp. 160–1.
[41] E.g. R. W. Battenhouse, *Shakespeare's Tragedy: its Art and Christian Premises* (Bloomington: Indiana University Press, 1969), pp. 384–96.

(newly rediscovered and provocative) Augustinian view of Lucrece were at least suggested.

It is likely that there were as many questions about these presentations of the heroines for the original audience as there are for us. For Chaucer and his audience, the questions surrounding femininity, its status of ontological inferiority, its inherent pathos, its piquant relationship to actual women in the audience, were important debating points. They were also concepts that could be, and in a male-dominated society often were, approached by means of the joke: 'For no Lucretia lives in Rome today.' In the *Legend of Lucrece* Chaucer has not diminished male culpability for the oppression of women by flippancy – indeed he has gravely condemned it in two places (1819 ff., 1883 ff.). Nevertheless the Legend generates an ambivalent response, which can be demonstrated in the work of modern critics: for most *Lucrece* is an example of the pathos of a tale about a completely innocent and helpless victim beset by a malevolent and violent attacker (Robert Frank), others respond like (and possibly to) the barrack-room discussion of women (Goddard).[42] That the rapist's thoughts and feelings as he plans the rape of Lucrece are rendered so vividly by the narrator, verging on titillation, enhances this second response. In contrast to his largely sympathetic treatment of Lucrece, Chaucer in the *Legend of Phyllis* dismisses its heroine's plight with unmistakable comedy and firmly identifies his own role of poet and lover with that of the male villains of the *Legend*. And it is to this second last Legend of good women that we will now turn.

---

[42] Frank, *Chaucer and the 'Legend'* p. 95, and indeed his whole chapter on *Lucrece*, pp. 93–110; Goddard, 'Chaucer's *Legend*', pp. 77–80.

14

Phyllis and inherited male perfidy

I have used the creation of the literary Dido to discuss the association of Woman with matter, and thence the subject matter with which the poet deals. The history of the Lucretia story, and not least Chaucer's *Lucrece*, reminds us that the virtue of women was also eminently suitable matter for debate. The final Legend which I wish to examine is that of *Phyllis*, and in it Chaucer's treatment of the other stereotype in the *Legend of Good Women*, the seducer, the rapist, the betrayer and, in the end, the poet. Here Chaucer uses the same old story of the proclivity of the male to do with women 'what so that hym leste' as an analogue of the imposition of literary form on raw subject matter. *Phyllis* opens with a flippant allusion to the inherited and instinctual aspect of masculine depredations on women and ends with Chaucer's humorous acknowledgement of his own position in this illustrious lineage. In this Legend Chaucer the poet adopts an attitude towards his 'matere' which is fully consonant with Demophon's casual seduction and betrayal of Phillis. The flippancy, assumed boredom and sexual innuendo of the narrating voice continue to deflect any lingering desire the audience might have to identify with the sufferings of the betrayed heroine; indeed it is with the successful deployment of these techniques that the poet displays his ability to impose his will on this well-worn matter. In the affectionate and exaggerated abuse of 'bad men' which we have become accustomed to in the *Legend of Good Women*, Chaucer lays claim to his affinity with other authors (and particularly his master Ovid), *proving* the potency of his 'lynage and [his] fayre tonge' and a craft, subtlety and art the equal of false Demophon's 'feigned sorrow' (cf. 2526–9, 2546, 2559). This in the end is the significance of the opening lines of *Phyllis*:

By *preve* as wel as autorite,
That wicked fruit cometh of a wiked tre,
That may ye fynde, if that it like yow. . .
2394–6 (emphasis mine)

The Demophoon story will 'prove' how duplicitous men are, and have always been, and how ingenious and crafty is the long line of poets also.

Phyllis is the second last of the Legends of good women, and the last in the series of deserted women, the ladies who were seduced and then abandoned by the heroes, Aeneas, Jason, Theseus. Phillis' story is little more than a cipher of theirs. After the destruction of Troy, Demophon's storm-battered ship is cast up on the shores of Phillis' kingdom. He seeks her grace, promises her marriage, robs her, does with her 'what so that hym leste' and departs (2433, 2466, 2467, 2469, 2481). She writes him a letter of complaint and 'for dispeyr fordide hyreself, allas' (2557). Chaucer's main poetic strategy in *Phyllis* is the witty exploitation of the very triteness of this featureless heroine's predicament. The Phyllis and Demophoon story is indeed boringly similar to that of Ariadne and Theseus, Medea and Jason, Dido and Aeneas. Its very sameness is made to imply how natural it is for men to deceive women and for women to believe their false promises. The villain Demophon's falseness in love is untaught, amoral, inherited from his father with his father's face, stature and social position. Demophon takes to opportunistic seduction and betrayal like a duck to water:

For of Athenes duk and lord was he,
As Theseus his fader hadde be . . .
And lyk his fader of face and of stature,
And fals of love; it com hym of nature.
As doth the fox Renard, the foxes sone,
Of kynde he coude his olde faders wone,
Withoute lore, as can a drake swimme
Whan it is caught and caryed to the brymme.
2442–51

Or, with echoes of the fabliau tradition, like 'the fox Renard, the foxes sone'! On Phillis' part, too, it is the same old story of women's easy fall to the seduction of a nice appearance – 'This honurable Phillis doth him chere/ Hire liketh wel his port and his manere' (2452–3). It is more than the narrator can bear. He interjects that he is surfeited with stories

of those 'that ben in love forsworn' and weary of the penitential task
imposed upon him by the God of Love:

> But, for I am agroted herebyforn
> To wryte of hem that ben in love forsworn,
> And ek to haste me in my legende,
> (Which to performe God me grace sende)
> Therfore I passe shortly. . .
> 2454–8

This definitive declaration of boredom with the project of constructing
stories of good women by glorifying foolishness and gullibility is not of
course an expression of genuine boredom, as Frank effectively demonstrated two decades ago.[1] On the contrary, the masterly manipulation
of tonal effect and audience response is an index of the poet's powerful
control over his matter, his ability to create something completely new
out of such an old, old story. That critics for so long accepted the fiction
of boredom as reality in itself indexes the poet's skill. The affectation of
boredom, however, is another matter and there can be no doubt that its
effect is to preclude sympathy with the victim, and remove the story
from the field of high tragedy. The haste which impels the narrator to
reduce the story to the bare details of the stereotype has the same effect:

> At shorte wordes, ryght so Demophon
> The same wey, the same path hath gon,
> That dide his false fader Theseus.
> For unto Phillis hath he sworen thus
> To wedden hire, and hire his trouthe plyghte,
> And piked of hire al the good he myghte,
> Whan he was hol and sound, and hadde his reste;
> And doth with Phillis what so that hym leste . . .
> 2459–69

As earlier in the *Legend* the common practice of *abbreviatio* was given
the colour of expurgation, here it is made to suggest that the matter
abbreviated is not worth serious attention. It was in *Phyllis*, moreover,
that critics first began to suspect the considerable presence of sexual

---

[1] Frank, *Chaucer and the 'Legend'*, pp. 189–210. Dinshaw does not clearly distinguish
between actual boredom as 'a specifically masculine defense against the feminine', the
'flip side of aggression', and the narrator's fictional stance which exploits this covertly
aggressive act for poetic purposes, see *Sexual Poetics*, pp. 86, 229 (n. 43).

innuendo in the *Legend*, even before Delany's study – the pushing 'now up, now doun' (2420), the 'doynge to and fro' (2471), and, more obscurely, the anchor laid in Phillis' harbour which promises Demophon's return.[2] The imposition on the story of connotations of trivial sexual adventure make a further contribution to the literary betrayal of 'this honurable Phillis'.

In this Legend a higher proportion of the relevant Heroidean epistle (*Heroides* II) is translated than in any other story in the *Legend of Good Women*. The controlling hand of the translator to do whatever he likes with his matter is very much in evidence. He comments patronisingly on Phillis' ability to write well, criticises the length of the letter, picks and chooses just what passages he will bother to translate, and interrupts the flow of her letter with frequent flippant interjections:

> But al hire letter wryten I ne may
> By order, for it were to me a charge;
> Hire letter was ryght long and therto large.
> But here and ther in rym I have it layd,
> There as me thoughte that she wel hath sayd.
>
> 2513–17

In effect, by choosing only the best bits, he deflowers Phillis' letter and, like Demophon, 'piked of hire al the good he myghte'. Those parts of her letter he decides to translate are devoted more to the seducer Demophon's false feigning, his fair tongue, his art, his craft, his subtlety and his ancestral lineage, than to the sufferings of the heroine (2525–49).

The sentiment to which most of the Legends subscribe, the wholesale abuse of the inherent falseness of men and foolish credulity of women (in spite of the minatory force of ancient examples), is diffused with a remarkable anticlimax in the last lines of *Phyllis*:

> Be war, ye wemen, of your subtyl fo,
> Syn yit this day men may ensaumple se;
> And trusteth, as in love, no man but me.
>
> 2559–61

---

[2] Cowen says the anchor laid in Phillis' harbour which promises his return is a close translation of the relevant passage of Filippo's Italian translation of *Heroides* II. She thinks that, as both the Italian and the English make no literal sense, a sexual pun is intended (of the naval variety common in later literature), 'Chaucer's *Legend* 2501–3', pp. 298–9. Delany considers the possibility of several other allusions of a sexual kind in *Phyllis*, 'Logic of Obscenity', p. 197.

After the concluding *moralitas* advising women to beware of men and never trust any of them, the last line appears to be an artful and slightly ribald invitation to submit themselves to the poet's seductions.[3] The war in which he is their foe, it seems, is no more than a flirtatious skirmish, in which the negotiations are not unpleasant. The lines remind us of the fictional parameters set up for the composition of the Legends of good women in the Prologue, that is, as a move the poet is compelled to make in a sometimes disreputable courtly game. Disreputable at least in the eyes of Alceste, the Good Woman herself, the upholder of the orthodoxies of love and literary propriety:

> And telle of false men that hem bytraien,
> That al hir lyf ne don nat but assayen
> How many women they may doon a shame;
> For in youre world that is now holde a game.
> F 486–9

Alceste means, of course, to condemn comprehensively the casual seduction of women, but these lines also set up the possibility that the Legends will be composed in the ludic spirit of much polite courtly entertainment, in which a great deal of pleasure was clearly derived from casting aspersions on the virtue of either men or women, or from exaggerated claims in support of the excellence of one sex over the other. In such contexts the ineradicable perfidy of Jason is simply a recognisable stereotype, behaviour exactly like that of any number of other 'false lovers' listening to Chaucer's tales:

> But in this hous if any fals lovere be,
> Ryght as hymself now doth, ryght so dide he,
> With feynynge, and with every subtil dede.
> 1554–6

At the beginning of *Phyllis* Chaucer also includes in the game the ladies of this implied audience, who are well enough armed and, one suspects, able to detect the seductive ploys of the Jasons and Demophoons of their world:

---

[3] Krueger has noted how Hue de Rotelande concluded *Ipomedon* with a similar obscene invitation to his female readers to allow the poet to commit some kind of sexual act (obscurely described) on them, *Women Readers*, pp. 79–80.

'God, for his grace, fro swich oon kepe us!'
Thus may these women preyen that it here.
2401–2

One senses that all the participants in this game of courtly flirtation, the
men, the women, collude with the poet in despising the poor 'innocents' of the *Legend of Good Women*, so rarely has the pathos of their
betrayal escaped a cynical closure. (They had similarly been pitied by
Ovid for not having had the benefit of his instruction in matters of
love.) Chaucer has appropriated the tragic predicaments of the ancient
heroines of classical story to the leisure world of his English courtly
audience.

Moreover, Chaucer's frank acknowledgement of solidarity with the
male tribe in these final lines of *Phyllis*, and the inherited tendency to
betray women that it implies, is also a claim to a place in the lineage of
'authors'. When Phillis is amazed that Demophon's tears, by which she
was beguiled, could possibly have been 'feyned', the audience should
wonder whether Chaucer could also 'wepe by craft' (2528–30), whether
his frequent cries of 'Allas' were genuine when he describes yet another
tale of female suffering. The poet identifies with the masculine predatoriness of the Legends' villains, who gain their ends by the seductive
power of beautiful words. He does not totally distance himself from
masculine power as evidenced in rape – witness the flippant ending to
his story of the rape of Philomela (2387–93), and the cavalier and brutal
treatment shown towards the text in which the fate of poor Phillis is
represented. By this I mean that superficially we will respond to the
narrator's stance towards Phillis as an entertaining and rollicking
account of a gullible woman betrayed by a callous male (regrettably
entertaining, no doubt). The note of boredom, the flippancy and sexual
puns all suggest an attitude to seduction with which the audience is
familiar and in which it is not encouraged to feel ashamed by the
narrator's mock-horror. Second thoughts reveal the implications of the
fictional status of this stance – it is a way of dealing with a text, not just a
woman's person, which is also being enacted.[4] Moreover, the text which

---

4 Wallace has observed how difficult it is to disentangle the historical and the metaphorical in Petrarch's remarks about women/texts in *Familiares* 18. 7, see ' "Whan she
translated was" ', pp. 192–3. E.g., Petrarch compares the attractions of the unadorned
text to 'Lucretia when she enflamed the heart of Sextus Tarquinius', see A. S. Bernardo,

is 'betrayed' by this unscrupulous vernacular poet, fully confident of his power, is a revered classical story.

When Chaucer initiated the palinodal project of writing a new poem to defend women against men's infidelity, I have no doubt that his purpose was to entertain rather than to instruct; his flippancy, however, serves him well, enabling him to approach the difficult questions associated with writing in English. Palinodes are more often than not written in praise of women, but also at the same time to defend and display poetic method. The *Legend of Good Women* is no different, as it valorises the role of the vernacular poet, whose Legends in English result from his treating his illustrious foreign models with scant respect. The translating and imposing of his authorial will upon the matter of the classical heroines is troped under the figures of seduction and rape. Like Aeneas, Jason, Theseus, Demophoon, heroes involved in higher enterprises, Chaucer's seduction consists of fine words and 'feyninge', of art and of craft. Like Jason he leaves one lady and moves on to the next, despoiling them of their goods on the way. Like Aeneas he 'is wery of his craft withinne a throwe' (1286). Like Tarquin he robs Lucrece of her good name for chastity, which is in a sense her life (1810–11) – with poets as with men, 'the trewest ys full brotel for to triste' (1885). The same problematic quality which applies to the 'giver of the forms' mentioned in *Philomela*, applies also to the poet who conceives and then promulgates the ill-fame of evil acts (2228 ff.). Thus the vernacular translator despoils the literature of the past, takes of its substance, fills his barge with its treasure (cf. 1560, 2151, 2467), when he makes a new work in his own tongue.[5] In the *Legend of Good Women* this 'authorisation' of vernacularity is most spectacularly evidenced in the cavalier treatment which Chaucer accords Vergil in *Dido*, when he refuses to accept the master's account of the role of the gods in Aeneas' abandonment of Dido – 'I coude folwe, word for word, Virgile,/ But it wolde

---

trans., *Francesco Petrarca: Letters on Familiar Matters* (*Rerum Familiarum Libri*), 3 vols. (Baltimore: Johns Hopkins, 1985), III, p. 54. The association of Woman and text or textuality is a commonplace in feminist scholarship; for thorough discussion of the motif in critics with an interest in Chaucer and the *Legend of Good Women* see Dinshaw, *Sexual Poetics*, passim, and Hansen, *Fictions of Gender*, passim.

[5] Kiser, *Classical Tales*, pp. 104–31 and passim, and Rowe, *Through Nature to Eternity*, pp. 49–79 and passim, offer numerous other examples of Chaucer's dramatisation of his own poetic procedure in the actions of the *Legend*'s protagonists.

lasten al to longe while' (1002–3) – choosing to emphasise the transgressive aspect of the perfectly respectable procedure of *abbreviatio*. In offering instead a commonsense worldly-wise explanation for Aeneas' behaviour as that of a common seducer, the English *Dido* values 'experience' over authority, and implies that this experience is the same as that encountered by its listeners everyday.

If the language of the Legends is suffused with a certain element of free-floating sexuality, as Delany maintains, it is also permeated with the language of literary creativity, and the two are often enough connected. I spoke earlier about Chaucer's creation in the Prologue of the myth of the daisy/Alceste portrayed as a product of the poet's imagination or *ingenium*, the image-making faculty of his mind – the term is related etymologically through *gignere* (engender) to *genius*, in origin the 'spirit of male generation'.[6] The medieval allegorical figure Genius (as in Alain de Lille and Jean de Meun) is a writing figure, who of course bears a pen. The term 'engyn', which Chaucer uses in a cognitive sense in the *Second Nun's Tale* 339, elsewhere in Middle English and French frequently has the sense of contrivance or even trickery, a spirit thus shared by the unfaithful man and the creative poet. Among the most memorable images of the Legends were those of the penetrating of the labyrinth in *Ariadne* and, in *Hypsipyle and Medea*, the continual movement of matter from one form to another; both images were given a strongly sexual colouring. The labyrinth, creation of the master craftsman Daedalus, is often associated in medieval literature and particularly in Chaucer with the intricacies and deceitful pathways of the literary text (cf. *HF* 1920–3) and of confusing argumentation (cf. *Bo* III, Pr. 12, 154–9).[7] The transference to the procedure of the literary craftsman of the philosopher's notion of matter's 'appetite' for one form after another needs little explication, and I have already discussed the many forms which the matter of Jason and Medea took in Chaucer's own time. The virtual identification of the poet's powerful words and

[6] Lynch, *High Medieval Dream Vision*, p. 94.
[7] For representative discussion of the image and further references, see P. Boitani, *Chaucer and the Imaginary World of Fame* (Woodbridge: Brewer, 1984), esp. pp. 210, 242; Kiser, *Classical Tales*, pp. 116–17; Dinshaw, *Sexual Politics*, pp. 84–6.

the power of the seducer is particularly clear in *Phyllis*, as in Chaucer's comment about Demophon's treatment of Phillis:

> And doth with Phillis what so that hym leste,
> As wel coude I, if that me leste so . . .
> 2469–70

First the identification between Chaucer and Demophon is described as an identity in sexual intention, but the sentence concludes by inserting the notion of narrative 'telling' into the bawdy collaboration:

> As wel coude I, if that me leste so,
> Tellen al his doynge to and fro.
> 2470–1

The flippant dismissal of the 'matter' of Demophon with which the poet yet again interrupts Phillis' sad story also appears to have sexual as well as writerly connotations:

> Me lyste nat vouche-safe on hym to swynke,
> Nor spende on hym a penne ful of ynke . . .
> 2490–1

'Swynke' denotes hard work, presumably the hard work of mental composition and finding the appropriate words involved in poetry writing, but can also suggest 'to toil sexually, copulate', according to *MED* 2. e, while the pen was traditionally an icon of sexual activity as well as of writing, as I have noted above. 'Spende' meant to spend (often to squander) money, and has many connotations of one's strength being used up or exhausted, and several relating to bodily functions; at least as attested in later times (*OED* 15. c); it was a slang term for 'ejaculate, have an orgasm' and Ross thinks this a remote possibility in Chaucer (*Chaucer's Bawdy*, p. 207). While it is the *subject matter* of false lovers like Demophon that Chaucer declines to 'swynke' upon, passive and 'feminine' as matter traditionally is, the apparent shift in the male character Demophon's gender role is quite disconcerting. I take it, however, that most readers find the lines which this couplet introduces strongly derisive, if humorously so (an effect to which the mock imprecation of 2493 contributes), whether a sexual overtone is heard in Chaucer's lexical choice or not. If the outrageously vulgar edge *is* there, it only enhances the slight Chaucer is offering to the whole trivial business of false lovers' activities, on which he cannot bring himself to condescend to squander any more laborious effort or ink.

In *Anelida and Arcite* as well, as has recently been noted, Chaucer implicitly compared the establishment of one's own poetic voice and the subtlety and craft of the false lover. If new versions of old stories are to be made, unfaithfulness to the original is inevitable: 'men's betrayal of women represents poetic language's necessary betrayal of literal meaning. (It also represents the poet's necessary betrayal of his predecessors).'[8] Even today the notion of fidelity to or betrayal of an original is a cliché in any discourse about translation theory, and it is an ancient trope. I have noted in an earlier chapter how the idea of a *fidus interpres* or faithful translator was more often than not a pejorative term, implying a pedestrian attempt to translate the words rather than the sense of the original; on the contrary, Cicero had demanded the transgressive activity of imitation rather than a faithful reproduction. Indeed Copeland perceives a similarity between Cicero's desire to see Latin works which rivalled the splendour of their Greek originals and the desire of the serious vernacular poet of the late Middle Ages to carve out for himself an honourable place.[9]

The notion of the poet as treacherous seducer has clear affinities with the traditional concept of the poet or rhetor as Liar. In an age of profoundly metaphorical exploration of mental and compositional activity Chaucer chose, from many possible tropes such as the gathering of flowers or the activity of bees making honey, to develop in the *Legend* the notion of the unfaithful male to indicate what must be done if the old is to be made new.[10] No doubt this valorising of the man doing 'as hym leste' with the woman is offensive to modern readers, especially female ones, but it is really only another indication of the broadly recreational context of the *Legend of Good Women*. Throughout his telling of the Legends the poet is playing at being maligned on account of women by the God of Love and the good Alceste, and dramatising

---

[8] Favier, '*Anelida and Arcite*', pp. 83–92; esp. pp. 90, 80.

[9] Copeland, *Rhetoric, Hermeneutics, and Translation*, pp. 175, 202.

[10] Cf. 'The association of poetry, robbery, ruse, and fornication is a common one', R. H. Bloch, *The Scandal of the Fabliaux* (University of Chicago Press, 1986), p. 39. For discussion of further disreputable metaphoric associations with poetry writing, see pp. 22–58.

his valiant attempt to meet their demands, while inviting his audience to appreciate how impossible it is for any man to treat the goodness of women wholly seriously. As far as his women listeners are concerned this is a taunt of sorts but also an excuse for flirtation. In my next and final chapter I will be examining how the F Prologue in particular sets up an expectation of just such a battle of the sexes by evoking the kind of ludic social situation in which orthodox social values, such as the courtly praise of women, were subverted, and in the course of which, irreverent and tasteless a vehicle as the seduction of women appears to modern ears, a serious point would nevertheless be made. The transgressive nature of Chaucer's Legends of good women could thus be enjoyed as courtly entertainment at the same time as they demonstrated the power of a poet composing in English.

The notion of lineage in *Phyllis* is a further interesting metaphorical choice, again ancient, again also permeating modern discourse about the relationship of languages, authors and texts. As a son is like his father, according to this trope, so a new version of an old story is the same as its 'parent' but different. The son follows in his father's footsteps and, because he admires, imitates; yet he in his turn must stamp his work with his own likeness.[11] The motif speaks of continuity with the ancient past along with a certain daring rivalry. *Phyllis* celebrates above all a consciousness of authorial control, a sense of native ability and skill, if not of an ethical *auctoritas*. A. J. Minnis suggests that the last lines of *Phyllis* are 'Chaucer's version of the bravado of Ovid's self-presentation as *praeceptor amoris* in *Ars Amatoria*,[12] and indeed the narrator of *Phyllis* adopts a posture which has more than a glancing affinity with that of the Ovidian master of the poetic and erotic skills. Myerowitz has traced the many parallels between the student lover and his master in love, and between them and the poet, in the first two books of the *Ars Amatoria*, where the young man is taught how to hunt, catch and maintain the love of a mistress.[13] In the Ovidian work the

[11] See Copeland, *Rhetoric, Hermeneutics, and Translation*, pp. 26–30, for the adaptation of this motif by Roman theorists.
[12] A. J. Minnis, 'De Vulgari Auctoritate: Chaucer, Gower and the Men of Great Authority', in R. F. Yeager, ed., *Chaucer and Gower: Difference, Mutuality, Exchange* (Victoria, B.C.: English Literary Studies, 1991), pp. 45, 69–70 (n. 38).
[13] *Ovid's Games*, esp. chapter 3, 'The Progress of Love'.

lover's erotic impulse and the poet's *ingenium*, his natural talent, his creativity, his inspiration, are equated. The challenge for each is to apply the controlling power of *ars* in service of the desired end, the satisfactory love affair, the completed poem. To both projects the same ancient metaphor is addressed, that of the journey by sea or land, and of the necessity to be either helmsman or charioteer if one wishes to master the well-nigh overwhelming power of the sea or speed of the chariot, in order to reach one's destination safely. The image lends itself in Ovid's hands to sexual innuendo (for example, *Ars* II 725–32); similarly, Demophon's seduction of Phillis in the *Legend* is described in sea-faring terms and as 'the same wey, the same path' as his father, the unfaithful Theseus, has gone. In a highly erotic passage from the *Roman de la Rose* 21346 ff., which I discuss in my next chapter, Jean de Meun conflates the Lover's journey of seduction, of both old and young women (well trodden roads or newly broken paths), with the poet's project of choosing and mastering matter from old or new sources. It seems clear that in the *Legend* Chaucer, like Ovid and Jean, associates amoral masculine virility and easy conquest of women with the poet's natural talent, expressed with 'art', 'craft' and 'subtelty'. As we know of Chaucer's profound respect for his classical heritage (in spite of the irreverent attitude to it expressed in the *Legend*), so we need not doubt his respect for the conventional feminine ideal celebrated in the daisy/Alceste figure; the licence of game, however, allows him to admire, under the cover of the unscrupulous seduction of women, the challenge offered by the upstart vernacular poet to the literary eminence of the classical past.

At this point, then, I leave the Legends of good women to return to the Prologues to the *Legend of Good Women*, and the F Prologue in particular. This enterprise, perforce, will be two-sided. On the one hand I hope my discussion of the Legends will throw some light upon several obscure, if charming, aspects of the F Prologue. On the other hand the F Prologue's evocation of the intimacies and elegancies of courtly game-playing may be seen as an alternative but complementary aspect of the contextualisation of the Legends.

PART V

The Legend as courtly game

15

The Legend as courtly game

The early fifteenth-century literary society known as Charles VI's *cour amoureuse* was formed on St Valentine's Day, 1400, 'à l'onneur, loenge et recommendacion de toutes dames et damoiselles'.[1] Its members were strictly forbidden to compose 'ditties, complaints, rondeaux, virelais, ballades, lays [or] any other literary form, in rhyme or prose, to the dishonour, blame, disparagement or detraction of any lady or ladies, damsel or damsels, or of women as a whole, whether living or dead, for any cause whatsoever, such as may give serious and unpleasant offence'.[2] The penalties for disobeying were severe, although probably tongue-in-cheek, yet one imagines that such strictures only came into existence because the likelihood of their not being conformed to was a very real possibility. This pastime, *la louange des dames*, the praise of women, operated at one pole of the literary treatment of the 'matter of Woman'. It was in diametrical opposition to the strategies of clerical antifeminism with its store of jokes and exempla against women and its appeals to 'experience'. In the opening lines of the *Legend of Good Women* Chaucer contrasts faith in the verities of religion with the urgent questioning of experience, and this epistemological dilemma of the ordinary Christian is replicated playfully in the poet's response to the 'woman question'. In the body of the work two attitudes towards women are held together in the voice of the *Legend*'s narrator, whose genuine poetic service in praise of women and love is apparently spurned or misunderstood by the God of Love, in consequence of which the poet continues in a state of covert rebellion against Love's

[1] Quoted in Green, *'Familia Regis'*, p. 96. See also Piaget, 'La Cour Amoureuse', p. 417.
[2] Translation from Green, *'Familia Regis'*, p. 95.

tyrannical and unreasonable dictates about the literary treatment of women.

In the G Prologue of the *Legend of Good Women* Chaucer, by alluding to some of the chief practitioners of clerical antifeminism (G 246–340), prepares his audience for a tale collection which will tend to subvert the ideals of *la louange des dames*. Clerical antifeminism frequently contained a strong ludic element, and when it moved into the vernacular and was accompanied by a higher consciousness of women in the audience, the notion of 'game' became even more important, and the apology to women one of its necessary components. In my earlier chapters dealing with the Prologues I chose to discuss the G Prologue's version of the poet's confrontation with the God of Love. In the F Prologue, with its extended worship of the daisy, its dedication to the queen and its vivid sense of a listening audience whose members are practised in the forms of courtly loving, the ludic context is developed differently and much more informally: the God of Love is not made to refer to 'Valerye' and Jerome or to impotent old clerks, indeed the courtly conceit of love as a religion is an elaborate feature of the version. This feature of Prologue F is a marked one, essentially because almost every example, apart from the basic motifs of sin, intercession, forgiveness and penance and the idea of a 'legendary', is missing in G. This material specific to F includes details like the poet's 'knelyng' to await the daisy's 'resureccioun . . . with dredful hert and glad devocioun' (F 103–17); the God of Love's reference to the daisy as his 'relyke' (F 321), his extravagant pronouncement that 'Ne shal no trewe lover come in helle' (F 553), and his departure home to 'paradys' (F 564); phrases like 'other holynesse' (F 424's description of Chaucer's *Boece*), which in G become 'other besynesse' (G 412), and so on.[3]

Moreover, the intimate courtly ambience of the pre-dream section is developed at greater length, particularly the long passage of some fifty lines dealing with the seasonal setting and the lovemaking of the small birds (F 125–70). (This amplification of the passage in which the small birds defy the fowler does not appear in the G Prologue and the G Prologue's amplification of the God of Love's speech in condemnation

---

[3] See Griffith, 'An Interpretation of Chaucer's *Legend*', pp. 396–404, where the phenomenon was, I think, first noted. Griffith's explanation that Chaucer had become more formally religious in the revised G Prologue is not necessary.

of the poet, with the reference to Valerye and Jerome, does not appear in the F Prologue, yet each makes a distinctive contribution to the peculiar character of the Prologue in which it occurs.) In F 125–70 it appears we have an allusion to the games with which the 'lovers' whom Chaucer identifies as his audience disported themselves, and the qualification of the notion of Ideal Woman comes from deep within the courtly milieu. Both Prologues introduce the *Legend* as a product of 'game' and 'holiday' and associate it with a certain dereliction from the requirements of serious study and the belief systems of orthodox culture (F/G 29–39).

I turn now to the audience expectations fostered by the F Prologue and begin with the peculiar passage F 125–70 which is strongly impregnated with allusions to the *Roman de la Rose*, but which has never yielded easily to interpretation.[4] In these lines the worship of the daisy and the sovereign lady suddenly modulates in the direction of a far less idealised view of love and the relationship of the sexes. Even the astrological reference denominating the month of May in which the poet kneels before the daisy is remarkable less for its seasonal precision than for its evocation of sexual passion and the classical tale of the rape of Europa (F 112–14). At the beginning of the passage the small birds join with the earth in farewelling winter (F 130 ff.), and at its end they 'welcome, somer, our governour and lord' (F 170). In the middle they hymn St Valentine, the harbinger of the lovemaking which belongs to summer and, given his February feast day, patron of spring's rebellion against winter's still operative power. In these lines neither the praise of ladies nor the tenets of clerical antifeminism are given much attention, but a marked element of (enjoyable) sexual sparring is envisaged. If both Prologues speak of a conflict between faith and doubt, between serious study and holiday games, between winter and summer and the Flower and the Leaf, this passage makes allusion to many other traditional and often irresolvable literary conflicts, such as those between youth and experience, along with oppositions which, in this passage at least, admit of a specifically sexual resolution or 'acord'

---

[4] Delany is one of the few to have paid it attention, although her argument does not parallel mine, see 'Rewriting Woman Good' and 'Women, Nature and Language: Chaucer's *Legend of Good Women*', in *Medieval Literary Politics*, pp. 74–87, 151–65.

(F 159, 169) – pity and 'danger', mercy and right, love and hate, innocence and malice, 'trouthe' and 'newfangelnesse'.

The heroes and heroines of this seasonal celebration of renewed warmth and love, the 'smale foules, of the sesoun fayn', offer spirited defiance to the 'foule cherl', the fowler who attempted in winter to capture them in his nets and snares:

> The smale foules, of the sesoun fayn,
> That from the panter and the net ben scaped,
> Upon the foweler, that hem made awhaped
> In wynter, and distroyed hadde hire brood,
> In his dispit hem thoghte yt did hem good
> To synge of hym, and in hir song despise
> The foule cherl that, for his coveytise,
> Had hem betrayed with his sophistrye.
> This was hire song: 'The foweler we deffye,
> And al his craft.'
> F 130–9

The image of the small birds' escape from the fowler frequently has religious connotations, common in the Old Testament, in patristic commentary, and in devotional works like Clanvowe's *The Two Ways*.[5] Most commonly the birds would be interpreted as human souls, and the fowler the devil with his envy of God and many deceitful stratagems designed to entrap men. There can be no doubt, however, that in the phraseology of this passage Chaucer is indebted to the humorous use Jean de Meun makes of the imagery of the fowler luring foolish birds into his nets by his sophistry (*RR* 21491 ff.; cf. F 137), where it refers to the fate of inexperienced girls in the hands of smooth-talking men. This spirited digression of Jean's in the *Roman de la Rose* (*RR* 21435–520), interrupting most surprisingly and at the very last moment his account of the final penetration of the Rose, is a curious account of the advisability of avoiding telling lies to older women if one should want to seduce them rather than *tendres puceles*. This extraordinary passage

---

[5] See B. G. Koonce, 'Satan the Fowler', *MS* 21 (1959): 176–81; J. Gardner, 'The Two Prologues', pp. 601–2; J. Speirs, *Chaucer the Maker*, 2nd edn (London: Faber, 1960), pp. 88–9; V. J. Scattergood, ed., *The Works of Sir John Clanvowe* (Cambridge: Brewer, 1975), pp. 69–71.

indicates an attitude to love and poetry which is constantly alluded to in the *Legend of Good Women*, but which is not always thought of as a courtly posture. Here in the F Prologue Chaucer derives his description of the bird's joyful escape from the fowler from Jean's account of how the older quail know by dint of painful past experience how to escape the net the fowler spreads in the thick green grass of springtime:

> [These flatterers] attempt deceit
> As does the fowler hidden in the woods,
> Who with his whistled notes decoys the birds
> To come within the nets where they'll be caught,
> And is [approached] by all the foolish fowl
> Who don't know how to meet his sophistries
> But are deceived as by a metaphor . . .
> [*Qui ne set respondre au sofime*
> *Qui l'a mis en decepcion*
> *Par figure de diccion . . .*]
> Unless some older quail refuse the snare . . .
> So older women who have once been lured,
> And by their suitors tricked by flatteries,
> Hearing the words that they have heard before . . .
> The more they've been deceived, the more they're sly
> To recognize, far off, the trick again.
> *RR* 21491–520 (trans. Robbins)

Chaucer's small birds, then, have a close affinity to Jean's women of experience, those 'well instructed in the art of fraud' (*RR* 21472–4), in the sense not of being deceivers but of knowing through experience how to resist deceit and flattery. It is instructive to look at the context of this passage in the *Roman* to which Chaucer turns several times in the *Legend*. Jean has paused (*RR* 21346 ff.) to praise Nature for her gifts to him, for his sexual 'equipment' – his scrip and pilgrim staff which undoubtedly stand as well for his natural literary abilities – which he must learn to use and have much practice with, in order to become a good craftsman. His scrip and staff help him in his journeying along various pathways, the dangerous and the easy, the highways and the footpaths. In a clear reference to the dictum of medieval literary theory advising poets to attempt to treat traditional material differently and well, Jean advises that 'there's more productive gain in trodden roads than in new-broken paths' (*veauz chemins que nouveaus sentiers, RR*

21435–8),[6] and then remarks that both Juvenal and Ovid have recommended to him that to invest in some older woman with money is a more advantageous road to take than the difficult one of seducing virgins. Thus the hard work of making love to older and experienced women comes to stand for the poetic labour involved in treating old material with skill and discrimination. The older women are also associated with a sophisticated audience, trained in the arts of literary interpretation and of disentangling rhetorical ploys. Jean says they know what to do when approached by flatterers (*flajoleur*) with sweet and seductive tongues:

> They fear to swallow hook with bait,
> And listen close and try to figure out
> Whether it's truth or fable they are told.
> They weigh each word, so much they fear deceit
> Because they have experienced it before . . .
> *RR* 21529–36

On the other hand, the 'tender maids', inexperienced and gullible, are associated with new and untried matter (and undiscriminating audiences); Jean concludes that if the poet/lover chooses this road of seducing virgins he should try as many as possible so that he may be able to distinguish good from bad.

There is a dramatic identification of poet and lover (or man intent on seducing women) in Jean's passage; almost all the lover's strategies of seduction are described as linguistic ones, and the fowler's *sofime* and *figure de diccion* are particularly pertinent. There can be no doubt that Chaucer knew and admired this passage from the *Roman* and indeed employed similar metaphorical strategies throughout the *Legend*. Nevertheless, this pre-dream section describing the courting of the small birds remains obscure and was possibly somewhat obscure even to initial audiences, although Chaucer retains a brief reference to the fowler's sophistry in both versions of the Prologue. What does come through in the F Prologue's extended account is a ludic and counter-orthodox attitude to love characteristic of some of the literature

---

[6] Horace, *Ars Poetica* 131–4, associated 'lingering over a common and open way' with the fault of the 'faithful translator'. See Myerowitz's account of the ancient motif of the voyage or journey with its various pathways as metaphor for the pursuit of poetry, *Ovid's Games*, esp. pp. 87–90.

associated with courtly seasonal festivities. The birds who defy the
fowler are the ladies in Chaucer's audience whom he addresses in
Phyllis, and who he knows were experienced enough not to have fallen
prey to the wiles of Demophon. The men of the *Roman* passage who lie
and flatter and beg for pity in order to entrap their female victims (*RR*
21475–90) are the Legends' heroes, but also the men in Chaucer's
audience who know as well as Jason how to 'come to hous upon an
innocent' (*LGW* 1546). In the passage from the *Legend* under consideration they also figure prominently:

> . . . thoo that hadde doon unkyndenesse –
> As dooth the tydif, for newfangelnesse –
> Besoghte mercy of hir trespassynge,
> And humblely songen hire repentynge,
> And sworen on the blosmes to be trewe
> So that hire makes wolde upon hem rewe,
> And at the laste maden hire acord.
> F 153–9

The penitential language is humorous and light-hearted; the act of
swearing on the blossoms (F 157), commonly considered the most
insubstantial and transitory part of the plant, and made by lovers
(presumably male) who have already proved to be unfaithful, makes it
virtually certain that it is not true love that is here envisaged, but
calculated seduction or cooperative flirtation. Only the inexperienced –
the 'innocent' (cf. F 163) – believe oaths sworn on blossoms, and agree to
grant their sexual favours. They are Jean's *tendres puceles*, those 'who
suspect no trap when they listen to flatterers' (*RR* 21465 ff.). Of course, it
is not unlikely that the older experienced women (whom Jean also
writes about), the ones able to defy the cruel fowler, are prepared, for the
purposes of the game, to play at being innocents ripe for seduction. The
'acord' thus made between the small birds is described in terms of the
Roman's allegorical enactment and is effected when Daunger is overcome by Pity's 'stronge gentil myght', who made 'Mercy passen Ryght/
Thurgh innocence and ruled Curtesye' (F 160–3). That is to say, the
initial resistance of the women ('Daunger'), when approached by these
treacherous suitors, is overcome by the female propensity to pity and the
conventions of the courtly life, with its obsession with the correct
behaviour of Love's servants and especially with talking well about love.

Pity and Courtesy are both warriors engaged in the God of Love's onslaught on the Rose in the *Roman*. The *Roman* does not mention 'innocence' as one of its amatory personifications, but lest we should miss the tone of the passage, it is a term which Chaucer further glosses:

> But I ne clepe nat innocence folye,
> Ne fals pitee, for vertu is the mene,
> As Etik seith; in swich maner I mene.
>
> F 164–6

This passage mysteriously implies that at least some of the audience will be inclined to equate innocence with folly and/or false pity. I suspect the terminology is ultimately a reference to Aristotle's telling account, in *Rhetorica* II (1389a–1390b II), of youth, old age and the virtuous mean of maturity, which also seems to subtend Jean de Meun's passage about tender young maids and experienced women. This account,[7] which was acutely observed, full of commonsense and did not require any philosophical training to appreciate, would appeal to the anthologiser in any age and was in fact adapted in Giles of Rome's *De Regimine Principum* (I IV I–IV), which Chaucer could have known. Aristotle describes youth as having an excess of natural and emotional energy, but a defect in experience. Old age is marked by a defect in emotion and an excess of experience.[8] Chaucer's terms 'innocence', 'folye' and 'pity' all have equivalents in the Aristotelian complex of descriptive comments on youth. The young are prone to acting upon pity because they think all people good and judge their neighbours by their own *innocentia* – usually translated 'harmlessness' or 'guilelessness'.[9] Other parts of Aristotle's passage are also relevant.[10] For example, the young are described as *non maligni* – Chaucer consistently uses 'not malicious' or 'voide of al malice' as an equivalent to 'innocent' (see F 167 and

---

[7] Cf. J. A. Burrow, *The Ages of Man: a Study in Medieval Writing and Thought* (Oxford: Clarendon, 1986), pp. 5–11. Burrow prints a translation of *Rhetorica* II 11–14 in an appendix, pp. 191–4.

[8] See J. E. C. Welldon, trans., *The Rhetoric of Aristotle* (London: Macmillan, 1886), pp. 164–70, and Bernhardus Schneider, ed., *Rhetorica: Translatio Anonyma sive Vetus et Translatio Guillelmi de Moerbeka. Aristoteles Latinus* (Leiden: Brill, 1978), XXXI 1–2, pp. 247–50.

[9] William of Moerbeck, *Rhetorica*, p. 248.

[10] For following quotations see Welldon, *Rhetoric*, p. 165; William of Moerbeck, *Rhetorica*, p. 247.

G 341, 345, 351) – because they have not so far seen many villainies. They are over-trustful, even gullible, 'because they have not yet been often deceived'. This shades into the meaning of Chaucer's third term 'folye', which has no exact equivalent in the Aristotelian passage. However, the notion of defect of experience, which is the inevitable concomitant of youth, leads to the idea of foolishness, imprudence, lack of wisdom, which is the primary meaning of the Middle English word 'folye'. The strong secondary meaning which *MED* gives for 'folye', and all its related forms, of lechery or lasciviousness is also represented in Aristotle. Youth, he says, has an excess of desire and emotion: 'of the bodily desires it is the sexual to which they are most disposed to give way, and in regard to sexual desire they exercise no self-restraint. They are changeful too and fickle in their desires which are as transitory as they are vehement.' Youth with its innocence, gullibility and fickleness is very clearly under the sway of the God of Love, as I described him in an earlier chapter.

If such an Aristotelian passage lies behind Chaucer's lines on innocence, virtue and the mean, then the poet has been somewhat disingenuous. Far from calling innocence virtue (although innocence is, of course, connected with goodness in many contexts), he is calling to mind that subsidiary meaning of innocence which connects it with foolishness growing out of lack of experience, and misplaced, even gullible, pity which derives from a youthful excess of emotion (Chaucer's 'folye' and 'fals pitee'). In Aristotle's schema, it should be noted, these concomitants of youth are not presented as vices, but simply as the mean not quite achieved, and likewise the Chaucerian passage is not marked conspicuously by a tone of moral condemnation. About the virtuous mean in this Aristotelian context – something like a right proportion of experience and emotion which comes with maturity – Chaucer has really nothing to say here, although among his other poems it would be true that Good Lady White represents a figure who has achieved the right mean or mixture of compassion and prudence in response to a suitor (*BD* 1269–72). It does seem likely, however, that the opposite position to innocence is envisaged in this passage in the *Legend*. That, it will be remembered, is the state of old age, marked by defect in emotion and too much experience. Not only do we see the marks of Jean's tender young maids, gullible and all too full of pity, but also, in the birds that defy the fowler, his older experienced women who, like Aristotle's description of the old, 'have lived many years and have been often the victims of deception and error . . . they do not trust anybody from having had experience of human wickedness'.[11] It is instructive to note that Lady White, albeit an idealised figure, operates in the serious realm of orthodox morality; on the other hand, the 'smale foules' of F 130–70 are humorously stereotyped as either 'youthful' or 'experienced' lovers, operating in the frivolous world of holiday flirtation which has little in common with marital fidelity. We should also observe that it is the type of behaviour which is being categorised here and not the actual ages of the participants, again as in the case of Lady White. Although Chaucer's schema probably derives from Aristotle's observations about the behaviour likely to be exhibited by the young, the middle-aged and the old, it has become dissociated from chronological age; Lady White is young, but behaves with the moral judgement of full maturity. Similarly Chaucer's 'smale foules' are not necessarily young or old; it is just that in their lovemaking they are not exhibiting the virtuous mean between gullibility and cynicism, but the tolerated sexual 'folly' characteristic of youth.

The audience of the F Prologue of the *Legend of Good Women*, we may be sure, was not conspicuously 'innocent' or inexperienced: the men knew the value of swearing false vows and promises and the women knew how to protect themselves from them. Both men and women will have been well versed in the language of love, with all its ambiguities and polite euphemisms. The birds' courting scene will signal to them, for example, a context in which Pity (and 'mercy', 'routhe', etc.) connotes the woman's sexual compliance,[12] and where promises of 'trouthe' are a likely marker of male duplicity, a playful and counterorthodox interpretation of terms whose moral status is normally unassailable. Above all, the attitude to love expressed here is not a tragic or pathetic one, but light-hearted and worldly-wise, naturalistic rather than idealistic. The experienced women defy the fowler because

---

[11] Welldon, *Rhetoric*, pp. 166–7; William of Moerbeck, *Rhetorica*, p. 248.

[12] Burnley makes the passing comment in his chapter on tyranny that 'the lady's pity (routhe, mercy, pitee, compassioun, grace) . . . in actuality means her sexual compliance' (*Chaucer's Language*, p. 34). *MED* does not mention the specifically sexual meaning of 'pite', although it is relatively common.

they understand the techniques of seduction. In the playful spirit of St Valentine's Day, however, they offer little resistance to those that 'sworen on the blosmes to be trewe', not because they are gullible but because they do not confuse earnest with game. If we needed any confirmation that the context of the *Legend* is ludic rather than serious, then we need only heed Prologue F's reference to the lovemaking of St Valentine's Day, for it is worth pursuing why the birds should recall their early Spring vows to St Valentine in a poem which is clearly set in May:

> In hire delyt they turned hem ful ofte,
> And songen, 'Blessed be Seynt Valentyn,
> For on his day I chees yow to be myn,
> Withouten repentyng, myn herte swete!'
> F 144–7

The celebration of St Valentine's Day was one of the most significant occasions for which courtly verse was written in England and France in the late Middle Ages. The origin of its customs, however, remains quite mysterious. They cannot be documented before the time of Chaucer, yet in a remarkably short time they achieved a far wider provenance than any similar court celebration, and are faintly remembered even today.[13] In spite of the fact that the earliest evidence is the poetic and aristocratic testimony of Chaucer and Oton de Grandson (supplemented by that of Gower and Clanvowe), the celebration of St Valentine's Day may have reflected much older folk customs. These customs were explicitly connected with the proverbial opinion that the birds met on February 14th to choose their mates for the following year.[14] It is unfashionable to accept this as a genuine proverb, since it is not found in writing before

---

[13] See W. Carew Hazlitt, *Faiths and Folklore of the British Isles: a Descriptive and Historical Dictionary*, 2 vols. (1905; rpt. New York: Blom, 1965), II, pp. 608–11. Cf. J. B. Oruch, 'St Valentine, Chaucer, and Spring in February', *Speculum* 56 (1981): 534–65, and A. L. Kellogg (with R. C. Cox), 'Chaucer's St Valentine: a Conjecture', in *Chaucer, Langland, Arthur* (New Brunswick: Rutgers University Press, 1972), pp. 108–45.

[14] H. A. Kelly doubts that Chaucer could have associated his St Valentine's Day and the actual mating of birds with the month of February, see *Chaucer and the Cult of Saint Valentine* (Leiden: Brill, 1986). My interest in the Valentine reference in the *Legend*, however, is to tone and not date, except insofar as the February date coincides sometimes with pre-Lenten festivities. February 14th as a lovers' festival was confirmed by the year 1400, as I noted at the beginning of this chapter.

Chaucer's time, although few other proverbs are either, and their authenticity is not doubted. Homely observations on the progress of the natural year abound for early February[15] and the spirit of St Valentine's Day perhaps owes something to the feeling that, in spite of the inclement weather of February, Spring was at hand and could be welcomed in anticipation. It is certainly true that the festivities of the pre-Lenten season retained elements of the desire to ensure fertility for beasts and crops in the ensuing period. St Valentine's Day sometimes falls just before Lent and sometimes just inside Lent, and in many Valentine poems there is more than a hint of the spirit of Carnival, a point which is made quite explicit in the early fifteenth-century poems of Charles d'Orléans, who writes of a conflict between Carnival and Lent in four of his Valentine's Day rondeaux.[16] Although the celebration of Carnival (English Shrovetide) was a weaker phenomenon in England than in other parts of Europe, Peter Burke makes some cautious generalisations which apply to the whole region: 'Carnival was a time of particularly intense sexual activity . . . Weddings often took place during Carnival, and mock weddings were a popular form of game. Songs with double meanings were not only permitted at this time, but were virtually obligatory.'[17]

The traditional connection between singing birds and lovers was perhaps enough to promote the idea that lovers, too, should celebrate St Valentine's Day with games involving choosing mates (probably by lottery), and with poetry – 'And somme songen clere layes of love . . . in worship and in preysinge of hir make . . .'(F 139–41). It is futile to bemoan the fact that the evidence for Valentine celebrations is almost solely literary, because poetry writing came to be seen as an almost obligatory feature of St Valentine's Day. The poems are demonstrations of metrical skill and inventive treatment of familiar themes, and were very probably competitive productions. The collection of annual

---

[15] See G. L. Apperson's entries for Candlemas day and St Valentine's Day, *English Proverbs and Proverbial Phrases: a Historical Dictionary* (London: Dent, 1929).

[16] P. Champion ed., *Charles d'Orléans: Poésies*, 2 vols. (Paris: CFMA, 1966), Rondeaux CLXI, CCCLV, CLXII, CCXLVII.

[17] P. Burke, *Popular Culture in Early Modern Europe* (London: Temple Smith, 1978), p. 186.

Valentine poems by Charles d'Orléans and his circle puts this point beyond doubt, as in Charles' own Valentine rondeau CCXLVIII which begins with an invitation to his confrères to come into the world of 'fine language', making poems of joy or sorrow in French or Latin:

> A ce jour de saint Valentin
> Venez avant, nouveaux faiseurs,
> Faictes de plaisirs ou douleurs
> Rymes en francoys ou latin . . .

The tonality of the poetry produced for Valentine's Day is wide-ranging, and is often marked by irony, humour and wit. The 'fidelity' which is almost obsessively celebrated in Valentine poetry is clearly only a relative matter, since the choosing of a mate for the limit of a year must have been a fairly light-hearted business (notwithstanding the impression usually derived from the *Parliament of Fowls*), and lack of fidelity is often treated with humour. There is something of an association between St Valentine and youthful love, even immature love.[18] Thomas Reed suggests that 'widespread and abiding concern for soul and lineage make it . . . likely that the rite [of choosing Valentine mates] allowed superabundant male courtiers and members of the household to declare their love for the few "formels" in attendance . . . through a ritually controlled – and because controlled, tolerated – flirtation'.[19]

The Valentine passage in the F Prologue continues with lines whose significance is often ignored, although D. S. Brewer cites F 152 as 'a rather feeble leer about sexual functions':[20]

> And therwithalle hire bekes gonnen meete,
> Yeldyng honour and humble obeysaunces
> To love, and diden hire other observaunces
> That longeth onto love and to nature;
> Construeth that as yow lyst, I do no cure.
> F 148–52

---

[18] Cf. Charles d'Orléans, *La Retinue d'Amours* (Champion, I, pp. 2, 16); Oton de Grandson, *A l'entree de ma jeunesse* (Piaget, pp. 428–34).
[19] Reed, *Middle English Debate Poetry*, p. 346.
[20] D. S. Brewer, *Chaucer*, 3rd edn (London: Longman, 1973), p. 101.

Chaucer's invitation in the last line to give an explicitly sexual connotation to his description of the birds' kisses and other observances of love and nature is not unknown to the spirit of Valentine poetry. The Valentine poems of Charles d'Orléans, for example, are characterised by one critic as 'sometimes vaguely bawdy'.[21]

The humorous association between love and nature (cf. F 151) is made in many St Valentine poems. Grandson says, in *Songe Saint Valentin* 338–49, that the love which makes people, as well as birds, join together in pairs is a natural thing, but is not so faithful between birds. Lydgate agrees, in *Flour of Curtesye* 50–70, but laments that Nature gives the birds freedom to choose whichever mates they desire from year to year. He questions, rather surprisingly and lumberingly, why the mating of human beings, alone of all creatures, is hedged about with rules and prohibitions, 'agayn al ryght of kynde'. The women of Dunbar's *Twa Mariit Wemen* 56–63 and 205–8 are frankly envious of the birds' Valentine's Day licence, and the 'privilege' which Nature gives them of dispensing with old husbands after a year; it is 'agane the law of luf, of kynd and of nature' to make mates stay together longer: 'Birdis hes ane better law.'[22] Here in the F Prologue Chaucer links the passage about love and nature to the passage dealing with the summertime renewal of the small birds' lovemaking with lines containing an allusion to the animal world: those who have been unfaithful to their St Valentine's Day pledges, he writes (and, if the conventions of the day were essentially literary and playful, this might include most of his audience), are like the 'tydif', a small bird renowned for its 'new-fangelnesse' and, probably, lechery (F 153 ff.).[23] It would seem that the association of nature and the sexual, although not often foregrounded in English courtly poetry, was nevertheless an available possibility. On St Valentine's Day one could countenance, it appears, what John Burrow characterises in other contexts as the 'seditious idea that youthful exuberance and sexuality was only natural'.[24]

---

[21] Kellogg, 'Chaucer's St Valentine', p. 134.

[22] Piaget, *Grandson*, p. 320; MacCracken, *Lydgate's Minor Poems*, I, pp. 410–18; J. Kinsley, ed., *Poems of William Dunbar* (Oxford University Press, 1979), pp. 42–59.

[23] Chaucer mentions the infidelity of the 'tydif' in *SqT* V 648. For the association of small birds and lechery, see Ross, *Chaucer's Bawdy*, pp. 206–7.

[24] Burrow, *Ages of Man*, p. 146.

René Nelli believes that the spirit of Valentinage in northern France and Savoy, where it had quickly spread from England, took over some of the liberties enjoyed in the ancient celebrations of May. In the France of the eighteenth century the licentiousness of St Valentine's Day was still commented on.[25] The same could not be said of England at an equivalent time, but that the original celebration of St Valentine was not entirely innocent is suggested by much of the early Valentine poetry and by observations like that of Shakespeare's Ophelia:

> To-morrow is Saint Valentine's day,
>   All in the morning betime,
> And I a maid at your window,
>   To be your Valentine.
> Then up he rose and donned his clothes,
>   And dupped the chamber door,
> Let in the maid, that out a maid
>   Never departed more.
> *Hamlet* IV v 46–53

Although the tone of the poems which mention St Valentine's Day varies widely in the period close to Chaucer's time, we should not be surprised at one which treats love with humour and irony, and where wry comment is made on the difficulty of being faithful to one mate unto death. The seemingly superfluous reference to the mating of St Valentine's day in the Prologue to the *Legend* appears another gesture inviting the audience to view the unfaithful heroes of the Legends with the tolerance usually accorded the licensed infidelity of this aristocratic holiday courting game.

Earlier in this chapter I spoke of the series of oppositions which mark the passage F 125–70, most of which end in 'acord'. The Prologue to the *Legend* inscribes conflict between several other such opposing terms. Such a one informs the cult of the Flower and the Leaf, another courtly game played by the 'lovers' of the French and English courts of the late fourteenth and early fifteenth century, which is a more prominent

---

[25] R. Nelli, *L'érotique des Troubadours*, 2 vols. (Paris: Union Générale d'Éditions, 1974), I, pp. 47–66.

feature in the F Prologue than in G. Like the celebrations surrounding St Valentine's Day it involved a strong literary component, and indeed nothing is known about it except from literary references. The game seems to have consisted in dividing the courtly participants into two 'orders', one of the Leaf and one of the Flower, after which each order vied in praising its own symbol more highly than the other. In 1386–8 it may have been a very recent custom, as Chaucer implies that he does not know much about it or its members, and certainly was not involved in it:

> But natheles, ne wene nat that I make
> In preysing of the flour agayn the leef . . .
> For, as to me, nys lever noon ne lother;
> I nam witholden yit with never nother;
> Ne I not who serveth leef ne who the flour.
> F 188–93

A series of poems by Eustache Deschamps is the earliest witness to what was understood by the Flower and by the Leaf.[26] One balade, *Des deux Ordres de la Feuille et de la Fleur (Eloge de la Fleur)*, tells us that Philippa of Lancaster, daughter of John of Gaunt, was a *tresdoulx nom* among those who worship the Flower, and since Philippa went to Portugal and marriage in 1386,[27] it is thought that the vogue for the Flower and the Leaf appeared in the early 1380s. Gower refers to companies of young people at Cupid's court wearing garlands, 'som o the lef, som of the flour'. If one important patroness of the Flower dwelt *en l'ille d'Albion*, according to this poem of Deschamps's, nevertheless his opening lines tell us that it was *en France* that the poet heard of these two orders in the amorous law, an indication of the intimate traffic that existed between the two courts, both in personnel and poetic productions:

[26] All the French Flower and Leaf poems are printed in G. L. Marsh, 'Sources and Analogues of *The Flower and the Leaf*', *MP* 4 (1906–7): 121–67 and 281–326. See also D. A. Pearsall's Introduction to *The Floure and the Leafe and the Assembly of Ladies* (London: Nelson, 1962). For Deschamps, see Saint-Hilaire/Raynaud, *Deschamps: Œuvres* VI, pp. 257 ff. and for Charles d'Orléans, Champion, *Charles d'Orléans* I, pp. 85–8.

[27] G. L. Kittredge, 'Chaucer and Some of His Friends', *MP* 1 (1903): 4.

Pour ce que j'ay oy parler en France
De deux ordres en l'amoureuse loy,
Que dames ont chascune en defferance,
L'une fueille et l'autre fleur, j'octroy
Mon corps, mon cuer a la fleur . . .
Éloge de la Fleur 1–5

These lines suggest that it was the women who originated the game, but certainly men could be enrolled in the order of the Flower. A rondeau of Deschamps's, purporting to be written by a woman, addresses a councillor and chamberlain of Charles VI as *tresdouce flour*, and goes on to describe him in terminology more commonly used to describe women. On the other hand, the envoy of Deschamps's matching balade, *Des deux ordres de la Feuille et de la Fleur (Eloge de la Feuille)*, contains a long list of distinguished gentlemen of the French court as supporters of the Leaf, the party, as will be seen, likely to seem more suitable for men to embrace.

When Deschamps praises the Flower above the Leaf, he comments on the Flower's beauty and goodness, fresh colour and perfume, and the fruit it produces (*Eloge de la Fleur* 14–16). Although the Leaf is long-lasting and gives pleasure through its greenness, he says, its only use is to honour the Flower and to protect it night and day from rain, tempest and wind. It is only a servant (24–7). All this is pure rhetoric, for in the poem where he praises the Leaf, the grounds for praise are the same ones for which he condemned it in the balade in praise of the Flower. Now the Leaf's long-lasting greenness is contrasted favourably with the fading beauty and fragility of the Flower and symbolises its strength, firmness and loyalty (*Eloge de la Feuille* 24–7). Moreover, he insists on the reasonableness of his argument, whichever side he takes. Clearly such poems were appreciated more for the wit of their argumentation and the elegance of the accompanying expression than for any objective truth of their content.

The symbolism of the Flower and the Leaf is quite straightforward and even commonplace, and commentators agree that the game of the Flower and Leaf was probably concerned with contrasting the virtues of the two sexes. The virtues of the Flower symbolised effectively the general view of woman as beautiful but fatally weak, whereas those of the Leaf symbolised the strength and faithfulness of the man. Charles d'Orléans has a pair of poems which lend support to this interpretation. The first tells how on the first day of May, when lovers have to make their annual choice between the 'leef so fresshe and fulle of gret verdure' and the 'flowre so fayre and soot to smelle', he took the Leaf. It was quite appropriate that this was his lot, he says, because his lady was dead.[28] In the next poem he has a dream on the second day of May in which a flower appears to him and chides him for forgetting her, and 'strengthist lo the leef agayn me sore'.[29] The flower does not seem to symbolise the dead lady but some kind of idea of women in general. Charles, it should be noted, associates the Flower and the Leaf with the celebrations of May but speaks of the custom of serving the Flower or the Leaf as if it were similar to that of St Valentine's Day, insofar as one has to make one's choice for the year (again by lot, it seems), of a party rather than of an individual mate. The author of the fifteenth-century poem *The Floure and the Leafe* also associates the game with May. This poem debates the merits of two kinds of love: the one chaste, faithful and honourable, represented by the Leaf and by Diana; the other idle, pleasure-loving and buffeted by the extremes of weather, and represented by the Flower and Flora. In the light of the present study, it is paradoxical that here the attributes of the Flower, and the courtly hymning of its merits, are treated pejoratively, because the Flower is described as a daisy (346–50). It has been suggested that the poem is the extant member of a matched pair of poems, the other one of which would have favoured the Flower.[30]

The kind of game in which male and female are typified by various kinds of plant material and set over against each other is well attested, and the Flower and Leaf game of summer seems to mimic the much better-known Holly and Ivy game of winter,[31] which endured for many centuries after the Flower and Leaf was forgotten. Although extant versions of the Holly and Ivy poems date from the fifteenth century, they seem to point to much older folk beliefs and customs, in which

---

[28] Ballade 65, 2240–1, R. Steele, ed., *The English Poems of Charles of Orleans* (London: EETS, 215, 220, 1940); cf. Champion, *Charles d'Orléans* I, 65, p. 85.

[29] Ballade 66, 2270; cf. Champion, *Charles d'Orléans* I, 62, p. 87.

[30] Reed, *Debate Poetry*, pp. 183–4.

[31] Ibid., pp. 162, 181–3; Pearsall, *Floure and Leafe*, p. 26.

prickly holly stood for man and his 'maistrie', and contended with pliant ivy representing malleable woman.[32] The gathering of holly and ivy for decorating houses was of course usually associated with Christmas celebrations, as the gathering of greenery and blossom was an essential part of the celebration of May, but R. L. Greene notes the Shrovetide burning of effigies known as the 'Holly Boy' and the 'Ivy Girl' respectively, as well as a Holly and Ivy verse for St Valentine's Day. The contention between Holly and Ivy in the Christmas game seems to centre on 'whether master or dame wears the britches'.[33] One of the best known of the group is a carol which has the taunting refrain: 'Nay, Iuy, nay, hyt shal not be, iwys/ Let Holy hafe the maystry, as the maner ys.' The verses of the carol suggest it is to be sung during a game in which the party of 'Iuy and hure maydenys [who] wepyn and . . . wryng' have to stand outside the door in the cold, while 'Holy and hys mery men [who] dawnseyn and . . . syng' remain inside the hall 'fayre to behold'.[34] Holly undoubtedly has the better of it in these poems, although there are a few poems of semi-learned and religious, if rather querulous, tone which celebrate the virtues of ivy.[35] In what scanty evidence we have concerning the Flower and the Leaf, however, the Flower seems to have been the favoured side. This may be a result of the marguerite having appropriated the traditional virtues of the Leaf – its stability and 'loyalty' – to the Flower's virtues of beauty, sweetness and perfume. In the last poem which is known to allude to the Flower and the Leaf, *The Floure and the Leafe*, the traditional hierarchy of values has been restored, as noted earlier, and the respective virtues and deficiencies of Flower and Leaf are applied to male and female indiscriminately. It is only in Charles d'Orléans that the association of Flower and Leaf and men and women is explicit, but the traditional gender-based character of the opposition of these characteristics, the analogy of such festive games as the Holly and the Ivy, and the nature of the controversy which is seen to be at issue later in the *Legend of Good Women*, all make

---

[32] See R. L. Greene, ed., *The Early English Carols* (Oxford: Clarendon, 1935), 'Introduction', page c.

[33] Ibid., pp. c–ci; the quotation is a seventeenth-century allusion.

[34] Ibid., no. 136, pp. 93–4, and p. xcix.

[35] Ibid., no. 139, p. 96.

it seem likely that the reference to the Flower and the Leaf in the Prologue alludes to the same kind of social game.

In sum, what we know for certain is that the game of the Flower and the Leaf was a polite pastime during which poems were made which celebrated alternately the virtues of the Flower and the Leaf. Allegiance to one or the other was not permanent, as both Deschamps and Charles d'Orléans suggest. When Chaucer says he does not know who 'serveth leef, ne who the flour' (F 193), it may be because he was not up with the current state of the game, if participants could be now on one side, now on the other. He also hopes flippantly that they will receive the (probably amatory) rewards they expect – for their labour of 'makyng', presumably (F 194). Chaucer's claim that he neither knows about nor is committed to either side in this 'stryf' (F 191–3) is a protest of sorts against the futility of setting in opposition two parts of a single organism, or the parts to the whole, such as the corn against the sheaf[36] (which requires a mental process comparable to not seeing the wood for the trees). It may well be that the poet is complaining about the God of Love's demand that the propagandist and reductionist stencil of the Good Woman be imposed on the irreducible complexity of the natural world. The passage about the Flower and the Leaf is separated in Prologue F from the scene of the small birds' courting by a few lines (F 171 ff.) evoking the prelapsarian 'acord' of the Golden Age, as Jean de Meun had described it, when Zepherus and Flora ruled and man and woman loved *sans rapine et sans covoitise* (*RR* 8431), a time without hierarchy and without conquest, before 'swich stryf was begonne' (F 196). I am assuming that 'swich stryf' connotes the game of stereotyped contention between male and female, flower and leaf. The significance of the mention of the Flower and the Leaf here is that it demands not that the opposition between male and female be denied but that it be approached in the spirit of joy and ultimate 'acord' which marks the small birds' lovemaking.

Chaucer's protest is to be received with caution. He is aware that his effusive praise of the daisy may suggest that he takes the side of the Flower, but the pun in 'for, as to me, nys lever noon ne lother' (F 191) might indicate a sympathy with the point of view of the Leaf. While he

---

[36] Delany, 'Rewriting Woman Good', p. 78.

can in some sense say correctly of the legendary he is about to compose in penance, 'For this thing is al of another tonne,/ Of olde storye, er swich stryf was begonne' (F 195–6), it is nevertheless not true that the tales which comprise it will be told without bias. The spirit of the game and the overtones of 'amorous strife' are everywhere to be noted in the Legends, as the partisan references to 'ye wemen' and 'us men' make clear. The wholesale abuse of men, which in so many places adorns the Legends, is readily perceived as tongue-in-cheek because so exaggerated. The concomitant praise of the faithfulness of all women is much less often thought to be humorous hyperbole nowadays, even though the audience to which the Legend was first addressed was well trained in this kind of point-scoring off the opposite side, and found it the most pleasant of pastimes.

That Alceste herself, in her reprimand to Chaucer later in the Prologue, remarks that contemporary men thought the conquest of as many women as possible was a game (F 486–9) should alert us to the fact that, even for medieval people, betrayed women and wicked seducers do not inevitably belong to a tragic or pathetic register. Moreover, there are other contemporary 'choosing' games which corroborate the characteristic bent of many extant poems associated with the seasonal festivities of St Valentine's Day, May Day and Christmas. That male infidelity and women's easy virtue (the too ready granting of pity) were popular topics in the discussions with which courtly ladies and gentlemen diverted themselves can be demonstrated by a poem like *The Chaunce of the Dice*.[37] This game for telling one's fortune occupies folios 148–54 of the fifteenth-century MS Fairfax 16, one of the most important of the *Legend of Good Women* manuscripts. The participants, both men and women, had to throw three dice and then look up their 'fortune' in the poem, where each throw, diagrammatically represented in the margin, was accompanied by a stanza purporting to give the player's character. This might be effusively laudatory or quite scurrilously rude and indicates the content and manner of much courtly entertainment. The second 'fortune', stanza 5, lines 29–35, for example, reads:

---

[37] The poem is printed in Eleanor Prescott Hammond, 'The Chance of the Dice', *Englische Studien* 59 (1925): 1–16.

To thinke vpon/ so double a creature
Myn hande ashamed/ [ys] I may not write
And in trouthe pleynly/ y yow ensure
My tonge ne may/ sufficen for to endyte
ffor vnto love/ ye do so grete dispite
There Jason falseth oon/ ye falsen twoo
Be god yet herde I neuer/ of such no moo

The second last line is, of course, a quotation from the *Legend of Good Women*. Another unfavourable 'fortune', stanza 55, accusingly informs the player who throws 3+1+1, 'Creseyde is here in worde bothe thought and dede.' A throw of 5+1+1 casts aspersions on a lady's virtue insofar that when she is dead, 'pitee', always so freely given to anyone who asked, will be lost to the world. We can hardly doubt that such chances of the dice were greeted with anything but laughter. That the players were well versed in Chaucer's works is evident from the quotations noted above, but there are several more: 'Was neuer wight set in no gretter ioye/ Syn that Troylus wanne first Creseyde in Troy' (139–40); 'Ther is no beter pandare as I trowe' (160); 'Now spronge ys newe Grisildes pacience' (206); 'Ye kan by rote the wifes lyfe of Bathe' (298). If Chaucer's poems offered endless material for participants in courtly diversions, it seems more than likely that the poems themselves often derive from just this kind of courtly entertainment.

Another fortune-telling game in the Fairfax MS[38] has a similar mixture of fervent praise and scurrility. *Ragman Roll* does not allude to Chaucerian or classical personages, but its verses exploit the same ludic courtly register as does the F Prologue to the *Legend*, and a connection between the game and the celebrations of St Valentine's Day or New Year has been postulated.[39] When a lady playing this game pulled out her fortune by a seal attached to a long ribbon, she might choose the verse beginning 'Ryght as the sonne is the worldys eye' (fo. 48ᵛ), which, in language similar to Chaucer's praise of the daisy, commends her beauty shining with its brightness in the 'hert of euery jentylman'; but another might be discomfited to read how she takes 'compassion' on all

---

[38] *MS Fairfax 16: a Facsimile, Bodleian Library, Oxford University* (London: Scolar, 1979), intro. J. Norton-Smith.
[39] C. Baskerville, 'Dramatic Aspects of Medieval Folk Festivals in England', *SP* 17 (1920): 38–9.

and sundry – each estate, high and low, cleric and lay, on which she confers her favours is minutely and even obscenely detailed (fo. 48ʳ); another fortune focuses on the 'experienced' lady's knowledge of the 'gret untrouth of man', so that she believes 'no mannys sleight ne flatere' and is a 'werry foo to coveytise' (fo. 49ᵛ), as do Jean de Meun's older quail or Chaucer's small birds who despised the fowler 'that, for his coveytise, had hem betrayed with his sophistrye' (F 136–7). This is a game specifically directed to women, although the scurrilous verses are sometimes attributed to 'kynge Ragman Holly',[40] indicating that humorously negative views of women were readily attributed to a male spokesperson and that any kind of playful gender-based sparring tended to be associated with the kind of seasonal festivity in which the Holly and Ivy game was enjoyed. As women were hardly forced to play it, one imagines that the slurs on their persons and characters were enjoyed as much as such games are by children today. The defiance which the small birds offer to the 'foule cherle' is probably marked by similar good humour and anticipation of ultimate accord:

> And thus thise foweles, voide of al malice,
> Acordeden to love, and laften vice
> Of hate, and songen alle of oon acord,
> 'Welcome, somer, oure governour and lord!'
> F 167–70

There are, then, obscure passages in the F Prologue which suggest that the poet knew his intended audience well and trusted that his playful hints of erotic conflict would develop in it an appropriate climate of anticipation with which to approach the body of the poem with its cargo of pathetic heroines and triumphant male villains. They imply an audience that could debate the merits and misdemeanours of the male and female protagonists of the stories, and appreciate the narrator's comic stance as a biased champion of the side not natural to him as a male poet. The tribute to the 'sovereign lady' and Queen Anne, the elaboration of the poetry in praise of the daisy and the religion of love, all add to our sense that this was a courtly audience and possibly a small

---

40 See F. L. Utley, *The Crooked Rib: an Analytical Index to the Argument about Women in English and Scots Literature to the End of the Year 1568* (1944, rpt. New York: Octagon, 1970), p. 201.

coterie audience. In spite of its obscure passages and rather haphazard construction, I would venture to suggest that the majority of readers have always derived more enjoyment from Prologue F, preferring its sense of shared understanding between poet and audience to the G Prologue's more precise articulation of the poem's issues.

The distinctive passage about the birds' flirtation and the Golden Age is missing in the G Prologue. In G the poet comes quickly to his flower-strewn bed and, dreaming that he is again looking for the daisy in the meadow, hears the birds welcoming spring and hymning St Valentine. The omission of F 152–87 markedly alters the effect of this passage. The dreaming poet then sees the God of Love and the daisy lady and describes them in exactly the same lines as in F. The poet admires the daisy perfunctorily (G 40–60), and the remaining section is devoted to the problems of writing in English and the Flower and Leaf debate (G 61–80). Although the pre-dream section is so short in G, it nevertheless includes the poem's introductory lines unchanged (G 1–39), together with the appendage warning the readers against uncritically believing all 'that autours seyn' (G 81–8). It appears, then, that what is common to both versions of the pre-dream section of the Prologue is the notion of debate, and the opposition envisaged is the one that the introduction suggests, that between what courtly authority enjoins and what experience suggests (probably contrasting idealising and sceptical views of women's virtue). In both versions, of course, the Legends they introduce, with all their problematic features, remain the same.

Both Prologues set up a climate of debate which is ludic and recreational in spirit.[41] The oppositions of the F Prologue derive from the gentler aspects of the cycle of nature and sexual negotiation: warmth, love, innocence and mercy overcoming cold, hate, malice and strict justice, conflicts which are dialectically related rather than hierarchically resolved. It is disturbing that Chaucer can in the G Prologue so readily substitute a passage evoking the masters of misogyny for the F Prologue's scene of avian lovemaking. The allusion to scholarly *jeu d'esprit* in G 258–315 (the antifeminist jokes characteristic

---

[41] Reed's discussion of Bakhtin and 'Carnival Laughter' in the context of late medieval debate poetry is a useful one, *Debate Poetry*, pp. 27–40.

of old worn-out clerks signalling an easily recognisable rhetorical position) may have opened the poem to a wider audience, one with less sympathy for, or knowledge of, courtly pastime and the religion of love. To locate the Legends of good women more formally within the parameters of the debate about women, as is the effect of the G Prologue, may have enhanced Chaucer's self-dramatisation as serious vernacular translator/poet and adviser to princes, but the change in emphasis inevitably encourages its audience to debate more acerbically the notion of woman's essential 'unstedefastnesse' rather than to empathise with her suffering at the hands of unfaithful men.

Epilogue

How serious was Chaucer in his desire to defend women's virtue in the *Legend of Good Women*? All the evidence adduced in the various aspects of my study suggests that he was not entirely serious. Rather, when he indicates that the purpose of his poem was to speak well of women, he was inviting his audience to participate with him in a familiar game, one of the age's most popular. Literary versions of the game of discussing the nature of Woman had many permutations. For example, in the *Legend* it finds expression in the elegant phrasemaking in praise of the daisy/Alceste, the Good Woman par excellence. By contrast, it includes Chaucer's reworkings of classical stories, which tended to subvert the God of Love's contention that ninety-nine per cent of women are virtuous. When medieval gentlemen were not praising women or laughing at them, they were often pitying them, and thus an emotional engagement with women's position in the world is also encompassed in the *Legend of Good Women*'s version of the debate about women. It was a game which could be adapted for many different purposes and responses: thus Chaucer used the daisy motif to pay tribute to some important female personage, his 'lady sovereyne', very likely Queen Anne; again, the strongly affective portrayals of women's suffering indulged, I would suggest, his audience's impulse to give vent to that pity which infallibly indicated a noble heart; moreover, the stories in whose heroines *we* find so much to argue about were designed, I believe, to promote partisan, gender-biased argument in his original audience. The pleasure in fine language, the tearshedding, the laughter and shocked debate caused by Chaucer's stories about women all had high entertainment value for many medieval audiences.

The challenge for modern readers is to accept this peculiar amalgam of adulation, compassion and scepticism as wholly consonant with medieval responses to women. Above all, we should not attempt to interpret the *Legend* by privileging one attitude to women over the others. In the past critics were inclined to ignore the rather questionable virtue of the heroines of the Legends in favour of the indisputable goodness of the heroine of the Prologue, and to view the Legends as a monolithic exercise in pathos, enlivened perhaps by the odd humorous or ironic side-comment. I have shown that the Legends are not straight-forwardly laudatory or even overly sympathetic to the suffering of women, but neither are they an 'unmerciful satire' on women, as an early scholar would have had it. Critics today are more likely to feel that since the humorous passages in any Legend frequently occupy focal positions – the beginning or end – that this immediately relativises and ironises the pathetic passages, ignoring the fact that very many readers even today are able to read the Legends as genuinely pathetic. It seems indisputable that for at least a century, most people have found humour antithetic to pathos, so that many readings of the *Legend of Good Women* consequently falsify the text because of the need to produce either a seriously pathetic reading or a wholeheartedly humorous or ironic one. It is no accident, however, that Chaucer insists on treating the heroines with *both* pathos and humour, and gives little indication which is to be the dominant mode. It is necessary to acknowledge that the idealisation of women and the joking questioning and trivialising of their essential virtue are consistently held in tension in the *Legend of Good Women*, with the balance shifting from Legend to Legend, and from Prologue to Legends, and is a deliberate structural principle of the poem.

Indeed the narrator's persona holds these competing voices in suspension: the poet presents himself as a humble adherent of the orthodox courtly praise of women, but one who is occasionally sceptical of the notion that women were once as completely good as Alceste and the God of Love maintain. The idea of love as a religion, parallel at every point with orthodox Christianity and one which permeates the F Prologue, provides the poet with his elucidatory metaphor: as the orthodox Christian believes in the existence of Heaven and Hell which Scripture requires, although he can have no supporting evidence in his everyday experience, so a gentleman praises and honours women and believes in the virtue of women which old books talk about, although he purports to have little experience of good women in his own experience. A provocative fiction which can be relied on to promote audience participation, an enjoyable aspect of the courtly world at play! The use of the word *Legend* in the title of the poem speaks to us of this religious metaphor; a 'legend' is a reading of morally improving stories, and came to describe a collection of such stories, usually of saints' lives with all the heroic excesses of piety which that genre denominates. The modern usage of the word has developed shades of meaning which encapsulate Chaucer's joke quite neatly: to describe something as 'legendary' (or 'fabulous' or 'mythical') is to mean it is extraordinary, but it can also mean that it is so extraordinary that its literal truth could not normally be believed. So Chaucer warns about his translations of old classical stories: 'Beleve hem if yow leste!'

Modern readers wonder whether they are supposed to laugh or cry at Chaucer's legendary good women. I am suggesting that readers' conflicting responses to the *Legend* over the last hundred years or so tell us something about the text which is intrinsic to its nature. Humour is there, but pathos is there also, as well as genuine respect for women, and there is no reason to doubt that Chaucer offers his praise of the daisy/Alceste figure as a serious tribute to Queen Anne or some other lady simply because there is little sympathy today for the kind of heroic and self-sacrificing virtue which Alceste embodies. Nor does modern distaste for the pathetic mean that Chaucer and his audience were not genuinely saddened (although not angered as modern people are likely to be) by the position in which women found themselves in the stories he tells. In fact, medieval responses to the poem were not entirely different from modern attempts to read the poem as exercises in either pathos or irony, or (in my own reading) a debate between a presentation of idealised feminine virtue in the Prologue versus a somewhat compromised, certainly more naturalistic, view of women's goodness in the Legends. The manuscript tradition suggests that the *Legend of Good Women* was able to fit into almost directly opposed contexts; in one it sits happily with works that praise the virtues of married love in all earnest, like the *Kingis Quair* (MS Bodley Arch. Selden B 24); in another its companions are heavily antifeminist (MS Trinity College 3. 19); in most, the surrounding works are the standard fare of light courtly entertainment (MSS Fairfax 16, Tanner 346, Bodley 638 and so on). But, as I have said, it seems likely to me that the audience for which it was originally designed, probably a courtly one as the reference to the Queen in Prologue F suggests, and almost certainly in playful mode (intimated by the passage in F about the birds' less than serious love-making), took a deal of pleasure in the juxtaposition of disparate views of women, and in the debates which followed, with the opportunities they offered for teasing and flirtation.

All audiences, of course, even in Chaucer's own time, may not have responded in similar ways. Perhaps the poet in effect envisaged several kinds of audience, some, for example, which may have regarded the Legends as serious examples of the pathetic genre, and others, more sophisticated and better educated, hence predominantly male audiences, which would have been well able to debate the questions the Legends raise. The existence of the G Prologue provides evidence that the poem could be adapted to emphasise the jokes about women dear to learned men's hearts, dispensing almost entirely with the elegancies of the religion of love and the complimentary references to a specific woman. It would seem logical to suppose that different audiences could be presented with differently modulated performances of the poem – the text is such that a live reading could emphasise or deemphasise the pathos or the occasional vulgarity, according to the response desired in a particular audience. In any case it is more useful to think of the stories as deliberately ambiguous than as having any controlling ironic purpose. They all promote a debate about women and love, or insofar as the poem is a genuine reply to *Troilus and Criseyde* and the *Roman de la Rose*, a continuation of the debate about women and love.

In the end the *Legend* is dealing with a literary construct of Woman, Woman as an ancient topic for discussion, and is not primarily concerned with the problems that real women faced. I have felt justified in referring to that complex of writing and talking and joking about women as the 'matter of Woman', a traditional field of discourse like the matter of Britain or the matter of Arthur, with a punning reference to the medieval belief that matter and bodies are feminine in contrast to masculine rationality and spirituality. The ambiguous responses which this text forces upon us are fully in tune with this idea of Woman, for medieval men seem to have hesitated endlessly between considering women as virtuous, gentle and full of pity, or as sub-rational creatures prone to sensuality and lust. It is the paradoxes inherent in the concept of Woman (in literary terms, its potential for palinode) which make her so attractive a subject. More than this, Chaucer in fact identifies his subject matter, women, with subject matter in general; subject matter is that which (male) writers treat and handle and master. How the poet handles his 'matere' to bring out his 'entente' is cited as the point at issue in the central scene of the Prologue, the poet's confrontation with the God of Love. Throughout the Legends men characters do what they want to women, and Chaucer *says* what he wants about women and does what he wants with his subject matter. Towards the end of the tale collection Chaucer finally makes the connection that the actions of the seducer/rapist and the poet/translator parallel each other.

This is an outrageous image, and a clear indication that the context was a ludic one, for the seduction and exploitation of women were not condoned in the moral strictures of orthodox medieval culture (indeed Chaucer *ostensibly* adopts this orthodox position during the course of the Legends). But Chaucer is making a relatively serious point about the control and detachment which anybody who handles subject matter needs to exercise over it in order to serve it effectively. No matter how well-meaning the motive, no matter how genuine the desire to be of service, there will always be a sense in which the subject matter is exploited, and, if mastery is achieved, an enhancement of the writer's reputation. If one wanted to find a disreputable image with which to make a similar point today, the most illuminating modern parallel that I can think of would be the kind of tabloid or television journalism in which the journalist pursues the grieving victim of a crime, ostensibly to bring the victim's case to a wider concern, but really providing the reporter with subject matter to exploit in his or her programme or article, for his or her own advancement. Acknowledgement of such unscrupulous commodification of human suffering does not preclude us from feeling sympathy with the victim's plight, the pain of a real person, as acknowledgement that Chaucer is using the victimisation of women as subject matter on which he can demonstrate his skill does not preclude us from responding with pity to their sad stories. I could have chosen less loaded illustrations of the same necessary compositional procedures in order to exemplify the paradox that service depends on mastery: these might include the service the academic offers his text, the preacher his scriptures, the practising musician the composer's work. So Chaucer's laudatory aim to restore balance by praising women instead of defaming them is subsumed under other agendas which include courtly entertainment and the valorisation of his own skills in putting a case. Presumably Chaucer could have used a different metaphoric structure to exemplify the paradoxes inherent in the humble service of women or of literary authorities, but it is instructive that he has chosen (as probably being more fun and more suitable to the ludic context) the disreputable example of the potency of the unfaithful male.

What is the really serious topic of concern in the *Legend of Good Women* is the poet's reputation for skill and learning. This concentration on poetic creativity and power may surprise us, but it was not dissimilar to what the fourteenth-century French poets were saying about the profession of poetry at the time. For an English writer, however, the notion could perhaps only find expression in the ludic, even carnivalesque, spirit which is evoked in the *Legend of Good Women*, something to be propounded not entirely seriously. Moreover, we mistake the situation if we see it as a simple statement of the god-like individuality and privileged cultural role of the modern 'artist', although in the *Legend* the narrator's 'I' seems to articulate a remarkably self-confident sense of the excellence of his powers and the impeccability of his intentions, almost of his *auctoritas*. It is more useful to observe that when the poet puts himself in opposition to the God of Love's simplistic notion that one's choice of subject matter determines one's meaning, he is setting up yet another dialogic pattern in the *Legend*, a conflict of official and unofficial cultural views, of which the debate about women is only a subordinate example. It is a way of articulating a debate about the value and procedures of literary works, analogous to those being conducted in Latin and French in other cultured groups of the period. It signifies not so much a serious critique of courtly culture, as an enhancement of the social group which can embrace such debate and appreciate the poet's creative effort, his mastery of language and learning, attributes which mesh with the group's own self-image. His listeners, too, the poem implies, have learned concerns and are appreciative of the well-turned phrase, they are capable of pity but also of engaging in witty dialogue.

The poet's opposing moves of resistance to and endorsement of the values of official culture are delicately managed, with nuances it is not now easy to analyse at this distance of time and culture. Let me recapitulate some aspects of this dialogue. Chaucer's narrator is presented as outside the genuinely noble life – the God of Love sees him as a 'worm' who should not dare approach the deity, he is a political rebel and religious heretic. It is difficult to know to what extent this represents social reality or is an expediency of the poem's central fiction. It is certainly expedient that the role of outsider allows the poet to explore different and somewhat subversive attitudes to the service of love. For the courtly audience Chaucer's stance is something like that occupied by the 'cherls' of the *Canterbury Tales*, opening the way to the listeners' enjoyment of topics not usually considered courtly. In the Prologue to the *Legend*, however, it is his role as a learned translator of the *Roman de la Rose* with its multiplicity of views on love (not all flattering) which marks him out from Love's servants. But there is also an entirely positive aspect of the poet's portrayal of his negotiations with Love's kingdom. He shows himself a master of the courtly forms of the praise of women, and no doubt offers his daisy poems as exemplars for his gentlemanly listeners to imitate. In instigating a goodhumoured debate about women he is also a facilitator of the graceful arts of health-giving recreation. Most importantly, he presents the Daisy Queen as the inspiration of his poetry and the God of Love as the one who leads his imagination on to the invention of the myth of Alceste's transformation into a daisy, the symbol of poetic creativity. Chaucer may be a learned outsider to truly noble society, but he offers it useful instruction and collaborates with its ideals. He maintains it has always been his intention to 'furthere trouthe in love'. The potentially disruptive intrusion of the realm of learning also has its positive side; the poet not only opens the world of Latinate culture to an English audience with his translation of the stories of the classical heroines but he also adorns his poem with the major passage incorporating traditional advice to a king. I call it an adornment because such material was so highly respected; it brought lustre to the society which received it and to the learned poet who produced it, as well as to the language in which it found expression. In a significant act of homage, it is also placed in the mouth of a woman, surely a profound compliment to whomever the daisy/Alceste figure was designed to compliment.

Finally, the poem consistently exploits the fact that a significant portion of the audience, ignoring all sense of social difference, must empathise totally with the poet on the basis of their shared gender. It is a matter of 'us men' and 'ye wemen'. It is unlikely that male listeners did not find an association of poetic skill with male potency exciting and something to be identified with, nor that they did not enjoy contemplating the possibility that authority and mastery over women could parade as humble service. (I forbear from speculating how closely this presentation of the poetic process mirrors the gender politics of Chaucer's audience.) Who knows what men may not dare, at least in the realm of fantasy? They too might deal with a Phaedra or a Medea, and live to tell the tale. By this means, when Chaucer speaks of his individual skill, all men could enter into the enjoyment of his representative status as an English writer, who, in the playful context of the *Legend of Good Women*, is an emulator of French elegance and the cheeky challenger of Latinate culture.

Index

Index

CAMBRIDGE STUDIES IN MEDIEVAL LITERATURE